Augustine

General Editors

John Baillie (1886–1960) served as President of the World Council of Churches, a member of the British Council of Churches, Moderator of the General Assembly of the Church of Scotland, and Dean of the Faculty of Divinity at the University of Edinburgh.

John T. McNeill (1885–1975) was Professor of the History of European Christianity at the University of Chicago and then Auburn Professor of Church History at Union Theological Seminary in New York.

Henry P. Van Dusen (1897–1975) was an early and influential member of the World Council of Churches and served at Union Theological Seminary in New York as Roosevelt Professor of Systematic Theology and later as President.

Augustine
Confessions and Enchiridion

Edited and translated by
ALBERT COOK OUTLER
PhD, DD

Westminster John Knox Press
LOUISVILLE • LONDON

Cover design by designpointinc.com

Published by Westminster John Knox Press
Louisville, Kentucky

This book is printed on acid-free paper that meets the American National Standards Institute Z39.48 standard.♾

PRINTED IN THE UNITED STATES OF AMERICA

Library of Congress Cataloging-in-Publication Data is on file at the Library of Congress, Washington, D.C.

ISBN-13: 978-0-664-23080-7
ISBN-10: 0-664-23080-6

GENERAL EDITORS' PREFACE

The Christian Church possesses in its literature an abundant and incomparable treasure. But it is an inheritance that must be reclaimed by each generation. THE LIBRARY OF CHRISTIAN CLASSICS is designed to present in the English language, and in twenty-six volumes of convenient size, a selection of the most indispensable Christian treatises written prior to the end of the sixteenth century.

The practice of giving circulation to writings selected for superior worth or special interest was adopted at the beginning of Christian history. The canonical Scriptures were themselves a selection from a much wider literature. In the Patristic era there began to appear a class of works of compilation (often designed for ready reference in controversy) of the opinions of well-reputed predecessors, and in the Middle Ages many such works were produced. These medieval anthologies actually preserve some noteworthy materials from works otherwise lost.

In modern times, with the increasing inability even of those trained in universities and theological colleges to read Latin and Greek texts with ease and familiarity, the translation of selected portions of earlier Christian literature into modern languages has become more necessary than ever; while the wide range of distinguished books written in vernaculars such as English makes selection there also needful. The efforts that have been made to meet this need are too numerous to be noted here, but none of these collections serves the purpose of the reader who desires a library of representative treatises spanning the Christian centuries as a whole. Most of them embrace only the age of the Church Fathers, and some of them have long been out of print. A fresh translation of a work already translated may shed much new light upon its meaning. This is true even of Bible translations despite the work of many experts through the centuries. In some instances old translations have been adopted in this series, but wherever necessary or desirable, new ones have been made. Notes have been supplied where these were needed to explain the author's meaning. The introductions provided for the several treatises and extracts will, we believe, furnish welcome guidance.

JOHN BAILLIE
JOHN T. McNEILL
HENRY P. VAN DUSEN

CONTENTS

Introduction

LIKE A COLOSSUS BESTRIDING TWO WORLDS,
Augustine stands as the last patristic and the first medieval
father of Western Christianity. He gathered together and
conserved all the main motifs of Latin Christianity from Ter-
tullian to Ambrose; he appropriated the heritage of Nicene
orthodoxy; he was a Chalcedonian before Chalcedon—and he
drew all this into an unsystematic synthesis which is still our best
mirror of the heart and mind of the Christian community in the
Roman Empire. More than this, he freely received and de-
liberately reconsecrated the religious philosophy of the Greco-
Roman world to a new apologetic use in maintaining the
intelligibility of the Christian proclamation. Yet, even in his
role as summator of tradition, he was no mere eclectic. The
center of his "system" is in the Holy Scriptures, as they
ordered and moved his heart and mind. It was in Scripture
that, first and last, Augustine found the focus of his religious
authority.

At the same time, it was this essentially conservative genius
who recast the patristic tradition into the new pattern by which
European Christianity would be largely shaped and who, with
relatively little interest in historical detail, wrought out the first
comprehensive "philosophy of history." Augustine regarded
himself as much less an innovator than a summator. He was less
a reformer of the Church than the defender of the Church's
faith. His own self-chosen project was to save Christianity from
the disruption of heresy and the calumnies of the pagans, and,
above everything else, to renew and exalt the faithful hearing of
the gospel of man's utter need and God's abundant grace. But
the unforeseen result of this enterprise was to furnish the motifs

13

of the Church's piety and doctrine for the next thousand years and more. Wherever one touches the Middle Ages, he finds the marks of Augustine's influence, powerful and pervasive—even Aquinas is more of an Augustinian at heart than a "proper" Aristotelian. In the Protestant Reformation, the evangelical elements in Augustine's thought were appealed to in condemnation of the corruptions of popular Catholicism—yet even those corruptions had a certain right of appeal to some of the non-evangelical aspects of Augustine's thought and life. And, still today, in the important theological revival of our own time, the influence of Augustine is obviously one of the most potent and productive impulses at work.

A succinct characterization of Augustine is impossible, not only because his thought is so extraordinarily complex and his expository method so incurably digressive, but also because throughout his entire career there were lively tensions and massive prejudices in his heart and head. His doctrine of God holds the Plotinian notions of divine unity and remotion in tension with the Biblical emphasis upon the sovereign God's active involvement in creation and redemption. For all his devotion to Jesus Christ, this theology was never adequately Christocentric, and this reflects itself in many ways in his practical conception of the Christian life. He did not invent the doctrines of original sin and seminal transmission of guilt but he did set them as cornerstones in his "system," matching them with a doctrine of infant baptism which cancels, *ex opere operato*, birth sin and hereditary guilt. He never wearied of celebrating God's abundant mercy and grace—but he was also fully persuaded that the vast majority of mankind are condemned to a wholly just and appalling damnation. He never denied the reality of human freedom and never allowed the excuse of human irresponsibility before God—but against all detractors of the primacy of God's grace, he vigorously insisted on both double predestination and irresistible grace.

For all this the Catholic Church was fully justified in giving Augustine his aptest title, *Doctor Gratiae*. The central theme in all Augustine's writings is the sovereign God of grace and the sovereign grace of God. Grace, for Augustine, is God's freedom to act without any external necessity whatsoever—to act in love beyond human understanding or control; to act in creation, judgment, and redemption; to give his Son freely as Mediator and Redeemer; to endue the Church with the indwelling power and guidance of the Holy Spirit; to shape the destinies of all creation and the ends of the two human societies, the "city of earth" and the "city of God." Grace is God's unmerited love and favor, prevenient and occurrent. It touches man's inmost heart and will. It guides and impels the pilgrimage of those called to be faithful. It draws and raises the soul to repentance, faith, and praise. It transforms the human will so that it is capable of doing good. It relieves man's religious anxiety by forgiveness and the gift of hope. It establishes the ground of Christian humility by abolishing the ground of human pride. God's grace became incarnate in Jesus Christ, and it remains immanent in the Holy Spirit in the Church.

Augustine had no system—but he did have a stable and coherent Christian outlook. Moreover, he had an unwearied, ardent concern: man's salvation from his hopeless plight, through the gracious action of God's redeeming love. To understand and interpret this was his one endeavor, and to this task he devoted his entire genius.

He was, of course, by conscious intent and profession, a Christian theologian, a pastor and teacher in the Christian community. And yet it has come about that his contributions to the larger heritage of Western civilization are hardly less important than his services to the Christian Church. He was far and away the best—if not the very first—psychologist in the ancient world. His observations and descriptions of human motives and emotions, his depth analyses of will and thought in their interaction, and his exploration of the inner nature of the human self—these have established one of the main traditions in European conceptions of human nature, even down to our own time. Augustine is an essential source for both contemporary depth psychology and existentialist philosophy. His view of the shape and process of human history has been more influential than any other single source in the development of the Western tradition which regards political order as inextricably involved in moral order. His conception of a *societas* as a community identified and held together by its loyalties and love has become an integral part of the general tradition of Christian social teaching and the Christian vision of "Christendom." His metaphysical explorations of the problems of being, the character of evil, the relation of faith and knowledge, of will and reason, of time and eternity, of creation and cosmic order, have not ceased to animate and enrich various philosophic reflections throughout the succeeding centuries. At the same time the hallmark of the Augustinian philosophy is its insistent demand that

reflective thought issue in practical consequence; no contemplation of the end of life suffices unless it discovers the means by
which men are brought to their proper goals. In sum, Augustine
is one of the very few men who simply cannot be ignored or
depreciated in any estimate of Western civilization without
serious distortion and impoverishment of one's historical and
religious understanding.

In the space of some forty-four years, from his conversion in
Milan (A.D. 386) to his death in Hippo Regius (A.D. 430),
Augustine wrote—mostly at dictation—a vast sprawling library
of books, sermons, and letters, the remains of which (in the
Benedictine edition of St. Maur) fill fourteen volumes as they
are reprinted in Migne, *Patrologiae cursus completus*, Series Latina
(Vols. 32–45). In his old age, Augustine reviewed his authorship
(in the *Retractations*) and has left us a critical review of ninety-three
of his works he judged most important. Even a cursory glance at
them shows how enormous was his range of interest. Yet almost
everything he wrote was in response to a specific problem or an
actual crisis in the immediate situation. One may mark off
significant developments in his thought over this twoscore years,
but one can hardly miss the fundamental consistency in his entire life's work. He was never interested in writing a systematic
summa theologica, and would have been incapable of producing a
balanced digest of his multifaceted teaching. Thus, if he is to be
read wisely, he must be read widely—and always in context,
with due attention to the specific aim in view in each particular
treatise.

For the general reader who wishes to approach Augustine as
directly as possible, however, it is a useful and fortunate thing
that at the very beginning of his Christian ministry and then
again at the very climax of it, Augustine set himself to focus his
experience and thought into what were, for him, summings up.
The result of the first effort is the *Confessions*, which is his most
familiar and widely read work. The second is in the *Enchiridion*,
written more than twenty years later. In the *Confessions*, he
stands on the threshold of his career in the Church. In the
Enchiridion, he stands forth as triumphant champion of orthodox
Christianity. In these two works—the nearest equivalent to
summation in the whole of the Augustinian corpus—we can
find all his essential themes and can sample the characteristic
flavor of his thought.

Augustine was baptized by Ambrose at Milan during Easter-
tide, A.D. 387. A short time later his mother, Monica, died at

Ostia on the journey back to Africa. A year later, Augustine was back in Roman Africa living in a monastery at Tagaste, his native town. In 391, he was ordained presbyter in the church of Hippo Regius (a small coastal town nearby). Here in 395—with grave misgivings on his own part (cf. *Sermon* CCCLV, 2) and in actual violation of the eighth canon of Nicea (cf. Mansi, *Sacrorum conciliorum*, II, 671, and IV, 1167)—he was consecrated assistant bishop to the aged Valerius, whom he succeeded the following year. Shortly after he entered into his episcopal duties he began his *Confessions*, completing them probably in 398 (cf. De Labriolle, I, vi (see Bibliography), and di Capua, *Miscellanea Agostiniana*, II, 678).

Augustine had a complex motive for undertaking such a self-analysis.[1] His pilgrimage of grace had led him to a most unexpected outcome. Now he felt a compelling need to retrace the crucial turnings of the way by which he had come. And since he was sure that it was God's grace that had been his prime mover on that way, it was a spontaneous expression of his heart that cast his self-recollection into the form of a sustained prayer to God.

The *Confessions* are not Augustine's autobiography. They are, instead, a deliberate effort, in the permissive atmosphere of God's felt presence, to recall those crucial episodes and events in which he can now see and celebrate the mysterious actions of God's prevenient and provident grace. Thus he follows the windings of his memory as it re-presents the upheavals of his youth and the stages of his disorderly quest for wisdom. He omits very much indeed. Yet he builds his successive climaxes so skillfully that the denouement in Book VIII is a vivid and believable convergence of influences, reconstructed and "placed" with consummate dramatic skill. We see how Cicero's *Hortensius* first awakened his thirst for wisdom, how the Manicheans deluded him with their promise of true wisdom, and how the Academics upset his confidence in certain knowledge—how they loosed him from the dogmatism of the Manicheans only to confront him with the opposite threat that all knowledge is uncertain. He shows us (Bk. V, Ch. X, 19) that almost the sole cause of his intellectual perplexity in religion was his stubborn, materialistic prejudice that if God existed he had to exist in a

---

[1] He had no models before him, for such earlier writings as the *Meditations* of Marcus Aurelius and the autobiographical sections in Hilary of Poitiers and Cyprian of Carthage have only to be compared with the *Confessions* to see how different they are.

body, and thus had to have extension, shape, and finite relation. He remembers how the "Platonists" rescued him from this "materialism" and taught him how to think of spiritual and immaterial reality—and so to become able to conceive of God in nondualistic categories. We can follow him in his extraordinarily candid and plain report of his Plotinian ecstasy, and his momentary communion with the One (Book VII). The "Platonists" liberated him from error, but they could not loose him from the fetters of incontinence. Thus, with a divided will, he continues to seek a stable peace in the Christian faith while he stubbornly clings to his pride and appetence.

In Book VIII, Augustine piles up a series of remembered incidents that inflamed his desire to imitate those who already seemed to have gained what he had so long been seeking. First of all, there had been Ambrose, who embodied for Augustine the dignity of Christian learning and the majesty of the authority of the Christian Scriptures. Then Simplicianus tells him the moving story of Victorinus (a more famous scholar than Augustine ever hoped to be), who finally came to the baptismal font in Milan as humbly as any other catechumen. Then, from Ponticianus he hears the story of Antony and about the increasing influence of the monastic calling. The story that stirs him most, perhaps, relates the dramatic conversion of the two "special agents of the imperial police" in the garden at Trèves—two unlikely prospects snatched abruptly from their worldly ways to the monastic life.

He makes it plain that these examples forced his own feelings to an intolerable tension. His intellectual perplexities had become resolved; the virtue of continence had been consciously preferred; there was a strong desire for the storms of his breast to be calmed; he longed to imitate these men who had done what he could not and who were enjoying the peace he longed for.

But the old habits were still strong and he could not muster a full act of the whole will to strike them down. Then comes the scene in the Milanese garden which is an interesting parallel to Ponticianus' story about the garden at Trèves. The long struggle is recapitulated in a brief moment; his will struggles against and within itself. The trivial distraction of a child's voice, chanting, "*Tolle, lege,*" precipitates the resolution of the conflict. There is a radical shift in mood and will, he turns eagerly to the chance text in Rom. 13: 13—and a new spirit rises in his heart.

After this radical change, there was only one more past event that had to be relived before his personal history could be seen in its right perspective. This was the death of his mother and the severance of his strongest earthly tie. Book IX tells us this story. The climactic moment in it is, of course, the vision at Ostia where mother and son are uplifted in an ecstasy that parallels— but also differs significantly from—the Plotinian vision of Book VII. After this, the mother dies and the son who had loved her almost too much goes on alone, now upheld and led by a greater and a wiser love.

We can observe two separate stages in Augustine's "conversion." The first was the dramatic striking off of the slavery of incontinence and pride which had so long held him from decisive commitment to the Christian faith. The second was the development of an adequate understanding of the Christian faith itself and his baptismal confession of Jesus Christ as Lord and Saviour. The former was achieved in the Milanese garden. The latter came more slowly and had no "dramatic moment." The dialogues that Augustine wrote at Cassiciacum the year following his conversion show few substantial signs of a theological understanding, decisively or distinctively Christian. But by the time of his ordination to the presbyterate we can see the basic lines of a comprehensive and orthodox theology firmly laid out. Augustine neglects to tell us (in 398) what had happened in his thought between 386 and 391. He had other questions, more interesting to him, with which to wrestle.

One does not read far in the *Confessions* before he recognizes that the term "confess" has a double range of meaning. On the one hand, it obviously refers to the free acknowledgment, before God, of the truth one knows about oneself—and this obviously meant, for Augustine, the "confession of sins." But, at the same time, and more importantly, *confiteri* means to acknowledge, to God, the truth one knows about God. To confess, then, is to praise and glorify God; it is an exercise in self-knowledge and true humility in the atmosphere of grace and reconciliation.

Thus the *Confessions* are by no means complete when the personal history is concluded at the end of Book IX. There are two more closely related problems to be explored: First, how does the finite self find the infinite God (or, how is it found of him?)? And, secondly, how may we interpret God's action in producing this created world in which such personal histories and revelations do occur? Book X, therefore, is an exploration of *man's way to God*, a way which begins in sense experience but swiftly passes beyond it, through and beyond the awesome mystery of memory, to the ineffable encounter between God and the soul in man's inmost subject-self. But such a journey is not complete until the process is reversed and man has looked as deeply as may be into the mystery of creation, on which all our history and experience depend. In Book XI, therefore, we discover why *time* is such a problem and how "*In the beginning God created the heavens and the earth*" is the basic formula of a massive Christian metaphysical world view. In Books XII and XIII, Augustine elaborates, in loving patience and with considerable allegorical license, the mysteries of creation—exegeting the first chapter of Genesis, verse by verse, until he is able to relate the whole round of creation to the point where we can view the drama of God's enterprise in human history on the vast stage of the cosmos itself. The Creator is the Redeemer! Man's end and the beginning meet at a single point!

The *Enchiridion* is a briefer treatise on the grace of God and represents Augustine's fully matured theological perspective— after the magnificent achievements of the *De Trinitate* and the greater part of the *De civitate Dei*, and after the tremendous turmoil of the Pelagian controversy in which the doctrine of grace was the exact epicenter. Sometime in 421, Augustine received a request from one Laurentius, a Christian layman who was the brother of the tribune Dulcitius (for whom Augustine wrote the *De octo dulcitii quaestionibus* in 423–425). This Laurentius wanted a handbook (*enchiridion*) that would sum up the essential Christian teaching in the briefest possible form. Augustine dryly comments that the shortest complete summary of the Christian faith is that God is to be served by man in faith, hope, and love. Then, acknowledging that this answer might indeed be *too* brief, he proceeds to expand it in an essay in which he tries unsuccessfully to subdue his natural digressive manner by imposing on it a patently artificial schematism. Despite its awkward form, however, the *Enchiridion* is one of the most important of all of Augustine's writings, for it is a conscious effort of the theological magistrate of the Western Church to stand on final ground of testimony to the Christian truth.

For his framework, Augustine chooses the Apostles' Creed and the Lord's Prayer. The treatise begins, naturally enough, with a discussion of God's work in creation. Augustine makes a firm distinction between the comparatively unimportant knowledge of nature and the supremely important acknowledgment of the Creator of nature. But creation lies under the shadow of sin and evil and Augustine reviews his famous (and borrowed!) doctrine of the privative character of evil. From this he digresses into an extended comment on error and lying as special instances of evil. He then returns to the hopeless case of fallen man, to which God's wholly unmerited grace has responded in the incarnation of the Mediator and Redeemer, Jesus Christ. The questions about the appropriation of God's grace lead naturally to a discussion of baptism and justification, and beyond these, to the Holy Spirit and the Church. Augustine then sets forth the benefits of redeeming grace and weighs the balance between faith and good works in the forgiven sinner. But redemption looks forward toward resurrection, and Augustine feels he must devote a good deal of energy and subtle speculation to the questions about the manner and mode of the life everlasting. From this he moves on to the problem of the destiny of the wicked and the mystery of predestination. Nor does he shrink from these grim topics; indeed, he actually *expands* some of his most rigid ideas of God's ruthless justice toward the damned. Having thus treated the Christian faith and Christian hope, he turns in a too-brief concluding section to the virtue of Christian love as the heart of the Christian life. This, then, is the "handbook" on faith, hope, and love which he hopes Laurence will put to use and not leave as "baggage on his bookshelf."

Taken together, the *Confessions* and the *Enchiridion* give us two very important vantage points from which to view the Augustinian perspective as a whole, since they represent both his early and his mature formulation. From them, we can gain a competent—though by no means complete—introduction to the heart and mind of this great Christian saint and sage. There are important differences between the two works, and these ought to be noted by the careful reader. But all the main themes of Augustinian Christianity appear in them, and through them we can penetrate to its inner dynamic core.

There is no need to justify a new English translation of these books, even though many good ones already exist. Every translation is, at best, only an approximation—and an interpretation too. There is small hope for a translation to end all translations. Augustine's Latin is, for the most part, comparatively easy to read. One feels directly the force of his constant wordplay, the artful balancing of his clauses, his laconic use of parataxis, and his deliberate involutions of thought and word order. He was always a Latin rhetor; artifice of style had come to be second nature with him—even though the Latin scriptures were powerful modifiers of his classical literary patterns. But it is a very tricky business to convey such a Latin style into anything like modern English without considerable violence one way or the other. A literal rendering of the text is simply not readable English. And this falsifies the text in another way, for Augustine's Latin is eminently readable! On the other side, when one resorts to the unavoidable paraphrase there is always the open question as to the point beyond which the thought itself is being recast. It has been my aim and hope that these translations will give the reader an accurate medium of contact with Augustine's temper and mode of argumentation. There has been no thought of trying to contrive an English equivalent for his style. If Augustine's ideas come through this translation with positive force and clarity, there can be no serious reproach if it is neither as eloquent nor as elegant as Augustine in his own language. In any case, those who will compare this translation with the others will get at least a faint notion of how complex and truly brilliant the original is!

The sensitive reader soon recognizes that Augustine will not willingly be inspected from a distance or by a neutral observer. In all his writings there is a strong concern and moving power to involve his reader in his own process of inquiry and perplexity. There is a manifest eagerness to have him share in his own flashes of insight and his sudden glimpses of God's glory. Augustine's style is deeply personal; it is therefore idiomatic, and often colloquial. Even in his knottiest arguments, or in the labyrinthine mazes of his allegorizing (e.g., *Confessions*, Bk. XIII, or *Enchiridion*, XVIII), he seeks to maintain contact with his reader in genuine respect and openness. He is never content to seek and find the truth in solitude. He must enlist his fellows in seeing and applying the truth as given. He is never the blind fideist; even in the face of mystery, there is a constant reliance on the limited but real powers of human reason, and a constant striving for clarity and intelligibility. In this sense, he was a consistent follower of his own principle of "Christian Socratism," developed in the *De Magistro* and the *De catechezandis rudibus*.

Even the best of Augustine's writing bears the marks of his own time and there is much in these old books that is of little interest to any but the specialist. There are many stones of stumbling in them for the modern secularist—and even for the modern Christian! Despite all this, it is impossible to read him with any attention at all without recognizing how his genius and his piety burst through the limitations of his times and his language—and even his English translations! He grips our hearts and minds and enlists us in the great enterprise to which his whole life was devoted: the search for and the celebration of God's grace and glory by which his faithful children are sustained and guided in their pilgrimage toward the true Light of us all.

The most useful critical text of the *Confessions* is that of Pierre de Labriolle (fifth edition, Paris, 1950). I have collated this with the other major critical editions: Martin Skutella, *S. Aureli Augustini Confessionum Libri Tredecim* (Leipzig, 1934)—itself a recension of the *Corpus Scriptorum ecclesiasticorum Latinorum XXXIII* text of Pius Knöll (Vienna, 1896)—and the second edition of John Gibb and William Montgomery (Cambridge, 1927).

There are two good critical texts of the *Enchiridion* and I have collated them: Otto Scheel, *Augustins Enchiridion* (zweite Auflage, Tübingen, 1930), and Jean Rivière, *Enchiridion* in the Bibliothèque Augustinienne, Œuvres de S. Augustin, première série: Opuscules, IX: *Exposés généraux de la foi* (Paris, 1947).

It remains for me to express my appreciation to the General Editors of this Library for their constructive help; to Professor Hollis W. Huston, who read the entire manuscript and made many valuable suggestions; and to Professor William A. Irwin, who greatly aided with parts of the *Enchiridion*. These men share the credit for preventing many flaws, but naturally no responsibility for those remaining. Professors Raymond P. Morris, of the Yale Divinity School Library; Robert Beach, of the Union Theological Seminary Library; and Decherd Turner, of our Bridwell Library here at Southern Methodist University, were especially generous in their bibliographical assistance. Last, but not least, Mrs. Hollis W. Huston and my wife, between them, managed the difficult task of putting the results of this project into fair copy. To them all I am most grateful.

AUGUSTINE'S TESTIMONY CONCERNING THE *CONFESSIONS*

I. The *Retractations*, II, 6 (A.D. 427)

1. My *Confessions*, in thirteen books, praise the righteous and good God as they speak either of my evil or good, and they are meant to excite men's minds and affections toward him. At least as far as I am concerned, this is what they did for me when they were being written and they still do this when read. What some people think of them is their own affair [*ipse viderint*]; but I do know that they have given pleasure to many of my brethren and still do so. The first through the tenth books were written about myself; the other three about Holy Scripture, from what is written there, *In the beginning God created the heaven and the earth,*[2] even as far as the reference to the Sabbath rest.[3]

2. In Book IV, when I confessed my soul's misery over the death of a friend and said that our soul had somehow been made one out of two souls, "But it may have been that I was afraid to die, lest he should then die wholly whom I had so greatly loved" (Ch. VI, 11)—this now seems to be more a trivial declamation than a serious confession, although this inept expression may be tempered somewhat by the "may have been" [*forte*] which I added. And in Book XIII what I said—"The firmament was made between the higher waters (and superior) and the lower (and inferior) waters"—was said without sufficient thought. In any case, the matter is very obscure.

This work begins thus: "Great art thou, O Lord."

II. *De Dono Perseverantiae*, XX, 53 (A.D. 428)

Which of my shorter works has been more widely known or given greater pleasure than the [thirteen] books of my *Confes*-

2 Gen. 1:1.   3 Gen. 2:2.

sions? And, although I published them long before the Pelagian heresy had even begun to be, it is plain that in them I said to my God, again and again, "Give what thou commandest and command what thou wilt." When these words of mine were repeated in Pelagius' presence at Rome by a certain brother of mine (an episcopal colleague), he could not bear them and contradicted him so excitedly that they nearly came to a quarrel. Now what, indeed, does God command, first and foremost, except that we believe in him? This faith, therefore, he himself gives; so that it is well said to him, "Give what thou commandest." Moreover, in those same books, concerning my account of my conversion when God turned me to that faith which I was laying waste with a very wretched and wild verbal assault,[4] do you not remember how the narration shows that I was given as a gift to the faithful and daily tears of my mother, who had been promised that I should not perish? I certainly declared there that God by his grace turns men's wills to the true faith when they are not only averse to it, but actually adverse. As for the other ways in which I sought God's aid in my growth in perseverance, you either know or can review them as you wish (*PL*, 45, c. 1026).

III. *Letter to Darius* (A.D. 429)

Thus, my son, take the books of my *Confessions* and use them as a good man should—not superficially, but as a Christian in Christian charity. Here see me as I am and do not praise me for more than I am. Here believe nothing else about me than my own testimony. Here observe what I have been in myself and through myself. And if something in me pleases you, here praise Him with me—him whom I desire to be praised on my account and not myself. "For it is he that hath made us, and not we ourselves."[5] Indeed, we were ourselves quite lost; but he who made us, remade us [*sed qui fecit, refecit*]. As, then, you find me in these pages, pray for me that I shall not fail but that I may go on to be perfected. Pray for me, my son, pray for me! (*Epist.* CCXXXI, *PL*, 33, c. 1025).

4 Notice the echo here of Acts 9:1.   5 Ps. 100:3.

AUGUSTINE'S TESTIMONY CONCERNING THE *ENCHIRIDION*

THE *Retractations*, II, 63

I also wrote a book "On Faith, Hope, and Love" since the one to whom it was written had asked me for a little treatise of mine that he might always have it "at hand"—the kind of book the Greeks call an *enchiridion*. In it I discussed with what I think was sufficient care what seems to me to be the right way in which God should be served; for it is the service of God that the divine Scripture defines as man's true wisdom.

This books begins: "I cannot tell you, my dearest son Laurence."

TABLE OF SIGNIFICANT DATES

354 (November 13) Birth of Augustine at Tagaste, Numidia Proconsularis, son of Patricius and Monica.

373 Augustine, aged 19, discovers Cicero's *Hortensius*, and is inspired to begin the quest for wisdom.

374–384 An "auditor" of the Manicheans.

375 First post as teacher of rhetoric, at Tagaste.

376 The year of the decisive battle of Hadrianople; Augustine transfers to Carthage.

383 Augustine leaves Africa for Rome, in hopes of improving his professional fortune.

384 Moves to Milan as professor of rhetoric, meets Ambrose and enrolls as catechumen in the Catholic Church.

385 Discovers "the books of the Platonists" and achieves a Plotinian ecstasy.

386 Christian conversion in Milan.

386–387 The sojourn at Cassiciacum.

387 Baptism at Milan of Augustine, Alypius, and Adeodatus. Death of Monica at Ostia.

388 Adeodatus dies. Augustine back in Africa in a monastic community at Tagaste.

391 Ordained presbyter at Hippo.

395 Consecrated assistant bishop to Valerius at Hippo—succeeded him as bishop in 396.

397–398 Composition of the *Confessions*.

403–412 Controversy with the Donatists, culminating in the famous Conference of Carthage in 411 and the imperial edict against Donatism in 412.

410 The sacking of Rome by Alaric.

412–421 The Pelagian controversy.

416 Publication of the *De Trinitate*.
413–426 Composition of the *De civitate Deo*.
421 The *Enchiridion* written for Laurentius.
427 Augustine reviews his authorship in the *Retractationes*.
430 (August 28) Death of Augustine at Hippo during the siege of the town by the Vandals.

THE CONFESSIONS OF SAINT AUGUSTINE

The Confessions of Saint Augustine

BOOK ONE

In God's searching presence, Augustine undertakes to plumb the depths of his memory to trace the mysterious pilgrimage of grace which his life has been—and to praise God for his constant and omnipotent grace. In a mood of sustained prayer, he recalls what he can of his infancy, his learning to speak, and his childhood experiences in school. He concludes with a paean of grateful praise to God.

CHAPTER I

1. "Great art thou, O Lord, and greatly to be praised; great is thy power, and infinite is thy wisdom."[1] And man desires to praise thee, for he is a part of thy creation; he bears his mortality about with him and carries the evidence of his sin and the proof that thou dost resist the proud. Still he desires to praise thee, this man who is only a small part of thy creation. Thou hast prompted him, that he should delight to praise thee, for thou hast made us for thyself and restless is our heart until it comes to rest in thee. Grant me, O Lord, to know and understand whether first to invoke thee or to praise thee; whether first to know thee or call upon thee. But who can invoke thee, knowing thee not? For he who knows thee not may invoke thee as another than thou art. It may be that we should invoke thee in order that we may come to know thee. But "how shall they call on him in whom they have not believed? Or how shall they believe without a preacher?"[2] Now, "they shall praise the Lord who seek him,"[3] for "those who seek shall find him,"[4] and,

---

[1] Cf. Ps. 145:3 and Ps. 147:5. [2] Rom. 10:14.
[3] Ps. 22:26. [4] Matt. 7:7.

finding him, shall praise him. I will seek thee, O Lord, and call upon thee. I call upon thee, O Lord, in my faith which thou hast given me, which thou hast inspired in me through the humanity of thy Son, and through the ministry of thy preacher.[5]

CHAPTER II

2. And how shall I call upon my God—my God and my Lord? For when I call on him I ask him to come into me. And what place is there in me into which my God can come? How could God, the God who made both heaven and earth, come into me? Is there anything in me, O Lord my God, that can contain thee? Do even the heaven and the earth, which thou hast made, and in which thou didst make me, contain thee? Is it possible that, since without thee nothing would be which does exist, thou didst make it so that whatever exists has some capacity to receive thee? Why, then, do I ask thee to come into me, since I also am and could not be if thou wert not in me? For I am not, after all, in hell—and yet thou art there too, for "if I go down into hell, thou art there." [6] Therefore I would not exist—I would simply not be at all—unless I exist in thee, from whom and by whom and in whom all things are. Even so, Lord; even so. Where do I call thee to, when I am already in thee? Or from whence wouldst thou come into me? Where, beyond heaven and earth, could I go that there my God might come to me—he who hath said, "I fill heaven and earth"? [7]

CHAPTER III

3. Since, then, thou dost fill the heaven and earth, do they contain thee? Or, dost thou fill and overflow them, because they cannot contain thee? And where dost thou pour out what remains of thee after heaven and earth are full? Or, indeed, is there no need that thou, who dost contain all things, shouldst be contained by any, since those things which thou dost fill thou fillest by containing them? For the vessels which thou dost fill do not confine thee, since even if they were broken, thou wouldst not be poured out. And, when thou art poured out on us, thou art not thereby brought down; rather, we are uplifted. Thou art

---

[5] A reference to Bishop Ambrose of Milan; see Bk. V, Ch. XIII; Bk. VIII, Ch. II, 3.
[6] Ps. 139:8.   [7] Jer. 23:24.

not scattered; rather, thou dost gather us together. But when thou dost fill all things, dost thou fill them with thy whole being? Or, since not even all things together could contain thee altogether, does any one thing contain a single part, and do all things contain that same part at the same time? Do singulars contain thee singly? Do greater things contain more of thee, and smaller things less? Or, is it not rather that thou art wholly present everywhere, yet in such a way that nothing contains thee wholly?

CHAPTER IV

4. What, therefore, is my God? What, I ask, but the Lord God? "For who is Lord but the Lord himself, or who is God besides our God?" [8] Most high, most excellent, most potent, most omnipotent; most merciful and most just; most secret and most truly present; most beautiful and most strong; stable, yet not supported; unchangeable, yet changing all things; never new, never old; making all things new, yet bringing old age upon the proud, and they know it not; always working, ever at rest; gathering, yet needing nothing; sustaining, pervading, and protecting; creating, nourishing, and developing; seeking, and yet possessing all things. Thou dost love, but without passion; art jealous, yet free from care; dost repent without remorse; art angry, yet remainest serene. Thou changest thy ways, leaving thy plans unchanged; thou recoverest what thou hast never really lost. Thou art never in need but still thou dost rejoice at thy gains; art never greedy, yet demandest dividends. Men pay more than is required so that thou dost become a debtor; yet who can possess anything at all which is not already thine? Thou owest men nothing, yet payest out to them as if in debt to thy creature, and when thou dost cancel debts thou losest nothing thereby. Yet, O my God, my life, my holy Joy, what is this that I have said? What can any man say when he speaks of thee? But woe to them that keep silence—since even those who say most are dumb.

CHAPTER V

5. Who shall bring me to rest in thee? Who will send thee into my heart so to overwhelm it that my sins shall be blotted out and I may embrace thee, my only good? What art thou to me? Have mercy that I may speak. What am I to thee that thou

[8] Cf. Ps. 18:31.

shouldst command me to love thee, and if I do it not, art angry and threatenest vast misery? Is it, then, a trifling sorrow not to love thee? It is not so to me. Tell me, by thy mercy, O Lord, my God, what thou art to me. "Say to my soul, I am your salvation." [9] So speak that I may hear. Behold, the ears of my heart are before thee, O Lord; open them and "say to my soul, I am your salvation." I will hasten after that voice, and I will lay hold upon thee. Hide not thy face from me. Even if I die, let me see thy face lest I die.

6. The house of my soul is too narrow for thee to come in to me; let it be enlarged by thee. It is in ruins; do thou restore it. There is much about it which must offend thy eyes; I confess and know it. But who will cleanse it? Or, to whom shall I cry but to thee? "Cleanse thou me from my secret faults," O Lord, "and keep back thy servant from strange sins." [10] "I believe, and therefore do I speak." [11] But thou, O Lord, thou knowest. Have I not confessed my transgressions unto thee, O my God; and hast thou not put away the iniquity of my heart? [12] I do not contend in judgment with thee, [13] who art Truth itself; and I would not deceive myself, lest my iniquity lie even to itself. I do not, therefore, contend in judgment with thee, for "if thou, Lord, shouldst mark iniquities, O Lord, who shall stand?" [14]

CHAPTER VI

7. Still, dust and ashes as I am, allow me to speak before thy mercy. Allow me to speak, for, behold, it is to thy mercy that I speak and not to a man who scorns me. Yet perhaps even thou mightest scorn me; but when thou dost turn and attend to me, thou wilt have mercy upon me. For what do I wish to say, O Lord my God, but that I know not whence I came hither into this life-in-death. Or should I call it death-in-life? I do not know. And yet the consolations of thy mercy have sustained me from the very beginning, as I have heard from my fleshly parents, from whom and in whom thou didst form me in time—for I cannot myself remember. Thus even though they sustained me by the consolation of woman's milk, neither my mother nor my nurses filled their own breasts but thou, through them, didst give me the food of infancy according to thy ordinance and thy bounty which underlie all things. For it was thou who didst

9 Ps. 35:3.
11 Ps. 116:10.
13 Cf. Job 9:2.
10 Cf. Ps. 19:12, 13.
12 Cf. Ps. 32:5.
14 Ps. 130:3.

cause me not to want more than thou gavest and it was thou who gavest to those who nourished me the will to give me what thou didst give them. And they, by an instinctive affection, were willing to give me what thou hadst supplied abundantly. It was, indeed, good for them that my good should come through them, though, in truth, it was not from them but by them. For it is from thee, O God, that all good things come—and from my God is all my health. This is what I have since learned, as thou hast made it abundantly clear by all that I have seen thee give, both to me and to those around me. For even at the very first I knew how to suck, to lie quiet when I was full, and to cry when in pain—nothing more.

8. Afterward I began to laugh—at first in my sleep, then when waking. For this I have been told about myself and I believe it—though I cannot remember it—for I see the same things in other infants. Then, little by little, I realized where I was and wished to tell my wishes to those who might satisfy them, but I could not! For my wants were inside me, and they were outside, and they could not by any power of theirs come into my soul. And so I would fling my arms and legs about and cry, making the few and feeble gestures that I could, though indeed the signs were not much like what I inwardly desired and when I was not satisfied—either from not being understood or because what I got was not good for me—I grew indignant that my elders were not subject to me and that those on whom I actually had no claim did not wait on me as slaves—and I avenged myself on them by crying. That infants are like this, I have myself been able to learn by watching them; and they, though they knew me not, have shown me better what I was like than my own nurses who knew me.

9. And, behold, my infancy died long ago, but I am still living. But thou, O Lord, whose life is forever and in whom nothing dies—since before the world was, indeed, before all that can be called "before," thou wast, and thou art the God and Lord of all thy creatures; and with thee abide all the stable causes of all unstable things, the unchanging sources of all changeable things, and the eternal reasons of all nonrational and temporal things—tell me, thy suppliant, O God, tell me, O merciful One, in pity tell a pitiful creature whether my infancy followed yet an earlier age of my life that had already passed away before it. Was it such another age which I spent in my mother's womb? For something of that sort has been suggested to me, and I have myself seen pregnant women. But what, O

God, my Joy, preceded *that* period of life? Was I, indeed, any-where, or anybody? No one can explain these things to me, neither father nor mother, nor the experience of others, nor my own memory. Dost thou laugh at me for asking such things? Or dost thou command me to praise and confess unto thee only what I know?

10. I give thanks to thee, O Lord of heaven and earth, giving praise to thee for that first being and my infancy of which I have no memory. For thou hast granted to man that he should come to self-knowledge through the knowledge of others, and that he should believe many things about himself on the authority of the womenfolk. Now, clearly, I had life and being; and, as my infancy closed, I was already learning signs by which my feelings could be communicated to others.

Whence could such a creature come but from thee, O Lord? Is any man skillful enough to have fashioned himself? Or is there any other source from which being and life could flow into us, save this, that thou, O Lord, hast made us— thou with whom being and life are one, since thou thyself art supreme being and supreme life both together. For thou art infinite and in thee there is no change, nor an end to this present day—although there is a sense in which it ends in thee since all things are in thee and there would be no such thing as days passing away unless thou didst sustain them. And since "thy years shall have no end,"[15] thy years are an ever-present day. And how many of ours and our fathers' days have passed through this thy day and have received from it what measure and fashion of being they had? And all the days to come shall so receive and so pass away. "But thou art the same"![16] And all the things of tomor-row and the days yet to come, and all of yesterday and the days that are past, thou wilt gather into this thy day. What is it to me if someone does not understand this? Let him still rejoice and continue to ask, "What is this?" Let him also rejoice and prefer to seek thee, even if he fails to find an answer, rather than to seek an answer and not find thee!

CHAPTER VII

11. "Hear me, O God! Woe to the sins of men!" When a man cries thus, thou showest him mercy, for thou didst create the man but not the sin in him. Who brings to remembrance the

15 Ps. 102:27.   16 Ps. 102:27.

sins of my infancy? For in thy sight there is none free from sin, not even the infant who has lived but a day upon this earth. Who brings this to my remembrance? Does not each little one, in whom I now observe what I no longer remember of myself? In what ways, in that time, did I sin? Was it that I cried for the breast? If I should now so cry—not indeed for the breast, but for food suitable to my condition—I should be most justly laughed at and rebuked. What I did then deserved rebuke but, since I could not understand those who rebuked me, neither custom nor common sense permitted me to be rebuked. As we grow we root out and cast away from us such childish habits. Yet I have not seen anyone who is wise who cast away the good when trying to purge the bad. Nor was it good, even in that time, to strive to get by crying what, if it had been given me, would have been hurtful; or to be bitterly indignant at those who, because they were older—not slaves, either, but free—and wiser than I, would not indulge my capricious desires. Was it a good thing for me to try, by struggling as hard as I could, to harm them for not obeying me, even when it would have done me harm to have been obeyed? Thus, the infant's innocence lies in the weakness of his body and not in the infant mind. I have myself observed a baby to be jealous, though it could not speak; it was livid as it watched another infant at the breast.

Who is ignorant of this? Mothers and nurses tell us that they cure these things by I know not what remedies. But is this innocence, when the fountain of milk is flowing fresh and abundant, that another who needs it should not be allowed to share it, even though he requires such nourishment to sustain his life? Yet we look leniently on such things, not because they are not faults, or even small faults, but because they will vanish as the years pass. For, although we allow for such things in an infant, the same things could not be tolerated patiently in an adult.

12. Therefore, O Lord my God, thou who gavest life to the infant, and a body which, as we see, thou hast furnished with senses, shaped with limbs, beautified with form, and endowed with all vital energies for its well-being and health—thou dost command me to praise thee for these things, to give thanks unto the Lord, and to sing praise unto his name, O Most High.[17] For thou art God, omnipotent and good, even if thou hadst done no more than these things, which no other but thou canst do— thou alone who madest all things fair and didst order everything according to thy law.

17 Cf. Ps. 92:1.

I am loath to dwell on this part of my life of which, O Lord, I have no remembrance, about which I must trust the word of others and what I can surmise from observing other infants, even if such guesses are trustworthy. For it lies in the deep murk of my forgetfulness and thus is like the period which I passed in my mother's womb. But if "I was conceived in iniquity, and in sin my mother nourished me in her womb,"[18] where, I pray thee, O my God, where, O Lord, or when was I, thy servant, ever innocent? But see now, I pass over that period, for what have I to do with a time from which I can recall no memories?

CHAPTER VIII

13. Did I not, then, as I grew out of infancy, come next to boyhood, or rather did it not come to me and succeed my infancy? My infancy did not go away (for where would it go?). It was simply no longer present; and I was no longer an infant who could not speak, but now a chattering boy. I remember this, and I have since observed how I learned to speak. My elders did not teach me words by rote, as they taught me my letters afterward. But I myself, when I was unable to communicate all I wished to say to whomever I wished by means of whimperings and grunts and various gestures of my limbs (which I used to reinforce my demands), I myself repeated the sounds already stored in my memory by the mind which thou, O my God, hadst given me. When they called some thing by name and pointed it out while they spoke, I saw it and realized that the thing they wished to indicate was called by the name they then uttered. And what they meant was made plain by the gestures of their bodies, by a kind of natural language, common to all nations, which expresses itself through changes of countenance, glances of the eye, gestures and intonations which indicate a disposition and attitude—either to seek or to possess, to reject or to avoid. So it was that by frequently hearing words, in different phrases, I gradually identified the objects which the words stood for and, having formed my mouth to repeat these signs, I was thereby able to express my will. Thus I exchanged with those about me the verbal signs by which we express our wishes and advanced deeper into the stormy fellowship of human life, depending all the while upon the authority of my parents and the behest of my elders.

[18] Cf. Ps. 51:5.

CHAPTER IX

14. O my God! What miseries and mockeries did I then experience when it was impressed on me that obedience to my teachers was proper to my boyhood estate if I was to flourish in this world and distinguish myself in those tricks of speech which would gain honor for me among men, and deceitful riches! To this end I was sent to school to get learning, the value of which I knew not—wretch that I was. Yet if I was slow to learn, I was flogged. For this was deemed praiseworthy by our forefathers and many had passed before us in the same course, and thus had built up the precedent for the sorrowful road on which we too were compelled to travel, multiplying labor and sorrow upon the sons of Adam. About this time, O Lord, I observed men praying to thee, and I learned from them to conceive thee— after my capacity for understanding as it was then—to be some great Being, who, though not visible to our senses, was able to hear and help us. Thus as a boy I began to pray to thee, my Help and my Refuge, and, in calling on thee, broke the bands of my tongue. Small as I was, I prayed with no slight earnestness that I might not be beaten at school. And when thou didst not heed me—for that would have been giving me over to my folly—my elders and even my parents too, who wished me no ill, treated my stripes as a joke, though they were then a great and grievous ill to me.

15. Is there anyone, O Lord, with a spirit so great, who cleaves to thee with such steadfast affection (or is there even a kind of obtuseness that has the same effect)—is there any man who, by cleaving devoutly to thee, is endowed with so great a courage that he can regard indifferently those racks and hooks and other torture weapons from which men throughout the world pray so fervently to be spared; and can they scorn those who so greatly fear these torments, just as my parents were amused at the torments with which our teachers punished us boys? For we were no less afraid of our pains, nor did we beseech thee less to escape them. Yet, even so, we were sinning by writing or reading or studying less than our assigned lessons.

For I did not, O Lord, lack memory or capacity, for, by thy will, I possessed enough for my age. However, my mind was absorbed only in play, and I was punished for this by those who were doing the same things themselves. But the idling of our elders is called business; the idling of boys, though quite like it, is punished by those same elders, and no one pities either the boys or the men. For will any common sense observer agree that I was rightly punished as a boy for playing ball—just because this hindered me from learning more quickly those lessons by means of which, as a man, I could play at more shameful games? And did he by whom I was beaten do anything different? When he was worsted in some small controversy with a fellow teacher, he was more tormented by anger and envy than I was when beaten by a playmate in the ball game.

CHAPTER X

16. And yet I sinned, O Lord my God, thou ruler and creator of all natural things—but of sins only the ruler—I sinned, O Lord my God, in acting against the precepts of my parents and of those teachers. For this learning which they wished me to acquire—no matter what their motives were—I might have put to good account afterward. I disobeyed them, not because I had chosen a better way, but from a sheer love of play. I loved the vanity of victory, and I loved to have my ears tickled with lying fables, which made them itch even more ardently, and a similar curiosity glowed more and more in my eyes for the shows and sports of my elders. Yet those who put on such shows are held in such high repute that almost all desire the same for their children. They are therefore willing to have them beaten, if their childhood games keep them from the studies by which their parents desire them to grow up to be able to give such shows. Look down on these things with mercy, O Lord, and deliver us who now call upon thee; deliver those also who do not call upon thee, that they may call upon thee, and thou mayest deliver them.

CHAPTER XI

17. Even as a boy I had heard of eternal life promised to us through the humility of the Lord our God, who came down to visit us in our pride, and I was signed with the sign of his cross, and was seasoned with his salt even from the womb of my mother, who greatly trusted in thee. Thou didst see, O Lord, how, once, while I was still a child, I was suddenly seized with stomach pains and was at the point of death—thou didst see, O my God, for even then thou wast my keeper, with what agitation and with what faith I solicited from the piety of my mother and from thy Church (which is the mother of us all) the baptism of

thy Christ, my Lord and my God. The mother of my flesh was much perplexed, for, with a heart pure in thy faith, she was always in deep travail for my eternal salvation. If I had not quickly recovered, she would have provided forthwith for my initiation and washing by thy life-giving sacraments, confessing thee, O Lord Jesus, for the forgiveness of sins. So my cleansing was deferred, as if it were inevitable that, if I should live, I would be further polluted; and, further, because the guilt contracted by sin after baptism would be still greater and more perilous.

Thus, at that time, I "believed" along with my mother and the whole household, except my father. But he did not overcome the influence of my mother's piety in me, nor did he prevent my believing in Christ, although he had not yet believed in him. For it was her desire, O my God, that I should acknowledge thee as my Father rather than him. In this thou didst aid her to overcome her husband, to whom, though his superior, she yielded obedience. In this way she also yielded obedience to thee, who dost so command.

18. I ask thee, O my God, for I would gladly know if it be thy will, to what good end my baptism was deferred at that time? Was it indeed for my good that the reins were slackened, as it were, to encourage me in sin? Or, were they not slackened? If not, then why is it still dinned into our ears on all sides, "Let him alone, let him do as he pleases, for he is not yet baptized"? In the matter of bodily health, no one says, "Let him alone; let him be worse wounded; for he is not yet cured"! How much better, then, would it have been for me to have been cured at once—and if thereafter, through the diligent care of friends and myself, my soul's restored health had been kept safe in thy keeping, who gave it in the first place! This would have been far better, in truth. But how many and great the waves of temptation which appeared to hang over me as I grew out of childhood! These were foreseen by my mother, and she preferred that the unformed clay should be risked to them rather than the clay molded after Christ's image.[19]

CHAPTER XII

19. But in this time of childhood—which was far less dreaded for me than my adolescence—I had no love of learning, and

[19] In baptism which, Augustine believed, established the *effigiem Christi* in the human soul.

hated to be driven to it. Yet I was driven to it just the same, and good was done for me, even though I did not do it well, for I would not have learned if I had not been forced to it. For no man does well against his will, even if what he does is a good thing. Neither did they who forced me do well, but the good that was done me came from thee, my God. For they did not care about the way in which I would use what they forced me to learn, and took it for granted that it was to satisfy the inordinate desires of a rich beggary and a shameful glory. But thou, Lord, by whom the hairs of our head are numbered, didst use for my good the error of all who pushed me on to study: but my error in not being willing to learn thou didst use for my punishment. And I—though so small a boy yet so great a sinner—was not punished without warrant. Thus by the instrumentality of those who did not do well, thou didst well for me; and by my own sin thou didst justly punish me. For it is even as thou hast ordained: that every inordinate affection brings on its own punishment.

CHAPTER XIII

20. But what were the causes for my strong dislike of Greek literature, which I studied from my boyhood? Even to this day I have not fully understood them. For Latin I loved exceedingly —not just the rudiments, but what the grammarians teach. For those beginner's lessons in reading, writing, and reckoning, I considered no less a burden and pain than Greek. Yet whence came this, unless from the sin and vanity of this life? For I was "but flesh, a wind that passeth away and cometh not again."[20] Those first lessons were better, assuredly, because they were more certain, and through them I acquired, and still retain, the power of reading what I find written and of writing for myself what I will. In the other subjects, however, I was compelled to learn about the wanderings of a certain Aeneas, oblivious of my own wanderings, and to weep for Dido dead, who slew herself for love. And all this while I bore with dry eyes my own wretched self dying to thee, O God, my life, in the midst of these things.

21. For what can be more wretched than the wretch who has no pity upon himself, who sheds tears over Dido, dead for the love of Aeneas, but who sheds no tears for his own death in not loving thee, O God, light of my heart, and bread of the inner

[20] Cf. Ps. 78:39.

mouth of my soul, O power that links together my mind with my inmost thoughts? I did not love thee, and thus committed fornication against thee.[21] Those around me, also sinning, thus cried out: "Well done! Well done!" The friendship of this world is fornication against thee; and "Well done! Well done!" is cried until one feels ashamed not to show himself a man in this way. For my own condition I shed no tears, though I wept for Dido, who "sought death at the sword's point,"[22] while I myself was seeking the lowest rung of thy creation, having forsaken thee; earth sinking back to earth again. And, if I had been forbidden to read these poems, I would have grieved that I was not allowed to read what grieved me. This sort of madness is considered more honorable and more fruitful learning than the beginner's course in which I learned to read and write.

22. But now, O my God, cry unto my soul, and let thy truth say to me: "Not so, not so! That first learning was far better." For, obviously, I would rather forget the wanderings of Aeneas, and all such things, than forget how to write and read. Still, over the entrance of the grammar school there hangs a veil. This is not so much the sign of a covering for a mystery as a curtain for error. Let them exclaim against me—those I no longer fear—while I confess to thee, my God, what my soul desires, and let me find some rest, for in blaming my own evil ways I may come to love thy holy ways. Neither let those cry out against me who buy and sell the baubles of literature. For if I ask them if it is true, as the poet says, that Aeneas once came to Carthage, the unlearned will reply that they do not know and the learned will deny that it is true. But if I ask with what letters the name Aeneas is written, all who have ever learned this will answer correctly, in accordance with the conventional understanding men have agreed upon as to these signs. Again, if I should ask which would cause the greatest inconvenience in our life, if it were forgotten: reading and writing, or these poetical fictions, who does not see what everyone would answer who had not entirely lost his own memory? I erred, then, when as a boy I preferred those vain studies to these more profitable ones, or rather loved the one and hated the other. "One and one are two, two and two are four": this was then a truly hateful song to me. But the wooden horse full of its armed soldiers, and the holocaust of Troy, and the spectral image of Creüsa were all a most delightful—and vain—show![23]

21 Cf. Ps. 72:27.   22 *Aeneid*, VI, 457.
23 Cf. *Aeneid*, II.

CHAPTER XIV

23. But why, then, did I dislike Greek learning, which was full of such tales? For Homer was skillful in inventing such poetic fictions and is most sweetly wanton; yet when I was a boy, he was most disagreeable to me. I believe that Virgil would have the same effect on Greek boys as Homer did on me if they were forced to learn him. For the tedium of learning a foreign language mingled gall into the sweetness of those Grecian myths. For I did not understand a word of the language, and yet I was driven with threats and cruel punishments to learn it. There was also a time when, as an infant, I knew no Latin; but this I acquired without any fear or tormenting, but merely by being alert to the blandishments of my nurses, the jests of those who smiled on me, and the sportiveness of those who toyed with me. I learned all this, indeed, without being urged by any pressure of punishment, for my own heart urged me to bring forth its own fashioning, which I could not do except by learning words: not from those who taught me but those who talked to me, into whose ears I could pour forth whatever I could fashion. From this it is sufficiently clear that a free curiosity is more effective in learning than a discipline based on fear. Yet, by thy ordinance, O God, discipline is given to restrain the excesses of freedom; this ranges from the ferule of the schoolmaster to the trials of the martyr and has the effect of mingling for us a wholesome bitterness, which calls us back to thee from the poisonous pleasures that first drew us from thee.

CHAPTER XV

24. Hear my prayer, O Lord; let not my soul faint under thy discipline, nor let me faint in confessing unto thee thy mercies, whereby thou hast saved me from all my most wicked ways till thou shouldst become sweet to me beyond all the allurements that I used to follow. Let me come to love thee wholly, and grasp thy hand with my whole heart that thou mayest deliver me from every temptation, even unto the last. And thus, O Lord, my King and my God, may all things useful that I learned as a boy now be offered in thy service—let it be that for thy service I now speak and write and reckon. For when I was learning vain things, thou didst impose thy discipline upon

me: and thou hast forgiven me my sin of delighting in those vanities. In those studies I learned many a useful word, but these might have been learned in matters not so vain; and surely that is the safe way for youths to walk in.

CHAPTER XVI

25. But woe unto you, O torrent of human custom! Who shall stay your course? When will you ever run dry? How long will you carry down the sons of Eve into that vast and hideous ocean, which even those who have the Tree (for an ark) [24] can scarcely pass over? Do I not read in you the stories of Jove the thunderer—and the adulterer? [25] How could he be both? But so it says, and the sham thunder served as a cloak for him to play at real adultery. Yet which of our gowned masters will give a tempered hearing to a man trained in their own schools who cries out and says: "These were Homer's fictions; he transfers things human to the gods. I could have wished that he would transfer divine things to us." [26] But it would have been more true if he said, "These are, indeed, his fictions, but he attributed divine attributes to sinful men, that crimes might not be accounted crimes, and that whoever committed such crimes might appear to imitate the celestial gods and not abandoned men."

26. And yet, O torrent of hell, the sons of men are still cast into you, and they pay fees for learning all these things. And much is made of it when this goes on in the forum under the auspices of laws which give a salary over and above the fees. And you beat against your rocky shore and roar: "Here words may be learned; here you can attain the eloquence which is so necessary to persuade people to your way of thinking; so helpful in unfolding your opinions." Verily, they seem to argue that we should never have understood these words, "golden shower," "bosom," "intrigue," "highest heavens," and other such words, if Terence had not introduced a good-for-nothing

---

24 *Lignum* is a common metaphor for the cross; and it was often joined to the figure of Noah's ark, as the means of safe transport from earth to heaven.

25 This apostrophe to "the torrent of human custom" now switches its focus to the poets who celebrated the philanderings of the gods; see *De civ. Dei*, II, vii–xi; IV, xxvi–xxviii.

26 Probably a contemporary disciple of Cicero (or the Academics) whom Augustine had heard levy a rather common philosopher's complaint against Olympian religion and the poetic myths about it. Cf. De Labriolle, I, 21 (see Bibl.).

youth upon the stage, setting up a picture of Jove as his example
of lewdness and telling the tale

> "Of Jove's descending in a golden shower
> Into Danae's bosom . . .
> With a woman to intrigue."

See how he excites himself to lust, as if by a heavenly authority,
when he says:

> "Great Jove,
> Who shakes the highest heavens with his thunder;
> Shall I, poor mortal man, not do the same?
> I've done it, and with all my heart, I'm glad." [27]

These words are not learned one whit more easily because of
this vileness, but through them the vileness is more boldly perpetrated. I do not blame the words, for they are, as it were,
choice and precious vessels, but I do deplore the wine of error
which was poured out to us by teachers already drunk. And,
unless we also drank we were beaten, without liberty of appeal
to a sober judge. And yet, O my God, in whose presence I can
now with security recall this, I learned these things willingly
and with delight, and for it I was called a boy of good promise.

CHAPTER XVII

27. Bear with me, O my God, while I speak a little of those
talents, thy gifts, and of the follies on which I wasted them. For
a lesson was given me that sufficiently disturbed my soul, for in
it there was both hope of praise and fear of shame or stripes. The
assignment was that I should declaim the words of Juno, as she
raged and sorrowed that she could not

> "Bar off Italy
> From all the approaches of the Teucrian king." [28]

I had learned that Juno had never uttered these words. Yet we
were compelled to stray in the footsteps of these poetic fictions,
and to turn into prose what the poet had said in verse. In the
declamation, the boy won most applause who most strikingly
reproduced the passions of anger and sorrow according to the
"character" of the persons presented and who clothed it all in

[27] Terence, *Eunuch.*, 584–591; quoted again in *De civ. Dei*, II, vii.
[28] *Aeneid*, I, 38.

the most suitable language. What is it now to me, O my true Life, my God, that my declaiming was applauded above that of many of my classmates and fellow students? Actually, was not all that smoke and wind? Besides, was there nothing else on which I could have exercised my wit and tongue? Thy praise, O Lord, thy praises might have propped up the tendrils of my heart by thy Scriptures; and it would not have been dragged away by these empty trifles, a shameful prey to the spirits of the air. For there is more than one way in which men sacrifice to the fallen angels.

CHAPTER XVIII

28. But it was no wonder that I was thus carried toward vanity and was estranged from thee, O my God, when men were held up as models to me who, when relating a deed of theirs— not in itself evil—were covered with confusion if found guilty of a barbarism or a solecism; but who could tell of their own licentiousness and be applauded for it, so long as they did it in a full and ornate oration of well-chosen words. Thou seest all this, O Lord, and dost keep silence—"long-suffering, and plenteous in mercy and truth" [29] as thou art. Wilt thou keep silence forever? Even now thou drawest from that vast deep the soul that seeks thee and thirsts after thy delight, whose "heart said unto thee, 'I have sought thy face; thy face, Lord, will I seek.' " [30] For I was far from thy face in the dark shadows of passion. For it is not by our feet, nor by change of place, that we either turn from thee or return to thee. That younger son did not charter horses or chariots, or ships, or fly away on visible wings, or journey by walking so that in the far country he might prodigally waste all that thou didst give him when he set out. [31] A kind Father when thou gavest; and kinder still when he returned destitute! To be wanton, that is to say, to be darkened in heart—this is to be far from thy face.

29. Look down, O Lord God, and see patiently, as thou art wont to do, how diligently the sons of men observe the conventional rules of letters and syllables, taught them by those who learned their letters beforehand, while they neglect the eternal rules of everlasting salvation taught by thee. They carry it so far that if he who practices or teaches the established rules of pronunciation should speak (contrary to grammatical usage)

[29] Cf. Ps. 103:8 and Ps. 86:15.   [30] Ps. 27:8.
[31] An interesting mixed reminiscence of *Enneads*, I, 5:8 and Luke 15:13-24.

without aspirating the first syllable of "*hominem*" ["*ominem*," and thus make it "a 'uman being"], he will offend men more than if he, a human being, were to *hate* another human being contrary to thy commandments. It is as if he should feel that there is an enemy who could be more destructive to himself than that hatred which excites him against his fellow man; or that he could destroy him whom he hates more completely than he destroys his own soul by this same hatred. Now, obviously, there is no knowledge of letters more innate than the writing of conscience—against doing unto another what one would not have done to himself.

How mysterious thou art, who "dwellest on high" [32] in silence. O thou, the only great God, who by an unwearied law hurlest down the penalty of blindness to unlawful desire! When a man seeking the reputation of eloquence stands before a human judge, while a thronging multitude surrounds him, and inveighs against his enemy with the most fierce hatred, he takes most vigilant heed that his tongue does not slip in a grammatical error, for example, and say *inter hominibus* [instead of *inter homines*], but he takes no heed lest, in the fury of his spirit, he cut off a man from his fellow men [*ex hominibus*].

30. These were the customs in the midst of which I was cast, an unhappy boy. This was the wrestling arena in which I was more fearful of perpetrating a barbarism than, having done so, of envying those who had not. These things I declare and confess to thee, my God. I was applauded by those whom I then thought it my whole duty to please, for I did not perceive the gulf of infamy wherein I was cast away from thy eyes.

For in thy eyes what was more infamous than I was already, since I displeased even my own kind and deceived, with endless lies, my tutor, my masters and parents—all from a love of play, a craving for frivolous spectacles, a stage-struck restlessness to imitate what I saw in these shows? I pilfered from my parents' cellar and table, sometimes driven by gluttony, sometimes just to have something to give to other boys in exchange for their baubles, which they were prepared to sell even though they liked them as well as I. Moreover, in this kind of play, I often sought dishonest victories, being myself conquered by the vain desire for pre-eminence. And what was I so unwilling to endure, and what was it that I censured so violently when I caught anyone, except the very things I did to others? And, when I was myself detected and censured, I preferred to quarrel rather than

[32] Ps. 123:1.

to yield. Is this the innocence of childhood? It is not, O Lord, it is not. I entreat thy mercy, O my God, for these same sins as we grow older are transferred from tutors and masters; they pass from nuts and balls and sparrows, to magistrates and kings, to gold and lands and slaves, just as the rod is succeeded by more severe chastisements. It was, then, the fact of humility in childhood that thou, O our King, didst approve as a symbol of humility when thou saidst, "Of such is the Kingdom of Heaven." [33]

CHAPTER XIX

31. However, O Lord, to thee most excellent and most good, thou Architect and Governor of the universe, thanks would be due thee, O our God, even if thou hadst not willed that I should survive my boyhood. For I existed even then; I lived and felt and was solicitous about my own well-being—a trace of that most mysterious unity from whence I had my being.[34] I kept watch, by my inner sense, over the integrity of my outer senses, and even in these trifles and also in my thoughts about trifles, I learned to take pleasure in truth. I was averse to being deceived; I had a vigorous memory; I was gifted with the power of speech, was softened by friendship, shunned sorrow, meanness, ignorance. Is not such an animated creature as this wonderful and praiseworthy? But all these are gifts of my God; I did not give them to myself. Moreover, they are good, and they all together constitute myself. Good, then, is he that made me, and he is my God; and before him will I rejoice exceedingly for every good gift which, even as a boy, I had. But herein lay my sin, that it was not in him, but in his creatures—myself and the rest—that I sought for pleasures, honors, and truths. And I fell thereby into sorrows, troubles, and errors. Thanks be to thee, my joy, my pride, my confidence, my God—thanks be to thee for thy gifts; but do thou preserve them in me. For thus wilt thou preserve me; and those things which thou hast given me shall be developed and perfected, and I myself shall be with thee, for from thee is my being.

[33] Matt. 19:14.
[34] Another Plotinian echo; cf. *Enneads*, III, 8:10.

BOOK TWO

He concentrates here on his sixteenth year, a year of idleness, lust, and adolescent mischief. The memory of stealing some pears prompts a deep probing of the motives and aims of sinful acts. "I became to myself a wasteland."

CHAPTER I

1. I wish now to review in memory my past wickedness and the carnal corruptions of my soul—not because I still love them, but that I may love thee, O my God. For love of thy love I do this, recalling in the bitterness of self-examination my wicked ways, that thou mayest grow sweet to me, thou sweetness without deception! Thou sweetness happy and assured! Thus thou mayest gather me up out of those fragments in which I was torn to pieces, while I turned away from thee, O Unity, and lost myself among "the many." [1] For as I became a youth, I longed to be satisfied with worldly things, and I dared to grow wild in a succession of various and shadowy loves. My form wasted away, and I became corrupt in thy eyes, yet I was still pleasing to my own eyes—and eager to please the eyes of men.

CHAPTER II

2. But what was it that delighted me save to love and to be loved? Still I did not keep the moderate way of the love of mind to mind—the bright path of friendship. Instead, the mists of passion steamed up out of the puddly concupiscence of the flesh, and the hot imagination of puberty, and they so obscured

---

[1] Yet another Plotinian phrase; cf. *Enneads*, I, 6, 9:1–2.

and overcast my heart that I was unable to distinguish pure affection from unholy desire. Both boiled confusedly within me, and dragged my unstable youth down over the cliffs of unchaste desires and plunged me into a gulf of infamy. Thy anger had come upon me, and I knew it not. I had been deafened by the clanking of the chains of my mortality, the punishment for my soul's pride, and I wandered farther from thee, and thou didst permit me to do so. I was tossed to and fro, and wasted, and poured out, and I boiled over in my fornications—and yet thou didst hold thy peace, O my tardy Joy! Thou didst still hold thy peace, and I wandered still farther from thee into more and yet more barren fields of sorrow, in proud dejection and restless lassitude.

3. If only there had been someone to regulate my disorder and turn to my profit the fleeting beauties of the things around me, and to fix a bound to their sweetness, so that the tides of my youth might have spent themselves upon the shore of marriage! Then they might have been tranquilized and satisfied with having children, as thy law prescribes, O Lord—O thou who dost form the offspring of our death and art able also with a tender hand to blunt the thorns which were excluded from thy paradise! [2] For thy omnipotence is not far from us even when we are far from thee. Now, on the other hand, I might have given more vigilant heed to the voice from the clouds: "Nevertheless, such shall have trouble in the flesh, but I spare you," [3] and, "It is good for a man not to touch a woman," [4] and, "He that is unmarried cares for the things that belong to the Lord, how he may please the Lord; but he that is married cares for the things that are of the world, how he may please his wife." [5] I should have listened more attentively to these words, and, thus having been "made a eunuch for the Kingdom of Heaven's sake," [6] I would have with greater happiness expected thy embraces.

4. But, fool that I was, I foamed in my wickedness as the sea and, forsaking thee, followed the rushing of my own tide, and burst out of all thy bounds. But I did not escape thy scourges. For what mortal can do so? Thou wast always by me, mercifully angry and flavoring all my unlawful pleasures with bitter discontent, in order that I might seek pleasures free from discontent. But where could I find such pleasure save in thee, O Lord—save in thee, who dost teach us by sorrow, who woundest

---

[2] Cf. Gen. 3:18 and *De bono conjugali*, 8-9, 32-35 (*N-PNF*, III, 396-413).
[3] I Cor. 7:28. [4] I Cor. 7:1.
[5] I Cor. 7:32, 33. [6] Cf. Matt. 19:12.

us to heal us, and dost kill us that we may not die apart from thee. Where was I, and how far was I exiled from the delights of thy house, in that sixteenth year of the age of my flesh, when the madness of lust held full sway in me—that madness which grants indulgence to human shamelessness, even though it is forbidden by thy laws—and I gave myself entirely to it? Meanwhile, my family took no care to save me from ruin by marriage, for their sole care was that I should learn how to make a powerful speech and become a persuasive orator.

CHAPTER III

5. Now, in that year my studies were interrupted. I had come back from Madaura, a neighboring city [7] where I had gone to study grammar and rhetoric; and the money for a further term at Carthage was being got together for me. This project was more a matter of my father's ambition than of his means, for he was only a poor citizen of Tagaste.

To whom am I narrating all this? Not to thee, O my God, but to my own kind in thy presence—to that small part of the human race who may chance to come upon these writings. And to what end? That I and all who read them may understand what depths there are from which we are to cry unto thee. [8] For what is more surely heard in thy ear than a confessing heart and a faithful life?

Who did not extol and praise my father, because he went quite beyond his means to supply his son with the necessary expenses for a far journey in the interest of his education? For many far richer citizens did not do so much for their children. Still, this same father troubled himself not at all as to how I was progressing toward thee nor how chaste I was, just so long as I was skillful in speaking—no matter how barren I was to thy tillage, O God, who art the one true and good Lord of my heart, which is thy field. [9]

6. During that sixteenth year of my age, I lived with my parents, having a holiday from school for a time—this idleness imposed upon me by my parents' straitened finances. The thornbushes of lust grew rank about my head, and there was no

---

[7] Twenty miles from Tagaste, famed as the birthplace of Apuleius, the only notable classical author produced by the province of Africa.

[8] Another echo of the *De profundis* (Ps. 130:1)—and the most explicit statement we have from Augustine of his motive and aim in writing these "confessions."   [9] Cf. I Cor. 3:9.

hand to root them out. Indeed, when my father saw me one day at the baths and perceived that I was becoming a man, and was showing the signs of adolescence, he joyfully told my mother about it as if already looking forward to grandchildren, rejoicing in that sort of inebriation in which the world so often forgets thee, its Creator, and falls in love with thy creature instead of thee—the inebriation of that invisible wine of a perverted will which turns and bows down to infamy. But in my mother's breast thou hadst already begun to build thy temple and the foundation of thy holy habitation—whereas my father was only a catechumen, and that but recently. She was, therefore, startled with a holy fear and trembling: for though I had not yet been baptized, she feared those crooked ways in which they walk who turn their backs to thee and not their faces.

7. Woe is me! Do I dare affirm that thou didst hold thy peace, O my God, while I wandered farther away from thee? Didst thou really then hold thy peace? Then whose words were they but thine which by my mother, thy faithful handmaid, thou didst pour into my ears? None of them, however, sank into my heart to make me do anything. She deplored and, as I remember, warned me privately with great solicitude, "not to commit fornication; but above all things never to defile another man's wife." These appeared to me but womanish counsels, which I would have blushed to obey. Yet they were from thee, and I knew it not. I thought that thou wast silent and that it was only she who spoke. Yet it was through her that thou didst not keep silence toward me; and in rejecting her counsel I was rejecting thee—I, her son, "the son of thy handmaid, thy servant." [10] But I did not realize this, and rushed on headlong with such blindness that, among my friends, I was ashamed to be less shameless than they, when I heard them boasting of their disgraceful exploits—yes, and glorying all the more the worse their baseness was. What is worse, I took pleasure in such exploits, not for the pleasure's sake only but mostly for praise. What is worthy of vituperation except vice itself? Yet I made myself out worse than I was, in order that I might not go lacking for praise. And when in anything I had not sinned as the worst ones in the group, I would still say that I had done what I had not done, in order not to appear contemptible because I was more innocent than they; and not to drop in their esteem because I was more chaste.

8. Behold with what companions I walked the streets of

[10] Ps. 116:16.

Babylon! I rolled in its mire and lolled about on it, as if on a bed of spices and precious ointments. And, drawing me more closely to the very center of that city, my invisible enemy trod me down and seduced me, for I was easy to seduce. My mother had already fled out of the midst of Babylon [11] and was progressing, albeit slowly, toward its outskirts. For in counseling me to chastity, she did not bear in mind what her husband had told her about me. And although she knew that my passions were destructive even then and dangerous for the future, she did not think they should be restrained by the bonds of conjugal affection—if, indeed, they could not be cut away to the quick. She took no heed of this, for she was afraid lest a wife should prove a hindrance and a burden to my hopes. These were not her hopes of the world to come, which my mother had in thee, but the hope of learning, which both my parents were too anxious that I should acquire—my father, because he had little or no thought of thee, and only vain thoughts for me; my mother, because she thought that the usual course of study would not only be no hindrance but actually a furtherance toward my eventual return to thee. This much I conjecture, recalling as well as I can the temperaments of my parents. Meantime, the reins of discipline were slackened on me, so that without the restraint of due severity, I might play at whatsoever I fancied, even to the point of dissoluteness. And in all this there was that mist which shut out from my sight the brightness of thy truth, O my God; and my iniquity bulged out, as it were, with fatness! [12]

CHAPTER IV

9. Theft is punished by thy law, O Lord, and by the law written in men's hearts, which not even ingrained wickedness can erase. For what thief will tolerate another thief stealing from him? Even a rich thief will not tolerate a poor thief who is driven to theft by want. Yet I had a desire to commit robbery, and did so, compelled to it by neither hunger nor poverty, but through a contempt for well-doing and a strong impulse to iniquity. For I pilfered something which I already had in sufficient measure, and of much better quality. I did not desire to enjoy what I stole, but only the theft and the sin itself.

There was a pear tree close to our own vineyard, heavily laden with fruit, which was not tempting either for its color or for its

<hr>

[11] Cf. Jer. 51:6; 50:8.   [12] Cf. Ps. 73:7.

flavor. Late one night—having prolonged our games in the streets until then, as our bad habit was—a group of young scoundrels, and I among them, went to shake and rob this tree. We carried off a huge load of pears, not to eat ourselves, but to dump out to the hogs, after barely tasting some of them ourselves. Doing this pleased us all the more because it was forbidden. Such was my heart, O God, such was my heart—which thou didst pity even in that bottomless pit. Behold, now let my heart confess to thee what it was seeking there, when I was being gratuitously wanton, having no inducement to evil but the evil itself. It was foul, and I loved it. I loved my own undoing. I loved my error—not that for which I erred but the error itself. A depraved soul, falling away from security in thee to destruction in itself, seeking nothing from the shameful deed but shame itself.

CHAPTER V

10. Now there is a comeliness in all beautiful bodies, and in gold and silver and all things. The sense of touch has its own power to please and the other senses find their proper objects in physical sensation. Worldly honor also has its own glory, and so do the powers to command and to overcome: and from these there springs up the desire for revenge. Yet, in seeking these pleasures, we must not depart from thee, O Lord, nor deviate from thy law. The life which we live here has its own peculiar attractiveness because it has a certain measure of comeliness of its own and a harmony with all these inferior values. The bond of human friendship has a sweetness of its own, binding many souls together as one. Yet because of these values, sin is committed, because we have an inordinate preference for these goods of a lower order and neglect the better and the higher good—neglecting thee, O our Lord God, and thy truth and thy law. For these inferior values have their delights, but not at all equal to my God, who hath made them all. For in him do the righteous delight and he is the sweetness of the upright in heart.

11. When, therefore, we inquire why a crime was committed, we do not accept the explanation unless it appears that there was the desire to obtain some of those values which we designate inferior, or else a fear of losing them. For truly they are beautiful and comely, though in comparison with the superior and celestial goods they are abject and contemptible. A man has murdered another man—what was his motive? Either he desired his wife or his property or else he would steal to support himself; or

else he was afraid of losing something to him; or else, having been injured, he was burning to be revenged. Would a man commit murder without a motive, taking delight simply in the act of murder? Who would believe such a thing? Even for that savage and brutal man [Catiline], of whom it was said that he was gratuitously wicked and cruel, there is still a motive assigned to his deeds. "Lest through idleness," he says, "hand or heart should grow inactive." [13] And to what purpose? Why, even this: that, having once got possession of the city through his practice of his wicked ways, he might gain honors, empire, and wealth, and thus be exempt from the fear of the laws and from financial difficulties in supplying the needs of his family— and from the consciousness of his own wickedness. So it seems that even Catiline himself loved not his own villainies, but something else, and it was this that gave him the motive for his crimes.

CHAPTER VI

12. What was it in you, O theft of mine, that I, poor wretch, doted on—you deed of darkness—in that sixteenth year of my age? Beautiful you were not, for you were a theft. But are you anything at all, so that I could analyze the case with you? Those pears that we stole were fair to the sight because they were thy creation, O Beauty beyond compare, O Creator of all, O thou good God—God the highest good and my true good. [14] Those pears were truly pleasant to the sight, but it was not for them that my miserable soul lusted, for I had an abundance of better pears. I stole those simply that I might steal, for, having stolen them, I threw them away. My sole gratification in them was my own sin, which I was pleased to enjoy; for, if any one of these pears entered my mouth, the only good flavor it had was my sin in eating it. And now, O Lord my God, I ask what it was in that theft of mine that caused me such delight; for behold it had no beauty of its own—certainly not the sort of beauty that exists in justice and wisdom, nor such as is in the mind, memory senses, and the animal life of man; nor yet the kind that is the glory and beauty of the stars in their courses; nor the beauty of the earth, or the sea—teeming with spawning life, replacing in birth that which dies and decays. Indeed, it did not have that false and shadowy beauty which attends the deceptions of vice.

13. For thus we see pride wearing the mask of high-spiritedness, although only thou, O God, art high above all. Ambition

[13] Cicero, *De Catiline*, 16.   [14] *Deus summum bonum et bonum verum meum.*

seeks honor and glory, whereas only thou shouldst be honored above all, and glorified forever. The powerful man seeks to be feared, because of his cruelty; but who ought really to be feared but God only? What can be forced away or withdrawn out of his power—when or where or whither or by whom? The entice-ments of the wanton claim the name of love; and yet nothing is more enticing than thy love, nor is anything loved more health-fully than thy truth, bright and beautiful above all. Curiosity prompts a desire for knowledge, whereas it is only thou who knowest all things supremely. Indeed, ignorance and foolishness themselves go masked under the names of simplicity and inno-cence; yet there is no being that has true simplicity like thine, and none is innocent as thou art. Thus it is that by a sinner's own deeds he is himself harmed. Human sloth pretends to long for rest, but what sure rest is there save in the Lord? Luxury would fain be called plenty and abundance; but thou art the fullness and unfailing abundance of unfading joy. Prodigality presents a show of liberality; but thou art the most lavish giver of all good things. Covetousness desires to possess much; but thou art already the possessor of all things. Envy contends that its aim is for excellence; but what is so excellent as thou? Anger seeks revenge; but who avenges more justly than thou? Fear recoils at the unfamiliar and the sudden changes which threaten things beloved, and is wary for its own security; but what can happen that is unfamiliar or sudden to thee? Or who can deprive thee of what thou lovest? Where, really, is there unshaken security save with thee? Grief languishes for things lost in which desire had taken delight, because it wills to have nothing taken from it, just as nothing can be taken from thee.

14. Thus the soul commits fornication when she is turned from thee,[15] and seeks apart from thee what she cannot find pure and untainted until she returns to thee. All things thus imitate thee—but pervertedly—when they separate themselves far from thee and raise themselves up against thee. But, even in this act of perverse imitation, they acknowledge thee to be the Creator of all nature, and recognize that there is no place whither they can altogether separate themselves from thee. What was it, then, that I loved in that theft? And wherein was I imitating my Lord, even in a corrupted and perverted way? Did I wish, if only by gesture, to rebel against thy law, even though I had no power to do so actually—so that, even as a

15 *Avertitur*, the opposite of *convertitur*: the evil will turns the soul *away* from God; this is sin. By grace it is turned *to* God; this is *conversion*.

captive, I might produce a sort of counterfeit liberty, by doing with impunity deeds that were forbidden, in a deluded sense of omnipotence? Behold this servant of thine, fleeing from his Lord and following a shadow! O rottenness! O monstrousness of life and abyss of death! Could I find pleasure only in what was unlawful, and only because it was unlawful?

CHAPTER VII

15. "What shall I render unto the Lord"[16] for the fact that while my memory recalls these things my soul no longer fears them? I will love thee, O Lord, and thank thee, and confess to thy name, because thou hast put away from me such wicked and evil deeds. To thy grace I attribute it and to thy mercy, that thou hast melted away my sin as if it were ice. To thy grace also I attribute whatsoever of evil I did *not* commit—for what might I not have done, loving sin as I did, just for the sake of sinning? Yea, all the sins that I confess now to have been forgiven me, both those which I committed willfully and those which, by thy providence, I did not commit. What man is there who, when reflecting upon his own infirmity, dares to ascribe his chastity and innocence to his own powers, so that he should love thee less—as if he were in less need of thy mercy in which thou forgivest the transgressions of those that return to thee? As for that man who, when called by thee, obeyed thy voice and shunned those things which he here reads of me as I recall and confess them of myself, let him not despise me—for I, who was sick, have been healed by the same Physician by whose aid it was that he did not fall sick, or rather was less sick than I. And for this let him love thee just as much—indeed, all the more—since he sees me restored from such a great weakness of sin by the selfsame Saviour by whom he sees himself preserved from such a weakness.

CHAPTER VIII

16. What profit did I, a wretched one, receive from those things which, when I remember them now, cause me shame—above all, from that theft, which I loved only for the theft's sake? And, as the theft itself was nothing, I was all the more wretched in that I loved it so. Yet by myself alone I would not

[16] Ps. 116:12.

have done it—I still recall how I felt about this then—I could not have done it alone. I loved it then because of the companionship of my accomplices with whom I did it. I did not, therefore, love the theft alone—yet, indeed, it was only the theft that I loved, for the companionship was nothing. What is this paradox? Who is it that can explain it to me but God, who illumines my heart and searches out the dark corners thereof? What is it that has prompted my mind to inquire about it, to discuss and to reflect upon all this? For had I at that time loved the pears that I stole and wished to enjoy them, I might have done so alone, if I could have been satisfied with the mere act of theft by which my pleasure was served. Nor did I need to have that itching of my own passions inflamed by the encouragement of my accomplices. But since the pleasure I got was not from the pears, it was in the crime itself, enhanced by the companionship of my fellow sinners.

CHAPTER IX

17. By what passion, then, was I animated? It was undoubtedly depraved and a great misfortune for me to feel it. But still, what was it? "Who can understand his errors?" [17]

We laughed because our hearts were tickled at the thought of deceiving the owners, who had no idea of what we were doing and would have strenuously objected. Yet, again, why did I find such delight in doing this which I would not have done alone? Is it that no one readily laughs alone? No one does so readily; but still sometimes, when men are by themselves and no one else is about, a fit of laughter will overcome them when something very droll presents itself to their sense or mind. Yet alone I would not have done it—alone I could not have done it at all.

Behold, my God, the lively review of my soul's career is laid bare before thee. I would not have committed that theft alone. My pleasure in it was not what I stole but, rather, the act of stealing. Nor would I have enjoyed doing it alone—indeed I would not have done it! O friendship all unfriendly! You strange seducer of the soul, who hungers for mischief from impulses of mirth and wantonness, who craves another's loss without any desire for one's own profit or revenge—so that, when they say, "Let's go, let's do it," we are ashamed not to be shameless.

[17] Ps. 19:12.

CHAPTER X

18. Who can unravel such a twisted and tangled knottiness? It is unclean. I hate to reflect upon it. I hate to look on it. But I do long for thee, O Righteousness and Innocence, so beautiful and comely to all virtuous eyes—I long for thee with an insatiable satiety. With thee is perfect rest, and life unchanging. He who enters into thee enters into the joy of his Lord,[18] and shall have no fear and shall achieve excellence in the Excellent. I fell away from thee, O my God, and in my youth I wandered too far from thee, my true support. And I became to myself a wasteland.

[18] Cf. Matt. 25:21.

BOOK THREE

The story of his student days in Carthage, his discovery of Cicero's Hortensius, *the enkindling of his philosophical interest, his infatuation with the Manichean heresy, and his mother's dream which foretold his eventual return to the true faith and to God.*

CHAPTER I

1. I came to Carthage, where a caldron of unholy loves was seething and bubbling all around me. I was not in love as yet, but I was in love with love; and, from a hidden hunger, I hated myself for not feeling more intensely a sense of hunger. I was looking for something to love, for I was in love with loving, and I hated security and a smooth way, free from snares. Within me I had a dearth of that inner food which is thyself, my God— although that dearth caused me no hunger. And I remained without any appetite for incorruptible food—not because I was already filled with it, but because the emptier I became the more I loathed it. Because of this my soul was unhealthy; and, full of sores, it exuded itself forth, itching to be scratched by scraping on the things of the senses.[1] Yet, had these things no soul, they would certainly not inspire our love.

To love and to be loved was sweet to me, and all the more when I gained the enjoyment of the body of the person I loved. Thus I polluted the spring of friendship with the filth of concupiscence and I dimmed its luster with the slime of lust. Yet, foul and unclean as I was, I still craved, in excessive vanity, to be thought elegant and urbane. And I did fall precipitately into the love I was longing for. My God, my mercy, with how much

---

[1] Cf. Job 2:7, 8.

bitterness didst thou, out of thy infinite goodness, flavor that sweetness for me! For I was not only beloved but also I secretly reached the climax of enjoyment; and yet I was joyfully bound with troublesome ties, so that I could be scourged with the burning iron rods of jealousy, suspicion, fear, anger, and strife.

CHAPTER II

2. Stage plays also captivated me, with their sights full of the images of my own miseries: fuel for my own fire. Now, why does a man like to be made sad by viewing doleful and tragic scenes, which he himself could not by any means endure? Yet, as a spectator, he wishes to experience from them a sense of grief, and in this very sense of grief his pleasure consists. What is this but wretched madness? For a man is more affected by these actions the more he is spuriously involved in these affections. Now, if he should suffer them in his own person, it is the custom to call this "misery." But when he suffers with another, then it is called "compassion." But what kind of compassion is it that arises from viewing fictitious and unreal sufferings? The spectator is not expected to aid the sufferer but merely to grieve for him. And the more he grieves the more he applauds the actor of these fictions. If the misfortunes of the characters—whether historical or entirely imaginary—are represented so as not to touch the feelings of the spectator, he goes away disgusted and complaining. But if his feelings are deeply touched, he sits it out attentively, and sheds tears of joy.

3. Tears and sorrow, then, are loved. Surely every man desires to be joyful. And, though no one is willingly miserable, one may, nevertheless, be pleased to be merciful so that we love their sorrows because without them we should have nothing to pity. This also springs from that same vein of friendship. But whither does it go? Whither does it flow? Why does it run into that torrent of pitch which seethes forth those huge tides of loathsome lusts in which it is changed and altered past recognition, being diverted and corrupted from its celestial purity by its own will? Shall, then, compassion be repudiated? By no means! Let us, however, love the sorrows of others. But let us beware of uncleanness, O my soul, under the protection of my God, the God of our fathers, who is to be praised and exalted—let us beware of uncleanness. I have not yet ceased to have compassion. But in those days in the theaters I sympathized with lovers when they sinfully enjoyed one another, although this was done

fictitiously in the play. And when they lost one another, I grieved with them, as if pitying them, and yet had delight in both grief and pity. Nowadays I feel much more pity for one who delights in his wickedness than for one who counts himself unfortunate because he fails to obtain some harmful pleasure or suffers the loss of some miserable felicity. This, surely, is the truer compassion, but the sorrow I feel in it has no delight for me. For although he that grieves with the unhappy should be commended for his work of love, yet he who has the power of real compassion would still prefer that there be nothing for him to grieve about. For if good will were to be ill will—which it cannot be—only then could he who is truly and sincerely compassionate wish that there were some unhappy people so that he might commiserate them. Some grief may then be justified, but none of it loved. Thus it is that thou dost act, O Lord God, for thou lovest souls far more purely than we do and art more incorruptibly compassionate, although thou art never wounded by any sorrow. Now "who is sufficient for these things?" [2]

4. But at that time, in my wretchedness, I loved to grieve; and I sought for things to grieve about. In another man's misery, even though it was feigned and impersonated on the stage, that performance of the actor pleased me best and attracted me most powerfully which moved me to tears. What marvel then was it that an unhappy sheep, straying from thy flock and impatient of thy care, I became infected with a foul disease? This is the reason for my love of griefs: that they would not probe into me too deeply (for I did not love to suffer in myself such things as I loved to look at), and they were the sort of grief which came from hearing those fictions, which affected only the surface of my emotion. Still, just as if they had been poisoned fingernails, their scratching was followed by inflammation, swelling, putrefaction, and corruption. Such was my life! But was it life, O my God?

CHAPTER III

5. And still thy faithful mercy hovered over me from afar. In what unseemly iniquities did I wear myself out, following a sacrilegious curiosity, which, having deserted thee, then began to drag me down into the treacherous abyss, into the beguiling obedience of devils, to whom I made offerings of my wicked deeds. And still in all this thou didst not fail to scourge me. I

[2] II Cor. 2:16.

dared, even while thy solemn rites were being celebrated inside the walls of thy church, to desire and to plan a project which merited death as its fruit. For this thou didst chastise me with grievous punishments, but nothing in comparison with my fault, O thou my greatest mercy, my God, my refuge from those terrible dangers in which I wandered with stiff neck, receding farther from thee, loving my own ways and not thine—loving a vagrant liberty!

6. Those studies I was then pursuing, generally accounted as respectable, were aimed at distinction in the courts of law—to excel in which, the more crafty I was, the more I should be praised. Such is the blindness of men that they even glory in their blindness. And by this time I had become a master in the School of Rhetoric, and I rejoiced proudly in this honor and became inflated with arrogance. Still I was relatively sedate, O Lord, as thou knowest, and had no share in the wreckings of "The Wreckers" [3] (for this stupid and diabolical name was regarded as the very badge of gallantry) among whom I lived with a sort of ashamed embarrassment that I was not even as they were. But I lived with them, and at times I was delighted with their friendship, even when I abhorred their acts (that is, their "wrecking") in which they insolently attacked the modesty of strangers, tormenting them by uncalled-for jeers, gratifying their mischievous mirth. Nothing could more nearly resemble the actions of devils than these fellows. By what name, therefore, could they be more aptly called than "wreckers"?—being themselves wrecked first, and altogether turned upside down. They were secretly mocked at and seduced by the deceiving spirits, in the very acts by which they amused themselves in jeering and horseplay at the expense of others.

CHAPTER IV

7. Among such as these, in that unstable period of my life, I studied the books of eloquence, for it was in eloquence that I was eager to be eminent, though from a reprehensible and vainglorious motive, and a delight in human vanity. In the ordinary course of study I came upon a certain book of Cicero's, whose language almost all admire, though not his heart. This particular book of his contains an exhortation to philosophy and

---

[3] *Eversores*, "overturners," from *evertere*, to overthrow or ruin. This was the nickname of a gang of young hoodlums in Carthage, made up largely, it seems, of students in the schools.

was called *Hortensius*.[4] Now it was this book which quite definitely changed my whole attitude and turned my prayers toward thee, O Lord, and gave me new hope and new desires. Suddenly every vain hope became worthless to me, and with an incredible warmth of heart I yearned for an immortality of wisdom and began now to arise that I might return to thee. It was not to sharpen my tongue further that I made use of that book. I was now nineteen; my father had been dead two years,[5] and my mother was providing the money for my study of rhetoric. What won me in it [i.e., the *Hortensius*] was not its style but its substance.

8. How ardent was I then, my God, how ardent to fly from earthly things to thee! Nor did I know how thou wast even then dealing with me. For with thee is wisdom. In Greek the love of wisdom is called "philosophy," and it was with this love that that book inflamed me. There are some who seduce through philosophy, under a great, alluring, and honorable name, using it to color and adorn their own errors. And almost all who did this, in Cicero's own time and earlier, are censored and pointed out in his book. In it there is also manifest that most salutary admonition of thy Spirit, spoken by thy good and pious servant: "Beware lest any man spoil you through philosophy and vain deceit, after the tradition of men, after the rudiments of the world, and not after Christ: for in him all the fullness of the Godhead dwells bodily."[6] Since at that time, as thou knowest, O Light of my heart, the words of the apostle were unknown to me, I was delighted with Cicero's exhortation, at least enough so that I was stimulated by it, and enkindled and inflamed to love, to seek, to obtain, to hold, and to embrace, not this or that sect, but wisdom itself, wherever it might be. Only this checked my ardor: that the name of Christ was not in it. For this name, by thy mercy, O Lord, this name of my Saviour thy Son, my tender heart had piously drunk in, deeply treasured even with my mother's milk. And whatsoever was lacking that name, no matter how erudite, polished, and truthful, did not quite take complete hold of me.

[4] A minor essay now lost. We know of its existence from other writers, but the only fragments that remain are in Augustine's works: *Contra Academicos*, III, 14:31; *De beata vita*, X; *Soliloquia*, I, 17; *De civitate Dei*, III, 15; *Contra Julianum*, IV, 15:78; *De Trinitate*, XIII, 4:7, 5:8; XIV, 9:12, 19:26; *Epist.* CXXX, 10.
[5] Note this merely parenthetical reference to his father's death and contrast it with the account of his mother's death in Bk. IX, Chs. X–XII.
[6] Col. 2:8, 9.

CHAPTER V

9. I resolved, therefore, to direct my mind to the Holy Scriptures, that I might see what they were. And behold, I saw something not comprehended by the proud, not disclosed to children, something lowly in the hearing, but sublime in the doing, and veiled in mysteries. Yet I was not of the number of those who could enter into it or bend my neck to follow its steps. For then it was quite different from what I now feel. When I then turned toward the Scriptures, they appeared to me to be quite unworthy to be compared with the dignity of Tully.[7] For my inflated pride was repelled by their style, nor could the sharpness of my wit penetrate their inner meaning. Truly they were of a sort to aid the growth of little ones, but I scorned to be a little one and, swollen with pride, I looked upon myself as fully grown.

CHAPTER VI

10. Thus I fell among men, delirious in their pride, carnal and voluble, whose mouths were the snares of the devil—a trap made out of a mixture of the syllables of thy name and the names of our Lord Jesus Christ and of the Paraclete.[8] These names were never out of their mouths, but only as sound and the clatter of tongues, for their heart was empty of truth. Still they cried, "Truth, Truth," and were forever speaking the word to me. But the thing itself was not in them. Indeed, they spoke falsely not only of thee—who truly art the Truth—but also about the basic elements of this world, thy creation. And, indeed, I should have passed by the philosophers themselves even when they were speaking truth concerning thy creatures,

---

[7] I.e., Marcus Tullius Cicero.

[8] These were the Manicheans, a pseudo-Christian sect founded by a Persian religious teacher, Mani (c. A.D. 216–277). They professed a highly eclectic religious system chiefly distinguished by its radical dualism and its elaborate cosmogony in which good was co-ordinated with light and evil with darkness. In the sect, there was an esoteric minority called *perfecti*, who were supposed to obey the strict rules of an ascetic ethic; the rest were *auditores*, who followed, at a distance, the doctrines of the *perfecti* but not their rules. The chief attraction of Manicheism lay in the fact that it appeared to offer a straightforward, apparently profound and rational solution to the problem of evil, both in nature and in human experience. Cf. H. C. Puech, *Le Manichéisme, son fondateur—sa doctrine* (Paris, 1949); F. C. Burkitt, *The Religion of the Manichees* (Cambridge, 1925); and Steven Runciman, *The Medieval Manichee* (Cambridge, 1947).

for the sake of thy love, O Highest Good, and my Father, O Beauty of all things beautiful.

O Truth, Truth, how inwardly even then did the marrow of my soul sigh for thee when, frequently and in manifold ways, in numerous and vast books, [the Manicheans] sounded out thy name though it was only a sound! And in these dishes—while I starved for thee—they served up to me, in thy stead, the sun and moon thy beauteous works—but still only thy works and not thyself; indeed, not even thy first work. For thy spiritual works came before these material creations, celestial and shining though they are. But I was hungering and thirsting, not even after those first works of thine, but after thyself the Truth, "with whom is no variableness, neither shadow of turning."[9] Yet they still served me glowing fantasies in those dishes. And, truly, it would have been better to have loved this very sun—which at least is true to our sight—than those illusions of theirs which deceive the mind through the eye. And yet because I supposed the illusions to be from thee I fed on them—not with avidity, for thou didst not taste in my mouth as thou art, and thou wast not these empty fictions. Neither was I nourished by them, but was instead exhausted. Food in dreams appears like our food awake; yet the sleepers are not nourished by it, for they are asleep. But the fantasies of the Manicheans were not in any way like thee as thou hast spoken to me now. They were simply fantastic and false. In comparison to them the actual bodies which we see with our fleshly sight, both celestial and terrestrial, are far more certain. These true bodies even the beasts and birds perceive as well as we do and they are more certain than the images we form about them. And again, we do with more certainty form our conceptions about them than, from them, we go on by means of them to imagine of other greater and infinite bodies which have no existence. With such empty husks was I then fed, and yet was not fed.

But thou, my Love, for whom I longed in order that I might be strong, neither art those bodies that we see in heaven nor art thou those which we do not see there, for thou hast created them all and yet thou reckonest them not among thy greatest works. How far, then, art thou from those fantasies of mine, fantasies of bodies which have no real being at all! The images of those bodies which actually exist are far more certain than these fantasies. The bodies themselves are more certain than the images, yet even these thou art not. Thou art not even the

[9] James 1:17.

soul, which is the life of bodies; and, clearly, the life of the body is better than the body itself. But thou art the life of souls, life of lives, having life in thyself, and never changing, O Life of my soul.[10]

11. Where, then, wast thou and how far from me? Far, indeed, was I wandering away from thee, being barred even from the husks of those swine whom I fed with husks.[11] For how much better were the fables of the grammarians and poets than these snares [of the Manicheans]! For verses and poems and "the flying Medea"[12] are still more profitable truly than these men's "five elements," with their various colors, answering to "the five caves of darkness"[13] (none of which exist and yet in which they slay the one who believes in them). For verses and poems I can turn into food for the mind, for though I sang about "the flying Medea" I never believed it, but those other things [the fantasies of the Manicheans] I did believe. Woe, woe, by what steps I was dragged down to "the depths of hell"[14]—toiling and fuming because of my lack of the truth, even when I was seeking after thee, my God! To thee I now confess it, for thou didst have mercy on me when I had not yet confessed it. I sought after thee, but not according to the understanding of the mind, by means of which thou hast willed that I should excel the beasts, but only after the guidance of my physical senses. Thou wast more inward to me than the most inward part of me; and higher than my highest reach. I came upon that brazen woman, devoid of prudence, who, in Solomon's obscure parable, sits at the door of the house on a seat and says, "Stolen waters are sweet, and bread eaten in secret is pleasant."[15] This woman seduced me, because she found my soul outside its own door, dwelling on the sensations of my flesh and ruminating on such food as I had swallowed through these physical senses.

CHAPTER VII

12. For I was ignorant of that other reality, true Being. And so it was that I was subtly persuaded to agree with these foolish deceivers when they put their questions to me: "Whence comes evil?" and, "Is God limited by a bodily shape, and has he hairs and nails?" and, "Are those patriarchs to be esteemed righteous

---

10 Cf. Plotinus, *Enneads*, V, 3:14.   11 Cf. Luke 15:16.
12 Cf. Ovid, *Metamorphoses*, VII, 219–224.
13 For the details of the Manichean cosmogony, see Burkitt, *op. cit.*, ch. 4.
14 Prov. 9:18.   15 Cf. Prov. 9:17; see also Prov. 9:13 (Vulgate text).

who had many wives at one time, and who killed men and who sacrificed living creatures?" In my ignorance I was much disturbed over these things and, though I was retreating from the truth, I appeared to myself to be going toward it, because I did not yet know that evil was nothing but a privation of good (that, indeed, it has no being)[16]; and how should I have seen this when the sight of my eyes went no farther than physical objects, and the sight of my mind reached no farther than to fantasms? And I did not know that God is a spirit who has no parts extended in length and breadth, whose being has no mass—for every mass is less in a part than in a whole—and if it be an infinite mass it must be less in such parts as are limited by a certain space than in its infinity. It cannot therefore be wholly everywhere as Spirit is, as God is. And I was entirely ignorant as to what is that principle within us by which we are like God, and which is rightly said in Scripture to be made "after God's image."

13. Nor did I know that true inner righteousness—which does not judge according to custom but by the measure of the most perfect law of God Almighty—by which the mores of various places and times were adapted to those places and times (though the law itself is the same always and everywhere, not one thing in one place and another in another). By this inner righteousness Abraham and Isaac, and Jacob and Moses and David, and all those commended by the mouth of God were righteous and were judged unrighteous only by foolish men who were judging by human judgment and gauging their judgment of the mores of the whole human race by the narrow norms of their own mores. It is as if a man in an armory, not knowing what piece goes on what part of the body, should put a greave on his head and a helmet on his shin and then complain because they did not fit. Or as if, on some holiday when afternoon business was forbidden, one were to grumble at not being allowed to go on selling as it had been lawful for him to do in the forenoon. Or, again, as if, in a house, he sees a servant handle something that the butler is not permitted to touch, or when something is done behind a stable that would be prohibited in a dining room, and then a person should be indignant that in one house and one family the same things are not allowed to every member of the household. Such is the case with those who cannot endure to hear that something was lawful for righteous men in former times that is not so now; or that God, for certain temporal

[16] Cf. *Enchiridion*, IV.

reasons, commanded then one thing to them and another now to these: yet both would be serving the same righteous will. These people should see that in one man, one day, and one house, different things are fit for different members; and a thing that was formerly lawful may become, after a time, unlawful—and something allowed or commanded in one place that is justly prohibited and punished in another. Is justice, then, variable and changeable? No, but the times over which she presides are not all alike because they are different times. But men, whose days upon the earth are few, cannot by their own perception harmonize the causes of former ages and other nations, of which they had no experience, and compare them with these of which they do have experience; although in one and the same body, or day, or family, they can readily see that what is suitable for each member, season, part, and person may differ. To the one they take exception; to the other they submit.

14. These things I did not know then, nor had I observed their import. They met my eyes on every side, and I did not see. I composed poems, in which I was not free to place each foot just anywhere, but in one meter one way, and in another meter another way, nor even in any one verse was the same foot allowed in all places. Yet the art by which I composed did not have different principles for each of these different cases, but the same law throughout. Still I did not see how, by that righteousness to which good and holy men submitted, all those things that God had commanded were gathered, in a far more excellent and sublime way, into one moral order; and it did not vary in any essential respect, though it did not in varying times prescribe all things at once but, rather, distributed and prescribed what was proper for each. And, being blind, I blamed those pious fathers, not only for making use of present things as God had commanded and inspired them to do, but also for foreshadowing things to come, as God revealed it to them.

CHAPTER VIII

15. Can it ever, at any time or place, be unrighteous for a man to love God with all his heart, with all his soul, and with all his mind; and his neighbor as himself?[17] Similarly, offenses against nature are everywhere and at all times to be held in detestation and should be punished. Such offenses, for example, were those of the Sodomites; and, even if all nations should

17 Cf. Matt. 22:37–39.

commit them, they would all be judged guilty of the same crime
by the divine law, which has not made men so that they should
ever abuse one another in that way. For the fellowship that
should be between God and us is violated whenever that nature
of which he is the author is polluted by perverted lust. But these
offenses against customary morality are to be avoided according
to the variety of such customs. Thus, what is agreed upon by
convention, and confirmed by custom or the law of any city or
nation, may not be violated at the lawless pleasure of any,
whether citizen or stranger. For any part that is not consistent
with its whole is unseemly. Nevertheless,when God commands
anything contrary to the customs or compacts of any nation,
even though it were never done by them before, it is to be done;
and if it has been interrupted, it is to be restored; and if it has
never been established, it is to be established. For it is lawful for
a king, in the state over which he reigns, to command that which
neither he himself nor anyone before him had commanded.
And if it cannot be held to be inimical to the public interest to
obey him—and, in truth, it would be inimical if he were not
obeyed, since obedience to princes is a general compact of
human society—how much more, then, ought we unhesitatingly
to obey God, the Governor of all his creatures! For, just as
among the authorities in human society, the greater authority
is obeyed before the lesser, so also must God be above all.

16. This applies as well to deeds of violence where there is a
real desire to harm another, either by humiliating treatment
or by injury. Either of these may be done for reasons of revenge,
as one enemy against another, or in order to obtain some advan-
tage over another, as in the case of the highwayman and the
traveler; else they may be done in order to avoid some other
evil, as in the case of one who fears another; or through envy as,
for example, an unfortunate man harming a happy one just
because he is happy; or they may be done by a prosperous man
against someone whom he fears will become equal to himself or
whose equality he resents. They may even be done for the mere
pleasure in another man's pain, as the spectators of gladiatorial
shows or the people who deride and mock at others. These are
the major forms of iniquity that spring out of the lust of the
flesh, and of the eye, and of power.[18] Sometimes there is just
one; sometimes two together; sometimes all of them at once.
Thus we live, offending against the Three and the Seven, that

[18] Cf. I John 2:16. And see also Bk. X, Chs. XXX–XLI, for an elaborate
analysis of them.

harp of ten strings, thy Decalogue, O God most high and most sweet.[19] But now how can offenses of vileness harm thee who canst not be defiled; or how can deeds of violence harm thee who canst not be harmed? Still thou dost punish these sins which men commit against themselves because, even when they sin against thee, they are also committing impiety against their own souls. Iniquity gives itself the lie, either by corrupting or by perverting that nature which thou hast made and ordained. And they do this by an immoderate use of lawful things; or by lustful desire for things forbidden, as "against nature"; or when they are guilty of sin by raging with heart and voice against thee, rebelling against thee, "kicking against the pricks"[20]; or when they cast aside respect for human society and take audacious delight in conspiracies and feuds according to their private likes and dislikes.

This is what happens whenever thou art forsaken, O Fountain of Life, who art the one and true Creator and Ruler of the universe. This is what happens when through self-willed pride a part is loved under the false assumption that it is the whole. Therefore, we must return to thee in humble piety and let thee purge us from our evil ways, and be merciful to those who confess their sins to thee, and hear the groanings of the prisoners and loosen us from those fetters which we have forged for ourselves. This thou wilt do, provided we do not raise up against thee the arrogance of a false freedom—for thus we lose all through craving more, by loving our own good more than thee, the common good of all.

CHAPTER IX

17. But among all these vices and crimes and manifold iniquities, there are also the sins that are committed by men who are, on the whole, making progress toward the good. When these are judged rightly and after the rule of perfection, the sins are censored but the men are to be commended because they show the hope of bearing fruit, like the green shoot of the growing corn. And there are some deeds that resemble vice and crime and yet are not sin because they offend neither thee, our Lord God, nor social custom. For example, when suitable reserves for hard times are provided, we cannot judge that this is done

[19] Cf. Ex. 20:3–8; Ps. 144:9. In Augustine's *Sermon* IX, he points out that in the Decalogue *three* commandments pertain to God and *seven* to men.
[20] Acts 9:5.

merely from a hoarding impulse. Or, again, when acts are punished by constituted authority for the sake of correction, we cannot judge that they are done merely out of a desire to inflict pain. Thus, many a deed which is disapproved in man's sight may be approved by thy testimony. And many a man who is praised by men is condemned—as thou art witness—because frequently the deed itself, the mind of the doer, and the hidden exigency of the situation all vary among themselves. But when, contrary to human expectation, thou commandest something unusual or unthought of—indeed, something thou mayest formerly have forbidden, about which thou mayest conceal the reason for thy command at that particular time; and even though it may be contrary to the ordinance of some society of men [21]— who doubts but that it should be done because only that society of men is righteous which obeys thee? But blessed are they who know what thou dost command. For all things done by those who obey thee either exhibit something necessary at that particular time or they foreshow things to come.

CHAPTER X

18. But I was ignorant of all this, and so I mocked those holy servants and prophets of thine. Yet what did I gain by mocking them save to be mocked in turn by thee? Insensibly and little by little, I was led on to such follies as to believe that a fig tree wept when it was plucked and that the sap of the mother tree was tears. Notwithstanding this, if a fig was plucked, by not his own but another man's wickedness, some Manichean saint might eat it, digest it in his stomach, and breathe it out again in the form of angels. Indeed, in his prayers he would assuredly groan and sigh forth particles of God, although these particles of the most high and true God would have remained bound in that fig unless they had been set free by the teeth and belly of some "elect saint" [22]! And, wretch that I was, I believed that more mercy was to be shown to the fruits of the earth than unto men, for whom these fruits were created. For, if a hungry man— who was not a Manichean—should beg for any food, the morsel that we gave to him would seem condemned, as it were, to capital punishment.

[21] An example of this which Augustine doubtless had in mind is God's command to Abraham to offer up his son Isaac as a human sacrifice. Cf. Gen. 22:1, 2.
[22] *Electi sancti.* Another Manichean term for the *perfecti*, the elite and "perfect" among them.

CHAPTER XI

19. And now thou didst "stretch forth thy hand from above"[23] and didst draw up my soul out of that profound darkness [of Manicheism] because my mother, thy faithful one, wept to thee on my behalf more than mothers are accustomed to weep for the bodily deaths of their children. For by the light of the faith and spirit which she received from thee, she saw that I was dead. And thou didst hear her, O Lord, thou didst hear her and despised not her tears when, pouring down, they watered the earth under her eyes in every place where she prayed. Thou didst truly hear her.

For what other source was there for that dream by which thou didst console her, so that she permitted me to live with her, to have my meals in the same house at the table which she had begun to avoid, even while she hated and detested the blasphemies of my error? In her dream she saw herself standing on a sort of wooden rule, and saw a bright youth approaching her, joyous and smiling at her, while she was grieving and bowed down with sorrow. But when he inquired of her the cause of her sorrow and daily weeping (not to learn from her, but to teach her, as is customary in visions), and when she answered that it was my soul's doom she was lamenting, he bade her rest content and told her to look and see that where she was there I was also. And when she looked she saw me standing near her on the same rule.

Whence came this vision unless it was that thy ears were inclined toward her heart? O thou Omnipotent Good, thou carest for every one of us as if thou didst care for him only, and so for all as if they were but one!

20. And what was the reason for this also, that, when she told me of this vision, and I tried to put this construction on it: "that she should not despair of being someday what I was," she replied immediately, without hesitation, "No; for it was not told me that 'where he is, there you shall be' but 'where you are, there he will be' "? I confess my remembrance of this to thee, O Lord, as far as I can recall it—and I have often mentioned it. Thy answer, given through my watchful mother, in the fact that she was not disturbed by the plausibility of my false interpretation but saw immediately what should have been seen— and which I certainly had not seen until she spoke—this answer moved me more deeply than the dream itself. Still, by that dream, the joy that was to come to that pious woman so

[23] Ps. 144:7.

long after was predicted long before, as a consolation for her present anguish.

Nearly nine years passed in which I wallowed in the mud of that deep pit and in the darkness of falsehood, striving often to rise, but being all the more heavily dashed down. But all that time this chaste, pious, and sober widow—such as thou dost love—was now more buoyed up with hope, though no less zealous in her weeping and mourning; and she did not cease to bewail my case before thee, in all the hours of her supplication. Her prayers entered thy presence, and yet thou didst allow me still to tumble and toss around in that darkness.

CHAPTER XII

21. Meanwhile, thou gavest her yet another answer, as I remember—for I pass over many things, hastening on to those things which more strongly impel me to confess to thee—and many things I have simply forgotten. But thou gavest her then another answer, by a priest of thine, a certain bishop reared in thy Church and well versed in thy books. When that woman had begged him to agree to have some discussion with me, to refute my errors, to help me to unlearn evil and to learn the good [24]— for it was his habit to do this when he found people ready to receive it—he refused, very prudently, as I afterward realized. For he answered that I was still unteachable, being inflated with the novelty of that heresy, and that I had already per- plexed divers inexperienced persons with vexatious questions, as she herself had told him. "But let him alone for a time," he said, "only pray God for him. He will of his own accord, by reading, come to discover what an error it is and how great its impiety is." He went on to tell her at the same time how he himself, as a boy, had been given over to the Manicheans by his misguided mother and not only had read but had even copied out almost all their books. Yet he had come to see, without external argu- ment or proof from anyone else, how much that sect was to be shunned—and had shunned it. When he had said this she was not satisfied, but repeated more earnestly her entreaties, and shed copious tears, still beseeching him to see and talk with me. Finally the bishop, a little vexed at her importunity, exclaimed, "Go your way; as you live, it cannot be that the son of these tears should perish." As she often told me afterward, she accepted this answer as though it were a voice from heaven.

[24] *Dedocere me mala ac docere bona*; a typical Augustinian wordplay.

BOOK FOUR

This is the story of his years among the Manicheans. It includes the account of his teaching at Tagaste, his taking a mistress, the attractions of astrology, the poignant loss of a friend which leads to a searching analysis of grief and transience. He reports on his first book, De pulchro et apto, *and his introduction to Aristotle's* Categories *and other books of philosophy and theology, which he mastered with great ease and little profit.*

CHAPTER I

1. During this period of nine years, from my nineteenth year to my twenty-eighth, I went astray and led others astray. I was deceived and deceived others, in varied lustful projects—sometimes publicly, by the teaching of what men style "the liberal arts"; sometimes secretly, under the false guise of religion. In the one, I was proud of myself; in the other, superstitious; in all, vain! In my public life I was striving after the emptiness of popular fame, going so far as to seek theatrical applause, entering poetic contests, striving for the straw garlands and the vanity of theatricals and intemperate desires. In my private life I was seeking to be purged from these corruptions of ours by carrying food to those who were called "elect" and "holy," which, in the laboratory of their stomachs, they should make into angels and gods for us, and by them we might be set free. These projects I followed out and practiced with my friends, who were both deceived with me and by me. Let the proud laugh at me, and those who have not yet been savingly cast down and stricken by thee, O my God. Nevertheless, I would confess to thee my shame to thy glory. Bear with me, I beseech thee, and give me the grace to retrace in my present memory

the devious ways of my past errors and thus be able to "offer to thee the sacrifice of thanksgiving."[1] For what am I to myself without thee but a guide to my own downfall? Or what am I, even at the best, but one suckled on thy milk and feeding on thee, O Food that never perishes?[2] What indeed is any man, seeing that he is but a man? Therefore, let the strong and the mighty laugh at us, but let us who are "poor and needy"[3] confess to thee.

CHAPTER II

2. During those years I taught the art of rhetoric. Conquered by the desire for gain, I offered for sale speaking skills with which to conquer others. And yet, O Lord, thou knowest that I really preferred to have honest scholars (or what were esteemed as such) and, without tricks of speech, I taught these scholars the tricks of speech—not to be used against the life of the innocent, but sometimes to save the life of a guilty man. And thou, O God, didst see me from afar, stumbling on that slippery path and sending out some flashes of fidelity amid much smoke —guiding those who loved vanity and sought after lying,[4] being myself their companion.

In those years I had a mistress, to whom I was not joined in lawful marriage. She was a woman I had discovered in my wayward passion, void as it was of understanding, yet she was the only one; and I remained faithful to her and with her I discovered, by my own experience, what a great difference there is between the restraint of the marriage bond contracted with a view to having children and the compact of a lustful love, where children are born against the parents' will—although once they are born they compel our love.

3. I remember too that, when I decided to compete for a theatrical prize, some magician—I do not remember him now —asked me what I would give him to be certain to win. But I detested and abominated such filthy mysteries,[5] and answered "that, even if the garland was of imperishable gold, I would still not permit a fly to be killed to win it for me." For he would have slain certain living creatures in his sacrifices, and by those honors would have invited the devils to help me. This evil thing I refused, but not out of a pure love of thee, O God of

[1] Ps. 50:14.   [2] Cf. John 6:27.
[3] Ps. 74:21.   [4] Cf. Ps. 4:2.
[5] The rites of the soothsayers, in which animals were killed, for auguries and propitiation of the gods.

my heart, for I knew not how to love thee because I knew not how to conceive of anything beyond corporeal splendors. And does not a soul, sighing after such idle fictions, commit fornication against thee, trust in false things, and "feed on the winds"[6]? But still I would not have sacrifices offered to devils on my behalf, though I was myself still offering them sacrifices of a sort by my own [Manichean] superstition. For what else is it "to feed on the winds" but to feed on the devils, that is, in our wanderings to become their sport and mockery?

CHAPTER III

4. And yet, without scruple, I consulted those other impostors, whom they call "astrologers" [*mathematicos*], because they used no sacrifices and invoked the aid of no spirit for their divinations. Still, true Christian piety must necessarily reject and condemn their art.

It is good to confess to thee and to say, "Have mercy on me; heal my soul; for I have sinned against thee"[7]—not to abuse thy goodness as a license to sin, but to remember the words of the Lord, "Behold, you are made whole: sin no more, lest a worse thing befall you."[8] All this wholesome advice [the astrologers] labor to destroy when they say, "The cause of your sin is inevitably fixed in the heavens," and, "This is the doing of Venus, or of Saturn, or of Mars"—all this in order that a man, who is only flesh and blood and proud corruption, may regard himself as blameless, while the Creator and Ordainer of heaven and the stars must bear the blame of our ills and misfortunes. But who is this Creator but thou, our God, the sweetness and wellspring of righteousness, who renderest to every man according to his works and despisest not "a broken and a contrite heart"[9]?

5. There was at that time a wise man, very skillful and quite famous in medicine.[10] He was proconsul then, and with his own hand he placed on my distempered head the crown I had won in a rhetorical contest. He did not do this as a physician, however; and for this distemper "only thou canst heal who resisteth the proud and giveth grace to the humble."[11] But didst

---

[6] Cf. Hos. 12:1.   [7] Ps. 41:4.
[8] John 5:14.   [9] Ps. 51:17.
[10] Vindicianus; see below, Bk. VII, Ch. VI, 8.
[11] James 4:6; I Peter 5:5.

thou fail me in that old man, or forbear from healing my soul? Actually when I became better acquainted with him, I used to listen, rapt and eager, to his words; for, though he spoke in simple language, his conversation was replete with vivacity, life, and earnestness. He recognized from my own talk that I was given to books of the horoscope-casters, but he, in a kind and fatherly way, advised me to throw them away and not to spend idly on these vanities care and labor that might otherwise go into useful things. He said that he himself in his earlier years had studied the astrologers' art with a view to gaining his living by it as a profession. Since he had already understood Hippocrates, he was fully qualified to understand this too. Yet, he had given it up and followed medicine for the simple reason that he had discovered astrology to be utterly false and, as a man of honest character, he was unwilling to gain his living by beguiling people. "But you," he said, "have the profession of rhetoric to support yourself by, so that you are following this delusion in free will and not necessity. All the more, therefore, you ought to believe me, since I worked at it to learn the art perfectly because I wished to gain my living by it." When I asked him to account for the fact that many true things are foretold by astrology, he answered me, reasonably enough, that the force of chance, diffused through the whole order of nature, brought these things about. For when a man, by accident, opens the leaves of some poet (who sang and intended something far different) a verse oftentimes turns out to be wondrously apposite to the reader's present business. "It is not to be wondered at," he continued, "if out of the human mind, by some higher instinct which does not know what goes on within itself, an answer should be arrived at, by chance and not art, which would fit both the business and the action of the inquirer."

6. And thus truly, either by him or through him, thou wast looking after me. And thou didst fix all this in my memory so that afterward I might search it out for myself.

But at that time, neither the proconsul nor my most dear Nebridius—a splendid youth and most circumspect, who scoffed at the whole business of divination—could persuade me to give it up, for the authority of the astrological authors influenced me more than they did. And, thus far, I had come upon no certain proof—such as I sought—by which it could be shown without doubt that what had been truly foretold by those consulted came from accident or chance, and not from the art of the star-gazers.

CHAPTER IV

7. In those years, when I first began to teach rhetoric in my native town, I had gained a very dear friend, about my own age, who was associated with me in the same studies. Like myself, he was just rising up into the flower of youth. He had grown up with me from childhood and we had been both schoolfellows and playmates. But he was not then my friend, nor indeed ever became my friend, in the true sense of the term; for there is no true friendship save between those thou dost bind together and who cleave to thee by that love which is "shed abroad in our hearts through the Holy Spirit who is given to us." [12] Still, it was a sweet friendship, being ripened by the zeal of common studies. Moreover, I had turned him away from the true faith—which he had not soundly and thoroughly mastered as a youth—and turned him toward those superstitious and harmful fables which my mother mourned in me. With me this man went wandering off in error and my soul could not exist without him. But behold thou wast close behind thy fugitives— at once a God of vengeance and a Fountain of mercies, who dost turn us to thyself by ways that make us marvel. Thus, thou didst take that man out of this life when he had scarcely completed one whole year of friendship with me, sweeter to me than all the sweetness of my life thus far.

8. Who can show forth all thy praise [13] for that which he has experienced in himself alone? What was it that thou didst do at that time, O my God; how unsearchable are the depths of thy judgments! For when, sore sick of a fever, he long lay unconscious in a death sweat and everyone despaired of his recovery, he was baptized without his knowledge. And I myself cared little, at the time, presuming that his soul would retain what it had taken from me rather than what was done to his unconscious body. It turned out, however, far differently, for he was revived and restored. Immediately, as soon as I could talk to him—and I did this as soon as he was able, for I never left him and we hung on each other overmuch—I tried to jest with him, supposing that he also would jest in return about that baptism which he had received when his mind and senses were inactive, but which he had since learned that he had received. But he recoiled from me, as if I were his enemy, and, with a remarkable and unexpected freedom, he admonished me that, if

[12] Rom. 5:5. [13] Cf. Ps. 106:2.

I desired to continue as his friend, I must cease to say such things. Confounded and confused, I concealed my feelings till he should get well and his health recover enough to allow me to deal with him as I wished. But he was snatched away from my madness, that with thee he might be preserved for my consolation. A few days after, during my absence, the fever returned and he died.

9. My heart was utterly darkened by this sorrow and everywhere I looked I saw death. My native place was a torture room to me and my father's house a strange unhappiness. And all the things I had done with him—now that he was gone— became a frightful torment. My eyes sought him everywhere, but they did not see him; and I hated all places because he was not in them, because they could not say to me, "Look, he is coming," as they did when he was alive and absent. I became a hard riddle to myself, and I asked my soul why she was so downcast and why this disquieted me so sorely.[14] But she did not know how to answer me. And if I said, "Hope thou in God,"[15] she very properly disobeyed me, because that dearest friend she had lost was as an actual man, both truer and better than the imagined deity she was ordered to put her hope in. Nothing but tears were sweet to me and they took my friend's place in my heart's desire.

CHAPTER V

10. But now, O Lord, these things are past and time has healed my wound. Let me learn from thee, who art Truth, and put the ear of my heart to thy mouth, that thou mayest tell me why weeping should be so sweet to the unhappy. Hast thou— though omnipresent—dismissed our miseries from thy concern? Thou abidest in thyself while we are disquieted with trial after trial. Yet unless we wept in thy ears, there would be no hope for us remaining. How does it happen that such sweet fruit is plucked from the bitterness of life, from groans, tears, sighs, and lamentations? Is it the hope that thou wilt hear us that sweetens it? This is true in the case of prayer, for in a prayer there is a desire to approach thee. But is it also the case in grief for a lost love, and in the kind of sorrow that had then overwhelmed me? For I had neither a hope of his coming back to life, nor in all my tears did I seek this. I simply grieved and wept, for I was

---

[14] Cf. Ps. 42:5; 43:5.   [15] *Ibid.*

miserable and had lost my joy. Or is weeping a bitter thing that gives us pleasure because of our aversion to the things we once enjoyed and this only as long as we loathe them?

CHAPTER VI

11. But why do I speak of these things? Now is not the time to ask such questions, but rather to confess to thee. I was wretched; and every soul is wretched that is fettered in the friendship of mortal things—it is torn to pieces when it loses them, and then realizes the misery which it had even before it lost them. Thus it was at that time with me. I wept most bitterly, and found a rest in bitterness. I was wretched, and yet that wretched life I still held dearer than my friend. For though I would willingly have changed it, I was still more unwilling to lose it than to have lost him. Indeed, I doubt whether I was willing to lose it, even for him—as they tell (unless it be fiction) of the friendship of Orestes and Pylades[16]; they would have gladly died for one another, or both together, because not to love together was worse than death to them. But a strange kind of feeling had come over me, quite different from this, for now it was wearisome to live and a fearful thing to die. I suppose that the more I loved him the more I hated and feared, as the most cruel enemy, that death which had robbed me of him. I even imagined that it would suddenly annihilate all men, since it had had such a power over him. This is the way I remember it was with me.

Look into my heart, O God! Behold and look deep within me, for I remember it well, O my Hope who cleansest me from the uncleanness of such affections, directing my eyes toward thee and plucking my feet out of the snare. And I marveled that other mortals went on living since he whom I had loved as if he would never die was now dead. And I marveled all the more that I, who had been a second self to him, could go on living when he was dead. Someone spoke rightly of his friend as being "his soul's other half"[17]—for I felt that my soul and his soul were but one soul in two bodies. Consequently, my life was now a horror to me because I did not want to live as a half self. But it may have been that I was afraid to die, lest he should then die wholly whom I had so greatly loved.

16 Cf. Ovid, *Tristia*, IV, 4:74.
17 Cf. Horace, Ode I, 3:8, where he speaks of Virgil, *et serves animae dimidium meae*. Augustine's memory changes the text here to *dimidium animae suae*.

CHAPTER VII

12. O madness that knows not how to love men as they should be loved! O foolish man that I was then, enduring with so much rebellion the lot of every man! Thus I fretted, sighed, wept, tormented myself, and took neither rest nor counsel, for I was dragging around my torn and bloody soul. It was impatient of my dragging it around, and yet I could not find a place to lay it down. Not in pleasant groves, nor in sport or song, nor in fragrant bowers, nor in magnificent banquetings, nor in the pleasures of the bed or the couch; not even in books or poetry did it find rest. All things looked gloomy, even the very light itself. Whatsoever was not what he was, was now repulsive and hateful, except my groans and tears, for in those alone I found a little rest. But when my soul left off weeping, a heavy burden of misery weighed me down. It should have been raised up to thee, O Lord, for thee to lighten and to lift. This I knew, but I was neither willing nor able to do; especially since, in my thoughts of thee, thou wast not thyself but only an empty fantasm. Thus my error was my god. If I tried to cast off my burden on this fantasm, that it might find rest there, it sank through the vacuum and came rushing down again upon me. Thus I remained to myself an unhappy lodging where I could neither stay nor leave. For where could my heart fly from my heart? Where could I fly from my own self? Where would I not follow myself? And yet I did flee from my native place so that my eyes would look for him less in a place where they were not accustomed to see him. Thus I left the town of Tagaste and returned to Carthage.

CHAPTER VIII

13. Time never lapses, nor does it glide at leisure through our sense perceptions. It does strange things in the mind. Lo, time came and went from day to day, and by coming and going it brought to my mind other ideas and remembrances, and little by little they patched me up again with earlier kinds of pleasure and my sorrow yielded a bit to them. But yet there followed after this sorrow, not other sorrows just like it, but the causes of other sorrows. For why had that first sorrow so easily penetrated to the quick except that I had poured out my soul onto the dust, by loving a man as if he would never die who nevertheless had

to die? What revived and refreshed me, more than anything else, was the consolation of other friends, with whom I went on loving the things I loved instead of thee. This was a monstrous fable and a tedious lie which was corrupting my soul with its "itching ears" [18] by its adulterous rubbing. And that fable would not die to me as often as one of my friends died. And there were other things in our companionship that took strong hold of my mind: to discourse and jest with him; to indulge in courteous exchanges; to read pleasant books together; to trifle together; to be earnest together; to differ at times without ill-humor, as a man might do with himself, and even through these infrequent dissensions to find zest in our more frequent agreements; sometimes teaching, sometimes being taught; longing for someone absent with impatience and welcoming the homecomer with joy. These and similar tokens of friendship, which spring spontaneously from the hearts of those who love and are loved in return—in countenance, tongue, eyes, and a thousand ingratiating gestures—were all so much fuel to melt our souls together, and out of the many made us one.

CHAPTER IX

14. This is what we love in our friends, and we love it so much that a man's conscience accuses itself if he does not love one who loves him, or respond in love to love, seeking nothing from the other but the evidences of his love. This is the source of our moaning when one dies—the gloom of sorrow, the steeping of the heart in tears, all sweetness turned to bitterness—and the feeling of death in the living, because of the loss of the life of the dying.

Blessed is he who loves thee, and who loves his friend in thee, and his enemy also, for thy sake; for he alone loses none dear to him, if all are dear in Him who cannot be lost. And who is this but our God: the God that created heaven and earth, and filled them because he created them by filling them up? None loses thee but he who leaves thee; and he who leaves thee, where does he go, or where can he flee but from thee well-pleased to thee offended? For where does he not find thy law fulfilled in his own punishment? "Thy law is the truth" [19] and thou art Truth.

[18] II Tim. 4:3.   [19] Ps. 119:142.

CHAPTER X

15. "Turn us again, O Lord God of Hosts, cause thy face to shine; and we shall be saved." [20] For wherever the soul of man turns itself, unless toward thee, it is enmeshed in sorrows, even though it is surrounded by beautiful things outside thee and outside itself. For lovely things would simply not be unless they were from thee. They come to be and they pass away, and by coming they begin to be, and they grow toward perfection. Then, when perfect, they begin to wax old and perish, and, if all do not wax old, still all perish. Therefore, when they rise and grow toward being, the more rapidly they grow to maturity, so also the more rapidly they hasten back toward nonbeing. This is the way of things. This is the lot thou hast given them, because they are part of things which do not all exist at the same time, but by passing away and succeeding each other they all make up the universe, of which they are all parts. For example, our speech is accomplished by sounds which signify meanings, but a meaning is not complete unless one word passes away, when it has sounded its part, so that the next may follow after it. Let my soul praise thee, in all these things, O God, the Creator of all; but let not my soul be stuck to these things by the glue of love, through the senses of the body. For they go where they were meant to go, that they may exist no longer. And they rend the soul with pestilent desires because she longs to be and yet loves to rest secure in the created things she loves. But in these things there is no resting place to be found. They do not abide. They flee away; and who is he who can follow them with his physical senses? Or who can grasp them, even when they are present? For our physical sense is slow because it is a physical sense and bears its own limitations in itself. The physical sense is quite sufficient for what it was made to do; but it is not sufficient to stay things from running their courses from the beginning appointed to the end appointed. For in thy word, by which they were created, they hear their appointed bound: "From there—to here!"

CHAPTER XI

16. Be not foolish, O my soul, and do not let the tumult of your vanity deafen the ear of your heart. Be attentive. The Word itself calls you to return, and with him is a place of

[20] Ps. 80:3.

unperturbed rest, where love is not forsaken unless it first for-
sakes. Behold, these things pass away that others may come to
be in their place. Thus even this lowest level of unity [21] may be
made complete in all its parts. "But do I ever pass away?" asks
the Word of God. Fix your habitation in him. O my soul, commit
whatsoever you have to him. For at long last you are now becoming tired of deceit. Commit to truth whatever you have received from the truth, and you will lose nothing. What is de-
cayed will flourish again; your diseases will be healed; your
perishable parts shall be reshaped and renovated, and made
whole again in you. And these perishable things will not carry
you with them down to where they go when they perish, but
shall stand and abide, and you with them, before God, who
abides and continues forever.

17. Why then, my perverse soul, do you go on following your
flesh? Instead, let it be converted so as to follow you. Whatever
you feel through it is but partial. You do not know the whole, of
which sensations are but parts; and yet the parts delight you.
But if my physical senses had been able to comprehend the
whole—and had not as a part of their punishment received only
a portion of the whole as their own province—you would then
desire that whatever exists in the present time should also pass
away so that the whole might please you more. For what we
speak, you also hear through physical sensation, and yet you
would not wish that the syllables should remain. Instead, you
wish them to fly past so that others may follow them, and the
whole be heard. Thus it is always that when any single thing is
composed of many parts which do not coexist simultaneously,
the whole gives more delight than the parts could ever do perceived separately. But far better than all this is He who made
it all. He is our God and he does not pass away, for there is
nothing to take his place.

CHAPTER XII

18. If physical objects please you, praise God for them,
but turn back your love to their Creator, lest, in those things
which please you, you displease him. If souls please you, let
them be loved in God; for in themselves they are mutable,
but in him firmly established—without him they would
simply cease to exist. In him, then, let them be loved; and

---

[21] That is, our physical universe.

bring along to him with yourself as many souls as you can, and say to them: "Let us love him, for he himself created all these, and he is not far away from them. For he did not create them, and then go away. They are of him and in him. Behold, there he is, wherever truth is known. He is within the inmost heart, yet the heart has wandered away from him. Return to your heart, O you transgressors, and hold fast to him who made you. Stand with him and you shall stand fast. Rest in him and you shall be at rest. Where do you go along these rugged paths? Where are you going? The good that you love is from him, and insofar as it is also for him, it is both good and pleasant. But it will rightly be turned to bitterness if whatever comes from him is not rightly loved and if he is deserted for the love of the creature. Why then will you wander farther and farther in these difficult and toilsome ways? There is no rest where you seek it. Seek what you seek; but remember that it is not where you seek it. You seek for a blessed life in the land of death. It is not there. For how can there be a blessed life where life itself is not?"

19. But our very Life came down to earth and bore our death, and slew it with the very abundance of his own life. And, thundering, he called us to return to him into that secret place from which he came forth to us—coming first into the virginal womb, where the human creature, our mortal flesh, was joined to him that it might not be forever mortal—and came "as a bridegroom coming out his chamber, rejoicing as a strong man to run a race." [22] For he did not delay, but ran through the world, crying out by words, deeds, death, life, descent, ascension—crying aloud to us to return to him. And he departed from our sight that we might return to our hearts and find him there. For he left us, and behold, he is here. He could not be with us long, yet he did not leave us. He went back to the place that he had never left, for "the world was made by him." [23] In this world he was, and into this world he came, to save sinners. To him my soul confesses, and he heals it, because it had sinned against him. O sons of men, how long will you be so slow of heart? Even now after Life itself has come down to you, will you not ascend and live? But where will you climb if you are already on a pinnacle and have set your mouth against the heavens? First come down that you may climb up, climb up to God. For you have fallen by trying to climb against him. Tell this to the souls you love that they may weep in the valley of tears, and so

[22] Ps. 19:5.   [23] John 1:10.

bring them along with you to God, because it is by his spirit that you speak thus to them, if, as you speak, you burn with the fire of love.

CHAPTER XIII

20. These things I did not understand at that time, and I loved those inferior beauties, and I was sinking down to the very depths. And I said to my friends: "Do we love anything but the beautiful? What then is the beautiful? And what is beauty? What is it that allures and unites us to the things we love; for unless there were a grace and beauty in them, they could not possibly attract us to them?" And I reflected on this and saw that in the objects themselves there is a kind of beauty which comes from their forming a whole and another kind of beauty that comes from mutual fitness—as the harmony of one part of the body with its whole, or a shoe with a foot, and so on. And this idea sprang up in my mind out of my inmost heart, and I wrote some books—two or three, I think—*On the Beautiful and the Fitting*.[24] Thou knowest them, O Lord; they have escaped my memory. I no longer have them; somehow they have been mislaid.

CHAPTER XIV

21. What was it, O Lord my God, that prompted me to dedicate these books to Hierius, an orator of Rome, a man I did not know by sight but whom I loved for his reputation of learning, in which he was famous—and also for some words of his that I had heard which had pleased me? But he pleased me more because he pleased others, who gave him high praise and expressed amazement that a Syrian, who had first studied Greek eloquence, should thereafter become so wonderful a Latin orator and also so well versed in philosophy. Thus a man we have never seen is commended and loved. Does a love like this come into the heart of the hearer from the mouth of him who sings the other's praise? Not so. Instead, one catches the spark of love from one who loves. This is why we love one who is praised when the eulogist is believed to give his praise from an unfeigned heart; that is, when he who loves him praises him.

22. Thus it was that I loved men on the basis of other men's

---

[24] *De pulchro et apto*; a lost essay with no other record save echoes in the rest of Augustine's aesthetic theories. Cf. *The Nature of the Good Against the Manicheans*, VIII–XV; *City of God*, XI, 18; *De ordine*, I, 7:18; II, 19:51; *Enchiridion*, III, 10; I, 5.

judgment, and not thine, O my God, in whom no man is deceived. But why is it that the feeling I had for such men was not like my feeling toward the renowned charioteer, or the great gladiatorial hunter, famed far and wide and popular with the mob? Actually, I admired the orator in a different and more serious fashion, as I would myself desire to be admired. For I did not want them to praise and love me as actors were praised and loved—although I myself praise and love them too. I would prefer being unknown than known in that way, or even being hated than loved that way. How are these various influences and divers sorts of loves distributed within one soul? What is it that I am in love with in another which, if I did not hate, I should neither detest nor repel from myself, seeing that we are equally men? For it does not follow that because the good horse is admired by a man who would not be that horse— even if he could—the same kind of admiration should be given to an actor, who shares our nature. Do I then love that in a man, which I also, a man, would hate to be? Man is himself a great deep. Thou dost number his very hairs, O Lord, and they do not fall to the ground without thee, and yet the hairs of his head are more readily numbered than are his affections and the movements of his heart.

23. But that orator whom I admired so much was the kind of man I wished myself to be. Thus I erred through a swelling pride and "was carried about with every wind," [25] but through it all I was being piloted by thee, though most secretly. And how is it that I know—whence comes my confident confession to thee—that I loved him more because of the love of those who praised him than for the things they praised in him? Because if he had gone unpraised, and these same people had criticized him and had spoken the same things of him in a tone of scorn and disapproval, I should never have been kindled and provoked to love him. And yet his qualities would not have been different, nor would he have been different himself; only the appraisals of the spectators. See where the helpless soul lies prostrate that is not yet sustained by the stability of truth! Just as the breezes of speech blow from the breast of the opinionated, so also the soul is tossed this way and that, driven forward and backward, and the light is obscured to it and the truth not seen. And yet, there it is in front of us.

And to me it was a great matter that both my literary work and my zest for learning should be known by that man. For if

[25] Eph. 4:14.

he approved them, I would be even more fond of him; but if he disapproved, this vain heart of mine, devoid of thy steadfastness, would have been offended. And so I meditated on the problem "of the beautiful and the fitting" and dedicated my essay on it to him. I regarded it admiringly, though no one else joined me in doing so.

CHAPTER XV

24. But I had not seen how the main point in these great issues [concerning the nature of beauty] lay really in thy craftsmanship, O Omnipotent One, "who alone doest great wonders."[26] And so my mind ranged through the corporeal forms, and I defined and distinguished as "beautiful" that which is so in itself and as "fit" that which is beautiful in relation to some other thing. This argument I supported by corporeal examples. And I turned my attention to the nature of the mind, but the false opinions which I held concerning spiritual things prevented me from seeing the truth. Still, the very power of truth forced itself on my gaze, and I turned my throbbing soul away from incorporeal substance to qualities of line and color and shape, and, because I could not perceive these with my mind, I concluded that I could not perceive my mind. And since I loved the peace which is in virtue, and hated the discord which is in vice, I distinguished between the unity there is in virtue and the discord there is in vice. I conceived that unity consisted of the rational soul and the nature of truth and the highest good. But I imagined that in the disunity there was some kind of substance of irrational life and some kind of entity in the supreme evil. This evil I thought was not only a substance but real life as well, and yet I believed that it did not come from thee, O my God, from whom are all things. And the first I called a Monad, as if it were a soul without sex. The other I called a Dyad, which showed itself in anger in deeds of violence, in deeds of passion and lust—but I did not know what I was talking about. For I had not understood nor had I been taught that evil is not a substance at all and that our soul is not that supreme and unchangeable good.

25. For just as in violent acts, if the emotion of the soul from whence the violent impulse springs is depraved and asserts itself insolently and mutinously—and just as in the acts of passion, if the affection of the soul which gives rise to carnal desires

[26] Ps. 72:18.

is unrestrained—so also, in the same way, errors and false opinions contaminate life if the rational soul itself is depraved. Thus it was then with me, for I was ignorant that my soul had to be enlightened by another light, if it was to be partaker of the truth, since it is not itself the essence of truth. "For thou wilt light my lamp; the Lord my God will lighten my darkness" [27]; and "of his fullness have we all received," [28] for "that was the true Light that lighteth every man that cometh into the world" [29]; for "in thee there is no variableness, neither shadow of turning." [30]

26. But I pushed on toward thee, and was pressed back by thee that I might know the taste of death, for "thou resistest the proud." [31] And what greater pride could there be for me than, with a marvelous madness, to assert myself to be that nature which thou art? I was mutable—this much was clear enough to me because my very longing to become wise arose out of a wish to change from worse to better—yet I chose rather to think thee mutable than to think that I was not as thou art. For this reason I was thrust back; thou didst resist my fickle pride. Thus I went on imagining corporeal forms, and, since I was flesh I accused the flesh, and, since I was "a wind that passes away," [32] I did not return to thee but went wandering and wandering on toward those things that have no being—neither in thee nor in me, nor in the body. These fancies were not created for me by thy truth but conceived by my own vain conceit out of sensory notions. And I used to ask thy faithful children—my own fellow citizens, from whom I stood unconsciously exiled—I used flippantly and foolishly to ask them, "Why, then, does the soul, which God created, err?" But I would not allow anyone to ask me, "Why, then, does God err?" I preferred to contend that thy immutable substance was involved in error through necessity rather than admit that my own mutable substance had gone astray of its own free will and had fallen into error as its punishment.

27. I was about twenty-six or twenty-seven when I wrote those books, analyzing and reflecting upon those sensory images which clamored in the ears of my heart. I was straining those ears to hear thy inward melody, O sweet Truth, pondering on "the beautiful and the fitting" and longing to stay and hear thee, and to rejoice greatly at "the Bridegroom's voice." [33] Yet

---

[27] Ps. 18:28.   [28] John 1:16.   [29] John 1:9.
[30] Cf. James 1:17.   [31] Cf. James 4:6; I Peter 5:5.   [32] Ps. 78:39.
[33] Cf. Jer. 25:10; 33:11; John 3:29; Rev. 18:23.

I could not, for by the clamor of my own errors I was hurried outside myself, and by the weight of my own pride I was sinking ever lower. You did not "make me to hear joy and gladness," nor did the bones rejoice which were not yet humbled.[34]

28. And what did it profit me that, when I was scarcely twenty years old, a book of Aristotle's entitled *The Ten Categories*[35] fell into my hands? On the very title of this I hung as on something great and divine, since my rhetoric master at Carthage and others who had reputations for learning were always referring to it with such swelling pride. I read it by myself and understood it. And what did it mean that when I discussed it with others they said that even with the assistance of tutors—who not only explained it orally, but drew many diagrams in the sand—they scarcely understood it and could tell me no more about it than I had acquired in the reading of it by myself alone? For the book appeared to me to speak plainly enough about substances, such as a man; and of their qualities, such as the shape of a man, his kind, his stature, how many feet high, and his family relationship, his status, when born, whether he is sitting or standing, is shod or armed, or is doing something or having something done to him—and all the innumerable things that are are classified under these nine categories (of which I have given some examples) or under the chief category of substance.

29. What did all this profit me, since it actually hindered me when I imagined that whatever existed was comprehended within those ten categories? I tried to interpret them, O my God, so that even thy wonderful and unchangeable unity could be understood as subjected to thy own magnitude or beauty, as if they existed in thee as their subject—as they do in corporeal bodies—whereas thou art thyself thy own magnitude and beauty. A body is not great or fair because it is a body, because, even if it were less great or less beautiful, it would still be a body. But my conception of thee was falsity, not truth. It was a figment of my own misery, not the stable ground of thy blessedness. For thou hadst commanded, and it was carried out in me, that the earth should bring forth briars and thorns for me, and that with heavy labor I should gain my bread.[36]

[34] Cf. Ps. 51:8.
[35] The first section of the *Organon*, which analyzes the problem of predication and develops "the ten categories" of *essence* and the nine "accidents." This existed in a Latin translation by Victorinus, who also translated the *Enneads* of Plotinus, to which Augustine refers infra, Bk. VIII, Ch. II, 3.
[36] Cf. Gen. 3:18.

30. And what did it profit me that I could read and understand for myself all the books I could get in the so-called "liberal arts," when I was actually a worthless slave of wicked lust? I took delight in them, not knowing the real source of what it was in them that was true and certain. For I had my back toward the light, and my face toward the things on which the light falls, so that my face, which looked toward the illuminated things, was not itself illuminated. Whatever was written in any of the fields of rhetoric or logic, geometry, music, or arithmetic, I could understand without any great difficulty and without the instruction of another man. All this thou knowest, O Lord my God, because both quickness in understanding and acuteness in insight are thy gifts. Yet for such gifts I made no thank offering to thee. Therefore, my abilities served not my profit but rather my loss, since I went about trying to bring so large a part of my substance into my own power. And I did not store up my strength for thee, but went away from thee into the far country to prostitute my gifts in disordered appetite.[37] And what did these abilities profit me, if I did not put them to good use? I did not realize that those arts were understood with great difficulty, even by the studious and the intelligent, until I tried to explain them to others and discovered that even the most proficient in them followed my explanations all too slowly.

31. And yet what did this profit me, since I still supposed that thou, O Lord God, the Truth, wert a bright and vast body and that I was a particle of that body? O perversity gone too far! But so it was with me. And I do not blush, O my God, to confess thy mercies to me in thy presence, or to call upon thee— any more than I did not blush when I openly avowed my blasphemies before men, and bayed, houndlike, against thee. What good was it for me that my nimble wit could run through those studies and disentangle all those knotty volumes, without help from a human teacher, since all the while I was erring so hatefully and with such sacrilege as far as the right substance of pious faith was concerned? And what kind of burden was it for thy little ones to have a far slower wit, since they did not use it to depart from thee, and since they remained in the nest of thy Church to become safely fledged and to nourish the wings of love by the food of a sound faith.

O Lord our God, under the shadow of thy wings let us hope —defend us and support us.[38] Thou wilt bear us up when we are little and even down to our gray hairs thou wilt carry us.

[37] Again, the Prodigal Son theme; cf. Luke 15:13.   [38] Cf. Ps. 17:8.

For our stability, when it is in thee, is stability indeed; but when it is in ourselves, then it is all unstable. Our good lives forever with thee, and when we turn from thee with aversion, we fall into our own perversion. Let us now, O Lord, return that we be not overturned, because with thee our good lives without blemish—for our good is thee thyself. And we need not fear that we shall find no place to return to because we fell away from it. For, in our absence, our home—which is thy eternity—does not fall away.

BOOK FIVE

A year of decision. Faustus comes to Carthage and Augustine is disen-
chanted in his hope for solid demonstration of the truth of Manichean
doctrine. He decides to flee from his known troubles at Carthage to
troubles yet unknown at Rome. His experiences at Rome prove disappoint-
ing and he applies for a teaching post at Milan. Here he meets Ambrose,
who confronts him as an impressive witness for Catholic Christianity and
opens out the possibilities of the allegorical interpretation of Scripture.
Augustine decides to become a Christian catechumen.

CHAPTER I

1. Accept this sacrifice of my confessions from the hand of my
tongue. Thou didst form it and hast prompted it to praise thy
name. Heal all my bones and let them say, "O Lord, who is
like unto thee?"[1] It is not that one who confesses to thee instructs thee as to what goes on within him. For the closed heart
does not bar thy sight into it, nor does the hardness of our heart
hold back thy hands, for thou canst soften it at will, either by
mercy or in vengeance, "and there is no one who can hide himself from thy heat."[2] But let my soul praise thee, that it may
love thee, and let it confess thy mercies to thee, that it may
praise thee. Thy whole creation praises thee without ceasing:
the spirit of man, by his own lips, by his own voice, lifted up to
thee; animals and lifeless matter by the mouths of those who
meditate upon them. Thus our souls may climb out of their
weariness toward thee and lean on those things which thou hast
created and pass through them to thee, who didst create them in a
marvelous way. With thee, there is refreshment and true strength.

[1] Ps. 35:10.　　　　　　　　　[2] Cf. Ps. 19:6.

CHAPTER II

2. Let the restless and the unrighteous depart, and flee away from thee. Even so, thou seest them and thy eye pierces through the shadows in which they run. For lo, they live in a world of beauty and yet are themselves most foul. And how have they harmed thee? Or in what way have they discredited thy power, which is just and perfect in its rule even to the last item in creation? Indeed, where would they fly when they fled from thy presence? Wouldst thou be unable to find them? But they fled that they might not see thee, who sawest them; that they might be blinded and stumble into thee. But thou forsakest nothing that thou hast made. The unrighteous stumble against thee that they may be justly plagued, fleeing from thy gentleness and colliding with thy justice, and falling on their own rough paths. For in truth they do not know that thou art everywhere; that no place contains thee, and that only thou art near even to those who go farthest from thee. Let them, therefore, turn back and seek thee, because even if they have abandoned thee, their Creator, thou hast not abandoned thy creatures. Let them turn back and seek thee—and lo, thou art there in their hearts, there in the hearts of those who confess to thee. Let them cast themselves upon thee, and weep on thy bosom, after all their weary wanderings; and thou wilt gently wipe away their tears.[3] And they weep the more and rejoice in their weeping, since thou, O Lord, art not a man of flesh and blood. Thou art the Lord, who canst remake what thou didst make and canst comfort them. And where was I when I was seeking thee? There thou wast, before me; but I had gone away, even from myself, and I could not find myself, much less thee.

CHAPTER III

3. Let me now lay bare in the sight of God the twenty-ninth year of my age. There had just come to Carthage a certain bishop of the Manicheans, Faustus by name, a great snare of the devil; and many were entangled by him through the charm of his eloquence. Now, even though I found this eloquence admirable, I was beginning to distinguish the charm of words from the truth of things, which I was eager to learn. Nor did I consider the dish as much as I did the kind of meat that their

[3] Cf. Rev. 21:4.

famous Faustus served up to me in it. His fame had run before him, as one very skilled in an honorable learning and preeminently skilled in the liberal arts.

And as I had already read and stored up in memory many of the injunctions of the philosophers, I began to compare some of their doctrines with the tedious fables of the Manicheans; and it struck me that the probability was on the side of the philosophers, whose power reached far enough to enable them to form a fair judgment of the world, even though they had not discovered the sovereign Lord of it all. For thou art great, O Lord, and thou hast respect unto the lowly, but the proud thou knowest afar off.[4] Thou drawest near to none but the contrite in heart, and canst not be found by the proud, even if in their inquisitive skill they may number the stars and the sands, and map out the constellations, and trace the courses of the planets.

4. For it is by the mind and the intelligence which thou gavest them that they investigate these things. They have discovered much; and have foretold, many years in advance, the day, the hour, and the extent of the eclipses of those luminaries, the sun and the moon. Their calculations did not fail, and it came to pass as they predicted. And they wrote down the rules they had discovered, so that to this day they may be read and from them may be calculated in what year and month and day and hour of the day, and at what quarter of its light, either the moon or the sun will be eclipsed, and it will come to pass just as predicted. And men who are ignorant in these matters marvel and are amazed; and those who understand them exult and are exalted. Both, by an impious pride, withdraw from thee and forsake thy light. They foretell an eclipse of the sun before it happens, but they do not see their own eclipse which is even now occurring. For they do not ask, as religious men should, what is the source of the intelligence by which they investigate these matters. Moreover, when they discover that thou didst make them, they do not give themselves up to thee that thou mightest preserve what thou hast made. Nor do they offer, as sacrifice to thee, what they have made of themselves. For they do not slaughter their own pride—as they do the sacrificial fowls—nor their own curiosities by which, like the fishes of the sea, they wander through the unknown paths of the deep. Nor do they curb their own extravagances as they do those of "the beasts of the field,"[5] so that thou, O Lord, "a consuming fire,"[6]

4 Cf. Ps. 138:6.   5 Ps. 8:7.   6 Heb. 12:29.

mayest burn up their mortal cares and renew them unto immortality.

5. They do not know the way which is thy word, by which thou didst create all the things that are and also the men who measure them, and the senses by which they perceive what they measure, and the intelligence whereby they discern the patterns of measure. Thus they know not that thy wisdom is not a matter of measure.[7] But the Only Begotten hath been "made unto us wisdom, and righteousness, and sanctification"[8] and hath been numbered among us and paid tribute to Caesar.[9] And they do not know this "Way" by which they could descend from themselves to him in order to ascend through him to him. They did not know this "Way," and so they fancied themselves exalted to the stars and the shining heavens. And lo, they fell upon the earth, and "their foolish heart was darkened."[10] They saw many true things about the creature but they do not seek with true piety for the Truth, the Architect of Creation, and hence they do not find him. Or, if they do find him, and know that he is God, they do not glorify him as God; neither are they thankful but become vain in their imagination, and say that they themselves are wise, and attribute to themselves what is thine. At the same time, with the most perverse blindness, they wish to attribute to thee their own quality—so that they load their lies on thee who art the Truth, "changing the glory of the incorruptible God for an image of corruptible man, and birds, and four-footed beasts, and creeping things."[11] "They exchanged thy truth for a lie, and worshiped and served the creature rather than the Creator."[12]

6. Yet I remembered many a true saying of the philosophers about the creation, and I saw the confirmation of their calculations in the orderly sequence of seasons and in the visible evidence of the stars. And I compared this with the doctrines of Mani, who in his voluminous folly wrote many books on these subjects. But I could not discover there any account, of either the solstices or the equinoxes, or the eclipses of the sun and moon, or anything of the sort that I had learned in the books of secular philosophy. But still I was ordered to believe, even where the ideas did not correspond with—even when they contradicted—the rational theories established by mathematics and my own eyes, but were very different.

---

[7] An echo of the opening sentence, Bk. I, Ch. I, 1. [8] Cf. I Cor. 1:30.
[9] Cf. Matt. 22:21. [10] Cf. Rom. 1:21 ff.
[11] Cf. Rom. 1:23. [12] Cf. Rom. 1:25.

CHAPTER IV

7. Yet, O Lord God of Truth, is any man pleasing to thee because he knows these things? No, for surely that man is unhappy who knows these things and does not know thee. And that man is happy who knows thee, even though he does not know these things. He who knows both thee and these things is not the more blessed for his learning, for thou only art his blessing, if knowing thee as God he glorifies thee and gives thanks and does not become vain in his thoughts.

For just as that man who knows how to possess a tree, and give thanks to thee for the use of it—although he may not know how many feet high it is or how wide it spreads—is better than the man who can measure it and count all its branches, but neither owns it nor knows or loves its Creator: just so is a faithful man who possesses the world's wealth as though he had nothing, and possesses all things through his union through thee, whom all things serve, even though he does not know the circlings of the Great Bear. Just so it is foolish to doubt that this faithful man may truly be better than the one who can measure the heavens and number the stars and weigh the elements, but who is forgetful of thee "who hast set in order all things in number, weight, and measure." [13]

CHAPTER V

8. And who ordered this Mani to write about these things, knowledge of which is not necessary to piety? For thou hast said to man, "Behold, godliness is wisdom" [14]—and of this he might have been ignorant, however perfectly he may have known these other things. Yet, since he did not know even these other things, and most impudently dared to teach them, it is clear that he had no knowledge of piety. For, even when we have a knowledge of this worldly lore, it is folly to make a *profession* of it, when piety comes from *confession* to thee. From piety, therefore, Mani had gone astray, and all his show of learning only enabled the truly learned to perceive, from his ignorance of what they knew, how little he was to be trusted to make plain these more really difficult matters. For he did not aim to be lightly esteemed, but went around trying to persuade men that the Holy Spirit, the Comforter and Enricher of thy

[13] Wis. 11:20.   [14] Cf. Job 28:28.

faithful ones, was personally resident in him with full authority. And, therefore, when he was detected in manifest errors about the sky, the stars, the movements of the sun and moon, even though these things do not relate to religious doctrine, the impious presumption of the man became clearly evident; for he not only taught things about which he was ignorant but also perverted them, and this with pride so foolish and mad that he sought to claim that his own utterances were as if they had been those of a divine person.

9. When I hear of a Christian brother, ignorant of these things, or in error concerning them, I can tolerate his uninformed opinion; and I do not see that any lack of knowledge as to the form or nature of this material creation can do him much harm, as long as he does not hold a belief in anything which is unworthy of thee, O Lord, the Creator of all. But if he thinks that his secular knowledge pertains to the essence of the doctrine of piety, or ventures to assert dogmatic opinions in matters in which he is ignorant—there lies the injury. And yet even a weakness such as this, in the infancy of our faith, is tolerated by our Mother Charity until the new man can grow up "unto a perfect man," and not be "carried away with every wind of doctrine." [15]

But Mani had presumed to be at once the teacher, author, guide, and leader of all whom he could persuade to believe this, so that all who followed him believed that they were following not an ordinary man but thy Holy Spirit. And who would not judge that such great madness, when it once stood convicted of false teaching, should then be abhorred and utterly rejected? But I had not yet clearly decided whether the alternation of day and night, and of longer and shorter days and nights, and the eclipses of sun and moon, and whatever else I read about in other books could be explained consistently with his theories. If they could have been so explained, there would still have remained a doubt in my mind whether the theories were right or wrong. Yet I was prepared, on the strength of his reputed godliness, to rest my faith on his authority.

CHAPTER VI

10. For almost the whole of the nine years that I listened with unsettled mind to the Manichean teaching I had been looking forward with unbounded eagerness to the arrival of this

[15] Eph. 4:13, 14.

Faustus. For all the other members of the sect that I happened to meet, when they were unable to answer the questions I raised, always referred me to his coming. They promised that, in discussion with him, these and even greater difficulties, if I had them, would be quite easily and amply cleared away. When at last he did come, I found him to be a man of pleasant speech, who spoke of the very same things they themselves did, although more fluently and in a more agreeable style. But what profit was there to me in the elegance of my cupbearer, since he could not offer me the more precious draught for which I thirsted? My ears had already had their fill of such stuff, and now it did not seem any better because it was better expressed nor more true because it was dressed up in rhetoric; nor could I think the man's soul necessarily wise because his face was comely and his language eloquent. But they who extolled him to me were not competent judges. They thought him able and wise because his eloquence delighted them. At the same time I realized that there is another kind of man who is suspicious even of truth itself, if it is expressed in smooth and flowing language. But thou, O my God, hadst already taught me in wonderful and marvelous ways, and therefore I believed—because it is true—that thou didst teach me and that beside thee there is no other teacher of truth, wherever truth shines forth. Already I had learned from thee that because a thing is eloquently expressed it should not be taken to be as necessarily true; nor because it is uttered with stammering lips should it be supposed false. Nor, again, is it necessarily true because rudely uttered, nor untrue because the language is brilliant. Wisdom and folly both are like meats that are wholesome and unwholesome, and courtly or simple words are like town-made or rustic vessels—both kinds of food may be served in either kind of dish.

11. That eagerness, therefore, with which I had so long awaited this man, was in truth delighted with his action and feeling in a disputation, and with the fluent and apt words with which he clothed his ideas. I was delighted, therefore, and I joined with others—and even exceeded them—in exalting and praising him. Yet it was a source of annoyance to me that, in his lecture room, I was not allowed to introduce and raise any of those questions that troubled me, in a familiar exchange of discussion with him. As soon as I found an opportunity for this, and gained his ear at a time when it was not inconvenient for him to enter into a discussion with me and my friends, I laid before him some of my doubts. I discovered at once that he

knew nothing of the liberal arts except grammar, and that only in an ordinary way. He had, however, read some of Tully's orations, a very few books of Seneca, and some of the poets, and such few books of his own sect as were written in good Latin. With this meager learning and his daily practice in speaking, he had acquired a sort of eloquence which proved the more delightful and enticing because it was under the direction of a ready wit and a sort of native grace. Was this not even as I now recall it, O Lord my God, Judge of my conscience? My heart and my memory are laid open before thee, who wast even then guiding me by the secret impulse of thy providence and wast setting my shameful errors before my face so that I might see and hate them.

CHAPTER VII

12. For as soon as it became plain to me that Faustus was ignorant in those arts in which I had believed him eminent, I began to despair of his being able to clarify and explain all these perplexities that troubled me—though I realized that such ignorance need not have affected the authenticity of his piety, if he had not been a Manichean. For their books are full of long fables about the sky and the stars, the sun and the moon; and I had ceased to believe him able to show me in any satisfactory fashion what I so ardently desired: whether the explanations contained in the Manichean books were better or at least as good as the mathematical explanations I had read elsewhere. But when I proposed that these subjects should be considered and discussed, he quite modestly did not dare to undertake the task, for he was aware that he had no knowledge of these things and was not ashamed to confess it. For he was not one of those talkative people—from whom I had endured so much—who undertook to teach me what I wanted to know, and then said nothing. Faustus had a heart which, if not right toward thee, was at least not altogether false toward himself; for he was not ignorant of his own ignorance, and he did not choose to be entangled in a controversy from which he could not draw back or retire gracefully. For this I liked him all the more. For the modesty of an ingenious mind is a finer thing than the acquisition of that knowledge I desired; and this I found to be his attitude toward all abstruse and difficult questions.

13. Thus the zeal with which I had plunged into the Manichean system was checked, and I despaired even more of their other teachers, because Faustus who was so famous among

them had turned out so poorly in the various matters that puzzled me. And so I began to occupy myself with him in the study of his own favorite pursuit, that of literature, in which I was already teaching a class as a professor of rhetoric among the young Carthaginian students. With Faustus then I read whatever he himself wished to read, or what I judged suitable to his bent of mind. But all my endeavors to make further progress in Manicheism came completely to an end through my acquaintance with that man. I did not wholly separate myself from them, but as one who had not yet found anything better I decided to content myself, for the time being, with what I had stumbled upon one way or another, until by chance something more desirable should present itself. Thus that Faustus who had entrapped so many to their death—though neither willing nor witting it— now began to loosen the snare in which I had been caught. For thy hands, O my God, in the hidden design of thy providence did not desert my soul; and out of the blood of my mother's heart, through the tears that she poured out by day and by night, there was a sacrifice offered to thee for me, and by marvelous ways thou didst deal with me. For it was thou, O my God, who didst it: for "the steps of a man are ordered by the Lord, and he shall choose his way." [16] How shall we attain salvation without thy hand remaking what it had already made?

CHAPTER VIII

14. Thou didst so deal with me, therefore, that I was persuaded to go to Rome and teach there what I had been teaching at Carthage. And how I was persuaded to do this I will not omit to confess to thee, for in this also the profoundest workings of thy wisdom and thy constant mercy toward us must be pondered and acknowledged. I did not wish to go to Rome because of the richer fees and the higher dignity which my friends promised me there—though these considerations did affect my decision. My principal and almost sole motive was that I had been informed that the students there studied more quietly and were better kept under the control of stern discipline, so that they did not capriciously and impudently rush into the classroom of a teacher not their own—indeed, they were not admitted at all without the permission of the teacher. At Carthage, on the contrary, there was a shameful and intemperate license among the students. They burst in rudely and, with furious

16 Ps. 36:23 (Vulgate).

gestures, would disrupt the discipline which the teacher had established for the good of his pupils. Many outrages they perpetrated with astounding effrontery, things that would be punishable by law if they were not sustained by custom. Thus custom makes plain that such behavior is all the more worthless because it allows men to do what thy eternal law never will allow. They think that they act thus with impunity, though the very blindness with which they act is their punishment, and they suffer far greater harm than they inflict.

The manners that I would not adopt as a student I was compelled as a teacher to endure in others. And so I was glad to go where all who knew the situation assured me that such conduct was not allowed. But thou, "O my refuge and my portion in the land of the living," [17] didst goad me thus at Carthage so that I might thereby be pulled away from it and change my worldly habitation for the preservation of my soul. At the same time, thou didst offer me at Rome an enticement, through the agency of men enchanted with this death-in-life—by their insane conduct in the one place and their empty promises in the other. To correct my wandering footsteps, thou didst secretly employ their perversity and my own. For those who disturbed my tranquillity were blinded by shameful madness and also those who allured me elsewhere had nothing better than the earth's cunning. And I who hated actual misery in the one place sought fictitious happiness in the other.

15. Thou knewest the cause of my going from one country to the other, O God, but thou didst not disclose it either to me or to my mother, who grieved deeply over my departure and followed me down to the sea. She clasped me tight in her embrace, willing either to keep me back or to go with me, but I deceived her, pretending that I had a friend whom I could not leave until he had a favorable wind to set sail. Thus I lied to my mother—and such a mother!—and escaped. For this too thou didst mercifully pardon me—fool that I was—and didst preserve me from the waters of the sea for the water of thy grace; so that, when I was purified by that, the fountain of my mother's eyes, from which she had daily watered the ground for me as she prayed to thee, should be dried. And, since she refused to return without me, I persuaded her, with some difficulty, to remain that night in a place quite close to our ship, where there was a shrine in memory of the blessed Cyprian. That night I slipped away secretly, and she remained to pray and weep. And

17 Ps. 142:5.

what was it, O Lord, that she was asking of thee in such a flood of tears but that thou wouldst not allow me to sail? But thou, taking thy own secret counsel and noting the real point to her desire, didst not grant what she was then asking in order to grant to her the thing that she had always been asking.

The wind blew and filled our sails, and the shore dropped out of sight. Wild with grief, she was there the next morning and filled thy ears with complaints and groans which thou didst disregard, although, at the very same time, thou wast using my longings as a means and wast hastening me on to the fulfillment of all longing. Thus the earthly part of her love to me was justly purged by the scourge of sorrow. Still, like all mothers—though even more than others—she loved to have me with her, and did not know what joy thou wast preparing for her through my going away. Not knowing this secret end, she wept and mourned and saw in her agony the inheritance of Eve—seeking in sorrow what she had brought forth in sorrow. And yet, after accusing me of perfidy and cruelty, she still continued her intercessions for me to thee. She returned to her own home, and I went on to Rome.

CHAPTER IX

16. And lo, I was received in Rome by the scourge of bodily sickness; and I was very near to falling into hell, burdened with all the many and grievous sins I had committed against thee, myself, and others—all over and above that fetter of original sin whereby we all die in Adam. For thou hadst forgiven me none of these things in Christ, neither had he abolished by his cross the enmity[18] that I had incurred from thee through my sins. For how could he do so by the crucifixion of a phantom, which was all I supposed him to be? The death of my soul was as real then as the death of his flesh appeared to me unreal. And the life of my soul was as false, because it was as unreal as the death of his flesh was real, though I believed it not.

My fever increased, and I was on the verge of passing away and perishing; for, if I had passed away then, where should I have gone but into the fiery torment which my misdeeds deserved, measured by the truth of thy rule? My mother knew nothing of this; yet, far away, she went on praying for me. And thou, present everywhere, didst hear her where she was and had pity on me where I was, so that I regained my bodily health, although I was still disordered in my sacrilegious heart. For

[18] Cf. Eph. 2:15.

that peril of death did not make me wish to be baptized. I was even better when, as a lad, I entreated baptism of my mother's devotion, as I have already related and confessed.[19] But now I had since increased in dishonor, and I madly scoffed at all the purposes of thy medicine which would not have allowed me, though a sinner such as I was, to die a double death. Had my mother's heart been pierced with this wound, it never could have been cured, for I cannot adequately tell of the love she had for me, or how she still travailed for me in the spirit with a far keener anguish than when she bore me in the flesh.

17. I cannot conceive, therefore, how she could have been healed if my death (still in my sins) had pierced her inmost love. Where, then, would have been all her earnest, frequent, and ceaseless prayers to thee? Nowhere but with thee. But couldst thou, O most merciful God, despise the "contrite and humble heart"[20] of that pure and prudent widow, who was so constant in her alms, so gracious and attentive to thy saints, never missing a visit to church twice a day, morning and evening—and this not for vain gossiping, nor old wives' fables, but in order that she might listen to thee in thy sermons, and thou to her in her prayers? Couldst thou, by whose gifts she was so inspired, despise and disregard the tears of such a one without coming to her aid—those tears by which she entreated thee, not for gold or silver, and not for any changing or fleeting good, but for the salvation of the soul of her son? By no means, O Lord. It is certain that thou wast near and wast hearing and wast carrying out the plan by which thou hadst predetermined it should be done. Far be it from thee that thou shouldst have deluded her in those visions and the answers she had received from thee—some of which I have mentioned, and others not—which she kept in her faithful heart, and, forever beseeching, urged them on thee as if they had thy own signature. For thou, "because thy mercy endureth forever,"[21] hast so condescended to those whose debts thou hast pardoned that thou likewise dost become a debtor by thy promises.

CHAPTER X

18. Thou didst restore me then from that illness, and didst heal the son of thy handmaid in his body, that he might live for

[19] Bk. I, Ch. XI, 17.　　　　[20] Cf. Ps. 51:17.
[21] A constant theme in The Psalms and elsewhere; cf. Ps. 136.

thee and that thou mightest endow him with a better and more certain health. After this, at Rome, I again joined those deluding and deluded "saints"; and not their "hearers" only, such as the man was in whose house I had fallen sick, but also with those whom they called "the elect." For it still seemed to me "that it is not we who sin, but some other nature sinned in us." And it gratified my pride to be beyond blame, and when I did anything wrong not to have to confess that *I* had done wrong— "that thou mightest heal my soul because it had sinned against thee" 22—and I loved to excuse my soul and to accuse something else inside me (I knew not what) but which was not I. But, assuredly, it was I, and it was my impiety that had divided me against myself. That sin then was all the more incurable because I did not deem myself a sinner. It was an execrable iniquity, O God Omnipotent, that I would have preferred to have thee defeated in me, to my destruction, than to be defeated by thee to my salvation. Not yet, therefore, hadst thou set a watch upon my mouth and a door around my lips that my heart might not incline to evil speech, to make excuse for sin with men that work iniquity.23 And, therefore, I continued still in the company of their "elect."

19. But now, hopeless of gaining any profit from that false doctrine, I began to hold more loosely and negligently even to those points which I had decided to rest content with, if I could find nothing better. I was now half inclined to believe that those philosophers whom they call "The Academics" 24 were wiser than the rest in holding that we ought to doubt everything, and in maintaining that man does not have the power of comprehending any certain truth, for, although I had not yet understood their meaning, I was fully persuaded that they thought just as they are commonly reputed to do. And I did not fail openly to dissuade my host from his confidence which I observed that he had in those fictions of which the works of Mani are full. For all this, I was still on terms of more intimate friendship with these people than with others who were not of their heresy.

22 Cf. Ps. 41:4.   23 Cf. Ps. 141:3f.
24 Followers of the skeptical tradition established in the Platonic Academy by Arcesilaus and Carneades in the third century B.C. They taught the necessity of ἐποχή, suspended judgment, in all questions of truth, and would allow nothing more than the consent of probability. This tradition was known in Augustine's time chiefly through the writings of Cicero; cf. his *Academica*. This kind of skepticism shook Augustine's complacency severely, and he wrote one of his first dialogues, *Contra Academicos*, in an effort to clear up the problem posed thereby.

I did not indeed defend it with my former ardor; but my familiarity with that group—and there were many of them concealed in Rome at that time [25]—made me slower to seek any other way. This was particularly easy since I had no hope of finding in thy Church the truth from which they had turned me aside, O Lord of heaven and earth, Creator of all things visible and invisible. And it still seemed to me most unseemly to believe that thou couldst have the form of human flesh and be bounded by the bodily shape of our limbs. And when I desired to meditate on my God, I did not know what to think of but a huge extended body—for what did not have bodily extension did not seem to me to exist—and this was the greatest and almost the sole cause of my unavoidable errors.

20. And thus I also believed that evil was a similar kind of substance, and that it had its own hideous and deformed extended body—either in a dense form which they called the earth or in a thin and subtle form as, for example, the substance of the air, which they imagined as some malignant spirit penetrating that earth. And because my piety—such as it was—still compelled me to believe that the good God never created any evil substance, I formed the idea of two masses, one opposed to the other, both infinite but with the evil more contracted and the good more expansive. And from this diseased beginning, the other sacrileges followed after.

For when my mind tried to turn back to the Catholic faith, I was cast down, since the Catholic faith was not what I judged it to be. And it seemed to me a greater piety to regard thee, my God—to whom I make confession of thy mercies—as infinite in all respects save that one: where the extended mass of evil stood opposed to thee, where I was compelled to confess that thou art finite—than if I should think that thou couldst be confined by the form of a human body on every side. And it seemed better to me to believe that no evil had been created by thee— for in my ignorance evil appeared not only to be some kind of substance but a corporeal one at that. This was because I had, thus far, no conception of mind, except as a subtle body diffused throughout local spaces. This seemed better than to believe that anything could emanate from thee which had the character that I considered evil to be in its nature. And I believed that our Saviour himself also—thy Only Begotten—had been brought forth, as it were, for our salvation out of the mass of thy bright shining substance. So that I could believe nothing about him

25 The Manicheans were under an official ban in Rome.

except what I was able to harmonize with these vain imaginations. I thought, therefore, that such a nature could not be born of the Virgin Mary without being mingled with the flesh, and I could not see how the divine substance, as I had conceived it, could be mingled thus without being contaminated. I was afraid, therefore, to believe that he had been born in the flesh, lest I should also be compelled to believe that he had been contaminated by the flesh. Now will thy spiritual ones smile blandly and lovingly at me if they read these confessions. Yet such was I.

CHAPTER XI

21. Furthermore, the things they censured in thy Scriptures I thought impossible to be defended. And yet, occasionally, I desired to confer on various matters with someone well learned in those books, to test what he thought of them. For already the words of one Elpidius, who spoke and disputed face to face against these same Manicheans, had begun to impress me, even when I was at Carthage; because he brought forth things out of the Scriptures that were not easily withstood, to which their answers appeared to me feeble. One of their answers they did not give forth publicly, but only to us in private—when they said that the writings of the New Testament had been tampered with by unknown persons who desired to ingraft the Jewish law into the Christian faith. But they themselves never brought forward any uncorrupted copies. Still thinking in corporeal categories and very much ensnared and to some extent stifled, I was borne down by those conceptions of bodily substance. I panted under this load for the air of thy truth, but I was not able to breathe it pure and undefiled.

CHAPTER XII

22. I set about diligently to practice what I came to Rome to do—the teaching of rhetoric. The first task was to bring together in my home a few people to whom and through whom I had begun to be known. And lo, I then began to learn that other offenses were committed in Rome which I had not had to bear in Africa. Just as I had been told, those riotous disruptions by young blackguards were not practiced here. Yet, now, my friends told me, many of the Roman students—breakers of faith, who, for the love of money, set a small value on justice—would conspire together and suddenly transfer to another

teacher, to evade paying their master's fees. My heart hated such people, though not with a "perfect hatred" [26]; for doubtless I hated them more because I was to suffer from them than on account of their own illicit acts. Still, such people are base indeed; they fornicate against thee, for they love the transitory mockeries of temporal things and the filthy gain which begrimes the hand that grabs it; they embrace the fleeting world and scorn thee, who abidest and invitest us to return to thee and who pardonest the prostituted human soul when it does return to thee. Now I hate such crooked and perverse men, although I love them if they will be corrected and come to prefer the learning they obtain to money and, above all, to prefer thee to such learning, O God, the truth and fullness of our positive good, and our most pure peace. But then the wish was stronger in me for my own sake not to suffer evil from them than was my desire that they should become good for thy sake.

CHAPTER XIII

23. When, therefore, the officials of Milan sent to Rome, to the prefect of the city, to ask that he provide them with a teacher of rhetoric for their city and to send him at the public expense, I applied for the job through those same persons, drunk with the Manichean vanities, to be freed from whom I was going away—though neither they nor I were aware of it at the time. They recommended that Symmachus, who was then prefect, after he had proved me by audition, should appoint me .

And to Milan I came, to Ambrose the bishop, famed through the whole world as one of the best of men, thy devoted servant. His eloquent discourse in those times abundantly provided thy people with the flour of thy wheat, the gladness of thy oil, and the sober intoxication of thy wine. [27] To him I was led by thee without my knowledge, that by him I might be led to thee in full knowledge. That man of God received me as a father would, and welcomed my coming as a good bishop should. And I began to love him, of course, not at the first as a teacher of the truth, for I had entirely despaired of finding that in thy Church—but

---

[26] Ps. 139:22.

[27] A mixed figure here, put together from Ps. 4:7; 45:7; 104:15; the phrase *sobriam vini ebrietatem* is almost certainly an echo of a stanza of one of Ambrose's own hymns, *Splendor paternae gloriae*, which Augustine had doubtless learned in Milan: "*Bibamus sobriam ebrietatem spiritus.*" Cf. W. I. Merrill, *Latin Hymns* (Boston, 1904), pp. 4, 5.

as a friendly man. And I studiously listened to him—though not with the right motive—as he preached to the people. I was trying to discover whether his eloquence came up to his reputation, and whether it flowed fuller or thinner than others said it did. And thus I hung on his words intently, but, as to his subject matter, I was only a careless and contemptuous listener. I was delighted with the charm of his speech, which was more erudite, though less cheerful and soothing, than Faustus' style. As for subject matter, however, there could be no comparison, for the latter was wandering around in Manichean deceptions, while the former was teaching salvation most soundly. But "salvation is far from the wicked," [28] such as I was then when I stood before him. Yet I was drawing nearer, gradually and unconsciously.

CHAPTER XIV

24. For, although I took no trouble to learn what he said, but only to hear how he said it—for this empty concern remained foremost with me as long as I despaired of finding a clear path from man to thee—yet, along with the eloquence I prized, there also came into my mind the ideas which I ignored; for I could not separate them. And, while I opened my heart to acknowledge how skillfully he spoke, there also came an awareness of how *truly* he spoke—but only gradually. First of all, his ideas had already begun to appear to me defensible; and the Catholic faith, for which I supposed that nothing could be said against the onslaught of the Manicheans, I now realized could be maintained without presumption. This was especially clear after I had heard one or two parts of the Old Testament explained allegorically—whereas before this, when I had interpreted them literally, they had "killed" me spiritually. [29] However, when many of these passages in those books were expounded to me thus, I came to blame my own despair for having believed that no reply could be given to those who hated and scoffed at the Law and the Prophets. Yet I did not see that this was reason enough to follow the Catholic way, just because it had learned advocates who could answer objections adequately and without absurdity. Nor could I see that what I had

---

[28] Ps. 119:155.
[29] Cf. II Cor. 3:6. The discovery of the allegorical method of interpretation opened new horizons for Augustine in Biblical interpretation and he adopted it as a settled principle in his sermons and commentaries; cf. M. Pontet, *L'Exégèse de Saint Augustin prédicateur* (Lyons, 1946).

held to heretofore should now be condemned, because both sides were equally defensible. For that way did not appear to me yet vanquished; but neither did it seem yet victorious.

25. But now I earnestly bent my mind to inquire if there was possible any way to prove the Manicheans guilty of falsehood. If I could have conceived of a spiritual substance, all their strongholds would have collapsed and been cast out of my mind. But I could not. Still, concerning the body of this world, nature as a whole—now that I was able to consider and compare such things more and more—I now decided that the majority of the philosophers held the more probable views. So, in what I thought was the method of the Academics—doubting everything and fluctuating between all the options—I came to the conclusion that the Manicheans were to be abandoned. For I judged, even in that period of doubt, that I could not remain in a sect to which I preferred some of the philosophers. But I refused to commit the cure of my fainting soul to the philosophers, because they were without the saving name of Christ. I resolved, therefore, to become a catechumen in the Catholic Church—which my parents had so much urged upon me—until something certain shone forth by which I might guide my course.

BOOK SIX

Turmoil in the twenties. Monica follows Augustine to Milan and finds him a catechumen in the Catholic Church. Both admire Ambrose but Augustine gets no help from him on his personal problems. Ambition spurs and Alypius and Nebridius join him in a confused quest for the happy life. Augustine becomes engaged, dismisses his first mistress, takes another, and continues his fruitless search for truth.

CHAPTER I

1. O Hope from my youth,[1] where wast thou to me and where hadst thou gone away?[2] For hadst thou not created me and differentiated me from the beasts of the field and the birds of the air, making me wiser than they? And yet I was wandering about in a dark and slippery way, seeking thee outside myself and thus not finding the God of my heart. I had gone down into the depths of the sea and had lost faith, and had despaired of ever finding the truth.

By this time my mother had come to me, having mustered the courage of piety, following over sea and land, secure in thee through all the perils of the journey. For in the dangers of the voyage she comforted the sailors—to whom the inexperienced voyagers, when alarmed, were accustomed to go for comfort—and assured them of a safe arrival because she had been so assured by thee in a vision.

She found me in deadly peril through my despair of ever finding the truth. But when I told her that I was now no longer a Manichean, though not yet a Catholic Christian, she did not leap for joy as if this were unexpected; for she had already been

[1] Cf. Ps. 71:5.　　　　　　[2] Cf. Ps. 10:1.

reassured about that part of my misery for which she had mourned me as one dead, but also as one who would be raised to thee. She had carried me out on the bier of her thoughts, that thou mightest say to the widow's son, "Young man, I say unto you, arise!" [3] and then he would revive and begin to speak, and thou wouldst deliver him to his mother. Therefore, her heart was not agitated with any violent exultation when she heard that so great a part of what she daily entreated thee to do had actually already been done—that, though I had not yet grasped the truth, I was rescued from falsehood. Instead, she was fully confident that thou who hadst promised the whole would give her the rest, and thus most calmly, and with a fully confident heart, she replied to me that she believed, in Christ, that before she died she would see me a faithful Catholic. And she said no more than this to me. But to thee, O Fountain of mercy, she poured out still more frequent prayers and tears that thou wouldst hasten thy aid and enlighten my darkness, and she hurried all the more zealously to the church and hung upon the words of Ambrose, praying for the fountain of water that springs up into everlasting life. [4] For she loved that man as an angel of God, since she knew that it was by him that I had been brought thus far to that wavering state of agitation I was now in, through which she was fully persuaded I should pass from sickness to health, even though it would be after a still sharper convulsion which physicians call "the crisis."

CHAPTER II

2. So also my mother brought to certain oratories, erected in the memory of the saints, offerings of porridge, bread, and wine—as had been her custom in Africa—and she was forbidden to do so by the doorkeeper [*ostiarius*]. And as soon as she learned that it was the bishop who had forbidden it, she acquiesced so devoutly and obediently that I myself marveled how readily she could bring herself to turn critic of her own customs, rather than question his prohibition. For winebibbing had not taken possession of her spirit, nor did the love of wine stimulate her to hate the truth, as it does too many, both male and female, who turn as sick at a hymn to sobriety as drunkards do at a draught of water. When she had brought her basket with the festive gifts, which she would taste first herself and give the rest away, she would never allow herself more than one

[3] Cf. Luke 7:11–17.   [4] Cf. John 4:14.

little cup of wine, diluted according to her own temperate palate, which she would taste out of courtesy. And, if there were many oratories of departed saints that ought to be honored in the same way, she still carried around with her the same little cup, to be used everywhere. This became not only very much watered but also quite tepid with carrying it about. She would distribute it by small sips to those around, for she sought to stimulate their devotion, not pleasure.

But as soon as she found that this custom was forbidden by that famous preacher and most pious prelate, even to those who would use it in moderation, lest thereby it might be an occasion of gluttony for those who were already drunken (and also because these funereal memorials were very much like some of the superstitious practices of the pagans), she most willingly abstained from it. And, in place of a basket filled with fruits of the earth, she had learned to bring to the oratories of the martyrs a heart full of purer petitions, and to give all that she could to the poor —so that the Communion of the Lord's body might be rightly celebrated in those places where, after the example of his Passion, the martyrs had been sacrificed and crowned. But yet it seems to me, O Lord my God—and my heart thinks of it this way in thy sight—that my mother would probably not have given way so easily to the rejection of this custom if it had been forbidden by another, whom she did not love as she did Ambrose. For, out of her concern for my salvation, she loved him most dearly; and he loved her truly, on account of her faithful religious life, in which she frequented the church with good works, "fervent in spirit."[5] Thus he would, when he saw me, often burst forth into praise of her, congratulating me that I had such a mother—little knowing what a son she had in me, who was still a skeptic in all these matters and who could not conceive that the way of life could be found out.

CHAPTER III

3. Nor had I come yet to groan in my prayers that thou wouldst help me. My mind was wholly intent on knowledge and eager for disputation. Ambrose himself I esteemed a happy man, as the world counted happiness, because great personages held him in honor. Only his celibacy appeared to me a painful burden. But what hope he cherished, what struggles he had against the temptations that beset his high station, what solace

[5] Rom. 12:11.

in adversity, and what savory joys thy bread possessed for the hidden mouth of his heart when feeding on it, I could neither conjecture nor experience.

Nor did he know my own frustrations, nor the pit of my danger. For I could not request of him what I wanted as I wanted it, because I was debarred from hearing and speaking to him by crowds of busy people to whose infirmities he devoted himself. And when he was not engaged with them—which was never for long at a time—he was either refreshing his body with necessary food or his mind with reading.

Now, as he read, his eyes glanced over the pages and his heart searched out the sense, but his voice and tongue were silent. Often when we came to his room—for no one was forbidden to enter, nor was it his custom that the arrival of visitors should be announced to him—we would see him thus reading to himself. After we had sat for a long time in silence—for who would dare interrupt one so intent?—we would then depart, realizing that he was unwilling to be distracted in the little time he could gain for the recruiting of his mind, free from the clamor of other men's business. Perhaps he was fearful lest, if the author he was studying should express himself vaguely, some doubtful and attentive hearer would ask him to expound it or discuss some of the more abstruse questions, so that he could not get over as much material as he wished, if his time was occupied with others. And even a truer reason for his reading to himself might have been the care for preserving his voice, which was very easily weakened. Whatever his motive was in so doing, it was doubtless, in such a man, a good one.

4. But actually I could find no opportunity of putting the questions I desired to that holy oracle of thine in his heart, unless it was a matter which could be dealt with briefly. However, those surgings in me required that he should give me his full leisure so that I might pour them out to him; but I never found him so. I heard him, indeed, every Lord's Day, "rightly dividing the word of truth"[6] among the people. And I became all the more convinced that all those knots of crafty calumnies which those deceivers of ours had knit together against the divine books could be unraveled.

I soon understood that the statement that man was made after the image of Him that created him[7] was not understood by thy spiritual sons—whom thou hadst regenerated through the Catholic Mother[8] through grace—as if they believed and

6 II Tim. 2:15.   7 Cf. Gen. 1:26f.   8 The Church.

imagined that thou wert bounded by a human form, although what was the nature of a spiritual substance I had not the faintest or vaguest notion. Still rejoicing, I blushed that for so many years I had bayed, not against the Catholic faith, but against the fables of fleshly imagination. For I had been both impious and rash in this, that I had condemned by pronouncement what I ought to have learned by inquiry. For thou, O Most High, and most near, most secret, yet most present, who dost not have limbs, some of which are larger and some smaller, but who art wholly everywhere and nowhere in space, and art not shaped by some corporeal form: thou didst create man after thy own image and, see, he dwells in space, both head and feet.

CHAPTER IV

5. Since I could not then understand how this image of thine could subsist, I should have knocked on the door and propounded the doubt as to how it was to be believed, and not have insultingly opposed it as if it were actually believed. Therefore, my anxiety as to what I could retain as certain gnawed all the more sharply into my soul, and I felt quite ashamed because during the long time I had been deluded and deceived by the [Manichean] promises of certainties, I had, with childish petulance, prated of so many uncertainties as if they were certain. That they were falsehoods became apparent to me only afterward. However, I was certain that they were uncertain and since I had held them as certainly uncertain I had accused thy Catholic Church with a blind contentiousness. I had not yet discovered that it taught the truth, but I now knew that it did not teach what I had so vehemently accused it of. In this respect, at least, I was confounded and converted; and I rejoiced, O my God, that the one Church, the body of thy only Son—in which the name of Christ had been sealed upon me as an infant—did not relish these childish trifles and did not maintain in its sound doctrine any tenet that would involve pressing thee, the Creator of all, into space, which, however extended and immense, would still be bounded on all sides—like the shape of a human body.

6. I was also glad that the old Scriptures of the Law and the Prophets were laid before me to be read, not now with an eye to what had seemed absurd in them when formerly I censured thy holy ones for thinking thus, when they actually did not think in that way. And I listened with delight to Ambrose, in his sermons

to the people, often recommending this text most diligently as a rule: "The letter kills, but the spirit gives life,"[9] while at the same time he drew aside the mystic veil and opened to view the spiritual meaning of what seemed to teach perverse doctrine if it were taken according to the letter. I found nothing in his teachings that offended me, though I could not yet know for certain whether what he taught was true. For all this time I restrained my heart from assenting to anything, fearing to fall headlong into error. Instead, by this hanging in suspense, I was being strangled.[10] For my desire was to be as certain of invisible things as I was that seven and three are ten. I was not so deranged as to believe that *this* could not be comprehended, but my desire was to have other things as clear as this, whether they were physical objects, which were not present to my senses, or spiritual objects, which I did not know how to conceive of except in physical terms.

If I could have believed, I might have been cured, and, with the sight of my soul cleared up, it might in some way have been directed toward thy truth, which always abides and fails in nothing. But, just as it happens that a man who has tried a bad physician fears to trust himself with a good one, so it was with the health of my soul, which could not be healed except by believing. But lest it should believe falsehoods, it refused to be cured, resisting thy hand, who hast prepared for us the medicines of faith and applied them to the maladies of the whole world, and endowed them with such great efficacy.

CHAPTER V

7. Still, from this time forward, I began to prefer the Catholic doctrine. I felt that it was with moderation and honesty that it commanded things to be believed that were not demonstrated —whether they could be demonstrated, but not to everyone, or whether they could not be demonstrated at all. This was far better than the method of the Manicheans, in which our credulity was mocked by an audacious promise of knowledge and then many fabulous and absurd things were forced upon believers *because* they were incapable of demonstration. After that, O Lord, little by little, with a gentle and most merciful hand, drawing and calming my heart, thou didst persuade me

---

[9] II Cor. 3:6.
[10] Another reference to the Academic doctrine of *suspendium* (ἐποχή); cf. Bk. V, Ch. X, 19, and also *Enchiridion*, VII, 20.

that, if I took into account the multitude of things I had never seen, nor been present when they were enacted—such as many of the events of secular history; and the numerous reports of places and cities which I had not seen; or such as my relations with many friends, or physicians, or with these men and those— that unless we should believe, we should do nothing at all in this life.[11] Finally, I was impressed with what an unalterable assurance I believed which two people were my parents, though this was impossible for me to know otherwise than by hearsay. By bringing all this into my consideration, thou didst persuade me that it was not the ones who believed thy books—which with so great authority thou hast established among nearly all nations—but those who did not believe them who were to be blamed. Moreover, those men were not to be listened to who would say to me, "How do you know that those Scriptures were imparted to mankind by the Spirit of the one and most true God?" For this was the point that was most of all to be believed, since no wranglings of blasphemous questions such as I had read in the books of the self-contradicting philosophers could once snatch from me the belief that thou dost exist—although *what* thou art I did not know—and that to thee belongs the governance of human affairs.

8. This much I believed, some times more strongly than other times. But I always believed both that thou art and that thou hast a care for us,[12] although I was ignorant both as to what should be thought about thy substance and as to which way led, or led back, to thee. Thus, since we are too weak by unaided reason to find out truth, and since, because of this, we need the authority of the Holy Writings, I had now begun to believe that thou wouldst not, under any circumstances, have given such eminent authority to those Scriptures throughout all lands if it had not been that through them thy will may be believed in and that thou mightest be sought. For, as to those passages in the Scripture which had heretofore appeared incongruous and offensive to me, now that I had heard several of them expounded reasonably, I could see that they were to be resolved by the mysteries of spiritual interpretation. The authority of Scripture seemed to me all the more revered and

---

11 *Nisi crederentur, omnino in hac vita nihil ageremus*, which should be set along-side the more famous *nisi credideritis, non intelligetis* (*Enchiridion*, XIII, 14). This is the basic assumption of Augustine's whole epistemology. See Robert E. Cushman, "Faith and Reason in the Thought of St. Augustine," in *Church History* (XIX, 4, 1950), pp. 271–294.
12 Cf. Heb. 11:6.

worthy of devout belief because, although it was visible for all to read, it reserved the full majesty of its secret wisdom within its spiritual profundity. While it stooped to all in the great plainness of its language and simplicity of style, it yet required the closest attention of the most serious-minded—so that it might receive all into its common bosom, and direct some few through its narrow passages toward thee, yet many more than would have been the case had there not been in it such a lofty authority, which nevertheless allured multitudes to its bosom by its holy humility. I continued to reflect upon these things, and thou wast with me. I sighed, and thou didst hear me. I vacillated, and thou guidedst me. I roamed the broad way of the world, and thou didst not desert me.

CHAPTER VI

9. I was still eagerly aspiring to honors, money, and matrimony; and thou didst mock me. In pursuit of these ambitions I endured the most bitter hardships, in which thou wast being the more gracious the less thou wouldst allow anything that was not thee to grow sweet to me. Look into my heart, O Lord, whose prompting it is that I should recall all this, and confess it to thee. Now let my soul cleave to thee, now that thou hast freed her from that fast-sticking glue of death.

How wretched she was! And thou didst irritate her sore wound so that she might forsake all else and turn to thee—who art above all and without whom all things would be nothing at all—so that she should be converted and healed. How wretched I was at that time, and how thou didst deal with me so as to make me aware of my wretchedness, I recall from the incident of the day on which I was preparing to recite a panegyric on the emperor. In it I was to deliver many a lie, and the lying was to be applauded by those who knew I was lying. My heart was agitated with this sense of guilt and it seethed with the fever of my uneasiness. For, while walking along one of the streets of Milan, I saw a poor beggar—with what I believe was a full belly—joking and hilarious. And I sighed and spoke to the friends around me of the many sorrows that flowed from our madness, because in spite of all our exertions—such as those I was then laboring in, dragging the burden of my unhappiness under the spur of ambition, and, by dragging it, increasing it at the same time—still and all we aimed only to attain that very happiness which this beggar had reached before us; and there was a grim chance that we should *never* attain it! For what he had obtained through a few coins, got by his begging, I was still scheming for by many a wretched and tortuous turning— namely, the joy of a passing felicity. He had not, indeed, gained true joy, but, at the same time, with all my ambitions, I was seeking one still more untrue. Anyhow, he was now joyous and I was anxious. He was free from care, and I was full of alarms. Now, if anyone should inquire of me whether I should prefer to be merry or anxious, I would reply, "Merry." Again, if I had been asked whether I should prefer to be as he was or as I myself then was, I would have chosen to be myself; though I was beset with cares and alarms. But would not this have been a false choice? Was the contrast valid? Actually, I ought not to prefer myself to him because I happened to be more learned than he was; for I got no great pleasure from my learning, but sought, rather, to please men by its exhibition—and this not to instruct, but only to please. Thus thou didst break my bones with the rod of thy correction.

10. Let my soul take its leave of those who say: "It makes a difference as to the object from which a man derives his joy. The beggar rejoiced in drunkenness; you longed to rejoice in glory." What glory, O Lord? The kind that is not in thee, for, just as his was no true joy, so was mine no true glory; but it turned my head all the more. He would get over his drunkenness that same night, but I had slept with mine many a night and risen again with it, and was to sleep again and rise again with it, I know not how many times. It does indeed make a difference as to the object from which a man's joy is gained. I know this is so, and I know that the joy of a faithful hope is incomparably beyond such vanity. Yet, at the same time, this beggar was beyond me, for he truly was the happier man—not only because he was thoroughly steeped in his mirth while I was torn to pieces with my cares, but because he had gotten his wine by giving good wishes to the passers-by while I was following after the ambition of my pride by lying. Much to this effect I said to my good companions, and I saw how readily they reacted pretty much as I did. Thus I found that it went ill with me; and I fretted, and doubled that very ill. And if any prosperity smiled upon me, I loathed to seize it, for almost before I could grasp it, it would fly away.

CHAPTER VII

11. Those of us who were living like friends together used to bemoan our lot in our common talk; but I discussed it with Alypius and Nebridius more especially and in very familiar terms. Alypius had been born in the same town as I; his parents were of the highest rank there, but he was a bit younger than I. He had studied under me when I first taught in our town, and then afterward at Carthage. He esteemed me highly because I appeared to him good and learned, and I esteemed him for his inborn love of virtue, which was uncommonly marked in a man so young. But in the whirlpool of Carthaginian fashion—where frivolous spectacles are hotly followed—he had been inveigled into the madness of the gladiatorial games. While he was miserably tossed about in this fad, I was teaching rhetoric there in a public school. At that time he was not attending my classes because of some ill feeling that had arisen between me and his father. I then came to discover how fatally he doted upon the circus, and I was deeply grieved, for he seemed likely to cast away his very great promise—if, indeed, he had not already done so. Yet I had no means of advising him, or any way of reclaiming him through restraint, either by the kindness of a friend or by the authority of a teacher. For I imagined that his feelings toward me were the same as his father's. But this turned out not to be the case. Indeed, disregarding his father's will in the matter, he began to be friendly and to visit my lecture room, to listen for a while and then depart.

12. But it slipped my memory to try to deal with his problem, to prevent him from ruining his excellent mind in his blind and headstrong passion for frivolous sport. But thou, O Lord, who holdest the helm of all that thou hast created,[13] thou hadst not forgotten him who was one day to be numbered among thy sons, a chief minister of thy sacrament.[14] And in order that his amendment might plainly be attributed to thee, thou broughtest it about through me while I knew nothing of it.

One day, when I was sitting in my accustomed place with my scholars before me, he came in, greeted me, sat himself

[13] Cf. Plato, *Politicus*, 273 D.
[14] Alypius was more than Augustine's close friend; he became bishop of Tagaste and was prominent in local Church affairs in the province of Africa.

down, and fixed his attention on the subject I was then discussing. It so happened that I had a passage in hand and, while I was interpreting it, a simile occurred to me, taken from the gladiatorial games. It struck me as relevant to make more pleasant and plain the point I wanted to convey by adding a biting gibe at those whom that madness had enthralled. Thou knowest, O our God, that I had no thought at that time of curing Alypius of that plague. But he took it to himself and thought that I would not have said it but for his sake. And what any other man would have taken as an occasion of offense against me, this worthy young man took as a reason for being offended at himself, and for loving me the more fervently. Thou hast said it long ago and written in thy Book, "Rebuke a wise man, and he will love you." [15] Now I had not rebuked him; but thou who canst make use of everything, both witting and unwitting, and in the order which thou thyself knowest to be best—and that order is right—thou madest my heart and tongue into burning coals with which thou mightest cauterize and cure the hopeful mind thus languishing. Let him be silent in thy praise who does not meditate on thy mercy, which rises up in my inmost parts to confess to thee. For after that speech Alypius rushed up out of that deep pit into which he had willfully plunged and in which he had been blinded by its miserable pleasures. And he roused his mind with a resolve to moderation. When he had done this, all the filth of the gladiatorial pleasures dropped away from him, and he went to them no more. Then he also prevailed upon his reluctant father to let him be my pupil. And, at the son's urging, the father at last consented. Thus Alypius began again to hear my lectures and became involved with me in the same superstition, loving in the Manicheans that outward display of ascetic discipline which he believed was true and unfeigned. It was, however, a senseless and seducing continence, which ensnared precious souls who were not able as yet to reach the height of true virtue, and who were easily beguiled with the veneer of what was only a shadowy and feigned virtue.

CHAPTER VIII

13. He had gone on to Rome before me to study law—which was the worldly way which his parents were forever urging him to pursue—and there he was carried away again with an incredible passion for the gladiatorial shows. For, although he

[15] Prov. 9:8.

had been utterly opposed to such spectacles and detested them, one day he met by chance a company of his acquaintances and fellow students returning from dinner; and, with a friendly violence, they drew him, resisting and objecting vehemently, into the amphitheater, on a day of those cruel and murderous shows. He protested to them: "Though you drag my body to that place and set me down there, you cannot force me to give my mind or lend my eyes to these shows. Thus I will be absent while present, and so overcome both you and them." When they heard this, they dragged him on in, probably interested to see whether he could do as he said. When they got to the arena, and had taken what seats they could get, the whole place became a tumult of inhuman frenzy. But Alypius kept his eyes closed and forbade his mind to roam abroad after such wickedness. Would that he had shut his ears also! For when one of the combatants fell in the fight, a mighty cry from the whole audience stirred him so strongly that, overcome by curiosity and still prepared (as he thought) to despise and rise superior to it no matter what it was, he opened his eyes and was struck with a deeper wound in his soul than the victim whom he desired to see had been in his body. Thus he fell more miserably than the one whose fall had raised that mighty clamor which had entered through his ears and unlocked his eyes to make way for the wounding and beating down of his soul, which was more audacious than truly valiant—also it was weaker because it presumed on its own strength when it ought to have depended on Thee. For, as soon as he saw the blood, he drank in with it a savage temper, and he did not turn away, but fixed his eyes on the bloody pastime, unwittingly drinking in the madness—delighted with the wicked contest and drunk with blood lust. He was now no longer the same man who came in, but was one of the mob he came into, a true companion of those who had brought him thither. Why need I say more? He looked, he shouted, he was excited, and he took away with him the madness that would stimulate him to come again: not only with those who first enticed him, but even without them; indeed, dragging in others besides. And yet from all this, with a most powerful and most merciful hand, thou didst pluck him and taught him not to rest his confidence in himself but in thee— but not till long after.

CHAPTER IX

14. But this was all being stored up in his memory as medicine for the future. So also was that other incident when he was still studying under me at Carthage and was meditating at noonday in the market place on what he had to recite—as scholars usually have to do for practice—and thou didst allow him to be arrested by the police officers in the market place as a thief. I believe, O my God, that thou didst allow this for no other reason than that this man who was in the future to prove so great should now begin to learn that, in making just decisions, a man should not readily be condemned by other men with reckless credulity.

For as he was walking up and down alone before the judgment seat with his tablets and pen, lo, a young man—another one of the scholars, who was the real thief—secretly brought a hatchet and, without Alypius seeing him, got in as far as the leaden bars which protected the silversmith shop and began to hack away at the lead gratings. But when the noise of the hatchet was heard the silversmiths below began to call to each other in whispers and sent men to arrest whomsoever they should find. The thief heard their voices and ran away, leaving his hatchet because he was afraid to be caught with it. Now Alypius, who had not seen him come in, got a glimpse of him as he went out and noticed that he went off in great haste. Being curious to know the reasons, he went up to the place, where he found the hatchet, and stood wondering and pondering when, behold, those that were sent caught him alone, holding the hatchet which had made the noise which had startled them and brought them there. They seized him and dragged him away, gathering the tenants of the market place about them and boasting that they had caught a notorious thief. Thereupon he was led away to appear before the judge.

15. But this is as far as his lesson was to go. For immediately, O Lord, thou didst come to the rescue of his innocence, of which thou wast the sole witness. As he was being led off to prison or punishment, they were met by the master builder who had charge of the public buildings. The captors were especially glad to meet him because he had more than once suspected them of stealing the goods that had been lost out of the market place. Now, at last, they thought they could convince him who it was that had committed the thefts. But the custodian had often met

Alypius at the house of a certain senator, whose receptions he used to attend. He recognized him at once and, taking his hand, led him apart from the throng, inquired the cause of all the trouble, and learned what had occurred. He then commanded all the rabble still around—and very uproarious and full of threatenings they were—to come along with him, and they came to the house of the young man who had committed the deed. There, before the door, was a slave boy so young that he was not restrained from telling the whole story by fear of harming his master. And he had followed his master to the market place. Alypius recognized him, and whispered to the architect, who showed the boy the hatchet and asked whose it was. "Ours," he answered directly. And, being further questioned, he disclosed the whole affair. Thus the guilt was shifted to that household and the rabble, who had begun to triumph over Alypius, were shamed. And so he went away home, this man who was to be the future steward of thy Word and judge of so many causes in thy Church—a wiser and more experienced man.

CHAPTER X

16. I found him at Rome, and he was bound to me with the strongest possible ties, and he went with me to Milan, in order that he might not be separated from me, and also that he might obtain some law practice, for which he had qualified with a view to pleasing his parents more than himself. He had already sat three times as assessor, showing an integrity that seemed strange to many others, though he thought them strange who could prefer gold to integrity. His character had also been tested, not only by the bait of covetousness, but by the spur of fear. At Rome he was assessor to the secretary of the Italian Treasury. There was at that time a very powerful senator to whose favors many were indebted, and of whom many stood in fear. In his usual highhanded way he demanded to have a favor granted him that was forbidden by the laws. This Alypius resisted. A bribe was promised, but he scorned it with all his heart. Threats were employed, but he trampled them underfoot—so that all men marveled at so rare a spirit, which neither coveted the friendship nor feared the enmity of a man at once so powerful and so widely known for his great resources of helping his friends and doing harm to his enemies. Even the official whose counselor Alypius was—although he was unwilling that the favor should be granted—would not openly refuse the request, but

passed the responsibility on to Alypius, alleging that he would not permit him to give his assent. And the truth was that even if the judge had agreed, Alypius would have simply left the court.

There was one matter, however, which appealed to his love of learning, in which he was very nearly led astray. He found out that he might have books copied for himself at praetorian rates [i.e., at public expense]. But his sense of justice prevailed, and he changed his mind for the better, thinking that the rule that forbade him was still more profitable than the privilege that his office would have allowed him. These are little things, but "he that is faithful in a little matter is faithful also in a great one."[16] Nor can that possibly be void which was uttered by the mouth of Thy truth: "If, therefore, you have not been faithful in the unrighteous mammon, who will commit to your trust the true riches? And if you have not been faithful in that which is another man's, who shall give you that which is your own?"[17] Such a man was Alypius, who clung to me at that time and who wavered in his purpose, just as I did, as to what course of life to follow.

17. Nebridius also had come to Milan for no other reason than that he might live with me in a most ardent search after truth and wisdom. He had left his native place near Carthage— and Carthage itself, where he usually lived—leaving behind his fine family estate, his house, and his mother, who would not follow him. Like me, he sighed; like me, he wavered; an ardent seeker after the true life and a most acute analyst of the most abstruse questions. So there were three begging mouths, sighing out their wants one to the other, and waiting upon thee, that thou mightest give them their meat in due season.[18] And in all the vexations with which thy mercy followed our worldly pursuits, we sought for the reason why we suffered so—and all was darkness! We turned away groaning and exclaiming, "How long shall these things be?" And this we often asked, yet for all our asking we did not relinquish them; for as yet we had not discovered anything certain which, when we gave those others up, we might grasp in their stead.

CHAPTER XI

18. And I especially puzzled and wondered when I remembered how long a time had passed since my nineteenth year, in

[16] Luke 16:10.   [17] Luke 16: 11, 12.   [18] Cf. Ps. 145:15.

which I had first fallen in love with wisdom and had determined
as soon as I could find her to abandon the empty hopes and
mad delusions of vain desires. Behold, I was now getting close
to thirty, still stuck fast in the same mire, still greedy of enjoying present goods which fly away and distract me; and I
was still saying, "Tomorrow I shall discover it; behold, it will
become plain, and I shall see it; behold, Faustus will come and
explain everything." Or I would say[19]: "O you mighty
Academics, is there no certainty that man can grasp for the
guidance of his life? No, let us search the more diligently, and
let us not despair. See, the things in the Church's books that
appeared so absurd to us before do not appear so now, and may
be otherwise and honestly interpreted. I will set my feet upon
that step where, as a child, my parents placed me, until the
clear truth is discovered. But where and when shall it be sought?
Ambrose has no leisure—we have no leisure to read. Where are
we to find the books? How or where could I get hold of them?
From whom could I borrow them? Let me set a schedule for
my days and set apart certain hours for the health of the soul.
A great hope has risen up in us, because the Catholic faith does
not teach what we thought it did, and vainly accused it of. Its
teachers hold it as an abomination to believe that God is
limited by the form of a human body. And do I doubt that I
should 'knock' in order for the rest also to be 'opened' unto me?
My pupils take up the morning hours; what am I doing with the
rest of the day? Why not do this? But, then, when am I to visit
my influential friends, whose favors I need? When am I to prepare the orations that I sell to the class? When would I get some
recreation and relax my mind from the strain of work?

19. "Perish everything and let us dismiss these idle triflings.
Let me devote myself solely to the search for truth. This life is
unhappy, death uncertain. If it comes upon me suddenly, in
what state shall I go hence and where shall I learn what here
I have neglected? Should I not indeed suffer the punishment of
my negligence here? But suppose death cuts off and finishes all
care and feeling. This too is a question that calls for inquiry.
God forbid that it should be so. It is not without reason, it is
not in vain, that the stately authority of the Christian faith has
spread over the entire world, and God would never have done
such great things for us if the life of the soul perished with the
death of the body. Why, therefore, do I delay in abandoning

---

[19] Here begins a long soliloquy which sums up his turmoil over the past
decade and his present plight of confusion and indecision.

my hopes of this world and giving myself wholly to seek after God and the blessed life?

"But wait a moment. This life also is pleasant, and it has a sweetness of its own, not at all negligible. We must not abandon it lightly, for it would be shameful to lapse back into it again. See now, it is important to gain some post of honor. And what more should I desire? I have crowds of influential friends, if nothing else; and, if I push my claims, a governorship may be offered me, and a wife with some money, so that she would not be an added expense. This would be the height of my desire. Many men, who are great and worthy of imitation, have combined the pursuit of wisdom with a marriage life."

20. While I talked about these things, and the winds of opinions veered about and tossed my heart hither and thither, time was slipping away. I delayed my conversion to the Lord; I postponed from day to day the life in thee, but I could not postpone the daily death in myself. I was enamored of a happy life, but I still feared to seek it in its own abode, and so I fled from it while I sought it. I thought I should be miserable if I were deprived of the embraces of a woman, and I never gave a thought to the medicine that thy mercy has provided for the healing of that infirmity, for I had never tried it. As for continence, I imagined that it depended on one's own strength, though I found no such strength in myself, for in my folly I knew not what is written, "None can be continent unless thou dost grant it." [20] Certainly thou wouldst have given it, if I had beseeched thy ears with heartfelt groaning, and if I had cast my care upon thee with firm faith.

CHAPTER XII

21. Actually, it was Alypius who prevented me from marrying, urging that if I did so it would not be possible for us to live together and to have as much undistracted leisure in the love of wisdom as we had long desired. For he himself was so chaste that it was wonderful, all the more because in his early youth he had entered upon the path of promiscuity, but had not continued in it. Instead, feeling sorrow and disgust at it, he had lived from that time down to the present most continently. I quoted against him the examples of men who had been married and still lovers of wisdom, who had pleased God and had been loyal and affectionate to their friends. I fell far short of them in

[20] Cf. Wis. 8:21 (LXX).

greatness of soul, and, enthralled with the disease of my carnality and its deadly sweetness, I dragged my chain along, fearing to be loosed of it. Thus I rejected the words of him who counseled me wisely, as if the hand that would have loosed the chain only hurt my wound. Moreover, the serpent spoke to Alypius himself by me, weaving and lying in his path, by my tongue to catch him with pleasant snares in which his honorable and free feet might be entangled.

22. For he wondered that I, for whom he had such a great esteem, should be stuck so fast in the gluepot of pleasure as to maintain, whenever we discussed the subject, that I could not possibly live a celibate life. And when I urged in my defense against his accusing questions that the hasty and stolen delight, which he had tasted and now hardly remembered, and therefore too easily disparaged, was not to be compared with a settled acquaintance with it; and that, if to this stable acquaintance were added the honorable name of marriage, he would not then be astonished at my inability to give it up—when I spoke thus, then he also began to wish to be married, not because he was overcome by the lust for such pleasures, but out of curiosity. For, he said, he longed to know what that could be without which my life, which he thought was so happy, seemed to me to be no life at all, but a punishment. For he who wore no chain was amazed at my slavery, and his amazement awoke the desire for experience, and from that he would have gone on to the experiment itself, and then perhaps he would have fallen into the very slavery that amazed him in me, since he was ready to enter into "a covenant with death," [21] for "he that loves danger shall fall into it." [22]

Now, the question of conjugal honor in the ordering of a good married life and the bringing up of children interested us but slightly. What afflicted me most and what had made me already a slave to it was the habit of satisfying an insatiable lust; but Alypius was about to be enslaved by a merely curious wonder. This is the state we were in until thou, O Most High, who never forsakest our lowliness, didst take pity on our misery and didst come to our rescue in wonderful and secret ways.

CHAPTER XIII

23. Active efforts were made to get me a wife. I wooed; I was engaged; and my mother took the greatest pains in the

[21] Isa. 28:15.   [22] Ecclus. 3:26.

matter. For her hope was that, when I was once married, I might be washed clean in health-giving baptism for which I was being daily prepared, as she joyfully saw, taking note that her desires and promises were being fulfilled in my faith. Yet, when, at my request and her own impulse, she called upon thee daily with strong, heartfelt cries, that thou wouldst, by a vision, disclose unto her a leading about my future marriage, thou wouldst not. She did, indeed, see certain vain and fantastic things, such as are conjured up by the strong preoccupation of the human spirit, and these she supposed had some reference to me. And she told me about them, but not with the confidence she usually had when thou hadst shown her anything. For she always said that she could distinguish, by a certain feeling impossible to describe, between thy revelations and the dreams of her own soul. Yet the matter was pressed forward, and proposals were made for a girl who was as yet some two years too young to marry.[23] And because she pleased me, I agreed to wait for her.

CHAPTER XIV

24. Many in my band of friends, consulting about and abhorring the turbulent vexations of human life, had often considered and were now almost determined to undertake a peaceful life, away from the turmoil of men. This we thought could be obtained by bringing together what we severally owned and thus making of it a common household, so that in the sincerity of our friendship nothing should belong more to one than to the other; but all were to have one purse and the whole was to belong to each and to all. We thought that this group might consist of ten persons, some of whom were very rich—especially Romanianus, my fellow townsman, an intimate friend from childhood days. He had been brought up to the court on grave business matters and he was the most earnest of us all about the project and his voice was of great weight in commending it because his estate was far more ample than that of the others. We had resolved, also, that each year two of us should be managers and provide all that was needful, while the rest were left undisturbed. But when we began to reflect whether this would be permitted by our wives, which some of us had already and others hoped to have, the whole plan, so excellently framed, collapsed in our hands and was utterly wrecked and cast aside.

---

[23] The normal minimum legal age for marriage was twelve! Cf. Justinian, *Institutiones*, I, 10:22.

From this we fell again into sighs and groans, and our steps followed the broad and beaten ways of the world; for many thoughts were in our hearts, but "Thy counsel standeth fast forever." [24] In thy counsel thou didst mock ours, and didst prepare thy own plan, for it was thy purpose "to give us meat in due season, to open thy hand, and to fill our souls with blessing." [25]

CHAPTER XV

25. Meanwhile my sins were being multiplied. My mistress was torn from my side as an impediment to my marriage, and my heart which clung to her was torn and wounded till it bled. And she went back to Africa, vowing to thee never to know any other man and leaving with me my natural son by her. But I, unhappy as I was, and weaker than a woman, could not bear the delay of the two years that should elapse before I could obtain the bride I sought. And so, since I was not a lover of wedlock so much as a slave of lust, I procured another mistress—not a wife, of course. Thus in bondage to a lasting habit, the disease of my soul might be nursed up and kept in its vigor or even increased until it reached the realm of matrimony. Nor indeed was the wound healed that had been caused by cutting away my former mistress; only it ceased to burn and throb, and began to fester, and was more dangerous because it was less painful.

CHAPTER XVI

26. Thine be the praise; unto thee be the glory, O Fountain of mercies. I became more wretched and thou didst come nearer. Thy right hand was ever ready to pluck me out of the mire and to cleanse me, but I did not know it. Nor did anything call me back from a still deeper plunge into carnal pleasure except the fear of death and of thy future judgment, which, amid all the waverings of my opinions, never faded from my breast. And I discussed with my friends, Alypius and Nebridius, the nature of good and evil, maintaining that, in my judgment, Epicurus would have carried off the palm if I had not believed what Epicurus would not believe: that after death there remains a life for the soul, and places of recompense. And I demanded of them: "Suppose we are immortal and live in the enjoyment of perpetual bodily pleasure, and that without any fear of losing it—why, then, should we not be happy, or why should we

[24] Cf. Ps. 33:11.   [25] Cf. Ps. 145:15, 16.

search for anything else?" I did not know that this was in fact the root of my misery: that I was so fallen and blinded that I could not discern the light of virtue and of beauty which must be embraced for its own sake, which the eye of flesh cannot see, and only the inner vision can see. Nor did I, alas, consider the reason why I found delight in discussing these very perplexities, shameful as they were, with my friends. For I could not be happy without friends, even according to the notions of happiness I had then, and no matter how rich the store of my carnal pleasures might be. Yet of a truth I loved my friends for their own sakes, and felt that they in turn loved me for my own sake.

O crooked ways! Woe to the audacious soul which hoped that by forsaking thee it would find some better thing! It tossed and turned, upon back and side and belly—but the bed is hard, and thou alone givest it rest.[26] And lo, thou art near, and thou deliverest us from our wretched wanderings and establishest us in thy way, and thou comfortest us and sayest, "Run, I will carry you; yea, I will lead you home and then I will set you free."[27]

[26] A variation on "restless is our heart until it comes to find rest in Thee," Bk. I, Ch. I, i.
[27] Isa. 46:4.

BOOK SEVEN

The conversion to Neoplatonism. Augustine traces his growing disenchantment with the Manichean conceptions of God and evil and the dawning understanding of God's incorruptibility. But his thought is still bound by his materialistic notions of reality. He rejects astrology and turns to the study of Neoplatonism. There follows an analysis of the differences between Platonism and Christianity and a remarkable account of his appropriation of Plotinian wisdom and his experience of a Plotinian ecstasy. From this, he comes finally to the diligent study of the Bible, especially the writings of the apostle Paul. His pilgrimage is drawing toward its goal, as he begins to know Jesus Christ and to be drawn to him in hesitant faith.

CHAPTER I

1. Dead now was that evil and shameful youth of mine, and I was passing into full manhood.[1] As I increased in years, the worse was my vanity. For I could not conceive of any substance but the sort I could see with my own eyes. I no longer thought of thee, O God, by the analogy of a human body. Ever since I inclined my ear to philosophy I had avoided this error —and the truth on this point I rejoiced to find in the faith of our spiritual mother, thy Catholic Church. Yet I could not see how else to conceive thee. And I, a man—and such a man!— sought to conceive thee, the sovereign and only true God. In my inmost heart, I believed that thou art incorruptible and inviolable and unchangeable, because—though I knew not how or why—I could still see plainly and without doubt that the

---

[1] Thirty years old; although the term "youth" (*juventus*) normally included the years twenty to forty.

corruptible is inferior to the incorruptible, the inviolable obviously superior to its opposite, and the unchangeable better than the changeable.

My heart cried out violently against all fantasms,[2] and with this one clear certainty I endeavored to brush away the swarm of unclean flies that swarmed around the eyes of my mind. But behold they were scarcely scattered before they gathered again, buzzed against my face, and beclouded my vision. I no longer thought of God in the analogy of a human body, yet I was constrained to conceive thee to be some kind of body in space, either infused into the world, or infinitely diffused beyond the world—and this was the incorruptible, inviolable, unchangeable substance, which I thought was better than the corruptible, the violable, and the changeable.[3] For whatever I conceived to be deprived of the dimensions of space appeared to me to be nothing, absolutely nothing; not even a void, for if a body is taken out of space, or if space is emptied of all its contents (of earth, water, air, or heaven), yet it remains an empty space—a spacious nothing, as it were.

2. Being thus gross-hearted and not clear even to myself, I then held that whatever had neither length nor breadth nor density nor solidity, and did not or could not receive such dimensions, was absolutely nothing. For at that time my mind dwelt only with ideas, which resembled the forms with which my eyes are still familiar, nor could I see that the act of thought, by which I formed those ideas, was itself immaterial, and yet it could not have formed them if it were not itself a measurable entity.

So also I thought about thee, O Life of my life, as stretched out through infinite space, interpenetrating the whole mass of the world, reaching out beyond in all directions, to immensity without end; so that the earth should have thee, the heaven have thee, all things have thee, and all of them be limited in thee, while thou art placed nowhere at all. As the body of the air above the earth does not bar the passage of the light of the sun, so that the light penetrates it, not by bursting nor dividing, but filling it entirely, so I imagined that the body of heaven and air and sea, and even of the earth, was all open to thee and, in all its greatest parts as well as the smallest, was ready to receive

---

[2] *Phantasmata*, mental constructs, which may be internally coherent but correspond to no reality outside the mind.

[3] Echoes here of Plato's *Timaeus* and Plotinus' *Enneads*, although with no effort to recall the sources or elaborate the ontological theory.

thy presence by a secret inspiration which, from within or without all, orders all things thou hast created. This was my conjecture, because I was unable to think of anything else; yet it was untrue. For in this way a greater part of the earth would contain a greater part of thee; a smaller part, a smaller fraction of thee. All things would be full of thee in such a sense that there would be more of thee in an elephant than in a sparrow, because one is larger than the other and fills a larger space. And this would make the portions of thyself present in the several portions of the world in fragments, great to the great, small to the small. But thou art not such a one. But as yet thou hadst not enlightened my darkness.

CHAPTER II

3. But it was not sufficient for me, O Lord, to be able to oppose those deceived deceivers and those dumb orators—dumb because thy Word did not sound forth from them—to oppose them with the answer which, in the old Carthaginian days, Nebridius used to propound, shaking all of us who heard it: "What could this imaginary people of darkness, which the Manicheans usually set up as an army opposed to thee, have done to thee if thou hadst declined the combat?" If they replied that it could have hurt thee, they would then have made thee violable and corruptible. If, on the other hand, the dark could have done thee no harm, then there was no cause for any battle at all; there was less cause for a battle in which a part of thee, one of thy members, a child of thy own substance, should be mixed up with opposing powers, not of thy creation; and should be corrupted and deteriorated and changed by them from happiness into misery, so that it could not be delivered and cleansed without thy help. This offspring of thy substance was supposed to be the human soul to which thy Word—free, pure, and entire—could bring help when it was being enslaved, contaminated, and corrupted. But on their hypothesis that Word was itself corruptible because it is one and the same substance as the soul.

And therefore if they admitted that thy nature—whatsoever thou art—is incorruptible, then all these assertions of theirs are false and should be rejected with horror. But if thy substance is corruptible, then this is self-evidently false and should be abhorred at first utterance. This line of argument, then, was enough against those deceivers who ought to be cast forth from a surfeited stomach—for out of this dilemma they could find no way of escape without dreadful sacrilege of mind and tongue, when they think and speak such things about thee.

CHAPTER III

4. But as yet, although I said and was firmly persuaded that thou our Lord, the true God, who madest not only our souls but our bodies as well—and not only our souls and bodies but all creatures and all things—wast free from stain and alteration and in no way mutable, yet I could not readily and clearly understand what was the cause of evil. Whatever it was, I realized that the question must be so analyzed as not to constrain me by any answer to believe that the immutable God was mutable, lest I should myself become the thing that I was seeking out. And so I pursued the search with a quiet mind, now in a confident feeling that what had been said by the Manicheans —and I shrank from them with my whole heart—could not be true. I now realized that when they asked what was the origin of evil their answer was dictated by a wicked pride, which would rather affirm that thy nature is capable of suffering evil than that their own nature is capable of doing it.

5. And I directed my attention to understand what I now was told, that free will is the cause of our doing evil and that thy just judgment is the cause of our having to suffer from its consequences. But I could not see this clearly. So then, trying to draw the eye of my mind up out of that pit, I was plunged back into it again, and trying often was just as often plunged back down. But one thing lifted me up toward thy light: it was that I had come to know that I had a will as certainly as I knew that I had life. When, therefore, I willed or was unwilling to do something, I was utterly certain that it was none but myself who willed or was unwilling—and immediately I realized that there was the cause of my sin. I could see that what I did against my will I suffered rather than did; and I did not regard such actions as faults, but rather as punishments in which I might quickly confess that I was not unjustly punished, since I believed thee to be most just. Who was it that put this in me, and implanted in me the root of bitterness, in spite of the fact that I was altogether the handiwork of my most sweet God? If the devil is to blame, who made the devil himself? And if he was a good angel who by his own wicked will became the devil, how did there happen to be in him that wicked will by which

he became a devil, since a good Creator made him wholly a good angel? By these reflections was I again cast down and stultified. Yet I was not plunged into that hell of error—where no man confesses to thee—where I thought that thou didst suffer evil, rather than that men do it.

CHAPTER IV

6. For in my struggle to solve the rest of my difficulties, I now assumed henceforth as settled truth that the incorruptible must be superior to the corruptible, and I did acknowledge that thou, whatever thou art, art incorruptible. For there never yet was, nor will be, a soul able to conceive of anything better than thee, who art the highest and best good.[4] And since most truly and certainly the incorruptible is to be placed above the corruptible—as I now admit it—it followed that I could rise in my thoughts to something better than my God, if thou wert not incorruptible. When, therefore, I saw that the incorruptible was to be preferred to the corruptible, I saw then where I ought to seek thee, and where I should look for the source of evil: that is, the corruption by which thy substance can in no way be profaned. For it is obvious that corruption in no way injures our God, by no inclination, by no necessity, by no unforeseen chance —because he is our God, and what he wills is good, and he himself is that good. But to be corrupted is not good. Nor art thou compelled to do anything against thy will, since thy will is not greater than thy power. But it would have to be greater if thou thyself wert greater than thyself—for the will and power of God are God himself. And what can take thee by surprise, since thou knowest all, and there is no sort of nature but thou knowest it? And what more should we say about why that substance which God is cannot be corrupted; because if this were so it could not be God?

CHAPTER V

7. And I kept seeking for an answer to the question, Whence is evil? And I sought it in an evil way, and I did not see the evil in my very search. I marshaled before the sight of my spirit all

---

4 Cf. the famous "definition" of God in Anselm's ontological argument: "that being than whom no greater can be conceived." Cf. *Proslogium*, II–V.

creation: all that we see of earth and sea and air and stars and trees and animals; and all that we do not see, the firmament of the sky above and all the angels and all spiritual things, for my imagination arranged these also, as if they were bodies, in this place or that. And I pictured to myself thy creation as one vast mass, composed of various kinds of bodies—some of which were actually bodies, some of those which I imagined spirits were like. I pictured this mass as vast—of course not in its full dimensions, for these I could not know—but as large as I could possibly think, still only finite on every side. But thou, O Lord, I imagined as environing the mass on every side and penetrating it, still infinite in every direction—as if there were a sea everywhere, and everywhere through measureless space nothing but an infinite sea; and it contained within itself some sort of sponge, huge but still finite, so that the sponge would in all its parts be filled from the immeasurable sea.[5]

Thus I conceived thy creation itself to be finite, and filled by thee, the infinite. And I said, "Behold God, and behold what God hath created!" God is good, yea, most mightily and incomparably better than all his works. But yet he who is good has created them good; behold how he encircles and fills them. Where, then, is evil, and whence does it come and how has it crept in? What is its root and what its seed? Has it no being at all? Why, then, do we fear and shun what has no being? Or if we fear it needlessly, then surely that fear is evil by which the heart is unnecessarily stabbed and tortured—and indeed a greater evil since we have nothing real to fear, and yet do fear. Therefore, either that is evil which we fear, or the act of fearing is in itself evil. But, then, whence does it come, since God who is good has made all these things good? Indeed, he is the greatest and chiefest Good, and hath created these lesser goods; but both Creator and created are all good. Whence, then, is evil? Or, again, was there some evil matter out of which he made and formed and ordered it, but left something in his creation that he did not convert into good? But why should this be? Was he powerless to change the whole lump so that no evil would remain in it, if he is the Omnipotent? Finally, why would he make anything at all out of such stuff? Why did he not, rather, annihilate it by his same almighty power? Could evil exist contrary to his will? And if it were from eternity, why did he permit it to be nonexistent for unmeasured intervals of time in the past, and

[5] This simile is Augustine's apparently original improvement on Plotinus' similar figure of the net in the sea; *Enneads*, IV, 3:9.

why, then, was he pleased to make something out of it after so long a time? Or, if he wished now all of a sudden to create something, would not an almighty being have chosen to annihilate this evil matter and live by himself—the perfect, true, sovereign, and infinite Good? Or, if it were not good that he who was good should not also be the framer and creator of what was good, then why was that evil matter not removed and brought to nothing, so that he might form good matter, out of which he might then create all things? For he would not be omnipotent if he were not able to create something good without being assisted by that matter which had not been created by himself.

Such perplexities I revolved in my wretched breast, overwhelmed with gnawing cares lest I die before I discovered the truth. And still the faith of thy Christ, our Lord and Saviour, as it was taught me by the Catholic Church, stuck fast in my heart. As yet it was unformed on many points and diverged from the rule of right doctrine, but my mind did not utterly lose it, and every day drank in more and more of it.

CHAPTER VI

8. By now I had also repudiated the lying divinations and impious absurdities of the astrologers. Let thy mercies, out of the depth of my soul, confess this to thee also, O my God. For thou, thou only (for who else is it who calls us back from the death of all errors except the Life which does not know how to die and the Wisdom which gives light to minds that need it, although it itself has no need of light—by which the whole universe is governed, even to the fluttering leaves of the trees?) —thou alone providedst also for my obstinacy with which I struggled against Vindicianus, a sagacious old man, and Nebridius, that remarkably talented young man. The former declared vehemently and the latter frequently—though with some reservation—that no art existed by which we foresee future things. But men's surmises have oftentimes the help of chance, and out of many things which they foretold some came to pass unawares to the predictors, who lighted on the truth by making so many guesses.

And thou also providedst a friend for me, who was not a negligent consulter of the astrologers even though he was not thoroughly skilled in the art either—as I said, one who consulted them out of curiosity. He knew a good deal about it,

which, he said, he had heard from his father, and he never realized how far his ideas would help to overthrow my estimation of
that art. His name was Firminus and he had received a liberal
education and was a cultivated rhetorician. It so happened that
he consulted me, as one very dear to him, as to what I thought
about some affairs of his in which his worldly hopes had risen,
viewed in the light of his so-called horoscope. Although I had
now begun to learn in this matter toward Nebridius' opinion, I
did not quite decline to speculate about the matter or to tell
him what thoughts still came into my irresolute mind, although
I did add that I was almost persuaded now that these were but
empty and ridiculous follies. He then told me that his father had
been very much interested in such books, and that he had a friend
who was as much interested in them as he was himself. They,
in combined study and consultation, fanned the flame of their
affection for this folly, going so far as to observe the moment
when the dumb animals which belonged to their household
gave birth to young, and then observed the position of the
heavens with regard to them, so as to gather fresh evidence for
this so-called art. Moreover, he reported that his father had told
him that, at the same time his mother was about to give birth
to him [Firminus], a female slave of a friend of his father's was
also pregnant. This could not be hidden from her master, who
kept records with the most diligent exactness of the birth dates
even of his dogs. And so it happened to pass that—under the
most careful observations, one for his wife and the other for his
servant, with exact calculations of the days, hours, and minutes
—both women were delivered at the same moment, so that
both were compelled to cast the selfsame horoscope, down to
the minute: the one for his son, the other for his young slave.
For as soon as the women began to be in labor, they each sent
word to the other as to what was happening in their respective
houses and had messengers ready to dispatch to one another as
soon as they had information of the actual birth—and each, of
course, knew instantly the exact time. It turned out, Firminus
said, that the messengers from the respective houses met one
another at a point equidistant from either house, so that neither
of them could discern any difference either in the position of the
stars or any other of the most minute points. And yet Firminus,
born in a high estate in his parents' house, ran his course
through the prosperous paths of this world, was increased in
wealth, and elevated to honors. At the same time, the slave,
the yoke of his condition being still unrelaxed, continued to

serve his masters as Firminus, who knew him, was able to report.

9. Upon hearing and believing these things related by so reliable a person all my resistance melted away. First, I endeavored to reclaim Firminus himself from his superstition by telling him that after inspecting his horoscope, I ought, if I could foretell truly, to have seen in it parents eminent among their neighbors, a noble family in its own city, a good birth, a proper education, and liberal learning. But if that servant had consulted me with the same horoscope, since he had the same one, I ought again to tell him likewise truly that I saw in it the lowliness of his origin, the abjectness of his condition, and everything else different and contrary to the former prediction. If, then, by casting up the same horoscopes I should, in order to speak the truth, make contrary analyses, or else speak falsely if I made identical readings, then surely it followed that whatever was truly foretold by the analysis of the horoscopes was not by art, but by chance. And whatever was said falsely was not from incompetence in the art, but from the error of chance.

10. An opening being thus made in my darkness, I began to consider other implications involved here. Suppose that one of the fools—who followed such an occupation and whom I longed to assail, and to reduce to confusion—should urge against me that Firminus had given me false information, or that his father had informed him falsely. I then turned my thoughts to those that are born twins, who generally come out of the womb so near the one to the other that the short interval between them—whatever importance they may ascribe to it in the nature of things—cannot be noted by human observation or expressed in those tables which the astrologer uses to examine when he undertakes to pronounce the truth. But such pronouncements cannot be true. For looking into the same horoscopes, he must have foretold the same future for Esau and Jacob,[6] whereas the same future did not turn out for them. He must therefore speak falsely. If he is to speak truly, then he must read contrary predictions into the same horoscopes. But this would mean that it was not by art, but by chance, that he would speak truly.

For thou, O Lord, most righteous ruler of the universe, dost work by a secret impulse—whether those who inquire or those inquired of know it or not—so that the inquirer may hear what, according to the secret merit of his soul, he ought to hear from

[6] Gen. 25:21 to 33:20.

the deeps of thy righteous judgment. Therefore let no man say to thee, "What is this?" or, "Why is that?" Let him not speak thus, for he is only a man.

CHAPTER VII

11. By now, O my Helper, thou hadst freed me from those fetters. But still I inquired, "Whence is evil?"—and found no answer. But thou didst not allow me to be carried away from the faith by these fluctuations of thought. I still believed both that thou dost exist and that thy substance is immutable, and that thou dost care for and wilt judge all men, and that in Christ, thy Son our Lord, and the Holy Scriptures, which the authority of thy Catholic Church pressed on me, thou hast planned the way of man's salvation to that life which is to come after this death.

With these convictions safe and immovably settled in my mind, I eagerly inquired, "Whence is evil?" What torments did my travailing heart then endure! What sighs, O my God! Yet even then thy ears were open and I knew it not, and when in stillness I sought earnestly, those silent contritions of my soul were loud cries to thy mercy. No man knew, but thou knewest what I endured. How little of it could I express in words to the ears of my dearest friends! How could the whole tumult of my soul, for which neither time nor speech was sufficient, come to them? Yet the whole of it went into thy ears, all of which I bellowed out in the anguish of my heart. My desire was before thee, and the light of my eyes was not with me; for it was within and I was without. Nor was that light in any place; but I still kept thinking only of things that are contained in a place, and could find among them no place to rest in. They did not receive me in such a way that I could say, "It is sufficient; it is well." Nor did they allow me to turn back to where it might be well enough with me. For I was higher than they, though lower than thou. Thou art my true joy if I depend upon thee, and thou hadst subjected to me what thou didst create lower than I. And this was the true mean and middle way of salvation for me, to continue in thy image and by serving thee have dominion over the body. But when I lifted myself proudly against thee, and "ran against the Lord, even against his neck, with the thick bosses of my buckler,"[7] even the lower things were placed above me and pressed down on me, so that there was no respite or

[7] Cf. Job 15:26 (Old Latin version).

breathing space. They thrust on my sight on every side, in crowds and masses, and when I tried to think, the images of bodies obtruded themselves into my way back to thee, as if they would say to me, "Where are you going, unworthy and unclean one?" And all these had sprung out of my wound, for thou hadst humbled the haughty as one that is wounded. By my swelling pride I was separated from thee, and my bloated cheeks blinded my eyes.

CHAPTER VIII

12. But thou, O Lord, art forever the same, yet thou art not forever angry with us, for thou hast compassion on our dust and ashes.[8] It was pleasing in thy sight to reform my deformity, and by inward stings thou didst disturb me so that I was impatient until thou wert made clear to my inward sight. By the secret hand of thy healing my swelling was lessened, the disordered and darkened eyesight of my mind was from day to day made whole by the stinging salve of wholesome grief.

CHAPTER IX

13. And first of all, willing to show me how thou dost "resist the proud, but give grace to the humble,"[9] and how mercifully thou hast made known to men the way of humility in that thy Word "was made flesh and dwelt among men,"[10] thou didst procure for me, through one inflated with the most monstrous pride, certain books of the Platonists, translated from Greek into Latin.[11] And therein I found, not indeed in the same words, but to the selfsame effect, enforced by many and various reasons that "in the beginning was the Word, and the Word was with God, and the Word was God. The same was in the beginning with God. All things were made by him; and without him was not anything made that was made." That which was made by him is "life, and the life was the light of men. And the light

---

[8] Cf. Ps. 103:9-14.   [9] James 4:6.   [10] Cf. John 1:14.

[11] It is not altogether clear as to which "books" and which "Platonists" are here referred to. The succeeding analysis of "Platonism" does not resemble any single known text closely enough to allow for identification. The most reasonable conjecture, as most authorities agree, is that the "books" here mentioned were the *Enneads* of Plotinus, which Marius Victorinus (q.v *infra*, Bk. VIII, Ch. II, 3-5) had translated into Latin several years before; cf. M. P. Garvey, *St. Augustine: Christian or Neo-Platonist* (Milwaukee, 1939). There is also a fair probability that Augustine had acquired some knowledge of the *Didaskalikos* of Albinus; cf. R. E. Witt, *Albinus and the History of Middle Platonism* (Cambridge, 1937).

shined in darkness; and the darkness comprehended it not." Furthermore, I read that the soul of man, though it "bears witness to the light," yet itself "is not the light; but the Word of God, being God, is that true light that lights every man who comes into the world." And further, that "he was in the world, and the world was made by him, and the world knew him not." [12] But that "he came unto his own, and his own received him not. And as many as received him, to them gave he power to become the sons of God, even to them that believed on his name" [13]—this I did not find there.

14. Similarly, I read there that God the Word was born "not of flesh nor of blood, nor of the will of man, nor the will of the flesh, but of God." [14] But, that "the Word was made flesh, and dwelt among us" [15]—I found this nowhere there. And I discovered in those books, expressed in many and various ways, that "the Son was in the form of God and thought it not robbery to be equal in God," [16] for he was naturally of the same substance. But, that "he emptied himself and took upon himself the form of a servant, and was made in the likeness of men: and being found in fashion as a man, he humbled himself, and became obedient unto death, even the death of the cross. Wherefore God also hath highly exalted him" from the dead, "and given him a name above every name; that at the name of Jesus every knee should bow, of things in heaven, and things in earth, and things under the earth; and that every tongue should confess that Jesus Christ is Lord, to the glory of God the Father" [17]—this those books have not. I read further in them that before all times and beyond all times, thy only Son remaineth unchangeably coeternal with thee, and that of his fullness all souls receive that they may be blessed, and that by participation in that wisdom which abides in them, they are renewed that they may be wise. But, that "in due time, Christ died for the ungodly" and that thou "sparedst not thy only Son, but deliveredst him up for us all" [18]—this is not there. "For thou hast hid these things from the wise and prudent, and hast revealed them unto babes" [19]; that they "that labor and are heavy laden" might "come unto him and he might refresh them" because he is "meek and lowly in heart." [20] "The meek will he

---

[12] Cf. this mixed quotation of John 1:1-10 with the Fifth *Ennead* and note Augustine's identification of *Logos*, in the Fourth Gospel, with *Nous* in Plotinus.   [13] John 1:11, 12.   [14] John 1:13.

[15] John 1:14.   [16] Phil. 2:6.   [17] Phil. 2:7-11.

[18] Rom. 5:6; 8:32.   [19] Luke 10:21.   [20] Cf. Matt. 11:28, 29.

guide in judgment; and the meek will he teach his way; beholding our lowliness and our trouble and forgiving all our sins."[21] But those who strut in the high boots of what they deem to be superior knowledge will not hear Him who says, "Learn of me, for I am meek and lowly in heart, and you shall find rest for your souls."[22] Thus, though they know God, yet they do not glorify him as God, nor are they thankful. Therefore, they "become vain in their imaginations; their foolish heart is darkened, and professing themselves to be wise they become fools."[23]

15. And, moreover, I also read there how "they changed the glory of thy incorruptible nature into idols and various images —into an image made like corruptible man and to birds and four-footed beasts, and creeping things"[24]: namely, into that Egyptian food[25] for which Esau lost his birthright; so that thy first-born people worshiped the head of a four-footed beast instead of thee, turning back in their hearts toward Egypt and prostrating thy image (their own soul) before the image of an ox that eats grass. These things I found there, but I fed not on them. For it pleased thee, O Lord, to take away the reproach of his minority from Jacob, that the elder should serve the younger and thou mightest call the Gentiles, and I had sought strenuously after that gold which thou didst allow thy people to take from Egypt, since wherever it was it was thine.[26] And thou saidst unto the Athenians by the mouth of thy apostle that in thee "we live and move and have our being," as one of their own poets had said.[27] And truly these books came from there. But I did not set my mind on the idols of Egypt which they fashioned of gold, "changing the truth of God into a lie and worshiping and serving the creature more than the Creator."[28]

CHAPTER X

16. And being admonished by these books to return into myself, I entered into my inward soul, guided by thee. This I

[21] Cf. Ps. 25:9, 18.   [22] Matt. 11:29.
[23] Rom. 1:21, 22.   [24] Rom. 1:23.
[25] An echo of Porphyry's *De abstinentia ab esu animalium.*
[26] The allegorical interpretation of the Israelites' despoiling the Egyptians (Ex. 12:35, 36) made it refer to the liberty of Christian thinkers in appropriating whatever was good and true from the pagan philosophers of the Greco-Roman world. This was a favorite theme of Clement of Alexandria and Origen and was quite explicitly developed in Origen's *Epistle to Gregory Thaumaturgus* (*ANF*, IX, pp. 295, 296); cf. Augustine, *On Christian Doctrine*, II, 41-42.
[27] Cf. Acts 17:28.   [28] Cf. Rom. 1:25.

could do because thou wast my helper. And I entered, and with the eye of my soul—such as it was—saw above the same eye of my soul and above my mind the Immutable Light. It was not the common light, which all flesh can see; nor was it simply a greater one of the same sort, as if the light of day were to grow brighter and brighter, and flood all space. It was not like that light, but different, yea, very different from all earthly light whatever. Nor was it above my mind in the same way as oil is above water, or heaven above earth, but it was higher, because it made me, and I was below it, because I was made by it. He who knows the Truth knows that Light, and he who knows it knows eternity. Love knows it, O Eternal Truth and True Love and Beloved Eternity! Thou art my God, to whom I sigh both night and day. When I first knew thee, thou didst lift me up, that I might see that there was something to be seen, though I was not yet fit to see it. And thou didst beat back the weakness of my sight, shining forth upon me thy dazzling beams of light, and I trembled with love and fear. I realized that I was far away from thee in the land of unlikeness, as if I heard thy voice from on high: "I am the food of strong men; grow and you shall feed on me; nor shall you change me, like the food of your flesh into yourself, but you shall be changed into my likeness." And I understood that thou chastenest man for his iniquity, and makest my soul to be eaten away as though by a spider.[29] And I said, "Is Truth, therefore, nothing, because it is not diffused through space—neither finite nor infinite?" And thou didst cry to me from afar, "I am that I am." [30] And I heard this, as things are heard in the heart, and there was no room for doubt. I should have more readily doubted that I am alive than that the Truth exists—the Truth which is "clearly seen, being understood by the things that are made." [31]

CHAPTER XI

17. And I viewed all the other things that are beneath thee, and I realized that they are neither wholly real nor wholly unreal. They are real in so far as they come from thee; but they are unreal in so far as they are not what thou art. For that is truly real which remains immutable. It is good, then, for me to

29 Cf. Ps. 39:11.
30 Some MSS. add "*immo vero*" ("yea, verily"), but not the best ones; cf. De Labriolle, *op. cit.*, I, p. 162.
31 Rom. 1:20.

hold fast to God, for if I do not remain in him, neither shall I abide in myself; but he, remaining in himself, renews all things. And thou art the Lord my God, since thou standest in no need of my goodness.

CHAPTER XII

18. And it was made clear to me that all things are good even if they are corrupted. They could not be corrupted if they were supremely good; but unless they were good they could not be corrupted. If they were supremely good, they would be incorruptible; if they were not good at all, there would be nothing in them to be corrupted. For corruption harms; but unless it could diminish goodness, it could not harm. Either, then, corruption does not harm—which cannot be—or, as is certain, all that is corrupted is thereby deprived of good. But if they are deprived of all good, they will cease to be. For if they are at all and cannot be at all corrupted, they will become better, because they will remain incorruptible. Now what can be more monstrous than to maintain that by losing all good they have become better? If, then, they are deprived of all good, they will cease to exist. So long as they are, therefore, they are good. Therefore, whatsoever is, is good. Evil, then, the origin of which I had been seeking, has no substance at all; for if it were a substance, it would be good. For either it would be an incorruptible substance and so a supreme good, or a corruptible substance, which could not be corrupted unless it were good. I understood, therefore, and it was made clear to me that thou madest all things good, nor is there any substance at all not made by thee. And because all that thou madest is not equal, each by itself is good, and the sum of all of them is very good, for our God made all things very good.[32]

CHAPTER XIII

19. To thee there is no such thing as evil, and even in thy whole creation taken as a whole, there is not; because there is nothing from beyond it that can burst in and destroy the order which thou hast appointed for it. But in the parts of creation, some things, because they do not harmonize with others, are

[32] A *locus classicus* of the doctrine of the privative character of evil and the positive character of the good. This is a fundamental premise in Augustine's metaphysics: it reappears in Bks. XII–XIII, in the *Enchiridion*, and elsewhere (see note, *infra*, p. 343). This doctrine of the goodness of all creation is taken up into the scholastic metaphysics; cf. *Confessions*, Bks. XII–XIII, and Thomas Aquinas, *Summa contra gentes*, II: 45.

considered evil. Yet those same things harmonize with others and are good, and in themselves are good. And all these things which do not harmonize with each other still harmonize with the inferior part of creation which we call the earth, having its own cloudy and windy sky of like nature with itself. Far be it from me, then, to say, "These things should not be." For if I could see nothing but these, I should indeed desire something better—but still I ought to praise thee, if only for these created things. For that thou art to be praised is shown from the fact that "earth, dragons, and all deeps; fire, and hail, snow and vapors, stormy winds fulfilling thy word; mountains, and all hills, fruitful trees, and all cedars; beasts and all cattle; creeping things, and flying fowl; things of the earth, and all people; princes, and all judges of the earth; both young men and maidens, old men and children," [33] praise thy name! But seeing also that in heaven all thy angels praise thee, O God, praise thee in the heights," and all thy hosts, sun and moon, all stars and light, the heavens of heavens, and the waters that are above the heavens," [34] praise thy name—seeing this, I say, I no longer desire a better world, because my thought ranged over all, and with a sounder judgment I reflected that the things above were better than those below, yet that all creation together was better than the higher things alone.

CHAPTER XIV

20. There is no health in those who find fault with any part of thy creation; as there was no health in me when I found fault with so many of thy works. And, because my soul dared not be displeased with my God, it would not allow that the things which displeased me were from thee. Hence it had wandered into the notion of two substances, and could find no rest, but talked foolishly, And turning from that error, it had then made for itself a god extended through infinite space; and it thought this was thou and set it up in its heart, and it became once more the temple of its own idol, an abomination to thee. But thou didst soothe my brain, though I was unaware of it, and closed my eyes lest they should behold vanity; and thus I ceased from preoccupation with self by a little and my madness was lulled to sleep; and I awoke in thee, and beheld thee as the Infinite, but not in the way I had thought —and this vision was not derived from the flesh.

[33] Ps. 148:7-12. [34] Ps. 148:1-5.

CHAPTER XV

21. And I looked around at other things, and I saw that it was to thee that all of them owed their being, and that they were all finite in thee; yet they are in thee not as in a space, but because thou holdest all things in the hand of thy truth, and because all things are true in so far as they are; and because falsehood is nothing except the existence in thought of what does not exist in fact. And I saw that all things harmonize, not only in their places but also in their seasons. And I saw that thou, who alone art eternal, didst not *begin* to work after un-numbered periods of time—because all ages, both those which are past and those which shall pass, neither go nor come except through thy working and abiding.

CHAPTER XVI

22. And I saw and found it no marvel that bread which is distasteful to an unhealthy palate is pleasant to a healthy one; or that the light, which is painful to sore eyes, is a delight to sound ones. Thy righteousness displeases the wicked, and they find even more fault with the viper and the little worm, which thou hast created good, fitting in as they do with the inferior parts of creation. The wicked themselves also fit in here, and pro-portionately more so as they become unlike thee—but they harmonize with the higher creation proportionately as they be-come like thee. And I asked what wickedness was, and I found that it was no substance, but a perversion of the will bent aside from thee, O God, the supreme substance, toward these lower things, casting away its inmost treasure and becoming bloated with external good.[35]

CHAPTER XVII

23. And I marveled that I now loved thee, and no fantasm in thy stead, and yet I was not stable enough to enjoy my God steadily. Instead I was transported to thee by thy beauty, and then presently torn away from thee by my own weight, sinking with grief into these lower things. This weight was carnal habit. But thy memory dwelt with me, and I never doubted in the least that there was One for me to cleave to; but I was not

[35] Cf. "The evil which overtakes us has its source in self-will, in the entry into the sphere of process and in the primal assertion of the desire for self-ownership" (Plotinus, *Enneads*, V, 1:1).

yet ready to cleave to thee firmly. For the body which is corrupted presses down the soul, and the earthly dwelling weighs down the mind, which muses upon many things. [36] My greatest certainty was that "the invisible things of thine from the creation of the world are clearly seen, being understood by the things that are made, even thy eternal power and Godhead." [37] For when I inquired how it was that I could appreciate the beauty of bodies, both celestial and terrestrial; and what it was that supported me in making correct judgments about things mutable; and when I concluded, "This ought to be thus; this ought not"—*then* when I inquired how it was that I could make such judgments (since I did, in fact, make them), I realized that I had found the unchangeable and true eternity of truth above my changeable mind.

And thus by degrees I was led upward from bodies to the soul which perceives them by means of the bodily senses, and from there on to the soul's inward faculty, to which the bodily senses report outward things—and this belongs even to the capacities of the beasts—and thence on up to the reasoning power, to whose judgment is referred the experience received from the bodily sense. And when this power of reason within me also found that it was changeable, it raised itself up to its own intellectual principle,[38] and withdrew its thoughts from experience, abstracting itself from the contradictory throng of fantasms in order to seek for that light in which it was bathed. Then, without any doubting, it cried out that the unchangeable was better than the changeable. From this it follows that the mind somehow knew the unchangeable, for, unless it had known it in some fashion, it could have had no sure ground for preferring it to the changeable. And thus with the flash of a trembling glance, it arrived at *that which is*.[39] And I saw thy invisibility [*invisibilia tua*] understood by means of the things that

---

[36] "We have gone weighed down from beneath; the vision is frustrated" (*Enneads*, VI, 9:4).

[37] Rom. 1:20.   [38] The Plotinian *Nous*.

[39] This is an astonishingly candid and plain account of a Plotinian ecstasy, the pilgrimage of the soul from its absorption in things to its rapturous but momentary vision of the One; cf. especially the Sixth *Ennead*, 9:3-11, for very close parallels in thought and echoes of language. This is one of two ecstatic visions reported in the *Confessions*; the other is, of course, the last great moment with his mother at Ostia (Bk. IX, Ch. X, 23-25). One comes before the "conversion" in the Milanese garden (Bk. VIII, Ch. XII, 28-29); the other, after. They ought to be compared with particular interest in their *similarities* as well as their significant differences. Cf. also K. E. Kirk, *The Vision of God* (London, 1932), pp. 319-346.

are made. But I was not able to sustain my gaze. My weakness was dashed back, and I lapsed again into my accustomed ways, carrying along with me nothing but a loving memory of my vision, and an appetite for what I had, as it were, smelled the odor of, but was not yet able to eat.

CHAPTER XVIII

24. I sought, therefore, some way to acquire the strength sufficient to enjoy thee; but I did not find it until I embraced that "Mediator between God and man, the man Christ Jesus,"[40] "who is over all, God blessed forever," [41] who came calling and saying, "I am the way, the truth, and the life," [42] and mingling with our fleshly humanity the heavenly food I was unable to receive. For "the Word was made flesh" in order that thy wisdom, by which thou didst create all things, might become milk for our infancy. And, as yet, I was not humble enough to hold the humble Jesus; nor did I understand what lesson his weakness was meant to teach us. For thy Word, the eternal Truth, far exalted above even the higher parts of thy creation, lifts his subjects up toward himself. But in this lower world, he built for himself a humble habitation of our own clay, so that he might pull down from themselves and win over to himself those whom he is to bring subject to him; lowering their pride and heightening their love, to the end that they might go on no farther in self-confidence—but rather should become weak, seeing at their feet the Deity made weak by sharing our coats of skin—so that they might cast themselves, exhausted, upon him and be uplifted by his rising.

CHAPTER XIX

25. But I thought otherwise. I saw in our Lord Christ only a man of eminent wisdom to whom no other man could be compared—especially because he was miraculously born of a virgin—sent to set us an example of despising worldly things for the attainment of immortality, and thus exhibiting his divine care for us. Because of this, I held that he had merited his great authority as leader. But concerning the mystery contained in "the Word was made flesh," I could not even form a notion. From what I learned from what has been handed down to us in the books about him—that he ate, drank, slept, walked, re-

---

[40] I Tim. 2:5.   [41] Rom. 9:5.   [42] John 14:6.

joiced in spirit, was sad, and discoursed with his fellows—I realized that his flesh alone was not bound unto thy Word, but also that there was a bond with the human soul and body. Everyone knows this who knows the unchangeableness of thy Word, and this I knew by now, as far as I was able, and I had no doubts at all about it. For at one time to move the limbs by an act of will, at another time not; at one time to feel some emotion, at another time not; at one time to speak intelligibly through verbal signs, at another, not—these are all properties of a soul and mind subject to change. And if these things were falsely written about him, all the rest would risk the imputation of falsehood, and there would remain in those books no saving faith for the human race.

Therefore, because they were written truthfully, I acknowledged a perfect man to be in Christ—not the body of a man only, nor, in the body, an animal soul without a rational one as well, but a true man. And this man I held to be superior to all others, not only because he was a form of the Truth, but also because of the great excellence and perfection of his human nature, due to his participation in wisdom.

Alypius, on the other hand, supposed the Catholics to believe that God was so clothed with flesh that besides God and the flesh there was no soul in Christ, and he did not think that a human mind was ascribed to him.[43] And because he was fully persuaded that the actions recorded of him could not have been performed except by a living rational creature, he moved the more slowly toward Christian faith.[44] But when he later learned that this was the error of the Apollinarian heretics, he rejoiced in the Catholic faith and accepted it. For myself, I must confess that it was even later that I learned how in the sentence, "The Word was made flesh," the Catholic truth can be distinguished from the falsehood of Photinus. For the refutation of heretics[45] makes the tenets of thy Church and sound doctrine to stand out boldly. "For there must also be heresies [factions] that those who are approved may be made manifest among the weak."[46]

---

43 An interesting reminder that the Apollinarian heresy was condemned but not extinct.

44 It is worth remembering that both Augustine and Alypius were catechumens and had presumably been receiving doctrinal instruction in preparation for their eventual baptism and full membership in the Catholic Church. That their ideas on the incarnation, at this stage, were in such confusion raises an interesting problem.

45 Cf. Augustine's *The Christian Combat* as an example of "the refutation of heretics."   46 Cf. I Cor. 11:19.

CHAPTER XX

26. By having thus read the books of the Platonists, and having been taught by them to search for the incorporeal Truth, I saw how thy invisible things are understood through the things that are made. And, even when I was thrown back, I still sensed what it was that the dullness of my soul would not allow me to contemplate. I was assured that thou wast, and wast infinite, though not diffused in finite space or infinity; that thou truly art, who art ever the same, varying neither in part nor motion; and that all things are from thee, as is proved by this sure cause alone: that they exist.

Of all this I was convinced, yet I was too weak to enjoy thee. I chattered away as if I were an expert; but if I had not sought thy Way in Christ our Saviour, my knowledge would have turned out to be not instruction but destruction.[47] For now full of what was in fact my punishment, I had begun to desire to seem wise. I did not mourn my ignorance, but rather was puffed up with knowledge. For where was that love which builds upon the foundation of humility, which is Jesus Christ?[48] Or, when would these books teach me this? I now believe that it was thy pleasure that I should fall upon these books before I studied thy Scriptures, that it might be impressed on my memory how I was affected by them; and then afterward, when I was subdued by thy Scriptures and when my wounds were touched by thy healing fingers, I might discern and distinguish what a difference there is between presumption and confession —between those who saw where they were to go even if they did not see the way, and the Way which leads, not only to the observing, but also the inhabiting of the blessed country. For had I first been molded in thy Holy Scriptures, and if thou hadst grown sweet to me through my familiar use of them, and if then I had afterward fallen on those volumes, they might have pushed me off the solid ground of godliness—or if I had stood firm in that wholesome disposition which I had there acquired, I might have thought that wisdom could be attained by the study of those [Platonist] books alone.

CHAPTER XXI

27. With great eagerness, then, I fastened upon the venerable writings of thy Spirit and principally upon the apostle

[47] *Non peritus, sed periturus essem.*   [48] Cf. I Cor. 3:11 f.

Paul. I had thought that he sometimes contradicted himself and that the text of his teaching did not agree with the testimonies of the Law and the Prophets; but now all these doubts vanished away. And I saw that those pure words had but one face, and I learned to rejoice with trembling. So I began, and I found that whatever truth I had read [in the Platonists] was here combined with the exaltation of thy grace. Thus, he who sees must not glory as if he had not received, not only the things that he sees, but the very power of sight—for what does he have that he has not received as a gift? By this he is not only exhorted to see, but also to be cleansed, that he may grasp thee, who art ever the same; and thus he who cannot see thee afar off may yet enter upon the road that leads to reaching, seeing, and possessing thee. For although a man may "delight in the law of God after the inward man," what shall he do with that other "law in his members which wars against the law of his mind, and brings him into captivity under the law of sin, which is in his members"? [49] Thou art righteous, O Lord; but we have sinned and committed iniquities, and have done wickedly. Thy hand has grown heavy upon us, and we are justly delivered over to that ancient sinner, the lord of death. For he persuaded our wills to become like his will, by which he remained not in thy truth. What shall "wretched man" do? "Who shall deliver him from the body of this death," [50] except thy grace through Jesus Christ our Lord; whom thou hast begotten, coeternal with thyself, and didst create in the beginning of thy ways [51]—in whom the prince of this world found nothing worthy of death, yet he killed him—and so the handwriting which was all against us was blotted out?

The books of the Platonists tell nothing of this. Their pages do not contain the expression of this kind of godliness—the tears of confession, thy sacrifice, a troubled spirit, a broken and a contrite heart, the salvation of thy people, the espoused City,

---

[49] Rom. 7:22, 23.   [50] Rom. 7:24, 25.
[51] Cf. Prov. 8:22 and Col. 1:15. Augustine is here identifying the figure of Wisdom in Proverbs with the figure of the Logos in the Prologue to the Fourth Gospel. In the Arian controversy both these references to God's Wisdom and Word as "created" caused great difficulty for the orthodox, for the Arians triumphantly appealed to them as proof that Jesus Christ was a "creature" of God. But Augustine was a Chalcedonian before Chalcedon, and there is no doubt that he is here quoting familiar Scripture and filling it with the interpretation achieved by the long struggle of the Church to affirm the coeternity and consubstantiality of Jesus Christ and God the Father.

the earnest of the Holy Spirit, the cup of our redemption. In them, no man sings: "Shall not my soul be subject unto God, for from him comes my salvation? He is my God and my salvation, my defender; I shall no more be moved." [52] In them, no one hears him calling, "Come unto me all you who labor." They scorn to learn of him because he is "meek and lowly of heart"; for "thou hast hidden those things from the wise and prudent, and hast revealed them unto babes." For it is one thing to see the land of peace from a wooded mountaintop, and fail to find the way thither—to attempt impassable ways in vain, opposed and waylaid by fugitives and deserters under their captain, the "lion" and "dragon" [53]; but it is quite another thing to keep to the highway that leads thither, guarded by the hosts of the heavenly Emperor, on which there are no deserters from the heavenly army to rob the passers-by, for they shun it as a torment. [54] These thoughts sank wondrously into my heart, when I read that "least of thy apostles" [55] and when I had considered all thy works and trembled.

[52] Cf. Ps. 62:1, 2, 5, 6.   [53] Cf. Ps. 91:13.
[54] A figure that compares the dangers of the solitary traveler in a bandit-infested land and the safety of an imperial convoy on a main highway to the capital city.
[55] Cf. I Cor. 15:9.

BOOK EIGHT

*Conversion to Christ. Augustine is deeply impressed by Simplicianus'
story of the conversion to Christ of the famous orator and philosopher,
Marius Victòrinus. He is stirred to emulate him, but finds himself still
enchained by his incontinence and preoccupation with worldly affairs. He
is then visited by a court official, Ponticianus, who tells him and Alypius
the stories of the conversion of Anthony and also of two imperial "secret
service agents." These stories throw him into a violent turmoil, in which
his divided will struggles against himself. He almost succeeds in making
the decision for continence, but is still held back. Finally, a child's song,
overheard by chance, sends him to the Bible; a text from Paul resolves the
crisis; the conversion is a fact. Alypius also makes his decision, and the
two inform the rejoicing Monica.*

CHAPTER I

1. O my God, let me remember with gratitude and confess
to thee thy mercies toward me. Let my bones be bathed in thy
love, and let them say: "Lord, who is like unto thee?[1] Thou
hast broken my bonds in sunder, I will offer unto thee the
sacrifice of thanksgiving."[2] And how thou didst break them I
will declare, and all who worship thee shall say, when they hear
these things: "Blessed be the Lord in heaven and earth, great
and wonderful is his name."[3]

Thy words had stuck fast in my breast, and I was hedged
round about by thee on every side. Of thy eternal life I was now
certain, although I had seen it "through a glass darkly."[4] And
I had been relieved of all doubt that there is an incorruptible

[1] Ps. 35:10.
[2] Cf. Ps. 116:16, 17.
[3] Cf. Ps. 8:1.
[4] I Cor. 13:12.

substance and that it is the source of every other substance. Nor did I any longer crave greater certainty about thee, but rather greater steadfastness in thee.

But as for my temporal life, everything was uncertain, and my heart had to be purged of the old leaven. "The Way"—the Saviour himself—pleased me well, but as yet I was reluctant to pass through the strait gate.

And thou didst put it into my mind, and it seemed good in my own sight, to go to Simplicianus, who appeared to me a faithful servant of thine, and thy grace shone forth in him. I had also been told that from his youth up he had lived in entire devotion to thee. He was already an old man, and because of his great age, which he had passed in such a zealous discipleship in thy way, he appeared to me likely to have gained much wisdom—and, indeed, he had. From all his experience, I desired him to tell me—setting before him all my agitations—which would be the most fitting way for one who felt as I did to walk in thy way.

2. For I saw the Church full; and one man was going this way and another that. Still, I could not be satisfied with the life I was living in the world. Now, indeed, my passions had ceased to excite me as of old with hopes of honor and wealth, and it was a grievous burden to go on in such servitude. For, compared with thy sweetness and the beauty of thy house—which I loved—those things delighted me no longer. But I was still tightly bound by the love of women; nor did the apostle forbid me to marry, although he exhorted me to something better, wishing earnestly that all men were as he himself was.

But I was weak and chose the easier way, and for this single reason my whole life was one of inner turbulence and listless indecision, because from so many influences I was compelled—even though unwilling—to agree to a married life which bound me hand and foot. I had heard from the mouth of Truth that "there are eunuchs who have made themselves eunuchs for the Kingdom of Heaven's sake" [5] but, said he, "He that is able to receive it, let him receive it." Of a certainty, all men are vain who do not have the knowledge of God, or have not been able, from the good things that are seen, to find him who is good. But I was no longer fettered in that vanity. I had surmounted it, and from the united testimony of thy whole creation had found thee, our Creator, and thy Word—God with thee, and together with thee and the Holy Spirit, one God—by whom thou hast

5 Matt. 19:12.

created all things. There is still another sort of wicked men, who "when they knew God, they glorified him not as God, neither were thankful." [6] Into this also I had fallen, but thy right hand held me up and bore me away, and thou didst place me where I might recover. For thou hast said to men, "Behold the fear of the Lord, this is wisdom," [7] and, "Be not wise in your own eyes," [8] because "they that profess themselves to be wise become fools." [9] But I had now found the goodly pearl; and I ought to have sold all that I had and bought it—yet I hesitated.

CHAPTER II

3. I went, therefore, to Simplicianus, the spiritual father of Ambrose (then a bishop), whom Ambrose truly loved as a father. I recounted to him all the mazes of my wanderings, but when I mentioned to him that I had read certain books of the Platonists which Victorinus—formerly professor of rhetoric at Rome, who died a Christian, as I had been told—had translated into Latin, Simplicianus congratulated me that I had not fallen upon the writings of other philosophers, which were full of fallacies and deceit, "after the beggarly elements of this world," [10] whereas in the Platonists, at every turn, the pathway led to belief in God and his Word.

Then, to encourage me to copy the humility of Christ, which is hidden from the wise and revealed to babes, he told me about Victorinus himself, whom he had known intimately at Rome. And I cannot refrain from repeating what he told me about him. For it contains a glorious proof of thy grace, which ought to be confessed to thee: how that old man, most learned, most skilled in all the liberal arts; who had read, criticized, and explained so many of the writings of the philosophers; the teacher of so many noble senators; one who, as a mark of his distinguished service in office had both merited and obtained a statue in the Roman Forum—which men of this world esteem a great honor—this man who, up to an advanced age, had been a worshiper of idols, a communicant in the sacrilegious rites to which almost all the nobility of Rome were wedded; and who had inspired the people with the love of Osiris and

> "The dog Anubis, and a medley crew
> Of monster gods who 'gainst Neptune stand in arms
> 'Gainst Venus and Minerva, steel-clad Mars," [11]

6 Rom. 1:21.   7 Job 28:28.   8 Prov. 3:7.
9 Rom. 1:22.   10 Col. 2:8.   11 Virgil, *Aeneid*, VIII, 698.

whom Rome once conquered, and now worshiped; all of which old Victorinus had with thundering eloquence defended for so many years—despite all this, he did not blush to become a child of thy Christ, a babe at thy font, bowing his neck to the yoke of humility and submitting his forehead to the ignominy of the cross.

4. O Lord, Lord, "who didst bow the heavens and didst descend, who didst touch the mountains and they smoked," [12] by what means didst thou find thy way into that breast? He used to read the Holy Scriptures, as Simplicianus said, and thought out and studied all the Christian writings most studiously. He said to Simplicianus—not openly but secretly as a friend—"You must know that I am a Christian." To which Simplicianus replied, "I shall not believe it, nor shall I count you among the Christians, until I see you in the Church of Christ." Victorinus then asked, with mild mockery, "Is it then the walls that make Christians?" Thus he often would affirm that he was already a Christian, and as often Simplicianus made the same answer; and just as often his jest about the walls was repeated. He was fearful of offending his friends, proud demon worshipers, from the height of whose Babylonian dignity, as from the tops of the cedars of Lebanon which the Lord had not yet broken down, he feared that a storm of enmity would descend upon him.

But he steadily gained strength from reading and inquiry, and came to fear lest he should be denied by Christ before the holy angels if he now was afraid to confess him before men. Thus he came to appear to himself guilty of a great fault, in being ashamed of the sacraments of the humility of thy Word, when he was not ashamed of the sacrilegious rites of those proud demons, whose pride he had imitated and whose rites he had shared. From this he became bold-faced against vanity and shamefaced toward the truth. Thus, suddenly and unexpectedly, he said to Simplicianus—as he himself told me—"Let us go to the church; I wish to become a Christian." Simplicianus went with him, scarcely able to contain himself for joy. He was admitted to the first sacraments of instruction, and not long afterward gave in his name that he might receive the baptism of regeneration. At this Rome marveled and the Church rejoiced. The proud saw and were enraged; they gnashed their teeth and melted away! But the Lord God was thy servant's hope and he paid no attention to their vanity and lying madness.

[12] Ps. 144:5.

5. Finally, when the hour arrived for him to make a public profession of his faith—which at Rome those who are about to enter into thy grace make from a platform in the full sight of the faithful people, in a set form of words learned by heart—the presbyters offered Victorinus the chance to make his profession more privately, for this was the custom for some who were likely to be afraid through bashfulness. But Victorinus chose rather to profess his salvation in the presence of the holy congregation. For there was no salvation in the rhetoric which he taught: yet he had professed that openly. Why, then, should he shrink from naming thy Word before the sheep of thy flock, when he had not shrunk from uttering his own words before the mad multitude?

So, then, when he ascended the platform to make his profession, everyone, as they recognized him, whispered his name one to the other, in tones of jubilation. Who was there among them that did not know him? And a low murmur ran through the mouths of all the rejoicing multitude: "Victorinus! Victorinus!" There was a sudden burst of exaltation at the sight of him, and suddenly they were hushed that they might hear him. He pronounced the true faith with an excellent boldness, and all desired to take him to their very heart—indeed, by their love and joy they did take him to their heart. And they received him with loving and joyful hands.

CHAPTER III

6. O good God, what happens in a man to make him rejoice more at the salvation of a soul that has been despaired of and then delivered from greater danger than over one who has never lost hope, or never been in such imminent danger? For thou also, O most merciful Father, "dost rejoice more over one that repents than over ninety and nine just persons that need no repentance."[13] And we listen with much delight whenever we hear how the lost sheep is brought home again on the shepherd's shoulders while the angels rejoice; or when the piece of money is restored to its place in the treasury and the neighbors rejoice with the woman who found it.[14] And the joy of the solemn festival of thy house constrains us to tears when it is read in thy house: about the younger son who "was dead and is alive again, was lost and is found." For it is thou who rejoicest both in us and in thy angels, who are holy through holy love.

[13] Luke 15:4.   [14] Cf. Luke, ch. 15.

For thou art ever the same because thou knowest unchangeably all things which remain neither the same nor forever.

7. What, then, happens in the soul when it takes more delight at finding or having restored to it the things it loves than if it had always possessed them? Indeed, many other things bear witness that this is so—all things are full of witnesses, crying out, "So it is." The commander triumphs in victory; yet he could not have conquered if he had not fought; and the greater the peril of the battle, the more the joy of the triumph. The storm tosses the voyagers, threatens shipwreck, and everyone turns pale in the presence of death. Then the sky and sea grow calm, and they rejoice as much as they had feared. A loved one is sick and his pulse indicates danger; all who desire his safety are themselves sick at heart; he recovers, though not able as yet to walk with his former strength; and there is more joy now than there was before when he walked sound and strong. Indeed, the very pleasures of human life—not only those which rush upon us unexpectedly and involuntarily, but also those which are voluntary and planned—men obtain by difficulties. There is no pleasure in eating and drinking unless the pains of hunger and thirst have preceded. Drunkards even eat certain salt meats in order to create a painful thirst—and when the drink allays this, it causes pleasure. It is also the custom that the affianced bride should not be immediately given in marriage so that the husband may not esteem her any less, whom as his betrothed he longed for.

8. This can be seen in the case of base and dishonorable pleasure. But it is also apparent in pleasures that are permitted and lawful: in the sincerity of honest friendship; and in him who was dead and lived again, who had been lost and was found. The greater joy is everywhere preceded by the greater pain. What does this mean, O Lord my God, when thou art an everlasting joy to thyself, and some creatures about thee are ever rejoicing in thee? What does it mean that this portion of creation thus ebbs and flows, alternately in want and satiety? Is this their mode of being and is this all thou hast allotted to them: that, from the highest heaven to the lowest earth, from the beginning of the world to the end, from the angels to the worm, from the first movement to the last, thou wast assigning to all their proper places and their proper seasons—to all the kinds of good things and to all thy just works? Alas, how high thou art in the highest and how deep in the deepest! Thou never departest from us, and yet only with difficulty do we return to thee.

CHAPTER IV

9. Go on, O Lord, and act: stir us up and call us back; inflame us and draw us to thee; stir us up and grow sweet to us; let us now love thee, let us run to thee. Are there not many men who, out of a deeper pit of darkness than that of Victorinus, return to thee—who draw near to thee and are illuminated by that light which gives those who receive it power from thee to become thy sons? But if they are less well-known, even those who know them rejoice less for them. For when many rejoice together the joy of each one is fuller, in that they warm one another, catch fire from each other; moreover, those who are well-known influence many toward salvation and take the lead with many to follow them. Therefore, even those who took the way before them rejoice over them greatly, because they do not rejoice over them alone. But it ought never to be that in thy tabernacle the persons of the rich should be welcome before the poor, or the nobly born before the rest—since "thou hast rather chosen the weak things of the world to confound the strong; and hast chosen the base things of the world and things that are despised, and the things that are not, in order to bring to nought the things that are."[15] It was even "the least of the apostles" by whose tongue thou didst sound forth these words. And when Paulus the proconsul had his pride overcome by the onslaught of the apostle and he was made to pass under the easy yoke of thy Christ and became an officer of the great King, he also desired to be called Paul instead of Saul, his former name, in testimony to such a great victory.[16] For the enemy is more overcome in one on whom he has a greater hold, and whom he has hold of more completely. But the proud he controls more readily through their concern about their rank and, through them, he controls more by means of their influence. The more, therefore, the world prized the heart of Victorinus (which the devil had held in an impregnable stronghold) and the tongue of Victorinus (that sharp, strong weapon with which the devil had slain so many), all the more exultingly should Thy sons rejoice because our King hath bound the strong man, and they saw his vessels taken from him and cleansed, and made fit for thy honor and "profitable to the Lord for every good work."[17]

[15] 1 Cor. 1:27.
[16] A garbled reference to the story of the conversion of Sergius Paulus, proconsul of Cyprus, in Acts 13:4–12.   [17] II Tim. 2:21.

CHAPTER V

10. Now when this man of thine, Simplicianus, told me the story of Victorinus, I was eager to imitate him. Indeed, this was Simplicianus' purpose in telling it to me. But when he went on to tell how, in the reign of the Emperor Julian, there was a law passed by which Christians were forbidden to teach literature and rhetoric; and how Victorinus, in ready obedience to the law, chose to abandon his "school of words" rather than thy Word, by which thou makest eloquent the tongues of the dumb—he appeared to me not so much brave as happy, because he had found a reason for giving his time wholly to thee. For this was what I was longing to do; but as yet I was bound by the iron chain of my own will. The enemy held fast my will, and had made of it a chain, and had bound me tight with it. For out of the perverse will came lust, and the service of lust ended in habit, and habit, not resisted, became necessity. By these links, as it were, forged together—which is why I called it "a chain"—a hard bondage held me in slavery. But that new will which had begun to spring up in me freely to worship thee and to enjoy thee, O my God, the only certain Joy, was not able as yet to overcome my former willfulness, made strong by long indulgence. Thus my two wills—the old and the new, the carnal and the spiritual—were in conflict within me; and by their discord they tore my soul apart.

11. Thus I came to understand from my own experience what I had read, how "the flesh lusts against the Spirit, and the Spirit against the flesh." [18] I truly lusted both ways, yet more in that which I approved in myself than in that which I disapproved in myself. For in the latter it was not now really I that was involved, because here I was rather an unwilling sufferer than a willing actor. And yet it was through me that habit had become an armed enemy against me, because I had willingly come to be what I unwillingly found myself to be.

Who, then, can with any justice speak against it, when just punishment follows the sinner? I had now no longer my accustomed excuse that, as yet, I hesitated to forsake the world and serve thee because my perception of the truth was uncertain. For now it was certain. But, still bound to the earth, I refused to be thy soldier; and was as much afraid of being freed from all entanglements as we ought to fear to be entangled.

[18] Gal. 5:17.

12. Thus with the baggage of the world I was sweetly burdened, as one in slumber, and my musings on thee were like the efforts of those who desire to awake, but who are still overpowered with drowsiness and fall back into deep slumber. And as no one wishes to sleep forever (for all men rightly count waking better)—yet a man will usually defer shaking off his drowsiness when there is a heavy lethargy in his limbs; and he is glad to sleep on even when his reason disapproves, and the hour for rising has struck—so was I assured that it was much better for me to give myself up to thy love than to go on yielding myself to my own lust. Thy love satisfied and vanquished me; my lust pleased and fettered me.[19] I had no answer to thy calling to me, "Awake, you who sleep, and arise from the dead, and Christ shall give you light."[20] On all sides, thou didst show me that thy words are true, and I, convicted by the truth, had nothing at all to reply but the drawling and drowsy words: "Presently; see, presently. Leave me alone a little while." But "presently, presently," had no present; and my "leave me alone a little while" went on for a long while. In vain did I "delight in thy law in the inner man" while "another law in my members warred against the law of my mind and brought me into captivity to the law of sin which is in my members." For the law of sin is the tyranny of habit, by which the mind is drawn and held, even against its will. Yet it deserves to be so held because it so willingly falls into the habit. "O wretched man that I am! Who shall deliver me from the body of this death" but thy grace alone, through Jesus Christ our Lord?[21]

CHAPTER VI

13. And now I will tell and confess unto thy name, O Lord, my helper and my redeemer, how thou didst deliver me from the chain of sexual desire by which I was so tightly held, and from the slavery of worldly business.[22] With increasing anxiety I was going about my usual affairs, and daily sighing to thee. I attended thy church as frequently as my business, under the

19 The text here is a typical example of Augustine's love of wordplay and assonance, as a conscious literary device: *tuae caritati me* dedere *quam meae cupiditati* cedere; *sed illud* placebat *et* vincebat, *hoc* libebat *et* vinciebat.
20 Eph. 5:14.   21 Rom. 7:22–25.
22 The last obstacles that remained. His intellectual difficulties had been cleared away and the intention to become a Christian had become strong. But incontinence and immersion in his career were too firmly fixed in habit to be overcome by an act of conscious resolution.

burden of which I groaned, left me free to do so. Alypius was with me, disengaged at last from his legal post, after a third term as assessor, and now waiting for private clients to whom he might sell his legal advice as I sold the power of speaking (as if it could be supplied by teaching). But Nebridius had consented, for the sake of our friendship, to teach under Verecundus—a citizen of Milan and professor of grammar, and a very intimate friend of us all—who ardently desired, and by right of friendship demanded from us, the faithful aid he greatly needed. Nebridius was not drawn to this by any desire of gain—for he could have made much more out of his learning had he been so inclined—but as he was a most sweet and kindly friend, he was unwilling, out of respect for the duties of friendship, to slight our request. But in this he acted very discreetly, taking care not to become known to those persons who had great reputations in the world. Thus he avoided all distractions of mind, and reserved as many hours as possible to pursue or read or listen to discussions about wisdom.

14. On a certain day, then, when Nebridius was away—for some reason I cannot remember—there came to visit Alypius and me at our house one Ponticianus, a fellow countryman of ours from Africa, who held high office in the emperor's court. What he wanted with us I do not know; but we sat down to talk together, and it chanced that he noticed a book on a game table before us. He took it up, opened it, and, contrary to his expectation, found it to be the apostle Paul, for he imagined that it was one of my wearisome rhetoric textbooks. At this, he looked up at me with a smile and expressed his delight and wonder that he had so unexpectedly found this book and only this one, lying before my eyes; for he was indeed a Christian and a faithful one at that, and often he prostrated himself before thee, our God, in the church in constant daily prayer. When I had told him that I had given much attention to these writings, a conversation followed in which he spoke of Anthony, the Egyptian monk, whose name was in high repute among thy servants, although up to that time not familiar to me. When he learned this, he lingered on the topic, giving us an account of this eminent man, and marveling at our ignorance. We in turn were amazed to hear of thy wonderful works so fully manifested in recent times—almost in our own—occurring in the true faith and the Catholic Church. We all wondered—we, that these things were so great, and he, that we had never heard of them.

15. From this, his conversation turned to the multitudes in

the monasteries and their manners so fragrant to thee, and to the teeming solitudes of the wilderness, of which we knew nothing at all. There was even a monastery at Milan, outside the city's walls, full of good brothers under the fostering care of Ambrose —and we were ignorant of it. He went on with his story, and we listened intently and in silence. He then told us how, on a certain afternoon, at Trier,[23] when the emperor was occupied watching the gladiatorial games, he and three comrades went out for a walk in the gardens close to the city walls. There, as they chanced to walk two by two, one strolled away with him, while the other two went on by themselves. As they rambled, these first two came upon a certain cottage where lived some of thy servants, some of the "poor in spirit" ("of such is the Kingdom of Heaven"), where they found the book in which was written the life of Anthony! One of them began to read it, to marvel and to be inflamed by it. While reading, he meditated on embracing just such a life, giving up his worldly employment to seek thee alone. These two belonged to the group of officials called "secret service agents."[24] Then, suddenly being overwhelmed with a holy love and a sober shame and as if in anger with himself, he fixed his eyes on his friend, exclaiming: "Tell me, I beg you, what goal are we seeking in all these toils of ours? What is it that we desire? What is our motive in public service? Can our hopes in the court rise higher than to be 'friends of the emperor'[25]? But how frail, how beset with peril, is that pride! Through what dangers must we climb to a greater danger? And when shall we succeed? But if I chose to become a friend of God, see, I can become one now." Thus he spoke, and in the pangs of the travail of the new life he turned his eyes again onto the page and continued reading; he was inwardly changed, as thou didst see, and the world dropped away from his mind, as soon became plain to others. For as he read with a heart like a stormy sea, more than once he groaned. Finally he saw the better course, and resolved on it. Then, having become thy servant,

---

23 Trèves, an important imperial town on the Moselle; the emperor referred to here was probably Gratian. Cf. E. A. Freeman, "Augusta Trevororum," in the *British Quarterly Review* (1875), 62, pp. 1–45.

24 *Agentes in rebus*, government agents whose duties ranged from postal inspection and tax collection to espionage and secret police work. They were ubiquitous and generally dreaded by the populace; cf. J. S. Reid, "Reorganization of the Empire," in *Cambridge Medieval History*, Vol. I, pp. 36–38.

25 The inner circle of imperial advisers; usually rather informally appointed and usually with precarious tenure.

he said to his friend: "Now I have broken loose from those hopes we had, and I am determined to serve God; and I enter into that service from this hour in this place. If you are reluctant to imitate me, do not oppose me." The other replied that he would continue bound in his friendship, to share in so great a service for so great a prize. So both became thine, and began to "build a tower", counting the cost—namely, of forsaking all that they had and following thee.[26] Shortly after, Ponticianus and his companion, who had walked with him in the other part of the garden, came in search of them to the same place, and having found them reminded them to return, as the day was declining. But the first two, making known to Ponticianus their resolution and purpose, and how a resolve had sprung up and become confirmed in them, entreated them not to take it ill if they refused to join themselves with them. But Ponticianus and his friend, although not changed from their former course, did nevertheless (as he told us) bewail themselves and congratulated their friends on their godliness, recommending themselves to their prayers. And with hearts inclining again toward earthly things, they returned to the palace. But the other two, setting their affections on heavenly things, remained in the cottage. Both of them had affianced brides who, when they heard of this, likewise dedicated their virginity to thee.

CHAPTER VII

16. Such was the story Ponticianus told. But while he was speaking, thou, O Lord, turned me toward myself, taking me from behind my back, where I had put myself while unwilling to exercise self-scrutiny. And now thou didst set me face to face with myself, that I might see how ugly I was, and how crooked and sordid, bespotted and ulcerous. And I looked and I loathed myself; but whither to fly from myself I could not discover. And if I sought to turn my gaze away from myself, he would continue his narrative, and thou wouldst oppose me to myself and thrust me before my own eyes that I might discover my iniquity and hate it. I had known it, but acted as though I knew it not—I winked at it and forgot it.

17. But now, the more ardently I loved those whose wholesome affections I heard reported—that they had given themselves up wholly to thee to be cured—the more did I abhor myself when compared with them. For many of my years—

[26] Cf. Luke 14:28–33.

perhaps twelve—had passed away since my nineteenth, when, upon the reading of Cicero's *Hortensius*, I was roused to a desire for wisdom. And here I was, still postponing the abandonment of this world's happiness to devote myself to the search. For not just the finding alone, but also the bare search for it, ought to have been preferred above the treasures and kingdoms of this world; better than all bodily pleasures, though they were to be had for the taking. But, wretched youth that I was—supremely wretched even in the very outset of my youth—I had entreated chastity of thee and had prayed, "Grant me chastity and continence, but not yet." For I was afraid lest thou shouldst hear me too soon, and too soon cure me of my disease of lust which I desired to have satisfied rather than extinguished. And I had wandered through perverse ways of godless superstition—not really sure of it, either, but preferring it to the other, which I did not seek in piety, but opposed in malice.

18. And I had thought that I delayed from day to day in rejecting those worldly hopes and following thee alone because there did not appear anything certain by which I could direct my course. And now the day had arrived in which I was laid bare to myself and my conscience was to chide me: "Where are you, O my tongue? You said indeed that you were not willing to cast off the baggage of vanity for uncertain truth. But behold now it is certain, and still that burden oppresses you. At the same time those who have not worn themselves out with searching for it as you have, nor spent ten years and more in thinking about it, have had their shoulders unburdened and have received wings to fly away." Thus was I inwardly confused, and mightily confounded with a horrible shame, while Ponticianus went ahead speaking such things. And when he had finished his story and the business he came for, he went his way. And then what did I not say to myself, within myself? With what scourges of rebuke did I not lash my soul to make it follow me, as I was struggling to go after thee? Yet it drew back. It refused. It would not make an effort. All its arguments were exhausted and confuted. Yet it resisted in sullen disquiet, fearing the cutting off of that habit by which it was being wasted to death, as if that were death itself.

CHAPTER VIII

19. Then, as this vehement quarrel, which I waged with my soul in the chamber of my heart, was raging inside my inner

dwelling, agitated both in mind and countenance, I seized upon Alypius and exclaimed: "What is the matter with us? What is this? What did you hear? The uninstructed start up and take heaven, and we—with all our learning but so little heart—see where we wallow in flesh and blood! Because others have gone before us, are we ashamed to follow, and not rather ashamed at our not following?" I scarcely knew what I said, and in my excitement I flung away from him, while he gazed at me in silent astonishment. For I did not sound like myself: my face, eyes, color, tone expressed my meaning more clearly than my words.

There was a little garden belonging to our lodging, of which we had the use—as of the whole house—for the master, our landlord, did not live there. The tempest in my breast hurried me out into this garden, where no one might interrupt the fiery struggle in which I was engaged with myself, until it came to the outcome that thou knewest though I did not. But I was mad for health, and dying for life; knowing what evil thing I was, but not knowing what good thing I was so shortly to become.

I fled into the garden, with Alypius following step by step; for I had no secret in which he did not share, and how could he leave me in such distress? We sat down, as far from the house as possible. I was greatly disturbed in spirit, angry at myself with a turbulent indignation because I had not entered thy will and covenant, O my God, while all my bones cried out to me to enter, extolling it to the skies. The way therein is not by ships or chariots or feet—indeed it was not as far as I had come from the house to the place where we were seated. For to go along that road and indeed to reach the goal is nothing else but the will to go. But it must be a strong and single will, not staggering and swaying about this way and that—a changeable, twisting, fluctuating will, wrestling with itself while one part falls as another rises.

20. Finally, in the very fever of my indecision, I made many motions with my body; like men do when they will to act but cannot, either because they do not have the limbs or because their limbs are bound or weakened by disease, or incapacitated in some other way. Thus if I tore my hair, struck my forehead, or, entwining my fingers, clasped my knee, these I did because I willed it. But I might have willed it and still not have done it, if the nerves had not obeyed my will. Many things then I did, in which the will and power to do were not the same. Yet I did not do that one thing which seemed to me infinitely more

desirable, which before long I should have power to will because shortly when I willed, I would will with a single will. For
in this, the power of willing is the power of doing; and as yet I
could not do it. Thus my body more readily obeyed the slightest
wish of the soul in moving its limbs at the order of my mind
than my soul obeyed itself to accomplish in the will alone its
great resolve.

CHAPTER IX

21. How can there be such a strange anomaly? And why is
it? Let thy mercy shine on me, that I may inquire and find an
answer, amid the dark labyrinth of human punishment and in
the darkest contritions of the sons of Adam. Whence such an
anomaly? And why should it be? The mind commands the body,
and the body obeys. The mind commands itself and is resisted.
The mind commands the hand to be moved and there is such
readiness that the command is scarcely distinguished from the
obedience in act. Yet the mind is mind, and the hand is body.
The mind commands the mind to will, and yet though it be
itself it does not obey itself. Whence this strange anomaly and
why should it be? I repeat: The will commands itself to will, and
could not give the command unless it wills; yet what is commanded is not done. But actually the will does not will entirely;
therefore it does not command entirely. For as far as it wills, it
commands. And as far as it does not will, the thing commanded
is not done. For the will commands that there be an act of
will—not another, but itself. But it does not command entirely.
Therefore, what is commanded does not happen; for if the will
were whole and entire, it would not even command it to be,
because it would already be. It is, therefore, no strange anomaly
partly to will and partly to be unwilling. This is actually an
infirmity of mind, which cannot wholly rise, while pressed down
by habit, even though it is supported by the truth. And so there
are two wills, because one of them is not whole, and what is
present in this one is lacking in the other.

CHAPTER X

22. Let them perish from thy presence, O God, as vain talkers
and deceivers of the soul perish, who, when they observe that
there are two wills in the act of deliberation, go on to affirm that
there are two kinds of minds in us: one good, the other evil.
They are indeed themselves evil when they hold these evil

opinions—and they shall become good only when they come to hold the truth and consent to the truth that thy apostle may say to them: "You were formerly in darkness, but now are you in the light in the Lord." [27] But they desired to be light, not "in the Lord," but in themselves. They conceived the nature of the soul to be the same as what God is, and thus have become a thicker darkness than they were; for in their dread arrogance they have gone farther away from thee, from thee "the true Light, that lights every man that comes into the world." Mark what you say and blush for shame; draw near to him and be enlightened, and your faces shall not be ashamed. [28]

While I was deliberating whether I would serve the Lord my God now, as I had long purposed to do, it was I who willed and it was also I who was unwilling. In either case, it was I. I neither willed with my whole will nor was I wholly unwilling. And so I was at war with myself and torn apart by myself. And this strife was against my will; yet it did not show the presence of another mind, but the punishment of my own. Thus it was no more I who did it, but the sin that dwelt in me—the punishment of a sin freely committed by Adam, and I was a son of Adam.

23. For if there are as many opposing natures as there are opposing wills, there will not be two but many more. If any man is trying to decide whether he should go to their conventicle or to the theater, the Manicheans at once cry out, "See, here are two natures—one good, drawing this way, another bad, drawing back that way; for how else can you explain this indecision between conflicting wills?" But I reply that both impulses are bad—that which draws to them and that which draws back to the theater. But they do not believe that the will which draws to them can be anything but good. Suppose, then, that one of us should try to decide, and through the conflict of his two wills should waver whether he should go to the theater or to our church. Would not those also waver about the answer here? For either they must confess, which they are unwilling to do, that the will that leads to our church is as good as that which carries their own adherents and those captivated by their mysteries; or else they must imagine that there are two evil natures and two evil minds in one man, both at war with each other, and then it will not be true what they say, that there is one good and another bad. Else they must be converted to the truth, and no longer deny that when anyone deliberates there is one soul fluctuating between conflicting wills.

[27] Eph. 5:8.   [28] Cf. Ps. 34:5.

24. Let them no longer maintain that when they perceive two wills to be contending with each other in the same man the contest is between two opposing minds, of two opposing substances, from two opposing principles, the one good and the other bad. Thus, O true God, thou dost reprove and confute and convict them. For both wills may be bad: as when a man tries to decide whether he should kill a man by poison or by the sword; whether he should take possession of this field or that one belonging to someone else, when he cannot get both; whether he should squander his money to buy pleasure or hold onto his money through the motive of covetousness; whether he should go to the circus or to the theater, if both are open on the same day; or, whether he should take a third course, open at the same time, and rob another man's house; or, a fourth option, whether he should commit adultery, if he has the opportunity—all these things concurring in the same space of time and all being equally longed for, although impossible to do at one time. For the mind is pulled four ways by four antagonistic wills—or even more, in view of the vast range of human desires—but even the Manicheans do not affirm that there are these many different substances. The same principle applies as in the action of good wills. For I ask them, "Is it a good thing to have delight in reading the apostle, or is it a good thing to delight in a sober psalm, or is it a good thing to discourse on the gospel?" To each of these, they will answer, "It is good." But what, then, if all delight us equally and all at the same time? Do not different wills distract the mind when a man is trying to decide what he should choose? Yet they are all good, and are at variance with each other until one is chosen. When this is done the whole united will may go forward on a single track instead of remaining as it was before, divided in many ways. So also, when eternity attracts us from above, and the pleasure of earthly delight pulls us down from below, the soul does not will either the one or the other with all its force, but still it is the same soul that does not will this or that with a united will, and is therefore pulled apart with grievous perplexities, because for truth's sake it prefers this, but for custom's sake it does not lay that aside.

CHAPTER XI

25. Thus I was sick and tormented, reproaching myself more bitterly than ever, rolling and writhing in my chain till it should be utterly broken. By now I was held but slightly, but still was

held. And thou, O Lord, didst press upon me in my inmost heart with a severe mercy, redoubling the lashes of fear and shame; lest I should again give way and that same slender remaining tie not be broken off, but recover strength and enchain me yet more securely.

I kept saying to myself, "See, let it be done now; let it be done now." And as I said this I all but came to a firm decision. I all but did it—yet I did not quite. Still I did not fall back to my old condition, but stood aside for a moment and drew breath. And I tried again, and lacked only a very little of reaching the resolve—and then somewhat less, and then all but touched and grasped it. Yet I still did not quite reach or touch or grasp the goal, because I hesitated to die to death and to live to life. And the worse way, to which I was habituated, was stronger in me than the better, which I had not tried. And up to the very moment in which I was to become another man, the nearer the moment approached, the greater horror did it strike in me. But it did not strike me back, nor turn me aside, but held me in suspense.

26. It was, in fact, my old mistresses, trifles of trifles and vanities of vanities, who still enthralled me. They tugged at my fleshly garments and softly whispered: "Are you going to part with us? And from that moment will we never be with you any more? And from that moment will not this and that be forbidden you forever?" What were they suggesting to me in those words "this or that"? What is it they suggested, O my God? Let thy mercy guard the soul of thy servant from the vileness and the shame they did suggest! And now I scarcely heard them, for they were not openly showing themselves and opposing me face to face; but muttering, as it were, behind my back; and furtively plucking at me as I was leaving, trying to make me look back at them. Still they delayed me, so that I hesitated to break loose and shake myself free of them and leap over to the place to which I was being called—for unruly habit kept saying to me, "Do you think you can live without them?"

27. But now it said this very faintly; for in the direction I had set my face, and yet toward which I still trembled to go, the chaste dignity of continence appeared to me—cheerful but not wanton, modestly alluring me to come and doubt nothing, extending her holy hands, full of a multitude of good examples —to receive and embrace me. There were there so many young men and maidens, a multitude of youth and every age, grave widows and ancient virgins; and continence herself in their

midst: not barren, but a fruitful mother of children—her joys—
by thee, O Lord, her husband. And she smiled on me with a
challenging smile as if to say: "Can you not do what these young
men and maidens can? Or can any of them do it of themselves,
and not rather in the Lord their God? The Lord their God gave
me to them. Why do you stand in your own strength, and so
stand not? Cast yourself on him; fear not. He will not flinch and
you will not fall. Cast yourself on him without fear, for he will
receive and heal you." And I blushed violently, for I still heard
the muttering of those "trifles" and hung suspended. Again she
seemed to speak: "Stop your ears against those unclean members of yours, that they may be mortified. They tell you of
delights, but not according to the law of the Lord thy God."
This struggle raging in my heart was nothing but the contest of
self against self. And Alypius kept close beside me, and awaited
in silence the outcome of my extraordinary agitation.

CHAPTER XII

28. Now when deep reflection had drawn up out of the secret
depths of my soul all my misery and had heaped it up before the
sight of my heart, there arose a mighty storm, accompanied by
a mighty rain of tears. That I might give way fully to my tears
and lamentations, I stole away from Alypius, for it seemed
to me that solitude was more appropriate for the business of
weeping. I went far enough away that I could feel that even his
presence was no restraint upon me. This was the way I felt at the
time, and he realized it. I suppose I had said something before
I started up and he noticed that the sound of my voice was
choked with weeping. And so he stayed alone, where we had
been sitting together, greatly astonished. I flung myself down
under a fig tree—how I know not—and gave free course to my
tears. The streams of my eyes gushed out an acceptable sacrifice
to thee. And, not indeed in these words, but to this effect, I
cried to thee: "And thou, O Lord, how long? How long, O
Lord? Wilt thou be angry forever? Oh, remember not against
us our former iniquities." [29] For I felt that I was still enthralled
by them. I sent up these sorrowful cries: "How long, how
long? Tomorrow and tomorrow? Why not now? Why not this
very hour make an end to my uncleanness?"

29. I was saying these things and weeping in the most bitter
contrition of my heart, when suddenly I heard the voice of a

[29] Cf. Ps. 6:3; 79:8.

boy or a girl—I know not which—coming from the neighboring house, chanting over and over again, "Pick it up, read it; pick it up, read it." [30] Immediately I ceased weeping and began most earnestly to think whether it was usual for children in some kind of game to sing such a song, but I could not remember ever having heard the like. So, damming the torrent of my tears, I got to my feet, for I could not but think that this was a divine command to open the Bible and read the first passage I should light upon. For I had heard [31] how Anthony, accidentally coming into church while the gospel was being read, received the admonition as if what was read had been addressed to him: "Go and sell what you have and give it to the poor, and you shall have treasure in heaven; and come and follow me." [32] By such an oracle he was forthwith converted to thee.

So I quickly returned to the bench where Alypius was sitting, for there I had put down the apostle's book when I had left there. I snatched it up, opened it, and in silence read the paragraph on which my eyes first fell: "Not in rioting and drunkenness, not in chambering and wantonness, not in strife and envying, but put on the Lord Jesus Christ, and make no provision for the flesh to fulfill the lusts thereof." [33] I wanted to read no further, nor did I need to. For instantly, as the sentence ended, there was infused in my heart something like the light of full certainty and all the gloom of doubt vanished away. [34]

30. Closing the book, then, and putting my finger or something else for a mark I began—now with a tranquil countenance—to tell it all to Alypius. And he in turn disclosed to me what had been going on in himself, of which I knew nothing. He asked to see what I had read. I showed him, and he looked on even further than I had read. I had not known what followed. But indeed it was this, "Him that is weak in the faith, receive." [35] This he applied to himself, and told me so. By these words of warning he was strengthened, and by exercising his good resolution and purpose—all very much in keeping with his character, in which, in these respects, he was always far different from and better than I—he joined me in full commitment without any restless hesitation.

Then we went in to my mother, and told her what happened,

---

[30] This is the famous *Tolle, lege; tolle, lege.*
[31] Doubtless from Ponticianus, in their earlier conversation.
[32] Matt. 19:21.   [33] Rom. 13:13.
[34] Note the parallels here to the conversion of Anthony and the *agentes in rebus.*   [35] Rom. 14:1.

to her great joy. We explained to her how it had occurred—and she leaped for joy triumphant; and she blessed thee, who art "able to do exceedingly abundantly above all that we ask or think." [36] For she saw that thou hadst granted her far more than she had ever asked for in all her pitiful and doleful lamentations. For thou didst so convert me to thee that I sought neither a wife nor any other of this world's hopes, but set my feet on that rule of faith which so many years before thou hadst showed her in her dream about me. And so thou didst turn her grief into gladness more plentiful than she had ventured to desire, and dearer and purer than the desire she used to cherish of having grandchildren of my flesh.

[36] Eph. 3:20.

BOOK NINE

The end of the autobiography. Augustine tells of his resigning from his professorship and of the days at Cassiciacum in preparation for baptism. He is baptized together with Adeodatus and Alypius. Shortly thereafter, they start back for Africa. Augustine recalls the ecstasy he and his mother shared in Ostia and then reports her death and burial and his grief. The book closes with a moving prayer for the souls of Monica, Patricius, and all his fellow citizens of the heavenly Jerusalem.

CHAPTER I

1. "O Lord, I am thy servant; I am thy servant and the son of thy handmaid. Thou hast loosed my bonds. I will offer to thee the sacrifice of thanksgiving." [1] Let my heart and my tongue praise thee, and let all my bones say, "Lord, who is like unto thee?" Let them say so, and answer thou me and say unto my soul, "I am your salvation."

Who am I, and what is my nature? What evil is there not in me and my deeds; or if not in my deeds, my words; or if not in my words, my will? But thou, O Lord, art good and merciful, and thy right hand didst reach into the depth of my death and didst empty out the abyss of corruption from the bottom of my heart. And this was the result: now I did not will to do what I willed, and began to will to do what thou didst will.

But where was my free will during all those years and from what deep and secret retreat was it called forth in a single moment, whereby I gave my neck to thy "easy yoke" and my shoulders to thy "light burden," O Christ Jesus, "my Strength and my Redeemer"? How sweet did it suddenly become to me

[1] Ps. 116:16, 17.

to be without the sweetness of trifles! And it was now a joy to put away what I formerly feared to lose. For thou didst cast them away from me, O true and highest Sweetness. Thou didst cast them away, and in their place thou didst enter in thyself— sweeter than all pleasure, though not to flesh and blood; brighter than all light, but more veiled than all mystery; more exalted than all honor, though not to them that are exalted in their own eyes. Now was my soul free from the gnawing cares of seeking and getting, of wallowing in the mire and scratching the itch of lust. And I prattled like a child to thee, O Lord my God—my light, my riches, and my salvation.

CHAPTER II

2. And it seemed right to me, in thy sight, not to snatch my tongue's service abruptly out of the speech market, but to withdraw quietly, so that the young men who were not concerned about thy law or thy peace, but with mendacious follies and forensic strifes, might no longer purchase from my mouth weapons for their frenzy. Fortunately, there were only a few days before the "vintage vacation" [2]; and I determined to endure them, so that I might resign in due form and, now bought by thee, return for sale no more.

My plan was known to thee, but, save for my own friends, it was not known to other men. For we had agreed that it should not be made public; although, in our ascent from the "valley of tears" and our singing of "the song of degrees," thou hadst given us sharp arrows and hot burning coals to stop that deceitful tongue which opposes under the guise of good counsel, and devours what it loves as though it were food.

3. Thou hadst pierced our heart with thy love, and we carried thy words, as it were, thrust through our vitals. The examples of thy servants whom thou hadst changed from black to shining white, and from death to life, crowded into the bosom of our thoughts and burned and consumed our sluggish temper, that we might not topple back into the abyss. And they fired us exceedingly, so that every breath of the deceitful tongue of our detractors might fan the flame and not blow it out.

Though this vow and purpose of ours should find those who would loudly praise it—for the sake of thy name, which thou hast sanctified throughout the earth—it nevertheless looked like a self-vaunting not to wait until the vacation time now so near.

2 An imperial holiday season, from late August to the middle of October.

For if I had left such a public office ahead of time, and had made the break in the eye of the general public, all who took notice of this act of mine and observed how near was the vintage time that I wished to anticipate would have talked about me a great deal, as if I were trying to appear a great person. And what purpose would it serve that people should consider and dispute about my conversion so that my good should be evil spoken of?

4. Furthermore, this same summer my lungs had begun to be weak from too much literary labor. Breathing was difficult; the pains in my chest showed that the lungs were affected and were soon fatigued by too loud or prolonged speaking. This had at first been a trial to me, for it would have compelled me almost of necessity to lay down that burden of teaching; or, if I was to be cured and become strong again, at least to take a leave for a while. But as soon as the full desire to be still that I might know that thou art the Lord [3] arose and was confirmed in me, thou knowest, my God, that I began to rejoice that I had this excuse ready—and not a feigned one, either—which might somewhat temper the displeasure of those who for their sons' freedom wished me never to have any freedom of my own.

Full of joy, then, I bore it until my time ran out—it was perhaps some twenty days—yet it was some strain to go through with it, for the greediness which helped to support the drudgery had gone, and I would have been overwhelmed had not its place been taken by patience. Some of thy servants, my brethren, may say that I sinned in this, since having once fully and from my heart enlisted in thy service, I permitted myself to sit a single hour in the chair of falsehood. I will not dispute it. But hast thou not, O most merciful Lord, pardoned and forgiven this sin in the holy water [4] also, along with all the others, horrible and deadly as they were?

CHAPTER III

5. Verecundus was severely disturbed by this new happiness of mine, since he was still firmly held by his bonds and saw that he would lose my companionship. For he was not yet a Christian, though his wife was; and, indeed, he was more firmly enchained by her than by anything else, and held back from that journey on which we had set out. Furthermore, he declared he did not wish to be a Christian on any terms except those that were impossible. However, he invited us most courteously to make use

[3] Cf. Ps. 46:10.   [4] His subsequent baptism; see below, Ch. VI.

of his country house so long as we would stay there. O Lord, thou wilt recompense him for this "in the resurrection of the just," [5] seeing that thou hast already given him "the lot of the righteous." [6] For while we were absent at Rome, he was overtaken with bodily sickness, and during it he was made a Christian and departed this life as one of the faithful. Thus thou hadst mercy on him, and not on him only, but on us as well; lest, remembering the exceeding kindness of our friend to us and not able to count him in thy flock, we should be tortured with intolerable grief. Thanks be unto thee, our God; we are thine. Thy exhortations, consolations, and faithful promises assure us that thou wilt repay Verecundus for that country house at Cassiciacum—where we found rest in thee from the fever of the world—with the perpetual freshness of thy paradise in which thou hast forgiven him his earthly sins, in that mountain flowing with milk, that fruitful mountain—thy own.

6. Thus Verecundus was full of grief; but Nebridius was joyous. For he was not yet a Christian, and had fallen into the pit of deadly error, believing that the flesh of thy Son, the Truth, was a phantom. [7] Yet he had come up out of that pit and now held the same belief that we did. And though he was not as yet initiated in any of the sacraments of thy Church, he was a most earnest inquirer after truth. Not long after our conversion and regeneration by thy baptism, he also became a faithful member of the Catholic Church, serving thee in perfect chastity and continence among his own people in Africa, and bringing his whole household with him to Christianity. Then thou didst release him from the flesh, and now he lives in Abraham's bosom. Whatever is signified by that term "bosom," there lives my Nebridius, my sweet friend, thy son by adoption, O Lord, and not a freedman any longer. There he lives; for what other place could there be for such a soul? There he lives in that abode about which he used to ask me so many questions—poor ignorant one that I was. Now he does not put his ear up to my mouth, but his spiritual mouth to thy fountain, and drinks wisdom as he desires and as he is able—happy without end. But I do not believe that he is so inebriated by that draught as to forget me; since thou, O Lord, who art the draught, art mindful of us.

Thus, then, we were comforting the unhappy Verecundus—

[5] Luke 14:14.   [6] Ps. 125:3.
[7] The heresy of Docetism, one of the earliest and most persistent of all Christological errors.

our friendship untouched—reconciling him to our conversion and exhorting him to a faith fit for his condition (that is, to his being married). We tarried for Nebridius to follow us, since he was so close, and this he was just about to do when at last the interim ended. The days had seemed long and many because of my eagerness for leisure and liberty in which I might sing to thee from my inmost part, "My heart has said to thee, I have sought thy face; thy face, O Lord, will I seek." [8]

CHAPTER IV

7. Finally the day came on which I was actually to be relieved from the professorship of rhetoric, from which I had already been released in intention. And it was done. And thou didst deliver my tongue as thou hadst already delivered my heart; and I blessed thee for it with great joy, and retired with my friends to the villa. [9] My books testify to what I got done there in writing, which was now hopefully devoted to thy service; though in this pause it was still as if I were panting from my exertions in the school of pride. [10] These were the books in which I engaged in dialogue with my friends, and also those in soliloquy before thee alone. [11] And there are my letters to Nebridius, who was still absent. [12]

When would there be enough time to recount all thy great blessings which thou didst bestow on us in that time, especially as I am hastening on to still greater mercies? For my memory recalls them to me and it is pleasant to confess them to thee, O Lord: the inward goads by which thou didst subdue me and how thou broughtest me low, leveling the mountains and hills of my thoughts, straightening my crookedness, and smoothing my rough ways. And I remember by what means thou also didst subdue Alypius, my heart's brother, to the name of thy

[8] Cf. Ps. 27:8.

[9] The group included Monica, Adeodatus (Augustine's fifteen-year-old son), Navigius (Augustine's brother), Rusticus and Fastidianus (relatives), Alypius, Trygetius, and Licentius (former pupils).

[10] A somewhat oblique acknowledgment of the fact that none of the Cassiciacum dialogues has any distinctive or substantial Christian content. This has often been pointed to as evidence that Augustine's conversion thus far had brought him no farther than to a kind of Christian Platonism; cf. P. Alfaric, L'Évolution intellectuelle de Saint Augustin (Paris, 1918).

[11] The dialogues written during this stay at Cassiciacum: Contra Academicos, De beata vita, De ordine, Soliloquia. See, in this series, Vol. VI, pp. 17–63, for an English translation of the Soliloquies.

[12] Cf. Epistles II and III.

only Son, our Lord and Saviour Jesus Christ—which he at first refused to have inserted in our writings. For at first he preferred that they should smell of the cedars of the schools[13] which the Lord hath now broken down, rather than of the wholesome herbs of the Church, hostile to serpents.[14]

8. O my God, how did I cry to thee when I read the psalms of David, those hymns of faith, those paeans of devotion which leave no room for swelling pride! I was still a novice in thy true love, a catechumen keeping holiday at the villa, with Alypius, a catechumen like myself. My mother was also with us—in woman's garb, but with a man's faith, with the peacefulness of age and the fullness of motherly love and Christian piety. What cries I used to send up to thee in those songs, and how I was enkindled toward thee by them! I burned to sing them if possible, throughout the whole world, against the pride of the human race. And yet, indeed, they are sung throughout the whole world, and none can hide himself from thy heat. With what strong and bitter regret was I indignant at the Manicheans! Yet I also pitied them; for they were ignorant of those sacraments, those medicines[15]—and raved insanely against the cure that might have made them sane! I wished they could have been somewhere close by, and—without my knowledge— could have seen my face and heard my words when, in that time of leisure, I pored over the Fourth Psalm. And I wish they could have seen how that psalm affected me.[16] "When I called upon thee, O God of my righteousness, thou didst hear me; thou didst enlarge me when I was in distress. Have mercy upon me and hear my prayer." I wish they might have heard what I said in comment on those words—without my knowing that they heard, lest they should think that I was speaking it just on their account. For, indeed, I should not have said quite the same things, nor quite in the same way, if I had known that I was heard and seen by them. And if I had so spoken, they would not have meant the same things to them as they did to me when I spoke by and for myself before thee, out of the private affections of my soul.

9. By turns I trembled with fear and warmed with hope and

13 A symbolic reference to the "cedars of Lebanon"; cf. Isa. 2:12–14; Ps. 29:5.
14 There is perhaps a remote connection here with Luke 10:18–20.
15 Ever since the time of Ignatius of Antioch who referred to the Eucharist as "the medicine of immortality," this had been a popular metaphor to refer to the sacraments; cf. Ignatius, *Ephesians* 20:2.
16 Here follows (8–11) a brief devotional commentary on Ps. 4.

rejoiced in thy mercy, O Father. And all these feelings showed forth in my eyes and voice when thy good Spirit turned to us and said, "O sons of men, how long will you be slow of heart, how long will you love vanity, and seek after falsehood?" For I had loved vanity and sought after falsehood. And thou, O Lord, had already magnified thy Holy One, raising him from the dead and setting him at thy right hand, that thence he should send forth from on high his promised "Paraclete, the Spirit of Truth." Already he had sent him, and I knew it not. He had sent him because he was now magnified, rising from the dead and ascending into heaven. For till then "the Holy Spirit was not yet given, because Jesus was not yet glorified."[17] And the prophet cried out: "How long will you be slow of heart? How long will you love vanity, and seek after falsehood? Know this, that the Lord hath magnified his Holy One." He cries, "How long?" He cries, "Know this," and I—so long "loving vanity, and seeking after falsehood"—heard and trembled, because these words were spoken to such a one as I remembered that I myself had been. For in those phantoms which I once held for truth there was vanity and falsehood. And I spoke many things loudly and earnestly—in the contrition of my memory —which I wish they had heard, who still "love vanity and seek after falsehood." Perhaps they would have been troubled, and have vomited up their error, and thou wouldst have heard them when they cried to thee; for by a real death in the flesh He died for us who now maketh intercession for us with thee.

10. I read on further, "Be angry, and sin not." And how deeply was I touched, O my God; for I had now learned to be angry with myself for the things past, so that in the future I might not sin. Yes, to be angry with good cause, for it was not another nature out of the race of darkness that had sinned for me—as they affirm who are not angry with themselves, and who store up for themselves dire wrath against the day of wrath and the revelation of thy righteous judgment. Nor were the good things I saw now outside me, nor were they to be seen with the eyes of flesh in the light of the earthly sun. For they that have their joys from without sink easily into emptiness and are spilled out on those things that are visible and temporal, and in their starving thoughts they lick their very shadows. If only they would grow weary with their hunger and would say, "Who will show us any good?" And we would answer, and they would hear, "O Lord, the light of thy countenance shines bright upon

[17] John 7:39.

us." For we are not that Light that enlightens every man, but we are enlightened by thee, so that we who were formerly in darkness may now be alight in thee. If only they could behold the inner Light Eternal which, now that I had tasted it, I gnashed my teeth because I could not show it to them unless they brought me their heart in their eyes—their roving eyes— and said, "Who will show us any good?" But even there, in the inner chamber of my soul—where I was angry with myself; where I was inwardly pricked, where I had offered my sacrifice, slaying my old man, and hoping in thee with the new resolve of a new life with my trust laid in thee—even there thou hadst begun to grow sweet to me and to "put gladness in my heart." And thus as I read all this, I cried aloud and felt its inward meaning. Nor did I wish to be increased in worldly goods which are wasted by time, for now I possessed, in thy eternal simplicity, other corn and wine and oil.

11. And with a loud cry from my heart, I read the following verse: "Oh, in peace! Oh, in the Selfsame!"[18] See how he says it: "I will lay me down and take my rest."[19] For who shall withstand us when the truth of this saying that is written is made manifest: "Death is swallowed up in victory"[20]? For surely thou, who dost not change, art the Selfsame, and in thee is rest and oblivion to all distress. There is none other beside thee, nor are we to toil for those many things which are not thee, for only thou, O Lord, makest me to dwell in hope."

These things I read and was enkindled—but still I could not discover what to do with those deaf and dead Manicheans to whom I myself had belonged; for I had been a bitter and blind reviler against these writings, honeyed with the honey of heaven and luminous with thy light. And I was sorely grieved at these enemies of this Scripture.

12. When shall I call to mind all that happened during those holidays? I have not forgotten them; nor will I be silent about the severity of thy scourge, and the amazing quickness of thy mercy. During that time thou didst torture me with a toothache; and when it had become so acute that I was not able to speak, it came into my heart to urge all my friends who were present to pray for me to thee, the God of all health. And I wrote it down on the tablet and gave it to them to read. Presently, as we bowed our knees in supplication, the pain was gone. But what pain? How did it go? I confess that I was terrified, O Lord

---

18 *Idipsum*—the oneness and immutability of God.
19 Cf. v. 9.   20 I Cor. 15:54.

my God, because from my earliest years I had never experienced such pain. And thy purposes were profoundly impressed upon me; and rejoicing in faith, I praised thy name. But that faith allowed me no rest in respect of my past sins, which were not yet forgiven me through thy baptism.

CHAPTER V

13. Now that the vintage vacation was ended, I gave notice to the citizens of Milan that they might provide their scholars with another word-merchant. I gave as my reasons my determination to serve thee and also my insufficiency for the task, because of the difficulty in breathing and the pain in my chest.

And by letters I notified thy bishop, the holy man Ambrose, of my former errors and my present resolution. And I asked his advice as to which of thy books it was best for me to read so that I might be the more ready and fit for the reception of so great a grace. He recommended Isaiah the prophet; and I believe it was because Isaiah foreshows more clearly than others the gospel, and the calling of the Gentiles. But because I could not understand the first part and because I imagined the rest to be like it, I laid it aside with the intention of taking it up again later, when better practiced in our Lord's words.

CHAPTER VI

14. When the time arrived for me to give in my name, we left the country and returned to Milan. Alypius also resolved to be born again in thee at the same time. He was already clothed with the humility that befits thy sacraments, and was so brave a tamer of his body that he would walk the frozen Italian soil with his naked feet, which called for unusual fortitude. We took with us the boy Adeodatus, my son after the flesh, the offspring of my sin. Thou hadst made of him a noble lad. He was barely fifteen years old, but his intelligence excelled that of many grave and learned men. I confess to thee thy gifts, O Lord my God, creator of all, who hast power to reform our deformities—for there was nothing of me in that boy but the sin. For it was thou who didst inspire us to foster him in thy discipline, and none other—thy gifts I confess to thee. There is a book of mine, entitled *De Magistro*.[21] It is a dialogue between Adeodatus and me, and thou knowest that all things there put into the mouth of

21 *Concerning the Teacher*; cf. Vol. VI of this series, pp. 64–101.

my interlocutor are his, though he was then only in his sixteenth year. Many other gifts even more wonderful I found in him. His talent was a source of awe to me. And who but thou couldst be the worker of such marvels? And thou didst quickly remove his life from the earth, and even now I recall him to mind with a sense of security, because I fear nothing for his childhood or youth, nor for his whole career. We took him for our companion, as if he were the same age in grace with ourselves, to be trained with ourselves in thy discipline. And so we were baptized and the anxiety about our past life left us.

Nor did I ever have enough in those days of the wondrous sweetness of meditating on the depth of thy counsels concerning the salvation of the human race. How freely did I weep in thy hymns and canticles; how deeply was I moved by the voices of thy sweet-speaking Church! The voices flowed into my ears; and the truth was poured forth into my heart, where the tide of my devotion overflowed, and my tears ran down, and I was happy in all these things.

CHAPTER VII

15. The church of Milan had only recently begun to employ this mode of consolation and exaltation with all the brethren singing together with great earnestness of voice and heart. For it was only about a year—not much more—since Justina, the mother of the boy-emperor Valentinian, had persecuted thy servant Ambrose on behalf of her heresy, in which she had been seduced by the Arians. The devoted people kept guard in the church, prepared to die with their bishop, thy servant. Among them my mother, thy handmaid, taking a leading part in those anxieties and vigils, lived there in prayer. And even though we were still not wholly melted by the heat of thy Spirit, we were nevertheless excited by the alarmed and disturbed city.

This was the time that the custom began, after the manner of the Eastern Church, that hymns and psalms should be sung, so that the people would not be worn out with the tedium of lamentation. This custom, retained from then till now, has been imitated by many, indeed, by almost all thy congregations throughout the rest of the world.[22]

16. Then by a vision thou madest known to thy renowned

22 This was apparently the first introduction into the West of antiphonal chanting, which was already widespread in the East. Ambrose brought it in; Gregory brought it to perfection.

bishop the spot where lay the bodies of Gervasius and Protasius, the martyrs, whom thou hadst preserved uncorrupted for so many years in thy secret storehouse, so that thou mightest produce them at a fit time to check a woman's fury—a woman indeed, but also a queen! When they were discovered and dug up and brought with due honor to the basilica of Ambrose, as they were borne along the road many who were troubled by unclean spirits—the devils confessing themselves—were healed. And there was also a certain man, a well-known citizen of the city, blind many years, who, when he had asked and learned the reason for the people's tumultuous joy, rushed out and begged his guide to lead him to the place. When he arrived there, he begged to be permitted to touch with his handkerchief the bier of thy saints, whose death is precious in thy sight. When he had done this, and put it to his eyes, they were immediately opened. The fame of all this spread abroad; from this thy glory shone more brightly. And also from this the mind of that angry woman, though not enlarged to the sanity of a full faith, was nevertheless restrained from the fury of persecution.

Thanks to thee, O my God. Whence and whither hast thou led my memory, that I should confess such things as these to thee—for great as they were, I had forgetfully passed them over? And yet at that time, when the sweet savor of thy ointment was so fragrant, I did not run after thee.[23] Therefore, I wept more bitterly as I listened to thy hymns, having so long panted after thee. And now at length I could breathe as much as the space allows in this our straw house.[24]

CHAPTER VIII

17. Thou, O Lord, who makest men of one mind to dwell in a single house, also broughtest Evodius to join our company. He was a young man of our city, who, while serving as a secret service agent, was converted to thee and baptized before us. He had relinquished his secular service, and prepared himself for thine. We were together, and we were resolved to live together in our devout purpose.

We cast about for some place where we might be most useful in our service to thee, and had planned on going back together to Africa. And when we had got as far as Ostia on the Tiber, my mother died.

[23] Cf. S. of Sol. 1:3, 4.
[24] Cf. Isa. 40:6; I Peter 1:24: "All flesh is grass." See Bk. XI, Ch. II, 3.

I am passing over many things, for I must hasten. Receive, O my God, my confessions and thanksgiving for the unnumbered things about which I am silent. But I will not omit anything my mind has brought back concerning thy handmaid who brought me forth—in her flesh, that I might be born into this world's light, and in her heart, that I might be born to life eternal. I will not speak of her gifts, but of thy gift in her; for she neither made herself nor trained herself. Thou didst create her, and neither her father nor her mother knew what kind of being was to come forth from them. And it was the rod of thy Christ, the discipline of thy only Son, that trained her in thy fear, in the house of one of thy faithful ones who was a sound member of thy Church. Yet my mother did not attribute this good training of hers as much to the diligence of her own mother as to that of a certain elderly maidservant who had nursed her father, carrying him around on her back, as big girls carried babies. Because of her long-time service and also because of her extreme age and excellent character, she was much respected by the heads of that Christian household. The care of her master's daughters was also committed to her, and she performed her task with diligence. She was quite earnest in restraining them with a holy severity when necessary and instructing them with a sober sagacity. Thus, except at mealtimes at their parents' table—when they were fed very temperately—she would not allow them to drink even water, however parched they were with thirst. In this way she took precautions against an evil custom and added the wholesome advice: "You drink water now only because you don't control the wine; but when you are married and mistresses of pantry and cellar, you may not care for water, but the habit of drinking will be fixed." By such a method of instruction, and her authority, she restrained the longing of their tender age, and regulated even the thirst of the girls to such a decorous control that they no longer wanted what they ought not to have.

18. And yet, as thy handmaid related to me, her son, there had stolen upon her a love of wine. For, in the ordinary course of things, when her parents sent her as a sober maiden to draw wine from the cask, she would hold a cup under the tap; and then, before she poured the wine into the bottle, she would wet the tips of her lips with a little of it, for more than this her taste refused. She did not do this out of any craving for drink, but out of the overflowing buoyancy of her time of life, which bubbles up with sportiveness and youthful spirits, but is usually

borne down by the gravity of the old folks. And so, adding daily a little to that little—for "he that contemns small things shall fall by a little here and a little there" [25]—she slipped into such a habit as to drink off eagerly her little cup nearly full of wine.

Where now was that wise old woman and her strict prohibition? Could anything prevail against our secret disease if thy medicine, O Lord, did not watch over us? Though father and mother and nurturers are absent, thou art present, who dost create, who callest, and who also workest some good for our salvation, through those who are set over us. What didst thou do at that time, O my God? How didst thou heal her? How didst thou make her whole? Didst thou not bring forth from another woman's soul a hard and bitter insult, like a surgeon's knife from thy secret store, and with one thrust drain off all that putrefaction? For the slave girl who used to accompany her to the cellar fell to quarreling with her little mistress, as it sometimes happened when she was alone with her, and cast in her teeth this vice of hers, along with a very bitter insult: calling her "a drunkard." Stung by this taunt, my mother saw her own vileness and immediately condemned and renounced it.

As the flattery of friends corrupts, so often do the taunts of enemies instruct. Yet thou repayest them, not for the good thou workest through their means, but for the malice they intended. That angry slave girl wanted to infuriate her young mistress, not to cure her; and that is why she spoke up when they were alone. Or perhaps it was because their quarrel just happened to break out at that time and place; or perhaps she was afraid of punishment for having told of it so late.

But thou, O Lord, ruler of heaven and earth, who changest to thy purposes the deepest floods and controls the turbulent tide of the ages, thou healest one soul by the unsoundness of another; so that no man, when he hears of such a happening, should attribute it to his own power if another person whom he wishes to reform is reformed through a word of his.

CHAPTER IX

19. Thus modestly and soberly brought up, she was made subject to her parents by thee, rather more than by her parents to thee. She arrived at a marriageable age, and she was given to a husband whom she served as her lord. And she busied herself

[25] Ecclus. 19:1.

to gain him to thee, preaching thee to him by her behavior, in which thou madest her fair and reverently amiable, and admirable to her husband. For she endured with patience his infidelity and never had any dissension with her husband on this account. For she waited for thy mercy upon him until, by believing in thee, he might become chaste.

Moreover, even though he was earnest in friendship, he was also violent in anger; but she had learned that an angry husband should not be resisted, either in deed or in word. But as soon as he had grown calm and was tranquil, and she saw a fitting moment, she would give him a reason for her conduct, if he had been excited unreasonably. As a result, while many matrons whose husbands were more gentle than hers bore the marks of blows on their disfigured faces, and would in private talk blame the behavior of their husbands, she would blame their tongues, admonishing them seriously—though in a jesting manner—that from the hour they heard what are called the matrimonial tablets read to them, they should think of them as instruments by which they were made servants. So, always being mindful of their condition, they ought not to set themselves up in opposition to their lords. And, knowing what a furious, bad-tempered husband she endured, they marveled that it had never been rumored, nor was there any mark to show, that Patricius had ever beaten his wife, or that there had been any domestic strife between them, even for a day. And when they asked her confidentially the reason for this, she taught them the rule I have mentioned. Those who observed it confirmed the wisdom of it and rejoiced; those who did not observe it were bullied and vexed.

20. Even her mother-in-law, who was at first prejudiced against her by the whisperings of malicious servants, she conquered by submission, persevering in it with patience and meekness; with the result that the mother-in-law told her son of the tales of the meddling servants which had disturbed the domestic peace between herself and her daughter-in-law and begged him to punish them for it. In conformity with his mother's wish, and in the interest of family discipline to insure the future harmony of its members, he had those servants beaten who were pointed out by her who had discovered them; and she promised a similar reward to anyone else who, thinking to please her, should say anything evil of her daughter-in-law. After this no one dared to do so, and they lived together with a wonderful sweetness of mutual good will.

21. This other great gift thou also didst bestow, O my God, my Mercy, upon that good handmaid of thine, in whose womb thou didst create me. It was that whenever she could she acted as a peacemaker between any differing and discordant spirits, and when she heard very bitter things on either side of a controversy—the kind of bloated and undigested discord which often belches forth bitter words, when crude malice is breathed out by sharp tongues to a present friend against an absent enemy—she would disclose nothing about the one to the other except what might serve toward their reconciliation. This might seem a small good to me if I did not know to my sorrow countless persons who, through the horrid and far-spreading infection of sin, not only repeat to enemies mutually enraged things said in passion against each other, but also add some things that were never said at all. It ought not to be enough in a truly humane man merely not to incite or increase the enmities of men by evil-speaking; he ought likewise to endeavor by kind words to extinguish them. Such a one was she—and thou, her most intimate instructor, didst teach her in the school of her heart.

22. Finally, her own husband, now toward the end of his earthly existence, she won over to thee. Henceforth, she had no cause to complain of unfaithfulness in him, which she had endured before he became one of the faithful. She was also the servant of thy servants. All those who knew her greatly praised, honored, and loved thee in her because, through the witness of the fruits of a holy life, they recognized thee present in her heart. For she had "been the wife of one man," [26] had honored her parents, had guided her house in piety, was highly reputed for good works, and brought up her children, travailing in labor with them as often as she saw them swerving from thee. Lastly, to all of us, O Lord—since of thy favor thou allowest thy servants to speak—to all of us who lived together in that association before her death in thee she devoted such care as she might have if she had been mother of us all; she served us as if she had been the daughter of us all.

CHAPTER X

23. As the day now approached on which she was to depart this life—a day which thou knewest, but which we did not—it happened (though I believe it was by thy secret ways arranged) that she and I stood alone, leaning in a certain window from

[26] I Tim. 5:9.

which the garden of the house we occupied at Ostia could be seen. Here in this place, removed from the crowd, we were resting ourselves for the voyage after the fatigues of a long journey.

We were conversing alone very pleasantly and "forgetting those things which are past, and reaching forward toward those things which are future." [27] We were in the present—and in the presence of Truth (which thou art)—discussing together what is the nature of the eternal life of the saints: which eye has not seen, nor ear heard, neither has entered into the heart of man. [28] We opened wide the mouth of our heart, thirsting for those supernal streams of thy fountain, "the fountain of life" which is with thee, [29] that we might be sprinkled with its waters according to our capacity and might in some measure weigh the truth of so profound a mystery.

24. And when our conversation had brought us to the point where the very highest of physical sense and the most intense illumination of physical light seemed, in comparison with the sweetness of that life to come, not worthy of comparison, nor even of mention, we lifted ourselves with a more ardent love toward the Selfsame, [30] and we gradually passed through all the levels of bodily objects, and even through the heaven itself, where the sun and moon and stars shine on the earth. Indeed, we soared higher yet by an inner musing, speaking and marveling at thy works.

And we came at last to our own minds and went beyond them, that we might climb as high as that region of unfailing plenty where thou feedest Israel forever with the food of truth, where life is that Wisdom by whom all things are made, both which have been and which are to be. Wisdom is not made, but is as she has been and forever shall be; for "to have been" and "to be hereafter" do not apply to her, but only "to be," because she is eternal and "to have been" and "to be hereafter" are not eternal.

And while we were thus speaking and straining after her, we just barely touched her with the whole effort of our hearts. Then with a sigh, leaving the first fruits of the Spirit bound to that ecstasy, we returned to the sounds of our own tongue, where the spoken word had both beginning and end. [31] But what is like to

[27] Phil. 3:13.   [28] Cf. I Cor. 2:9.
[29] Ps. 36:9.   [30] *Idipsum.*
[31] Cf. this report of a "Christian ecstasy" with the Plotinian ecstasy recounted in Bk. VII, Ch. XVII, 23, above.

thy Word, our Lord, who remaineth in himself without becoming old, and "makes all things new" [32]?

25. What we said went something like this: "If to any man the tumult of the flesh were silenced; and the phantoms of earth and waters and air were silenced; and the poles were silent as well; indeed, if the very soul grew silent to herself, and went beyond herself by not thinking of herself; if fancies and imaginary revelations were silenced; if every tongue and every sign and every transient thing—for actually if any man could hear them, all these would say, 'We did not create ourselves, but were created by Him who abides forever'—and if, having uttered this, they too should be silent, having stirred our ears to hear him who created them; and if then he alone spoke, not through them but by himself, that we might hear his word, not in fleshly tongue or angelic voice, nor sound of thunder, nor the obscurity of a parable, but might hear him—him for whose sake we love these things—if we could hear him without these, as we two now strained ourselves to do, we then with rapid thought might touch on that Eternal Wisdom which abides over all. And if this could be sustained, and other visions of a far different kind be taken away, and this one should so ravish and absorb and envelop its beholder in these inward joys that his life might be eternally like that one moment of knowledge which we now sighed after—would not *this* be the reality of the saying, 'Enter into the joy of thy Lord'[33]? But when shall such a thing be? Shall it not be 'when we all shall rise again,' and shall it not be that 'all things will be changed'[34]?"

26. Such a thought I was expressing, and if not in this manner and in these words, still, O Lord, thou knowest that on that day we were talking thus and that this world, with all its joys, seemed cheap to us even as we spoke. Then my mother said: "Son, for myself I have no longer any pleasure in anything in this life. Now that my hopes in this world are satisfied, I do not know what more I want here or why I am here. There was indeed one thing for which I wished to tarry a little in this life, and that was that I might see you a Catholic Christian before I died. My God hath answered this more than abundantly, so that I see you now made his servant and spurning all earthly happiness. What more am I to do here?"

---

[32] Cf. Wis. 7:21–30; see especially v. 27: "And being but one, she [Wisdom] can do all things: and remaining in herself the same, she makes all things new."

Matt. 25:21.   [34] I Cor. 15:51.

CHAPTER XI

27. I do not well remember what reply I made to her about this. However, it was scarcely five days later—certainly not much more—that she was prostrated by fever. While she was sick, she fainted one day and was for a short time quite unconscious. We hurried to her, and when she soon regained her senses, she looked at me and my brother [35] as we stood by her, and said, in inquiry, "Where was I?" Then looking intently at us, dumb in our grief, she said, "Here in this place shall you bury your mother." I was silent and held back my tears; but my brother said something, wishing her the happier lot of dying in her own country and not abroad. When she heard this, she fixed him with her eye and an anxious countenance, because he savored of such earthly concerns, and then gazing at me she said, "See how he speaks." Soon after, she said to us both: "Lay this body anywhere, and do not let the care of it be a trouble to you at all. Only this I ask: that you will remember me at the Lord's altar, wherever you are." And when she had expressed her wish in such words as she could, she fell silent, in heavy pain with her increasing sickness.

28. But as I thought about thy gifts, O invisible God, which thou plantest in the heart of thy faithful ones, from which such marvelous fruits spring up, I rejoiced and gave thanks to thee, remembering what I had known of how she had always been much concerned about her burial place, which she had provided and prepared for herself by the body of her husband. For as they had lived very peacefully together, her desire had always been—so little is the human mind capable of grasping things divine—that this last should be added to all that happiness, and commented on by others: that, after her pilgrimage beyond the sea, it would be granted her that the two of them, so united on earth, should lie in the same grave.

When this vanity, through the bounty of thy goodness, had begun to be no longer in her heart, I do not know; but I joyfully marveled at what she had thus disclosed to me—though indeed in our conversation in the window, when she said, "What is there here for me to do any more?" she appeared not to desire

35 Navigius, who had joined them in Milan, but about whom Augustine is curiously silent save for the brief and unrevealing references in *De beata vita*, I, 6, to II, 7, and *De ordine*, I, 2–3.

to die in her own country. I heard later on that, during our stay in Ostia, she had been talking in maternal confidence to some of my friends about her contempt of this life and the blessing of death. When they were amazed at the courage which was given her, a woman, and had asked her whether she did not dread having her body buried so far from her own city, she replied: "Nothing is far from God. I do not fear that, at the end of time, he should not know the place whence he is to resurrect me." And so on the ninth day of her sickness, in the fifty-sixth year of her life and the thirty-third of mine,[36] that religious and devout soul was set loose from the body.

CHAPTER XII

29. I closed her eyes; and there flowed in a great sadness on my heart and it was passing into tears, when at the strong behest of my mind my eyes sucked back the fountain dry, and sorrow was in me like a convulsion. As soon as she breathed her last, the boy Adeodatus burst out wailing; but he was checked by us all, and became quiet. Likewise, my own childish feeling which was, through the youthful voice of my heart, seeking escape in tears, was held back and silenced. For we did not consider it fitting to celebrate that death with tearful wails and groanings. This is the way those who die unhappy or are altogether dead are usually mourned. But she neither died unhappy nor did she altogether die.[37] For of this we were assured by the witness of her good life, her "faith unfeigned,"[38] and other manifest evidence.

30. What was it, then, that hurt me so grievously in my heart except the newly made wound, caused from having the sweet and dear habit of living together with her suddenly broken? I was full of joy because of her testimony in her last illness, when she praised my dutiful attention and called me kind, and recalled with great affection of love that she had never heard any harsh or reproachful sound from my mouth against her. But yet, O my God who made us, how can that honor I paid her be compared with her service to me? I was then left destitute of a great comfort in her, and my soul was stricken; and that life

---

[36] A.D. 387.
[37] *Nec omnino moriebatur.* Is this an echo of Horace's famous memorial ode, *Exegi monumentum aere perennius . . . non omnis moriar?* Cf. *Odes*, Book III, Ode XXX.   [38] I Tim. 1:5.

was torn apart, as it were, which had been made but one out of hers and mine together.[39]

31. When the boy was restrained from weeping, Evodius took up the Psalter and began to sing, with the whole household responding, the psalm, "I will sing of mercy and judgment unto thee, O Lord."[40] And when they heard what we were doing, many of the brethren and religious women came together. And while those whose office it was to prepare for the funeral went about their task according to custom, I discoursed in another part of the house, with those who thought I should not be left alone, on what was appropriate to the occasion. By this balm of truth, I softened the anguish known to thee. They were unconscious of it and listened intently and thought me free of any sense of sorrow. But in thy ears, where none of them heard, I reproached myself for the mildness of my feelings, and restrained the flow of my grief which bowed a little to my will. The paroxysm returned again, and I knew what I repressed in my heart, even though it did not make me burst forth into tears or even change my countenance; and I was greatly annoyed that these human things had such power over me, which in the due order and destiny of our natural condition must of necessity happen. And so with a new sorrow I sorrowed for my sorrow and was wasted with a twofold sadness.

32. So, when the body was carried forth, we both went and returned without tears. For neither in those prayers which we poured forth to thee, when the sacrifice of our redemption was offered up to thee for her—with the body placed by the side of the grave as the custom is there, before it is lowered down into it—neither in those prayers did I weep. But I was most grievously sad in secret all the day, and with a troubled mind entreated thee, as I could, to heal my sorrow; but thou didst not. I now believe that thou wast fixing in my memory, by this one lesson, the power of the bonds of all habit, even on a mind which now no longer feeds upon deception. It then occurred to me that it would be a good thing to go and bathe, for I had heard that the word for bath [*balneum*] took its name from the Greek *balaneion* [βαλανεῖον], because it washes anxiety from the mind. Now see, this also I confess to thy mercy, "O Father of the fatherless"[41]: I bathed and felt the same as I had done before.

---

[39] Cf. this passage, as Augustine doubtless intended, with the story of his morbid and immoderate grief at the death of his boyhood friend, above, Bk. IV, Chs. IV, 9, to VII, 12.

[40] Ps. 101:1.   [41] Ps. 68:5.

For the bitterness of my grief was not sweated from my heart.

Then I slept, and when I awoke I found my grief not a little assuaged. And as I lay there on my bed, those true verses of Ambrose came to my mind, for thou art truly,

> "Deus, creator omnium,
> Polique rector, vestiens
> Diem decoro lumine,
> Noctem sopora gratia;
>   Artus solutos ut quies
> Reddat laboris usui
> Mentesque fessas allevet,
> Luctusque solvat anxios."

> "O God, Creator of us all,
> Guiding the orbs celestial,
> Clothing the day with lovely light,
> Appointing gracious sleep by night:
>
> Thy grace our wearied limbs restore
> To strengthened labor, as before,
> And ease the grief of tired minds
> From that deep torment which it finds." [42]

33. And then, little by little, there came back to me my former memories of thy handmaid: her devout life toward thee, her holy tenderness and attentiveness toward us, which had suddenly been taken away from me—and it was a solace for me to weep in thy sight, for her and for myself, about her and about myself. Thus I set free the tears which before I repressed, that they might flow at will, spreading them out as a pillow beneath my heart. And it rested on them, for thy ears were near me—not those of a man, who would have made a scornful comment about my weeping. But now in writing I confess it to thee, O Lord! Read it who will, and comment how he will, and if he finds me to have sinned in weeping for my mother for part of an hour—that mother who was for a while dead to my eyes, who had for many years wept for me that I might live in thy eyes—let him

[42] Sir Tobie Matthew (adapted). For Augustine's own analysis of the scansion and structure of this hymn, see *De musica*, VI, 2:2–3; for a brief commentary on the Latin text, see A. S. Walpole, *Early Latin Hymns* (Cambridge, 1922), pp. 44–49.

not laugh at me; but if he be a man of generous love, let him weep for my sins against thee, the Father of all the brethren of thy Christ.

CHAPTER XIII

34. Now that my heart is healed of that wound—so far as it can be charged against me as a carnal affection—I pour out to thee, O our God, on behalf of thy handmaid, tears of a very different sort: those which flow from a spirit broken by the thoughts of the dangers of every soul that dies in Adam. And while she had been "made alive" in Christ[43] even before she was freed from the flesh, and had so lived as to praise thy name both by her faith and by her life, yet I would not dare say that from the time thou didst regenerate her by baptism no word came out of her mouth against thy precepts. But it has been declared by thy Son, the Truth, that "whosoever shall say to his brother, You fool, shall be in danger of hell-fire."[44] And there would be doom even for the life of a praiseworthy man if thou judgedst it with thy mercy set aside. But since thou dost not so stringently inquire after our sins, we hope with confidence to find some place in thy presence. But whoever recounts his actual and true merits to thee, what is he doing but recounting to thee thy own gifts? Oh, if only men would know themselves as men, then "he that glories" would "glory in the Lord"[45]!

35. Thus now, O my Praise and my Life, O God of my heart, forgetting for a little her good deeds for which I give joyful thanks to thee, I now beseech thee for the sins of my mother. Hearken unto me, through that Medicine of our wounds, who didst hang upon the tree and who sittest at thy right hand "making intercession for us."[46] I know that she acted in mercy, and from the heart forgave her debtors their debts.[47] I beseech thee also to forgive her debts, whatever she contracted during so many years since the water of salvation. Forgive her, O Lord, forgive her, I beseech thee; "enter not into judgment" with her.[48] Let thy mercy be exalted above thy justice, for thy words are true and thou hast promised mercy to the merciful, that the merciful shall obtain mercy.[49] This is thy gift, who hast mercy on whom thou wilt and who wilt have compassion on whom thou dost have compassion on.[50]

[43] I Cor. 15:22.
[45] II Cor. 10:17.
[47] Cf. Matt. 6:12.
[49] Matt. 5:7.
[44] Matt. 5:22.
[46] Rom. 8.34.
[48] Ps. 143:2.
[50] Cf. Rom. 9:15.

36. Indeed, I believe thou hast already done what I ask of thee, but "accept the freewill offerings of my mouth, O Lord." [51] For when the day of her dissolution was so close, she took no thought to have her body sumptuously wrapped or embalmed with spices. Nor did she covet a handsome monument, or even care to be buried in her own country. About these things she gave no commands at all, but only desired to have her name remembered at thy altar, where she had served without the omission of a single day, and where she knew that the holy sacrifice was dispensed by which that handwriting that was against us is blotted out; and that enemy vanquished who, when he summed up our offenses and searched for something to bring against us, could find nothing in Him, in whom we conquer.

Who will restore to him the innocent blood? Who will repay him the price with which he bought us, so as to take us from him? Thus to the sacrament of our redemption did thy handmaid bind her soul by the bond of faith. Let none separate her from thy protection. Let not the "lion" and "dragon" bar her way by force or fraud. For she will not reply that she owes nothing, lest she be convicted and duped by that cunning deceiver. Rather, she will answer that her sins are forgiven by Him to whom no one is able to repay the price which he, who owed us nothing, laid down for us all.

37. Therefore, let her rest in peace with her husband, before and after whom she was married to no other man; whom she obeyed with patience, bringing fruit to thee that she might also win him for thee. And inspire, O my Lord my God, inspire thy servants, my brothers; thy sons, my masters, who with voice and heart and writings I serve, that as many of them as shall read these confessions may also at thy altar remember Monica, thy handmaid, together with Patricius, once her husband; by whose flesh thou didst bring me into this life, in a manner I know not. May they with pious affection remember my parents in this transitory life, and remember my brothers under thee our Father in our Catholic mother; and remember my fellow citizens in the eternal Jerusalem, for which thy people sigh in their pilgrimage from birth until their return. So be fulfilled what my mother desired of me—more richly in the prayers of so many gained for her through these confessions of mine than by my prayers alone.

[51] Ps. 119:108.

BOOK TEN

From autobiography to self-analysis. Augustine turns from his memories of the past to the inner mysteries of memory itself. In doing so, he reviews his motives for these written "confessions," and seeks to chart the path by which men come to God. But this brings him into the intricate analysis of memory and its relation to the self and its powers. This done, he explores the meaning and mode of true prayer. In conclusion, he undertakes a detailed analysis of appetite and the temptations to which the flesh and the soul are heirs, and comes finally to see how necessary and right it was for the Mediator between God and man to have been the God-Man.

CHAPTER I

1. Let me know thee, O my Knower; let me know thee even as I am known.[1] O Strength of my soul, enter it and prepare it for thyself that thou mayest have and hold it, without "spot or blemish."[2] This is my hope, therefore have I spoken; and in this hope I rejoice whenever I rejoice aright. But as for the other things of this life, they deserve our lamentations less, the more we lament them; and some should be lamented all the more, the less men care for them. For see, "Thou desirest truth"[3] and "he who does the truth comes to the light."[4] This is what I wish to do through confession in my heart before thee, and in my writings before many witnesses.

CHAPTER II

2. And what is there in me that could be hidden from thee, O Lord, to whose eyes the abysses of man's conscience are

[1] Cf. I Cor. 13:12. [2] Eph. 5:27.
[3] Ps. 51:6. [4] John 3:21.

naked, even if I were unwilling to confess it to thee? In doing so I would only hide thee from myself, not myself from thee. But now that my groaning is witness to the fact that I am dissatisfied with myself, thou shinest forth and satisfiest. Thou art beloved and desired; so that I blush for myself, and renounce myself and choose thee, for I can neither please thee nor myself except in thee. To thee, then, O Lord, I am laid bare, whatever I am, and I have already said with what profit I may confess to thee. I do not do it with words and sounds of the flesh but with the words of the soul, and with the sound of my thoughts, which thy ear knows. For when I am wicked, to confess to thee means nothing less than to be dissatisfied with myself; but when I am truly devout, it means nothing less than not to attribute my virtue to myself; because thou, O Lord, blessest the righteous, but first thou justifiest him while he is yet ungodly. My confession therefore, O my God, is made unto thee silently in thy sight—and yet not silently. As far as sound is concerned, it is silent. But in strong affection it cries aloud. For neither do I give voice to something that sounds right to men, which thou hast not heard from me before, nor dost thou hear anything of the kind from me which thou didst not first say to me.

CHAPTER III

3. What is it to me that men should hear my confessions as if it were they who were going to cure all my infirmities? People are curious to know the lives of others, but slow to correct their own. Why are they anxious to hear from me what I am, when they are unwilling to hear from thee what they are? And how can they tell when they hear what I say about myself whether I speak the truth, since no man knows what is in a man "save the spirit of man which is in him"[5]? But if they were to hear from thee something concerning themselves, they would not be able to say, "The Lord is lying." For what does it mean to hear from thee about themselves but to know themselves? And who is he that knows himself and says, "This is false," unless he himself is lying? But, because "love believes all things"[6]—at least among those who are bound together in love by its bonds—I confess to thee, O Lord, so that men may also hear; for if I cannot prove to them that I confess the truth, yet those whose ears love opens to me will believe me.

---

[5] I Cor. 2:11.   [6] I Cor. 13:7.

4. But wilt thou, O my inner Physician, make clear to me what profit I am to gain in doing this? For the confessions of my past sins (which thou hast "forgiven and covered" [7] that thou mightest make me blessed in thee, transforming my soul by faith and thy sacrament), when *they* are read and heard, may stir up the heart so that it will stop dozing along in despair, saying, "I cannot"; but will instead awake in the love of thy mercy and the sweetness of thy grace, by which he that is weak is strong, provided he is made conscious of his own weakness. And it will please those who are good to hear about the past errors of those who are now freed from them. And they will take delight, not because they are errors, but because they were and are so no longer. What profit, then, O Lord my God—to whom my conscience makes her daily confession, far more confident in the hope of thy mercy than in her own innocence—what profit is there, I ask thee, in confessing to men in thy presence, through this book, both what I am now as well as what I have been? For I have seen and spoken of my harvest of things past. But what am I *now*, at this very moment of making my confessions? Many different people desire to know, both those who know me and those who do not know me. Some have heard about me or from me, but their ear is not close to my heart, where I am whatever it is that I am. They have the desire to hear me confess what I am within, where they can neither extend eye nor ear nor mind. They desire as those willing to believe—but will they understand? For the love by which they are good tells them that I am not lying in my confessions, and the love in them believes me.

CHAPTER IV

5. But for what profit do they desire this? Will they wish me happiness when they learn how near I have approached thee, by thy gifts? And will they pray for me when they learn how much I am still kept back by my own weight? To such as these I will declare myself. For it is no small profit, O Lord my God, that many people should give thanks to thee on my account and that many should entreat thee for my sake. Let the brotherly soul love in me what thou teachest him should be loved, and let him lament in me what thou teachest him should be lamented. Let it be the soul of a brother that does this, and not a

---

[7] Ps. 32:1.

stranger—not one of those "strange children, whose mouth speaks vanity, and whose right hand is the right hand of falsehood." [8] But let my brother do it who, when he approves of me, rejoices for me, but when he disapproves of me is sorry for me; because whether he approves or disapproves, he loves me. To such I will declare myself. Let them be refreshed by my good deeds and sigh over my evil ones. My good deeds are thy acts and thy gifts; my evil ones are my own faults and thy judgment. Let them breathe expansively at the one and sigh over the other. And let hymns and tears ascend in thy sight out of their brotherly hearts—which are thy censers. [9] And, O Lord, who takest delight in the incense of thy holy temple, have mercy upon me according to thy great mercy, for thy name's sake. And do not, on any account whatever, abandon what thou hast begun in me. Go on, rather, to complete what is yet imperfect in me.

6. This, then, is the fruit of my confessions (not of what I was, but of what I am), that I may not confess this before thee alone, in a secret exultation with trembling and a secret sorrow with hope, but also in the ears of the believing sons of men—who are the companions of my joy and sharers of my mortality, my fellow citizens and fellow pilgrims—those who have gone before and those who are to follow after, as well as the comrades of my present way. These are thy servants, my brothers, whom thou desirest to be thy sons. They are my masters, whom thou hast commanded me to serve if I desire to live with and in thee. But this thy Word would mean little to me if it commanded in words alone, without thy prevenient action. I do this, then, both in act and word. I do this under thy wings, in a danger too great to risk if it were not that under thy wings my soul is subject to thee, and my weakness known to thee. I am insufficient, but my Father liveth forever, and my Defender is sufficient for me. For he is the Selfsame who didst beget me and who watcheth over me; thou art the Selfsame who art all my good. Thou art the Omnipotent, who art with me, even before I am with thee. To those, therefore, whom thou commandest me to serve, I will declare, not what I was, but what I now am and what I will continue to be. But I do not judge myself. Thus, therefore, let me be heard.

[8] Ps. 144:7, 8.
[9] Cf. Rev. 8:3–5. "And the smoke of the incense with the prayers of the saints went up before God out of the angel's hand" (v. 4).

CHAPTER V

7. For it is thou, O Lord, who judgest me. For although no man "knows the things of a man, save the spirit of the man which is in him,"[10] yet there is something of man which "the spirit of the man which is in him" does not know itself. But thou, O Lord, who madest him, knowest him completely. And even I—though in thy sight I despise myself and count myself but dust and ashes—even I know something about thee which I do not know about myself. And it is certain that "now we see through a glass darkly," not yet "face to face."[11] Therefore, as long as I journey away from thee, I am more present with myself than with thee. I know that thou canst not suffer violence, but I myself do not know what temptations I can resist, and what I cannot. But there is hope, because thou art faithful and thou wilt not allow us to be tempted beyond our ability to resist, but wilt with the temptation also make a way of escape that we may be able to bear it. I would therefore confess what I know about myself; I will also confess what I do not know about myself. What I do know of myself, I know from thy enlightening of me; and what I do not know of myself, I will continue not to know until the time when my "darkness is as the noonday"[12] in thy sight.

CHAPTER VI

8. It is not with a doubtful consciousness, but one fully certain that I love thee, O Lord. Thou hast smitten my heart with thy Word, and I have loved thee. And see also the heaven, and earth, and all that is in them—on every side they tell me to love thee, and they do not cease to tell this to all men, "so that they are without excuse."[13] Wherefore, still more deeply wilt thou have mercy on whom thou wilt have mercy, and compassion on whom thou wilt have compassion.[14] For otherwise, both heaven and earth would tell abroad thy praises to deaf ears.

But what is it that I love in loving thee? Not physical beauty, nor the splendor of time, nor the radiance of the light—so pleasant to our eyes—nor the sweet melodies of the various kinds of songs, nor the fragrant smell of flowers and ointments and spices; not manna and honey, not the limbs embraced in physical love—it is not these I love when I love my God. Yet

[10] I Cor. 2:11.   [11] I Cor. 13:12.
[12] Isa. 58:10.   [13] Rom. 1:20.   [14] Cf. Rom. 9:15.

it is true that I love a certain kind of light and sound and fragrance and food and embrace in loving my God, who is the light and sound and fragrance and food and embracement of my inner man—where that light shines into my soul which no place can contain, where time does not snatch away the lovely sound, where no breeze disperses the sweet fragrance, where no eating diminishes the food there provided, and where there is an embrace that no satiety comes to sunder. This is what I love when I love my God.

9. And what is this God? I asked the earth, and it answered, "I am not he"; and everything in the earth made the same confession. I asked the sea and the deeps and the creeping things, and they replied, "We are not your God; seek above us." I asked the fleeting winds, and the whole air with its inhabitants answered, "Anaximenes[15] was deceived; I am not God." I asked the heavens, the sun, moon, and stars; and they answered, "Neither are we the God whom you seek." And I replied to all these things which stand around the door of my flesh: "You have told me about my God, that you are not he. Tell me something about him." And with a loud voice they all cried out, "He made us." My question had come from my observation of them, and their reply came from their beauty of order. And I turned my thoughts into myself and said, "Who are you?" And I answered, "A man." For see, there is in me both a body and a soul; the one without, the other within. In which of these should I have sought my God, whom I had already sought with my body from earth to heaven, as far as I was able to send those messengers—the beams of my eyes? But the inner part is the better part; for to it, as both ruler and judge, all these messengers of the senses report the answers of heaven and earth and all the things therein, who said, "We are not God, but he made us." My inner man knew these things through the ministry of the outer man, and I, the inner man, knew all this—I, the soul, through the senses of my body.[16] I asked the whole frame of

---

[15] One of the pre-Socratic "physiologers" who taught that αἰθήρ was the primary element in ἡ φύσις. Cf. Cicero's *On the Nature of the Gods* (a likely source for Augustine's knowledge of early Greek philosophy), I, 10: "After Anaximander comes Anaximenes, who taught that the air is God. . . ."

[16] An important text for Augustine's conception of sensation and the relation of body and mind. Cf. *On Music*, VI, 5:10; *The Magnitude of the Soul*, 25:48; *On the Trinity*, XII, 2:2; see also F. Coplestone, *A History of Philosophy* (London, 1950), II, 51–60, and E. Gilson, *Introduction à l'étude de Saint Augustin*, pp. 74–87.

earth about my God, and it answered, "I am not he, but he made me."

10. Is not this beauty of form visible to all whose senses are unimpaired? Why, then, does it not say the same things to all? Animals, both small and great, see it but they are unable to interrogate its meaning, because their senses are not endowed with the reason that would enable them to judge the evidence which the senses report. But man can interrogate it, so that "the invisible things of him . . . are clearly seen, being understood by the things that are made."[17] But men love these created things too much; they are brought into subjection to them—and, as subjects, are not able to judge. None of these created things reply to their questioners unless they can make rational judgments. The creatures will not alter their voice—that is, their beauty of form—if one man simply sees what another both sees and questions, so that the world appears one way to this man and another to that. It appears the same way to both; but it is mute to this one and it speaks to that one. Indeed, it actually speaks to all, but only they understand it who compare the voice received from without with the truth within. For the truth says to me, "Neither heaven nor earth nor anybody is your God." Their very nature tells this to the one who beholds[18] them. "They are a mass, less in part than the whole." Now, O my soul, you are my better part, and to you I speak; since you animate the whole mass of your body, giving it life, whereas no body furnishes life to a body. But your God is the life of your life.

CHAPTER VII

11. What is it, then, that I love when I love my God? Who is he that is beyond the topmost point of my soul? Yet by this very soul will I mount up to him. I will soar beyond that power of mine by which I am united to the body, and by which the whole structure of it is filled with life. Yet it is not by that vital power that I find my God. For then "the horse and the mule, that have no understanding,"[19] also might find him, since they have the same vital power, by which their bodies also live. But there is, besides the power by which I animate my body, another by which I endow my flesh with sense—a power that the Lord hath provided for me; commanding that the eye is not to

17 Rom. 1:20.
18 Reading *videnti* (with De Labriolle) instead of *vident* (as in Skutella).
19 Ps. 32:9.

hear and the ear is not to see, but that I am to see by the eye and to hear by the ear; and giving to each of the other senses its own proper place and function, through the diversity of which I, the single mind, act. I will soar also beyond this power of mine, for the horse and mule have this too, for they also perceive through their bodily senses.

CHAPTER VIII

12. I will soar, then, beyond this power of my nature also, still rising by degrees toward him who made me. And I enter the fields and spacious halls of memory, where are stored as treasures the countless images that have been brought into them from all manner of things by the senses. There, in the memory, is likewise stored what we cogitate, either by enlarging or reducing our perceptions, or by altering one way or another those things which the senses have made contact with; and everything else that has been entrusted to it and stored up in it, which oblivion has not yet swallowed up and buried.

When I go into this storehouse, I ask that what I want should be brought forth. Some things appear immediately, but others require to be searched for longer, and then dragged out, as it were, from some hidden recess. Other things hurry forth in crowds, on the other hand, and while something else is sought and inquired for, they leap into view as if to say, "Is it not we, perhaps?" These I brush away with the hand of my heart from the face of my memory, until finally the thing I want makes its appearance out of its secret cell. Some things suggest themselves without effort, and in continuous order, just as they are called for—the things that come first give place to those that follow, and in so doing are treasured up again to be forthcoming when I want them. All of this happens when I repeat a thing from memory.

13. All these things, each one of which came into memory in its own particular way, are stored up separately and under the general categories of understanding. For example, light and all colors and forms of bodies came in through the eyes; sounds of all kinds by the ears; all smells by the passages of the nostrils; all flavors by the gate of the mouth; by the sensation of the whole body, there is brought in what is hard or soft, hot or cold, smooth or rough, heavy or light, whether external or internal to the body. The vast cave of memory, with its numerous and mysterious recesses, receives all these things and stores them up,

to be recalled and brought forth when required. Each experience enters by its own door, and is stored up in the memory. And yet the things themselves do not enter it, but only the images of the things perceived are there for thought to remember. And who can tell how these images are formed, even if it is evident which of the senses brought which perception in and stored it up? For even when I am in darkness and silence I can bring out colors in my memory if I wish, and discern between black and white and the other shades as I wish; and at the same time, sounds do not break in and disturb what is drawn in by my eyes, and which I am considering, because the sounds which are also there are stored up, as it were, apart. And these too I can summon if I please and they are immediately present in memory. And though my tongue is at rest and my throat silent, yet I can sing as I will; and those images of color, which are as truly present as before, do not interpose themselves or interrupt while another treasure which had flowed in through the ears is being thought about. Similarly all the other things that were brought in and heaped up by all the other senses, I can recall at my pleasure. And I distinguish the scent of lilies from that of violets while actually smelling nothing; and I prefer honey to mead, a smooth thing to a rough, even though I am neither tasting nor handling them, but only remembering them.

14. All this I do within myself, in that huge hall of my memory. For in it, heaven, earth, and sea are present to me, and whatever I can cogitate about them—except what I have forgotten. There also I meet myself and recall myself[20]—what, when, or where I did a thing, and how I felt when I did it. There are all the things that I remember, either having experienced them myself or been told about them by others. Out of the same storehouse, with these past impressions, I can construct now this, now that, image of things that I either have experienced or have believed on the basis of experience—and from these I can further construct future actions, events, and hopes; and I can meditate on all these things as if they were present. "I will do this or that"—I say to myself in that vast recess of my mind, with its full store of so many and such great images—"and this or that will follow upon it." "O that this or that could happen!" "God prevent this or that." I speak to myself in this way; and

[20] The notion of the soul's immediate self-knowledge is a basic conception in Augustine's psychology and epistemology; cf. the refutation of skepticism, *Si fallor, sum* in *On Free Will*, II, 3:7; see also the *City of God*, XI, 26.

when I speak, the images of what I am speaking about are present out of the same store of memory; and if the images were absent I could say nothing at all about them.

15. Great is this power of memory, exceedingly great, O my God—a large and boundless inner hall! Who has plumbed the depths of it? Yet it is a power of my mind, and it belongs to my nature. But I do not myself grasp all that I am. Thus the mind is far too narrow to contain itself. But where can that part of it be which it does not contain? Is it outside and not in itself? How can it be, then, that the mind cannot grasp itself? A great marvel rises in me; astonishment seizes me. Men go forth to marvel at the heights of mountains and the huge waves of the sea, the broad flow of the rivers, the vastness of the ocean, the orbits of the stars, and yet they neglect to marvel at themselves. Nor do they wonder how it is that, when I spoke of all these things, I was not looking at them with my eyes—and yet I could not have spoken about them had it not been that I was actually seeing within, in my memory, those mountains and waves and rivers and stars which I have seen, and that ocean which I believe in—and with the same vast spaces between them as when I saw them outside me. But when I saw them outside me, I did not take them into me by seeing them; and the things themselves are not inside me, but only their images. And yet I knew through which physical sense each experience had made an impression on me.

CHAPTER IX

16. And yet this is not all that the unlimited capacity of my memory stores up. In memory, there are also all that one has learned of the liberal sciences, and has not forgotten—removed still further, so to say, into an inner place which is not a place. Of these things it is not the images that are retained, but the things themselves. For what literature and logic are, and what I know about how many different kinds of questions there are— all these are stored in my memory as they are, so that I have not taken in the image and left the thing outside. It is not as though a sound had sounded and passed away like a voice heard by the ear which leaves a trace by which it can be called into memory again, as if it were still sounding in mind while it did so no longer outside. Nor is it the same as an odor which, even after it has passed and vanished into the wind, affects the sense of smell— which then conveys into the memory the *image* of the smell

which is what we recall and re-create; or like food which, once in the belly, surely now has no taste and yet does have a kind of taste in the memory; or like anything that is felt by the body through the sense of touch, which still remains as an image in the memory after the external object is removed. For these things themselves are not put into the memory. Only the images of them are gathered with a marvelous quickness and stored, as it were, in the most wonderful filing system, and are thence produced in a marvelous way by the act of remembering.

CHAPTER X

17. But now when I hear that there are three kinds of questions—"Whether a thing is? What it is? Of what kind it is?"—I do indeed retain the images of the sounds of which these words are composed and I know that those sounds pass through the air with a noise and now no longer exist. But the things themselves which were signified by those sounds I never could reach by any sense of the body nor see them at all except by my mind. And what I have stored in my memory was not their signs, but the things signified.

How they got into me, let them tell who can. For I examine all the gates of my flesh, but I cannot find the door by which any of them entered. For the eyes say, "If they were colored, we reported that." The ears say, "If they gave any sound, we gave notice of that." The nostrils say, "If they smell, they passed in by us." The sense of taste says, "If they have no flavor, don't ask me about them." The sense of touch says, "If it had no bodily mass, I did not touch it, and if I never touched it, I gave no report about it."

Whence and how did these things enter into my memory? I do not know. For when I first learned them, it was not that I believed them on the credit of another man's mind, but I recognized them in my own; and I saw them as true, took them into my mind and laid them up, so to say, where I could get at them again whenever I willed. There they were, then, even before I learned them, but they were not in my memory. Where were they, then? How does it come about that when they were spoken of, I could acknowledge them and say, "So it is, it is true," unless they were already in the memory, though far back and hidden, as it were, in the more secret caves, so that unless they had been drawn out by the teaching of another person, I should perhaps never have been able to think of them at all?

CHAPTER XI

18. Thus we find that learning those things whose images we do not take in by our senses, but which we intuit within ourselves without images and as they actually are, is nothing else except the gathering together of those same things which the memory already contains—but in an indiscriminate and confused manner—and putting them together by careful observation as they are at hand in the memory; so that whereas they formerly lay hidden, scattered, or neglected, they now come easily to present themselves to the mind which is now familiar with them. And how many things of this sort my memory has stored up, which have already been discovered and, as I said, laid up for ready reference. These are the things we may be said to have learned and to know. Yet, if I cease to recall them even for short intervals of time, they are again so submerged—and slide back, as it were, into the further reaches of the memory—that they must be drawn out again as if new from the same place (for there is nowhere else for them to have gone) and must be collected [*cogenda*] so that they can become known. In other words, they must be gathered up [*colligenda*] from their dispersion. This is where we get the word *cogitate* [*cogitare*]. For *cogo* [collect] and *cogito* [to go on collecting] have the same relation to each other as *ago* [do] and *agito* [do frequently], and *facio* [make] and *factito* [make frequently]. But the mind has properly laid claim to this word [cogitate] so that not everything that is gathered together anywhere, but only what is collected and gathered together in the mind, is properly said to be "cogitated."

CHAPTER XII

19. The memory also contains the principles and the unnumbered laws of numbers and dimensions. None of these has been impressed on the memory by a physical sense, because they have neither color nor sound, nor taste, nor sense of touch. I have heard the sound of the words by which these things are signified when they are discussed: but the sounds are one thing, the things another. For the sounds are one thing in Greek, another in Latin; but the things themselves are neither Greek nor Latin nor any other language. I have seen the lines of the craftsmen, the finest of which are like a spider's web, but mathematical lines are different. They are not the images of

such things as the eye of my body has showed me. The man who knows them does so without any cogitation of physical objects whatever, but intuits them within himself. I have perceived with all the senses of my body the numbers we use in counting; but the numbers by which we count are far different from these. They are not the images of these; they simply are. Let the man who does not see these things mock me for saying them; and I will pity him while he laughs at me.

CHAPTER XIII

20. All these things I hold in my memory, and I remember how I learned them. I also remember many things that I have heard quite falsely urged against them, which, even if they are false, yet it is not false that I have remembered them. And I also remember that I have distinguished between the truths and the false objections, and now I see that it is one thing to distinguish these things and another to remember that I did distinguish them when I have cogitated on them. I remember, then, both that I have often understood these things and also that I am now storing away in my memory what I distinguish and comprehend of them so that later on I may remember just as I understand them now. Therefore, I remember that I remembered, so that if afterward I call to mind that I once was able to remember these things it will be through the power of memory that I recall it.

CHAPTER XIV

21. This same memory also contains the feelings of my mind; not in the manner in which the mind itself experienced them, but very differently according to a power peculiar to memory. For without being joyous now, I can remember that I once was joyous, and without being sad, I can recall my past sadness. I can remember past fears without fear, and former desires without desire. Again, the contrary happens. Sometimes when I am joyous I remember my past sadness, and when sad, remember past joy.

This is not to be marveled at as far as the body is concerned; for the mind is one thing and the body another.[21] If, therefore,

---

21 Again, the mind-body dualism typical of the Augustinian tradition. Cf. E. Gilson, *The Spirit of Medieval Philosophy* (Charles Scribner's Sons, New York, 1940), pp. 173–188; and E. Gilson, *The Philosophy of Saint Bonaventure* (Sheed & Ward, New York, 1938), ch. XI.

when I am happy, I recall some past bodily pain, it is not so strange. But even as this memory is experienced, it is identical with the mind—as when we tell someone to remember something we say, "See that you bear this in mind"; and when we forget a thing, we say, "It did not enter my mind" or "It slipped my mind." Thus we call memory itself mind.

Since this is so, how does it happen that when I am joyful I can still remember past sorrow? Thus the mind has joy, and the memory has sorrow; and the mind is joyful from the joy that is in it, yet the memory is not sad from the sadness that is in it. Is it possible that the memory does not belong to the mind? Who will say so? The memory doubtless is, so to say, the belly of the mind: and joy and sadness are like sweet and bitter food, which when they are committed to the memory are, so to say, passed into the belly where they can be stored but no longer tasted. It is ridiculous to consider this an analogy; yet they are not utterly unlike.

22. But look, it is from my memory that I produce it when I say that there are four basic emotions of the mind: desire, joy, fear, sadness. Whatever kind of analysis I may be able to make of these, by dividing each into its particular species, and by defining it, I still find what to say in my memory and it is from my memory that I draw it out. Yet I am not moved by any of these emotions when I call them to mind by remembering them. Moreover, before I recalled them and thought about them, they were there in the memory; and this is how they could be brought forth in remembrance. Perhaps, therefore, just as food is brought up out of the belly by rumination, so also these things are drawn up out of the memory by recall. But why, then, does not the man who is thinking about the emotions, and is thus recalling them, feel in the mouth of his reflection the sweetness of joy or the bitterness of sadness? Is the comparison unlike in this because it is not complete at every point? For who would willingly speak on these subjects, if as often as we used the term sadness or fear, we should thereby be compelled to be sad or fearful? And yet we could never speak of them if we did not find them in our memories, not merely as the sounds of the names, as their images are impressed on it by the physical senses, but also the notions of the things themselves—which we did not receive by any gate of the flesh, but which the mind itself recognizes by the experience of its own passions, and has entrusted to the memory; or else which the memory itself has retained without their being entrusted to it.

CHAPTER XV

23. Now whether all this is by means of images or not, who can rightly affirm? For I name a stone, I name the sun, and those things themselves are not present to my senses, but their images are present in my memory. I name some pain of the body, yet it is not present when there is no pain; yet if there were not some such image of it in my memory, I could not even speak of it, nor should I be able to distinguish it from pleasure. I name bodily health when I am sound in body, and the thing itself is indeed present in me. At the same time, unless there were some image of it in my memory, I could not possibly call to mind what the sound of this name signified. Nor would sick people know what was meant when health was named, unless the same image were preserved by the power of memory, even though the thing itself is absent from the body. I can name the numbers we use in counting, and it is not their images but themselves that are in my memory. I name the image of the sun, and this too is in my memory. For I do not recall the image of that image, but that image itself, for the image itself is present when I remember it. I name memory and I know what I name. But where do I know it, except in the memory itself? Is it also present to itself by its image, and not by itself?

CHAPTER XVI

24. When I name forgetfulness, and understand what I mean by the name, how could I understand it if I did not remember it? And if I refer not to the sound of the name, but to the thing which the term signifies, how could I know what that sound signified if I had forgotten what the name means? When, therefore, I remember memory, then memory is present to itself by itself, but when I remember forgetfulness then both memory and forgetfulness are present together—the memory by which I remember the forgetfulness which I remember. But what is forgetfulness except the privation of memory? How, then, is that present to my memory which, when it controls my mind, I cannot remember? But if what we remember we store up in our memory; and if, unless we remembered forgetfulness, we could never know the thing signified by the term when we heard it— then, forgetfulness is contained in the memory. It is present so that we do not forget it, but since it is present, we do forget. From this it is to be inferred that when we remember forgetfulness, it is not present to the memory through itself, but

through its image; because if forgetfulness were present through itself, it would not lead us to remember, but only to forget. Now who will someday work this out? Who can understand how it is?

25. Truly, O Lord, I toil with this and labor in myself. I have become a troublesome field that requires hard labor and heavy sweat. For we are not now searching out the tracts of heaven, or measuring the distances of the stars or inquiring about the weight of the earth. It is I myself—I, the mind— who remember. This is not much to marvel at, if what I myself am is not far from me. And what is nearer to me than myself? For see, I am not able to comprehend the force of my own memory, though I could not even call my own name without it. But what shall I say, when it is clear to me that I remember forgetfulness? Should I affirm that what I remember is not in my memory? Or should I say that forgetfulness is in my memory to the end that I should not forget? Both of these views are most absurd. But what third view is there? How can I say that the image of forgetfulness is retained by my memory, and not forgetfulness itself, when I remember it? How can I say this, since for the image of anything to be imprinted on the memory the thing itself must necessarily have been present first by which the image could have been imprinted? Thus I remember Carthage; thus, also, I remember all the other places where I have been. And I remember the faces of men whom I have seen and things reported by the other senses. I remember the health or sickness of the body. And when these objects were present, my memory received images from them so that they remain present in order for me to see them and reflect upon them in my mind, if I choose to remember them in their absence. If, therefore, forgetfulness is retained in the memory through its image and not through itself, then this means that it itself was once present, so that its image might have been imprinted. But when it was present, how did it write its image on the memory, since forgetfulness, by its presence, blots out even what it finds already written there? And yet in some way or other, even though it is incomprehensible and inexplicable, I am still quite certain that I also remember forgetfulness, by which we remember that something is blotted out.

CHAPTER XVII

26. Great is the power of memory. It is a true marvel, O my God, a profound and infinite multiplicity! And this is the mind,

and this I myself am. What, then, am I, O my God? Of what nature am I? A life various, and manifold, and exceedingly vast. Behold in the numberless halls and caves, in the innumerable fields and dens and caverns of my memory, full without measure of numberless kinds of things—present there either through images as all bodies are; or present in the things themselves as are our thoughts; or by some notion or observation as our emotions are, which the memory retains even though the mind feels them no longer, as long as whatever is in the memory is also in the mind—through all these I run and fly to and fro. I penetrate into them on this side and that as far as I can and yet there is nowhere any end.

So great is the power of memory, so great the power of life in man whose life is mortal! What, then, shall I do, O thou my true life, my God? I will pass even beyond this power of mine that is called memory—I will pass beyond it, that I may come to thee, O lovely Light. And what art thou saying to me? See, I soar by my mind toward thee, who remainest above me. I will also pass beyond this power of mine that is called memory, desiring to reach thee where thou canst be reached, and wishing to cleave to thee where it is possible to cleave to thee. For even beasts and birds possess memory, or else they could never find their lairs and nests again, nor display many other things they know and do by habit. Indeed, they could not even form their habits except by their memories. I will therefore pass even beyond memory that I may reach Him who has differentiated me from the four-footed beasts and the fowls of the air by making me a wiser creature. Thus I will pass beyond memory; but where shall I find thee, who art the true Good and the steadfast Sweetness? But where shall I find thee? If I find thee without memory, then I shall have no memory of thee; and how could I find thee at all, if I do not remember thee?

CHAPTER XVIII

27. For the woman who lost her small coin [22] and searched for it with a light would never have found it unless she had remembered it. For when it was found, how could she have known whether it was the same coin, if she had not remembered it? I remember having lost and found many things, and I have learned this from that experience: that when I was searching

22 Luke 15:8.

for any of them and was asked: "Is this it? Is that it?" I answered, "No," until finally what I was seeking was shown to me. But if I had not remembered it—whatever it was—even though it was shown to me, I still would not have found it because I could not have recognized it. And this is the way it always is when we search for and find anything that is lost. Still, if anything is accidentally lost from sight—not from memory, as a visible body might be—its image is retained within, and the thing is searched for until it is restored to sight. And when the thing is found, it is recognized by the image of it which is within. And we do not say that we have found what we have lost unless we can recognize it, and we cannot recognize it unless we remember it. But all the while the thing lost to the sight was retained in the memory.

CHAPTER XIX

28. But what happens when the memory itself loses something, as when we forget anything and try to recall it? Where, finally, do we search, but in the memory itself? And there, if by chance one thing is offered for another, we refuse it until we meet with what we are looking for; and when we do, we recognize that this is it. But we could not do this unless we recognized it, nor could we have recognized it unless we remembered it. Yet we had indeed forgotten it.

Perhaps the whole of it had not slipped out of our memory; but a part was retained by which the other lost part was sought for, because the memory realized that it was not operating as smoothly as usual and was being held up by the crippling of its habitual working; hence, it demanded the restoration of what was lacking.

For example, if we see or think of some man we know, and, having forgotten his name, try to recall it—if some other thing presents itself, we cannot tie it into the effort to remember, because it was not habitually thought of in association with him. It is consequently rejected, until something comes into the mind on which our knowledge can rightly rest as the familiar and sought-for object. And where does this name come back from, save from the memory itself? For even when we recognize it by another's reminding us of it, still it is from the memory that this comes, for we do not believe it as something new; but when we recall it, we admit that what was said was correct. But if the name had been entirely blotted out of the mind, we should not be able to recollect it even when reminded of it. For we have not entirely forgotten anything if we can remember that we have forgotten it. For a lost notion, one that we have entirely forgotten, we cannot even search for.

CHAPTER XX

29. How, then, do I seek thee, O Lord? For when I seek thee, my God, I seek a happy life. I will seek thee that my soul may live. [23] For my body lives by my soul, and my soul lives by thee. How, then, do I seek a happy life, since happiness is not mine till I can rightly say: "It is enough. This is it." How do I seek it? Is it by remembering, as though I had forgotten it and still knew that I had forgotten it? Do I seek it in longing to learn of it as though it were something unknown, which either I had never known or had so completely forgotten as not even to remember that I had forgotten it? Is not the happy life the thing that all desire, and is there anyone who does not desire it at all? [24] But where would they have gotten the knowledge of it, that they should so desire it? Where have they seen it that they should so love it? It is somehow true that we have it, but how I do not know. There is, indeed, a sense in which when anyone has his desire he is happy. And then there are some who are happy in hope. These are happy in an inferior degree to those that are actually happy; yet they are better off than those who are happy neither in actuality nor in hope. But even these, if they had not known happiness in some degree, would not then desire to be happy. And yet it is most certain that they do so desire. How they come to know happiness, I cannot tell, but they have it by some kind of knowledge unknown to me, for I am very much in doubt as to whether it is in the memory. For if it is in there, then we have been happy once on a time—either each of us individually or all of us in that man who first sinned and in whom also we all died and from whom we are all born in misery. How this is, I do not now ask; but I do ask whether the happy life is in the memory. For if we did not know it, we should not love it. We hear the name of it, and we all acknowledge that we desire the thing, for we are not delighted with the name only. For when a Greek hears it spoken in Latin, he does not feel delighted, for he does not know what has been spoken. But we are as delighted as he would be in turn if he heard it in Greek,

<hr>

23 Cf. Isa. 55:3.
24 Cf. the early dialogue "On the Happy Life" in Vol. I of The Fathers of the Church (New York, 1948).

because the thing itself is neither Greek nor Latin, this happiness which Greeks and Latins and men of all the other tongues long so earnestly to obtain. It is, then, known to all; and if all could with one voice be asked whether they wished to be happy, there is no doubt they would all answer that they would. And this would not be possible unless the thing itself, which we name "happiness," were held in the memory.

CHAPTER XXI

30. But is it the same kind of memory as one who having seen Carthage remembers it? No, for the happy life is not visible to the eye, since it is not a physical object. Is it the sort of memory we have for numbers? No, for the man who has these in his understanding does not keep striving to attain more. Now we know something about the happy life and therefore we love it, but still we wish to go on striving for it that we may be happy. Is the memory of happiness, then, something like the memory of eloquence? No, for although some, when they hear the term eloquence, call the thing to mind, even if they are not themselves eloquent—and further, there are many people who would like to be eloquent, from which it follows that they must know something about it—nevertheless, these people have noticed through their senses that others are eloquent and have been delighted to observe this and long to be this way themselves. But they would not be delighted if it were not some interior knowledge; and they would not desire to be delighted unless they had been delighted. But as for a happy life, there is no physical perception by which we experience it in others.

Do we remember happiness, then, as we remember joy? It may be so, for I remember my joy even when I am sad, just as I remember a happy life when I am miserable. And I have never, through physical perception, either seen, heard, smelled, tasted, or touched my joy. But I have experienced it in my mind when I rejoiced; and the knowledge of it clung to my memory so that I can call it to mind, sometimes with disdain and at other times with longing, depending on the different kinds of things I now remember that I rejoiced in. For I have been bathed with a certain joy even by unclean things, which I now detest and execrate as I call them to mind. At other times, I call to mind with longing good and honest things, which are not any longer near at hand, and I am therefore saddened when I recall my former joy.

31. Where and when did I ever experience my happy life that I can call it to mind and love it and long for it? It is not I alone or even a few others who wish to be happy, but absolutely everybody. Unless we knew happiness by a knowledge that is certain, we should not wish for it with a will which is so certain. Take this example: If two men were asked whether they wished to serve as soldiers, one of them might reply that he would, and the other that he would not; but if they were asked whether they wished to be happy, both of them would unhesitatingly say that they would. But the first one would wish to serve as a soldier and the other would not wish to serve, both from no other motive than to be happy. Is it, perhaps, that one finds his joy in this and another in that? Thus they agree in their wish for happiness just as they would also agree, if asked, in wishing for joy. Is this joy what they call a happy life? Although one could choose his joy in this way and another in that, all have one goal which they strive to attain, namely, to have joy. This joy, then, being something that no one can say he has not experienced, is therefore found in the memory and it is recognized whenever the phrase "a happy life" is heard.

CHAPTER XXII

32. Forbid it, O Lord, put it far from the heart of thy servant, who confesses to thee—far be it from me to think I am happy because of any and all the joy I have. For there is a joy not granted to the wicked but only to those who worship thee thankfully—and this joy thou thyself art. The happy life is this —to rejoice to thee, in thee, and for thee. This it is and there is no other. But those who think there is another follow after other joys, and not the true one. But their will is still not moved except by some image or shadow of joy.

CHAPTER XXIII

33. Is it, then, uncertain that all men wish to be happy, since those who do not wish to find their joy in thee—which is alone the happy life—do not actually desire the happy life? Or, is it rather that all desire this, but because "the flesh lusts against the spirit and the spirit against the flesh," so that they "prevent you from doing what you would," [25] you fall to doing what you are able to do and are content with that. For you do not want

[25] Gal. 5:17.

to do what you cannot do urgently enough to make you able to do it.

Now I ask all men whether they would rather rejoice in truth or in falsehood. They will no more hesitate to answer, "In truth," than to say that they wish to be happy. For a happy life is joy in the truth. Yet this is joy in thee, who art the Truth, O God my Light, "the health of my countenance and my God." [26] All wish for this happy life; all wish for this life which is the only happy one: joy in the truth is what all men wish.

I have had experience with many who wished to deceive, but not one who wished to be deceived. [27] Where, then, did they ever know about this happy life, except where they knew also what the truth is? For they love it, too, since they are not willing to be deceived. And when they love the happy life, which is nothing else but joy in the truth, then certainly they also love the truth. And yet they would not love it if there were not some knowledge of it in the memory.

Why, then, do they not rejoice in it? Why are they not happy? Because they are so fully preoccupied with other things which do more to make them miserable than those which would make them happy, which they remember so little about. Yet there is a little light in men. Let them walk—let them walk in it, lest the darkness overtake them.

34. Why, then, does truth generate hatred, and why does thy servant who preaches the truth come to be an enemy to them who also love the happy life, which is nothing else than joy in the truth—unless it be that truth is loved in such a way that those who love something else besides her wish that to be the truth which they do love. Since they are unwilling to be deceived, they are unwilling to be convinced that they have been deceived. Therefore, they hate the truth for the sake of whatever it is that they love in place of the truth. They love truth when she shines on them; and hate her when she rebukes them. And since they are not willing to be deceived, but do wish to deceive, they love truth when she reveals herself and hate her when she reveals them. On this account, she will so repay them that those who are unwilling to be exposed by her she will indeed expose against their will, and yet will not disclose herself to them.

Thus, thus, truly thus: the human mind so blind and sick, so base and ill-mannered, desires to lie hidden, but does not wish that anything should be hidden from it. And yet the

[26] Ps. 42:11.   [27] Cf. Enchiridion, VI, 19 ff.

opposite is what happens—the mind itself is not hidden from the truth, but the truth is hidden from it. Yet even so, for all its wretchedness, it still prefers to rejoice in truth rather than in known falsehoods. It will, then, be happy only when without other distractions it comes to rejoice in that single Truth through which all things else are true.

CHAPTER XXIV

35. Behold how great a territory I have explored in my memory seeking thee, O Lord! And in it all I have still not found thee. Nor have I found anything about thee, except what I had already retained in my memory from the time I learned of thee. For where I found Truth, there found I my God, who is the Truth. From the time I learned this I have not forgotten. And thus since the time I learned of thee, thou hast dwelt in my memory, and it is there that I find thee whenever I call thee to remembrance, and delight in thee. These are my holy delights, which thou hast bestowed on me in thy mercy, mindful of my poverty.

CHAPTER XXV

36. But where in my memory dost thou abide, O Lord? Where dost thou dwell there? What sort of lodging hast thou made for thyself there? What kind of sanctuary hast thou built for thyself? Thou hast done this honor to my memory to take up thy abode in it, but I must consider further in what part of it thou dost abide. For in calling thee to mind, I soared beyond those parts of memory which the beasts also possess, because I did not find thee there among the images of corporeal things. From there I went on to those parts where I had stored the remembered affections of my mind, and I did not find thee there. And I entered into the inmost seat of my mind, which is in my memory, since the mind remembers itself also—and thou wast not there. For just as thou art not a bodily image, nor the emotion of a living creature (such as we feel when we rejoice or are grief-stricken, when we desire, or fear, or remember, or forget, or anything of that kind), so neither art thou the mind itself. For thou art the Lord God of the mind and of all these things that are mutable; but thou abidest immutable over all. Yet thou hast elected to dwell in my memory from the time I learned of thee. But why do I now inquire about the part of my memory thou dost dwell in, as if indeed there were separate

parts in it? Assuredly, thou dwellest in it, since I have remembered thee from the time I learned of thee, and I find thee in my memory when I call thee to mind.

CHAPTER XXVI

37. Where, then, did I find thee so as to be able to learn of thee? For thou wast not in my memory before I learned of thee. Where, then, did I find thee so as to be able to learn of thee—save in thyself beyond me.[28] Place there is none. We go "backward" and "forward" and there is no place. Everywhere and at once, O Truth, thou guidest all who consult thee, and simultaneously answerest all even though they consult thee on quite different things. Thou answerest clearly, though all do not hear in clarity. All take counsel of thee on whatever point they wish, though they do not always hear what they wish. He is thy best servant who does not look to hear from thee what he himself wills, but who wills rather to will what he hears from thee.

CHAPTER XXVII

38. Belatedly I loved thee, O Beauty so ancient and so new, belatedly I loved thee. For see, thou wast within and I was without, and I sought thee out there. Unlovely, I rushed heedlessly among the lovely things thou hast made. Thou wast with me, but I was not with thee. These things kept me far from thee; even though they were not at all unless they were in thee. Thou didst call and cry aloud, and didst force open my deafness. Thou didst gleam and shine, and didst chase away my blindness. Thou didst breathe fragrant odors and I drew in my breath; and now I pant for thee. I tasted, and now I hunger and thirst. Thou didst touch me, and I burned for thy peace.

CHAPTER XXVIII

39. When I come to be united to thee with all my being, then there will be no more pain and toil for me, and my life shall be a real life, being wholly filled by thee. But since he whom

[28] When he is known at all, God is known as the Self-evident. This is, of course, not a doctrine of innate ideas but rather of the necessity, and reality, of divine illumination as the *dynamic source* of all our knowledge of divine reality. Cf. Coplestone, *op. cit.*, ch. IV, and Cushman, *op. cit.*

thou fillest is the one thou liftest up, I am still a burden to myself because I am not yet filled by thee. Joys of sorrow contend with sorrows of joy, and on which side the victory lies I do not know.

Woe is me! Lord, have pity on me; my evil sorrows contend with my good joys, and on which side the victory lies I do not know. Woe is me! Lord, have pity on me. Woe is me! Behold, I do not hide my wounds. Thou art the Physician, I am the sick man; thou art merciful, I need mercy. Is not the life of man on earth an ordeal? Who is he that wishes for vexations and difficulties? Thou commandest them to be endured, not to be loved. For no man loves what he endures, though he may love to endure. Yet even if he rejoices to endure, he would prefer that there were nothing for him to endure. In adversity, I desire prosperity; in prosperity, I fear adversity. What middle place is there, then, between these two, where human life is not an ordeal? There is woe in the prosperity of this world; there is woe in the fear of misfortune; there is woe in the distortion of joy. There is woe in the adversities of this world—a second woe, and a third, from the desire of prosperity—because adversity itself is a hard thing to bear and makes shipwreck of endurance. Is not the life of man upon the earth an ordeal, and that without surcease?

CHAPTER XXIX

40. My whole hope is in thy exceeding great mercy and that alone. Give what thou commandest and command what thou wilt. Thou commandest continence from us, and when I knew, as it is said, that no one could be continent unless God gave it to him, even this was a point of wisdom to know whose gift it was.[29] For by continence we are bound up and brought back together in the One, whereas before we were scattered abroad among the many.[30] For he loves thee too little who loves along with thee anything else that he does not love for thy sake, O Love, who dost burn forever and art never quenched. O Love, O my God, enkindle me! Thou commandest continence; give what thou commandest, and command what thou wilt.

CHAPTER XXX

41. Obviously thou commandest that I should be continent from "the lust of the flesh, and the lust of the eyes, and the pride

29 Cf. Wis. 8:21.   30 Cf. *Enneads*, VI, 9:4.

of life." [31] Thou commandest me to abstain from fornication, and as for marriage itself, thou hast counseled something better than what thou dost allow. And since thou gavest it, it was done—even before I became a minister of thy sacrament. But there still exist in my memory—of which I have spoken so much—the images of such things as my habits had fixed there. These things rush into my thoughts with no power when I am awake; but in sleep they rush in not only so as to give pleasure, but even to obtain consent and what very closely resembles the deed itself. Indeed, the illusion of the image prevails to such an extent, in both my soul and my flesh, that the illusion persuades me when sleeping to what the reality cannot do when I am awake. Am I not myself at such a time, O Lord my God? And is there so much of a difference between myself awake and myself in the moment when I pass from waking to sleeping, or return from sleeping to waking?

Where, then, is the power of reason which resists such suggestions when I am awake—for even if the things themselves be forced upon it I remain unmoved? Does reason cease when the eyes close? Is it put to sleep with the bodily senses? But in that case how does it come to pass that even in slumber we often resist, and with our conscious purposes in mind, continue most chastely in them, and yield no assent to such allurements? Yet there is at least this much difference: that when it happens otherwise in dreams, when we wake up, we return to peace of conscience. And it is by this difference between sleeping and waking that we discover that it was not we who did it, while we still feel sorry that in some way it was done in us.

42. Is not thy hand, O Almighty God, able to heal all the diseases of my soul and, by thy more and more abundant grace, to quench even the lascivious motions of my sleep? Thou wilt increase thy gifts in me more and more, O Lord, that my soul may follow me to thee, wrenched free from the sticky glue of lust so that it is no longer in rebellion against itself, even in dreams; that it neither commits nor consents to these debasing corruptions which come through sensual images and which result in the pollution of the flesh. For it is no great thing for the Almighty, who is "able to do . . . more than we can ask or think," [32] to bring it about that no such influence—not even one so slight that a nod might restrain it—should afford gratification to the feelings of a chaste person even when sleeping. This could come to pass not only in this life but even at my present

[31] I John 2:16. [32] Eph. 3:20.

age. But what I am still in this way of wickedness I have confessed unto my good Lord, rejoicing with trembling in what thou hast given me and grieving in myself for that in which I am still imperfect. I am trusting that thou wilt perfect thy mercies in me, to the fullness of that peace which both my inner and outward being shall have with thee when death is swallowed up in victory.[33]

CHAPTER XXXI

43. There is yet another "evil of the day"[34] to which I wish I were sufficient. By eating and drinking we restore the daily losses of the body until that day when thou destroyest both food and stomach, when thou wilt destroy this emptiness with an amazing fullness and wilt clothe this corruptible with an eternal incorruption. But now the necessity of habit is sweet to me, and against this sweetness must I fight, lest I be enthralled by it. Thus I carry on a daily war by fasting, constantly "bringing my body into subjection,"[35] after which my pains are banished by pleasure. For hunger and thirst are actual pain. They consume and destroy like fever does, unless the medicine of food is at hand to relieve us. And since this medicine at hand comes from the comfort we receive in thy gifts (by means of which land and water and air serve our infirmity), even our calamity is called pleasure.

44. This much thou hast taught me: that I should learn to take food as medicine. But during that time when I pass from the pinch of emptiness to the contentment of fullness, it is in that very moment that the snare of appetite lies baited for me. For the passage itself is pleasant; there is no other way of passing thither, and necessity compels us to pass. And while health is the reason for our eating and drinking, yet a perilous delight joins itself to them as a handmaid; and indeed, she tries to take precedence in order that I may want to do for her sake what I say I want to do for health's sake. They do not both have the same limit either. What is sufficient for health is not enough for pleasure. And it is often a matter of doubt whether it is the needful care of the body that still calls for food or whether it is the sensual snare of desire still wanting to be served. In this uncertainty my unhappy soul rejoices, and uses it to prepare an excuse as a defense. It is glad that it is not clear as to what is sufficient for the moderation of health, so that under the pretense of health it may conceal its projects for pleasure. These

[33] I Cor. 15:54.   [34] Cf. Matt. 6:34.   [35] I Cor. 9:27.

temptations I daily endeavor to resist and I summon thy right hand to my help and cast my perplexities onto thee, for I have not yet reached a firm conclusion in this matter.

45. I hear the voice of my God commanding: "Let not your heart be overcharged with surfeiting and drunkenness." [36] Drunkenness is far from me. Thou wilt have mercy that it does not come near me. But "surfeiting" sometimes creeps upon thy servant. Thou wilt have mercy that it may be put far from me. For no man can be continent unless thou give it. [37] Many things that we pray for thou givest us, and whatever good we receive before we prayed for it, we receive it from thee, so that we might afterward know that we did receive it from thee. I never was a drunkard, but I have known drunkards made into sober men by thee. It was also thy doing that those who never were drunkards have not been—and likewise, it was from thee that those who have been might not remain so always. And it was likewise from thee that both might know from whom all this came.

I heard another voice of thine: "Do not follow your lusts and refrain yourself from your pleasures." [38] And by thy favor I have also heard this saying in which I have taken much delight: "Neither if we eat are we the better; nor if we eat not are we the worse." [39] This is to say that neither shall the one make me to abound, nor the other to be wretched. I heard still another voice: "For I have learned, in whatsoever state I am, therewith to be content. I know how to be abased and I know how to abound. . . . I can do all things through Christ who strengtheneth me." [40] See here a soldier of the heavenly army; not the sort of dust we are. But remember, O Lord, "that we are dust" [41] and that thou didst create man out of the dust, [42] and that he "was lost, and is found." [43] Of course, he [the apostle Paul] could not do all this by his own power. He was of the same dust—he whom I loved so much and who spoke of these things through the afflatus of thy inspiration: "I can," he said, "do all things through him who strengtheneth me." Strengthen me, that I too may be able. Give what thou commandest, and command what thou wilt. This man [Paul] confesses that he received the gift of grace and that, when he glories, he glories in the Lord. I have heard yet another voice praying that he might receive. "Take from me," he said, "the greediness of the

---

[36] Cf. Luke 21:34.
[37] Cf. Wis. 8:21.
[38] Ecclus. 18:30.
[39] I Cor. 8:8.
[40] Phil. 4:11–13.
[41] Ps. 103:14.
[42] Cf. Gen. 3:19.
[43] Luke 15:24.

belly." [44] And from this it appears, O my holy God, that thou dost give it, when what thou commandest to be done is done.

46. Thou hast taught me, good Father, that "to the pure all things are pure" [45]; but "it is evil for that man who gives offense in eating" [46]; and that "every creature of thine is good, and nothing is to be refused if it is received with thanksgiving" [47]; and that "meat does not commend us to God" [48]; and that "no man should judge us in meat or in drink." [49] "Let not him who eats despise him who eats not, and let him that does not eat judge not him who does eat." [50] These things I have learned, thanks and praise be to thee, O my God and Master, who knockest at my ears and enlightenest my heart. Deliver me from all temptation!

It is not the uncleanness of meat that I fear, but the uncleanness of an incontinent appetite. I know that permission was granted Noah to eat every kind of flesh that was good for food; that Elijah was fed with flesh; that John, blessed with a wonderful abstinence, was not polluted by the living creatures (that is, the locusts) on which he fed. And I also know that Esau was deceived by his hungering after lentils and that David blamed himself for desiring water, and that our King was tempted not by flesh but by bread. And, thus, the people in the wilderness truly deserved their reproof, not because they desired meat, but because in their desire for food they murmured against the Lord.

47. Set down, then, in the midst of these temptations, I strive daily against my appetite for food and drink. For it is not the kind of appetite I am able to deal with by cutting it off once for all, and thereafter not touching it, as I was able to do with fornication. The bridle of the throat, therefore, must be held in the mean between slackness and tightness. And who, O Lord, is he who is not in some degree carried away beyond the bounds of necessity? Whoever he is, he is great; let him magnify thy name. But I am not such a one, "for I am a sinful man." [51] Yet I too magnify thy name, for he who hath "overcome the world" [52] intercedeth with thee for my sins, numbering me among the weak members of his body; for thy eyes did see what was imperfect in him, and in thy book all shall be written down. [53]

[44] Ecclus. 23:6.
[46] Rom. 14:20.
[48] I Cor. 8:8. [49] Cf. Col. 2:16.
[51] Luke 5:8. [52] John 16:33.

[45] Titus 1:15.
[47] I Tim. 4:4.
[50] Rom. 14:3.
[53] Cf. Ps. 139:16.

CHAPTER XXXII

48. I am not much troubled by the allurement of odors. When they are absent, I do not seek them; when they are present, I do not refuse them; and I am always prepared to go without them. At any rate, I appear thus to myself; it is quite possible that I am deceived. For there is a lamentable darkness in which my capabilities are concealed, so that when my mind inquires into itself concerning its own powers, it does not readily venture to believe itself, because what already is in it is largely concealed unless experience brings it to light. Thus no man ought to feel secure in this life, the whole of which is called an ordeal, ordered so that the man who could be made better from having been worse may not also from having been better become worse. Our sole hope, our sole confidence, our only assured promise, is thy mercy.

CHAPTER XXXIII

49. The delights of the ear drew and held me much more powerfully, but thou didst unbind and liberate me. In those melodies which thy words inspire when sung with a sweet and trained voice, I still find repose; yet not so as to cling to them, but always so as to be able to free myself as I wish. But it is because of the words which are their life that they gain entry into me and strive for a place of proper honor in my heart; and I can hardly assign them a fitting one. Sometimes, I seem to myself to give them more respect than is fitting, when I see that our minds are more devoutly and earnestly inflamed in piety by the holy words when they are sung than when they are not. And I recognize that all the diverse affections of our spirits have their appropriate measures in the voice and song, to which they are stimulated by I know not what secret correlation. But the pleasures of my flesh—to which the mind ought never to be surrendered nor by them enervated—often beguile me while physical sense does not attend on reason, to follow her patiently, but having once gained entry to help the reason, it strives to run on before her and be her leader. Thus in these things I sin unknowingly, but I come to know it afterward.

50. On the other hand, when I avoid very earnestly this kind of deception, I err out of too great austerity. Sometimes I go to the point of wishing that all the melodies of the pleasant

songs to which David's Psalter is adapted should be banished both from my ears and from those of the Church itself. In this mood, the safer way seemed to me the one I remember was once related to me concerning Athanasius, bishop of Alexandria, who required the readers of the psalm to use so slight an inflection of the voice that it was more like speaking than singing.

However, when I call to mind the tears I shed at the songs of thy Church at the outset of my recovered faith, and how even now I am moved, not by the singing but by what is sung (when they are sung with a clear and skillfully modulated voice), I then come to acknowledge the great utility of this custom. Thus I vacillate between dangerous pleasure and healthful exercise. I am inclined—though I pronounce no irrevocable opinion on the subject—to approve of the use of singing in the church, so that by the delights of the ear the weaker minds may be stimulated to a devotional mood.[54] Yet when it happens that I am more moved by the singing than by what is sung, I confess myself to have sinned wickedly, and then I would rather not have heard the singing. See now what a condition I am in! Weep with me, and weep for me, those of you who can so control your inward feelings that good results always come forth. As for you who do not act this way at all, such things do not concern you. But do thou, O Lord, my God, give ear; look and see, and have mercy upon me; and heal me—thou, in whose sight I am become an enigma to myself; this itself is my weakness.

CHAPTER XXXIV

51. There remain the delights of these eyes of my flesh, about which I must make my confession in the hearing of the ears of thy temple, brotherly and pious ears. Thus I will finish the list of the temptations of carnal appetite which still assail me—groaning and desiring as I am to be clothed upon with my house from heaven.[55]

The eyes delight in fair and varied forms, and bright and pleasing colors. Let these not take possession of my soul! Rather let God possess it, he who didst make all these things very good indeed. He is still my good, and not these. The pleasures of sight affect me all the time I am awake. There is no rest from them given me, as there is from the voices of melody, which I can occasionally find in silence. For daylight, that queen of the

[54] Cf. the evidence for Augustine's interest and proficiency in music in his essay *De musica*, written a decade earlier. [55] Cf. II Cor. 5:2.

colors, floods all that we look upon everywhere I go during the day. It flits about me in manifold forms and soothes me even when I am busy about other things, not noticing it. And it presents itself so forcibly that if it is suddenly withdrawn it is looked for with longing, and if it is long absent the mind is saddened.

52. O Light, which Tobit saw even with his eyes closed in blindness, when he taught his son the way of life—and went before him himself in the steps of love and never went astray[56]; or that Light which Isaac saw when his fleshly "eyes were dim, so that he could not see" [57] because of old age, and it was permitted him unknowingly to bless his sons, but in the blessing of them to know them; or that Light which Jacob saw, when he too, blind in old age yet with an enlightened heart, threw light on the nation of men yet to come—presignified in the persons of his own sons—and laid his hands mystically crossed upon his grandchildren by Joseph (not as their father, who saw them from without, but as though he were within them), and distinguished them aright [58]: this is the true Light; it is one, and all are one who see and love it.

But that corporeal light, of which I was speaking, seasons the life of the world for her blind lovers with a tempting and fatal sweetness. Those who know how to praise thee for it, "O God, Creator of Us All," take it up in thy hymn,[59] and are not taken over by it in their sleep. Such a man I desire to be. I resist the seductions of my eyes, lest my feet be entangled as I go forward in thy way; and I raise my invisible eyes to thee, that thou wouldst be pleased to "pluck my feet out of the net."[60] Thou dost continually pluck them out, for they are easily ensnared. Thou ceasest not to pluck them out, but I constantly remain fast in the snares set all around me. However, thou who "keepest Israel shall neither slumber nor sleep."[61]

53. What numberless things there are: products of the various arts and manufactures in our clothes, shoes, vessels, and all such things; besides such things as pictures and statuary—and all these far beyond the necessary and moderate use of them or their significance for the life of piety—which men have added

[56] Cf. Tobit, chs. 2 to 4.
[57] Gen. 27:1; cf. Augustine's *Sermon* IV, 20:21 f.
[58] Cf. Gen., ch. 48.
[59] Again, Ambrose, *Deus, creator omnium,* an obvious favorite of Augustine's. See above, Bk. IX, Ch. XII, 32.
[60] Ps. 25:15.   [61] Ps. 121:4.

for the delight of the eye, copying the outward forms of the things they make; but inwardly forsaking Him by whom they were made and destroying what they themselves have been made to be!

And I, O my God and my Joy, I also raise a hymn to thee for all these things, and offer a sacrifice of praise to my Sanctifier, because those beautiful forms which pass through the medium of the human soul into the artist's hands come from that beauty which is above our minds, which my soul sighs for day and night. But the craftsmen and devotees of these outward beauties discover the norm by which they judge them from that higher beauty, but not the measure of their use. Still, even if they do not see it, it is there nevertheless, to guard them from wandering astray, and to keep their strength for thee, and not dissipate it in delights that pass into boredom. And for myself, though I can see and understand this, I am still entangled in my own course with such beauty, but thou wilt rescue me, O Lord, thou wilt rescue me, "for thy loving-kindness is before my eyes." [62] For I am captivated in my weakness but thou in thy mercy dost rescue me: sometimes without my knowing it, because I had only lightly fallen; at other times, the rescue is painful because I was stuck fast.

CHAPTER XXXV

54. Besides this there is yet another form of temptation still more complex in its peril. For in addition to the fleshly appetite which strives for the gratification of all senses and pleasures—in which its slaves perish because they separate themselves from thee—there is also a certain vain and curious longing in the soul, rooted in the same bodily senses, which is cloaked under the name of knowledge and learning; not having pleasure in the flesh, but striving for new experiences through the flesh. This longing—since its origin is our appetite for learning, and since the sight is the chief of our senses in the acquisition of knowledge—is called in the divine language "the lust of the eyes." [63] For seeing is a function of the eyes; yet we also use this word for the other senses as well, when we exercise them in the search for knowledge. We do not say, "Listen how it glows," "Smell how it glistens," "Taste how it shines," or "Feel how it flashes," since all of these are said to be *seen*. And we do not simply say, "See how it shines," which only the eyes can perceive; but we

also say, "See how it sounds, see how it smells, see how it tastes, see how hard it is." Thus, as we said before, the whole round of sensory experience is called "the lust of the eyes" because the function of seeing, in which the eyes have the principal role, is applied by analogy to the other senses when they are seeking after any kind of knowledge.

55. From this, then, one can the more clearly distinguish whether it is pleasure or curiosity that is being pursued by the senses. For pleasure pursues objects that are beautiful, melodious, fragrant, savory, soft. But curiosity, seeking new experiences, will even seek out the contrary of these, not with the purpose of experiencing the discomfort that often accompanies them, but out of a passion for experimenting and knowledge.

For what pleasure is there in the sight of a lacerated corpse, which makes you shudder? And yet if there is one lying close by we flock to it, as if to be made sad and pale. People fear lest they should see such a thing even in sleep, just as they would if, when awake, someone compelled them to go and see it or if some rumor of its beauty had attracted them.

This is also the case with the other senses; it would be tedious to pursue a complete analysis of it. This malady of curiosity is the reason for all those strange sights exhibited in the theater. It is also the reason why we proceed to search out the secret powers of nature—those which have nothing to do with our destiny—which do not profit us to know about, and concerning which men desire to know only for the sake of knowing. And it is with this same motive of perverted curiosity for knowledge that we consult the magical arts. Even in religion itself, this prompting drives us to make trial of God when signs and wonders are eagerly asked of him—not desired for any saving end, but only to make trial of him.

56. In such a wilderness so vast, crammed with snares and dangers, behold how many of them I have lopped off and cast from my heart, as thou, O God of my salvation, hast enabled me to do. And yet, when would I dare to say, since so many things of this sort still buzz around our daily lives—when would I dare to say that no such motive prompts my seeing or creates a vain curiosity in me? It is true that now the theaters never attract me, nor do I now care to inquire about the courses of the stars, and my soul has never sought answers from the departed spirits. All sacrilegious oaths I abhor. And yet, O Lord my God, to whom I owe all humble and singlehearted service, with what subtle suggestion the enemy still influences me to

require some sign from thee! But by our King, and by Jerusalem, our pure and chaste homeland, I beseech thee that where any consenting to such thoughts is now far from me, so may it always be farther and farther. And when I entreat thee for the salvation of any man, the end I aim at is something more than the entreating: let it be that as thou dost what thou wilt, thou dost also give me the grace willingly to follow thy lead.

57. Now, really, in how many of the most minute and trivial things my curiosity is still daily tempted, and who can keep the tally on how often I succumb? How often, when people are telling idle tales, we begin by tolerating them lest we should give offense to the sensitive; and then gradually we come to listen willingly! I do not nowadays go to the circus to see a dog chase a rabbit, but if by chance I pass such a race in the fields, it quite easily distracts me even from some serious thought and draws me after it—not that I turn aside with my horse, but with the inclination of my mind. And unless, by showing me my weakness, thou dost speedily warn me to rise above such a sight to thee by a deliberate act of thought—or else to despise the whole thing and pass it by—then I become absorbed in the sight, vain creature that I am.

How is it that when I am sitting at home a lizard catching flies, or a spider entangling them as they fly into her webs, oftentimes arrests me? Is the feeling of curiosity not the same just because these are such tiny creatures? From them I proceed to praise thee, the wonderful Creator and Disposer of all things; but it is not this that first attracts my attention. It is one thing to get up quickly and another thing not to fall—and of both such things my life is full and my only hope is in thy exceeding great mercy. For when this heart of ours is made the depot of such things and is overrun by the throng of these abounding vanities, then our prayers are often interrupted and disturbed by them. Even while we are in thy presence and direct the voice of our hearts to thy ears, such a great business as this is broken off by the inroads of I know not what idle thoughts.

CHAPTER XXXVI

58. Shall we, then, also reckon this vain curiosity among the things that are to be but lightly esteemed? Shall anything restore us to hope except thy complete mercy since thou hast begun to change us? Thou knowest to what extent thou hast already changed me, for first of all thou didst heal me of the lust

for vindicating myself, so that thou mightest then forgive all my remaining iniquities and heal all my diseases, and "redeem my life from corruption and crown me with loving-kindness and tender mercies, and satisfy my desires with good things." [64] It was thou who didst restrain my pride with thy fear, and bowed my neck to thy "yoke." [65] And now I bear the yoke and it is "light" to me, because thou didst promise it to be so, and hast made it to be so. And so in truth it was, though I knew it not when I feared to take it up.

59. But, O Lord—thou who alone reignest without pride, because thou alone art the true Lord, who hast no Lord—has this third kind of temptation left me, or can it leave me during this life: the desire to be feared and loved of men, with no other view than that I may find in it a joy that is no joy? It is, rather, a wretched life and an unseemly ostentation. It is a special reason why we do not love thee, nor devotedly fear thee. Therefore "thou resistest the proud but givest grace to the humble." [66] Thou thunderest down on the ambitious designs of the world, and "the foundations of the hills" tremble. [67]

And yet certain offices in human society require the office-holder to be loved and feared of men, and through this the adversary of our true blessedness presses hard upon us, scattering everywhere his snares of "well done, well done"; so that while we are eagerly picking them up, we may be caught unawares and split off our joy from thy truth and fix it on the deceits of men. In this way we come to take pleasure in being loved and feared, not for thy sake but in thy stead. By such means as this, the adversary makes men like himself, that he may have them as his own, not in the harmony of love, but in the fellowship of punishment—the one who aspired to exalt his throne in the north,[68] that in the darkness and the cold men might have to serve him, mimicking thee in perverse and distorted ways.

But see, O Lord, we are thy little flock. Possess us, stretch thy wings above us, and let us take refuge under them. Be thou our glory; let us be loved for thy sake, and let thy word be feared in us. Those who desire to be commended by the men whom thou condemnest will not be defended by men when thou judgest, nor will they be delivered when thou dost condemn them. But when—not as a sinner is praised in the wicked desires of his soul nor when the unrighteous man is blessed in his unrighteousness

---

[64] Cf. Ps. 103: 3–5.
[65] Cf. Matt. 11:30.
[66] I Peter 5:5.
[67] Cf. Ps. 18:7, 13.
[68] Cf. Isa. 14:12–14.

—a man is praised for some gift that thou hast given him, and he is more gratified at the praise for himself than because he possesses the gift for which he is praised, such a one is praised while thou dost condemn him. In such a case the one who praised is truly better than the one who was praised. For the gift of God in man was pleasing to the one, while the other was better pleased with the gift of man than with the gift of God.

CHAPTER XXXVII

60. By these temptations we are daily tried, O Lord; we are tried unceasingly. Our daily "furnace" is the human tongue. [69] And also in this respect thou commandest us to be continent. Give what thou commandest and command what thou wilt. In this matter, thou knowest the groans of my heart and the rivers of my eyes, for I am not able to know for certain how far I am clean of this plague; and I stand in great fear of my "secret faults," [70] which thy eyes perceive, though mine do not. For in respect of the pleasures of my flesh and of idle curiosity, I see how far I have been able to hold my mind in check when I abstain from them either by voluntary act of the will or because they simply are not at hand; for then I can inquire of myself how much more or less frustrating it is to me not to have them. This is also true about riches, which are sought for in order that they may minister to one of these three "lusts," or two, or the whole complex of them. The mind is able to see clearly if, when it has them, it despises them so that they may be cast aside and it may prove itself.

But if we desire to test our power of doing without praise, must we then live wickedly or lead a life so atrocious and abandoned that everyone who knows us will detest us? What greater madness than this can be either said or conceived? And yet if praise, both by custom and right, is the companion of a good life and of good works, we should as little forgo its companionship as the good life itself. But unless a thing is absent I do not know whether I should be contented or troubled at having to do without it.

61. What is it, then, that I am confessing to thee, O Lord, concerning this sort of temptation? What else, than that I am delighted with praise, but more with the truth itself than with praise. For if I were to have any choice whether, if I were mad or utterly in the wrong, I would prefer to be praised by all men

---

[69] Cf. Prov. 27:21.   [70] Cf. Ps. 19:12.

or, if I were steadily and fully confident in the truth, would prefer to be blamed by all, I see which I should choose. Yet I wish I were unwilling that the approval of others should add anything to my joy for any good I have. Yet I admit that it does increase it; and, more than that, dispraise diminishes it. Then, when I am disturbed over this wretchedness of mine, an excuse presents itself to me, the value of which thou knowest, O God, for it renders me uncertain. For since it is not only continence that thou hast enjoined on us—that is, what things to hold back our love from—but righteousness as well—that is, what to bestow our love upon—and hast wished us to love not only thee, but also our neighbor, it often turns out that when I am gratified by intelligent praise I seem to myself to be gratified by the competence or insight of my neighbor; or, on the other hand, I am sorry for the defect in him when I hear him dispraise either what he does not understand or what is good. For I am sometimes grieved at the praise I get, either when those things that displease me in myself are praised in me, or when lesser and trifling goods are valued more highly than they should be. But, again, how do I know whether I feel this way because I am unwilling that he who praises me should differ from me concerning myself not because I am moved with any consideration for him, but because the good things that please me in myself are more pleasing to me when they also please another? For in a way, I am not praised when my judgment of myself is not praised, since either those things which are displeasing to me are praised, or those things which are less pleasing to me are more praised. Am I not, then, quite uncertain of myself in this respect?

62. Behold, O Truth, it is in thee that I see that I ought not to be moved at my own praises for my own sake, but for the sake of my neighbor's good. And whether this is actually my way, I truly do not know. On this score I know less of myself than thou dost. I beseech thee now, O my God, to reveal myself to me also, that I may confess to my brethren, who are to pray for me in those matters where I find myself weak.

Let me once again examine myself the more diligently. If, in my own praise, I am moved with concern for my neighbor, why am I less moved if some other man is unjustly dispraised than when it happens to me? Why am I more irritated at that reproach which is cast on me than at one which is, with equal injustice, cast upon another in my presence? Am I ignorant of this also? Or is it still true that I am deceiving myself, and do not keep the truth before thee in my heart and tongue? Put such madness far from me, O Lord, lest my mouth be to me "the oil of sinners, to anoint my head." [71]

CHAPTER XXXVIII

63. "I am needy and poor." [72] Still, I am better when in secret groanings I displease myself and seek thy mercy until what is lacking in me is renewed and made complete for that peace which the eye of the proud does not know. The reports that come from the mouth and from actions known to men have in them a most perilous temptation to the love of praise. This love builds up a certain complacency in one's own excellency, and then goes around collecting solicited compliments. It tempts me, even when I inwardly reprove myself for it, and this precisely because it is reproved. For a man may often glory vainly in the very scorn of vainglory—and in this case it is not any longer the scorn of vainglory in which he glories, for he does not truly despise it when he inwardly glories in it.

CHAPTER XXXIX

64. Within us there is yet another evil arising from the same sort of temptation. By it they become empty who please themselves in themselves, although they do not please or displease or aim at pleasing others. But in pleasing themselves they displease thee very much, not merely taking pleasure in things that are not good as if they were good, but taking pleasure in thy good things as if they were their own; or even as if they were thine but still as if they had received them through their own merit; or even as if they had them through thy grace, still without this grace with their friends, but as if they envied that grace to others. In all these and similar perils and labors, thou perceivest the agitation of my heart, and I would rather feel my wounds being cured by thee than not inflicted by me on myself.

CHAPTER XL

65. Where hast thou not accompanied me, O Truth, teaching me both what to avoid and what to desire, when I have submitted to thee what I could understand about matters here below, and have sought thy counsel about them?

[71] Cf. Ps. 141:5.   [72] Ps. 109:22.

With my external senses I have viewed the world as I was able and have noticed the life which my body derives from me and from these senses of mine. From that stage I advanced inwardly into the recesses of my memory—the manifold chambers of my mind, marvelously full of unmeasured wealth. And I reflected on this and was afraid, and could understand none of these things without thee and found thee to be none of them. Nor did I myself discover these things—I who went over them all and labored to distinguish and to value everything according to its dignity, accepting some things upon the report of my senses and questioning about others which I thought to be related to my inner self, distinguishing and numbering the reporters themselves; and in that vast storehouse of my memory, investigating some things, depositing other things, taking out still others. Neither was I myself when I did this—that is, that ability of mine by which I did it—nor was it thou, for thou art that never-failing light from which I took counsel about them all; whether they were what they were, and what was their real value. In all this I heard thee teaching and commanding me. And this I often do—and this is a delight to me—and as far as I can get relief from my necessary duties, I resort to this kind of pleasure. But in all these things which I review when I consult thee, I still do not find a secure place for my soul save in thee, in whom my scattered members may be gathered together and nothing of me escape from thee. And sometimes thou introducest me to a most rare and inward feeling, an inexplicable sweetness. If this were to come to perfection in me I do not know to what point life might not then arrive. But still, by these wretched weights of mine, I relapse into these common things, and am sucked in by my old customs and am held. I sorrow much, yet I am still closely held. To this extent, then, the burden of habit presses us down. I can exist in this fashion but I do not wish to do so. In that other way I wish I were, but cannot be—in both ways I am wretched.

CHAPTER XLI

66. And now I have thus considered the infirmities of my sins, under the headings of the three major "lusts," and I have called thy right hand to my aid. For with a wounded heart I have seen thy brightness, and having been beaten back I cried: "Who can attain to it? I am cut off from before thy eyes." [73]

73 Ps. 31:22.

Thou art the Truth, who presidest over all things, but I, because of my greed, did not wish to lose thee. But still, along with thee, I wished also to possess a lie—just as no one wishes to lie in such a way as to be ignorant of what is true. By this I lost thee, for thou wilt not condescend to be enjoyed along with a lie.

CHAPTER XLII

67. Whom could I find to reconcile me to thee? Should I have approached the angels? What kind of prayer? What kind of rites? Many who were striving to return to thee and were not able of themselves have, I am told, tried this and have fallen into a longing for curious visions and deserved to be deceived. Being exalted, they sought thee in their pride of learning, and they thrust themselves forward rather than beating their breasts.[74] And so by a likeness of heart, they drew to themselves the princes of the air,[75] their conspirators and companions in pride, by whom they were deceived by the power of magic. Thus they sought a mediator by whom they might be cleansed, but there was none. For the mediator they sought was the devil, disguising himself as an angel of light.[76] And he allured their proud flesh the more because he had no fleshly body.

They were mortal and sinful, but thou, O Lord, to whom they arrogantly sought to be reconciled, art immortal and sinless. But a mediator between God and man ought to have something in him like God and something in him like man, lest in being like man he should be far from God, or if only like God he should be far from man, and so should not be a mediator. That deceitful mediator, then, by whom, by thy secret judgment, human pride deserves to be deceived, had one thing in common with man, that is, his sin. In another respect, he would seem to have something in common with God, for not being clothed with the mortality of the flesh, he could boast that he was immortal. But since "the wages of sin is death," [77] what he really has in common with men is that, together with them, he is condemned to death.

CHAPTER XLIII

68. But the true Mediator, whom thou in thy secret mercy hast revealed to the humble, and hast sent to them so that

---

[74] Cf. the parable of the Pharisee and the Publican, Luke 18:9-14.
[75] Cf. Eph. 2:2.   [76] II Cor. 11:14.   [77] Rom. 6:23.

through his example they also might learn the same humility—
that "Mediator between God and man, the man Christ Jesus," [78]
appeared between mortal sinners and the immortal Just One.
He was mortal as men are mortal; he was righteous as God is
righteous; and because the reward of righteousness is life and
peace, he could, through his righteousness united with God,
cancel the death of justified sinners, which he was willing to
have in common with them. Hence he was manifested to holy
men of old, to the end that they might be saved through faith in
his Passion to come, even as we through faith in his Passion
which is past. As man he was Mediator, but as the Word he
was not something in between the two; because he was equal
to God, and God with God, and, with the Holy Spirit, one
God.

69. How hast thou loved us, O good Father, who didst not
spare thy only Son, but didst deliver him up for us wicked ones![79]
How hast thou loved us, for whom he who did not count it
robbery to be equal with thee "became obedient unto death,
even the death of the cross" [80]! He alone was "free among the
dead." [81] He alone had power to lay down his life and power to
take it up again, and for us he became to thee both Victor and
Victim; and Victor because he was the Victim. For us, he was
to thee both Priest and Sacrifice, and Priest because he was the
Sacrifice. Out of slaves, he maketh us thy sons, because he was
born of thee and did serve us. Rightly, then, is my hope fixed
strongly on him, that thou wilt "heal all my diseases" [82] through
him, who sitteth at thy right hand and maketh intercession for
us.[83] Otherwise I should utterly despair. For my infirmities
are many and great; indeed, they are very many and very
great. But thy medicine is still greater. Otherwise, we might
think that thy word was removed from union with man, and
despair of ourselves, if it had not been that he was "made flesh
and dwelt among us." [84]

70. Terrified by my sins and the load of my misery, I had
resolved in my heart and considered flight into the wilderness.
But thou didst forbid me, and thou didst strengthen me, saying
that "since Christ died for all, they who live should not henceforth live unto themselves, but unto him who died for them." [85]
Behold, O Lord, I cast all my care on thee, that I may live and

---

[78] I Tim. 2:5.   [79] Cf. Rom. 8:32.
[80] Phil. 2:6–8.   [81] Cf. Ps. 88:5; see Ps. 87:6 (Vulgate).
[82] Ps. 103:3.   [83] Cf. Rom. 8:34.
[84] John 1:14.   [85] II Cor. 5:15.

"behold wondrous things out of thy law." [86] Thou knowest my incompetence and my infirmities; teach me and heal me. Thy only Son—he "in whom are hid all the treasures of wisdom and knowledge" [87]—hath redeemed me with his blood. Let not the proud speak evil of me, because I keep my ransom before my mind, and eat and drink and share my food and drink. For, being poor, I desire to be satisfied from him, together with those who eat and are satisfied: "and they shall praise the Lord that seek Him." [88]

[86] Ps. 119:18.   [87] Col. 2:3.   [88] Cf. Ps. 21:27 (Vulgate).

BOOK ELEVEN

The eternal Creator and the Creation in time. Augustine ties together his memory of his past life, his present experience, and his ardent desire to comprehend the mystery of creation. This leads him to the questions of the mode and time of creation. He ponders the mode of creation and shows that it was de nihilo *and involved no alteration in the being of God. He then considers the question of the beginning of the world and time and shows that time and creation are cotemporal. But what is time? To this Augustine devotes a brilliant analysis of the subjectivity of time and the relation of all temporal process to the abiding eternity of God. From this, he prepares to turn to a detailed interpretation of Gen.* 1:1, 2.

CHAPTER I

1. Is it possible, O Lord, that, since thou art in eternity, thou art ignorant of what I am saying to thee? Or, dost thou see in time an event at the time it occurs? If not, then why am I recounting such a tale of things to thee? Certainly not in order to acquaint thee with them through me; but, instead, that through them I may stir up my own love and the love of my readers toward thee, so that all may say, "Great is the Lord and greatly to be praised." I have said this before[1] and will say it again: "For love of thy love I do it." So also we pray—and yet Truth tells us, "Your Father knoweth what things you need before you ask him."[2] Consequently, we lay bare our feelings before

---

[1] In the very first sentence of *Confessions*, Bk. I, Ch. I. Here we have a basic and recurrent motif of the *Confessions* from beginning to end: the celebration and praise of the greatness and goodness of God—Creator and Redeemer. The repetition of it here connects this concluding section of the *Confessions*, Bks. XI–XIII, with the preceding part.

[2] Matt. 6:8.

thee, that, through our confessing to thee our plight and thy
mercies toward us, thou mayest go on to free us altogether, as
thou hast already begun; and that we may cease to be wretched
in ourselves and blessed in thee—since thou hast called us to be
poor in spirit, meek, mourners, hungering and athirst for
righteousness, merciful and pure in heart.[3] Thus I have told
thee many things, as I could find ability and will to do so, since
it was thy will in the first place that I should confess to thee, O
Lord my God—for "Thou art good and thy mercy endureth
forever."[4]

CHAPTER II

2. But how long would it take for the voice of my pen to tell
enough of thy exhortations and of all thy terrors and comforts
and leadings by which thou didst bring me to preach thy Word
and to administer thy sacraments to thy people? And even if I
could do this sufficiently, the drops of time[5] are very precious
to me and I have for a long time been burning with the desire
to meditate on thy law, and to confess in thy presence my
knowledge and ignorance of it—from the first streaks of thy
light in my mind and the remaining darkness, until my weakness shall be swallowed up in thy strength. And I do not wish
to see those hours drained into anything else which I can find
free from the necessary care of the body, the exercise of the
mind, and the service we owe to our fellow men—and what we
give even if we do not owe it.

3. O Lord my God, hear my prayer and let thy mercy attend
my longing. It does not burn for itself alone but longs as well
to serve the cause of fraternal love. Thou seest in my heart that
this is so. Let me offer the service of my mind and my tongue—
and give me what I may in turn offer back to thee. For "I am
needy and poor"; thou art rich to all who call upon thee—
thou who, in thy freedom from care, carest for us. Trim away
from my lips, inwardly and outwardly, all rashness and lying.
Let thy Scriptures be my chaste delight. Let me not be deceived
in them, nor deceive others from them. O Lord, hear and pity!
O Lord my God, light of the blind, strength of the weak—and
also the light of those who see and the strength of the strong—
hearken to my soul and hear it crying from the depths.[6] Unless

---

[3] The "virtues" of the Beatitudes, the reward for which is blessedness; cf.
Matt. 5:1–11. [4] Ps. 118:1; cf. Ps. 136.
[5] An interesting symbol of time's ceaseless passage; the reference is to a
water clock (*clepsydra*). [6] Cf. Ps. 130:1, *De profundis,*

thy ears attend us even in the depths, where should we go? To whom should we cry?

"Thine is the day and the night is thine as well." [7] At thy bidding the moments fly by. Grant me in them, then, an interval for my meditations on the hidden things of thy law, nor close the door of thy law against us who knock. Thou hast not willed that the deep secrets of all those pages should have been written in vain. Those forests are not without their stags which keep retired within them, ranging and walking and feeding, lying down and ruminating. [8] Perfect me, O Lord, and reveal their secrets to me. Behold, thy voice is my joy; thy voice surpasses in abundance of delights. Give me what I love, for I do love it. And this too is thy gift. Abandon not thy gifts and despise not thy "grass" which thirsts for thee. [9] Let me confess to thee everything that I shall have found in thy books and "let me hear the voice of thy praise." [10] Let me drink from thee and "consider the wondrous things out of thy law" [11]—from the very beginning, when thou madest heaven and earth, and thenceforward to the everlasting reign of thy Holy City with thee.

4. O Lord, have mercy on me and hear my petition. For my prayer is not for earthly things, neither gold nor silver and precious stones, nor gorgeous apparel, nor honors and power, nor fleshly pleasures, nor of bodily necessities in this life of our pilgrimage: all of these things are "added" to those who seek thy Kingdom and thy righteousness. [12]

Observe, O God, from whence comes my desire. The unrighteous have told me of delights but not such as those in thy law, O Lord. Behold, this is the spring of my desire. See, O Father, look and see—and approve! Let it be pleasing in thy mercy's sight that I should find favor with thee—that the secret things of thy Word may be opened to me when I knock. I beg this of thee by our Lord Jesus Christ, thy Son, the Man of thy right hand, the Son of Man; whom thou madest strong for thy purpose as Mediator between thee and us; through whom thou didst seek us when we were not seeking thee, but didst seek us so that we might seek thee; thy Word, through whom thou madest all things, and me among them; thy only Son, through whom thou hast called thy faithful people to adoption, and me among them. I beseech it of thee through

---

[7] Ps. 74:16.   [8] This metaphor is probably from Ps. 29:9.
[9] A repetition of the metaphor above, Bk. IX, Ch. VII, 16.
[10] Ps. 26:7.   [11] Ps. 119:18.   [12] Cf. Matt. 6:33.

him who sitteth at thy right hand and maketh intercession for us, "in whom are hid all treasures of wisdom and knowledge." [13] It is he I seek in thy books. Moses wrote of him. He tells us so himself; the Truth tells us so.

CHAPTER III

5. Let me hear and understand how in the beginning thou madest heaven and earth.[14] Moses wrote of this; he wrote and passed on—moving from thee to thee—and he is now no longer before me. If he were, I would lay hold on him and ask him and entreat him solemnly that in thy name he would open out these things to me, and I would lend my bodily ears to the sounds that came forth out of his mouth. If, however, he spoke in the Hebrew language, the sounds would beat on my senses in vain, and nothing would touch my mind; but if he spoke in Latin, I would understand what he said. But how should I then know whether what he said was true? If I knew even this much, would it be that I knew it from him? Indeed, within me, deep inside the chambers of my thought, Truth itself—neither Hebrew, nor Greek, nor Latin, nor barbarian, without any organs of voice and tongue, without the sound of syllables—would say, "He speaks the truth," and I should be assured by this. Then I would confidently say to that man of thine, "You speak the truth." [15] However, since I cannot inquire of Moses, I beseech thee, O Truth, from whose fullness he spoke truth; I beseech thee, my God, forgive my sins, and as thou gavest thy servant the gift to speak these things, grant me also the gift to understand them.

CHAPTER IV

6. Look around; there are the heaven and the earth. They cry aloud that they were made, for they change and vary. Whatever there is that has not been made, and yet has being,

13 Col. 2:3.
14 Augustine was profoundly stirred, in mind and heart, by the great mystery of creation and the Scriptural testimony about it. In addition to this long and involved analysis of time and creation which follows here, he returned to the story in Genesis repeatedly: e.g., *De Genesi contra Manicheos*; *De Genesi ad litteram, liber imperfectus* (both written *before* the *Confessions*); *De Genesi ad litteram, libri* XII and *De civitate Dei*, XI–XII (both written *after* the *Confessions*).
15 The final test of truth, for Augustine, is self-evidence and the final source of truth is the indwelling Logos.

has nothing in it that was not there before. This having something not already existent is what it means to be changed and varied. Heaven and earth thus speak plainly that they did not make themselves: "We are, because we have been made; we did not exist before we came to be so that we could have made ourselves!" And the voice with which they speak is simply their visible presence. It was thou, O Lord, who madest these things. Thou art beautiful; thus they are beautiful. Thou art good, thus they are good. Thou art; thus they are. But they are not as beautiful, nor as good, nor as truly real as thou their Creator art. Compared with thee, they are neither beautiful nor good, nor do they even exist. These things we know, thanks be to thee. Yet our knowledge is ignorance when it is compared with thy knowledge.

CHAPTER V

7. But *how* didst thou make the heaven and the earth, and what was the tool of such a mighty work as thine? For it was not like a human worker fashioning body from body, according to the fancy of his mind, able somehow or other to impose on it a form which the mind perceived in itself by its inner eye (yet how should even he be able to do this, if thou hadst not made that mind?). He imposes the form on something already existing and having some sort of being, such as clay, or stone or wood or gold or such like (and where would these things come from if thou hadst not furnished them?). For thou madest his body for the artisan, and thou madest the mind which directs the limbs; thou madest the matter from which he makes anything; thou didst create the capacity by which he understands his art and sees within his mind what he may do with the things before him; thou gavest him his bodily sense by which, as if he had an interpreter, he may communicate from mind to matter what he proposes to do and report back to his mind what has been done, that the mind may consult with the Truth which presideth over it as to whether what is done is well done.

All these things praise thee, the Creator of them all. But how didst thou make them? How, O God, didst thou make the heaven and earth? For truly, neither in heaven nor on earth didst thou make heaven and earth—nor in the air nor in the waters, since all of these also belong to the heaven and the earth. Nowhere in the whole world didst thou make the whole world, because there was no place where it could be made before it was made. And thou didst not hold anything in thy hand from which to fashion the heaven and the earth,[16] for where couldst thou have gotten what thou hadst not made in order to make something with it? Is there, indeed, anything at all except because thou art? Thus thou didst speak and they were made,[17] and by thy Word thou didst make them all.

CHAPTER VI

8. But how didst thou speak? Was it in the same manner in which the voice came from the cloud saying, "This is my beloved Son"[18]? For that voice sounded forth and died away; it began and ended. The syllables sounded and passed away, the second after the first, the third after the second, and thence in order, till the very last after all the rest; and silence after the last. From this it is clear and plain that it was the action of a creature, itself in time, which sounded that voice, obeying thy eternal will. And what these words were which were formed at that time the outer ear conveyed to the conscious mind, whose inner ear lay attentively open to thy eternal Word. But it compared those words which sounded in time with thy eternal word sounding in silence and said: "This is different; quite different! These words are far below me; they are not even real, for they fly away and pass, but the Word of my God remains above me forever." If, then, in words that sound and fade away thou didst say that heaven and earth should be made, and thus madest heaven and earth, then there was already some kind of corporeal creature before heaven and earth by whose motions in time that voice might have had its occurrence in time. But there was nothing corporeal before the heaven and the earth; or if there was, then it is certain that already, without a time-bound voice, thou hadst created whatever it was out of which thou didst make the time-bound voice by which thou didst say, "Let the heaven and the earth be made!" For whatever it was out of which such a voice was made simply did not exist at all until it was made by thee. Was it decreed by thy Word that a body might be made from which such words might come?

16 Cf. the notion of creation in Plato's *Timaeus* (29D–30C; 48E–50C), in which the Demiurgos (craftsman) fashions the universe from pre-existent "matter" (τὸ ὑποδοχή) and imposes as much form as the Receptacle will receive. The notion of the world fashioned from pre-existent matter of some sort was a universal idea in Greco-Roman cosmology.

17 Cf. Ps. 33:9.   18 Matt. 3:17.

CHAPTER VII

9. Thou dost call us, then, to understand the Word—the God who is God with thee—which is spoken eternally and by which all things are spoken eternally. For what was first spoken was not finished, and then something else spoken until the whole series was spoken; but all things at the same time and forever. For, otherwise, we should have time and change and not a true eternity, nor a true immortality.

This I know, O my God, and I give thanks. I know, I confess to thee, O Lord, and whoever is not ungrateful for certain truths knows and blesses thee along with me. We know, O Lord, this much we know: that in the same proportion as anything is not what it was, and is what it was not, in that very same proportion it passes away or comes to be. But there is nothing in thy Word that passes away or returns to its place; for it is truly immortal and eternal. And, therefore, unto the Word coeternal with thee, at the same time and always thou sayest all that thou sayest. And whatever thou sayest shall be made is made, and thou makest nothing otherwise than by speaking. Still, not all the things that thou dost make by speaking are made at the same time and always.

CHAPTER VIII

10. Why is this, I ask of thee, O Lord my God? I see it after a fashion, but I do not know how to express it, unless I say that everything that begins to be and then ceases to be begins and ceases when it is known in thy eternal Reason that it ought to begin or cease—in thy eternal Reason where nothing begins or ceases. And this is thy Word, which is also "the Beginning," because it also speaks to us.[19] Thus, in the gospel, he spoke through the flesh; and this sounded in the outward ears of men so that it might be believed and sought for within, and so that it might be found in the eternal Truth, in which the good and only Master teacheth all his disciples.[20] There, O Lord, I hear thy voice, the voice of one speaking to me, since he who teacheth us speaketh to us. But he that doth not teach us doth not really speak to us even when he speaketh. Yet who is it that teacheth us unless it be the Truth immutable? For even when we are instructed by means of the mutable creation, we are thereby led

[19] Cf. the Vulgate of John 8:25.
[20] Cf. Augustine's emphasis on Christ as true Teacher in *De Magistro*.

to the Truth immutable. There we learn truly as we stand and hear him, and we rejoice greatly "because of the bridegroom's voice," [21] restoring us to the source whence our being comes. And therefore, unless the Beginning remained immutable, there would then not be a place to which we might return when we had wandered away. But when we return from error, it is through our gaining knowledge that we return. In order for us to gain knowledge he teacheth us, since he is the Beginning, and speaketh to us.

CHAPTER IX

11. In this Beginning, O God, thou hast made heaven and earth—through thy Word, thy Son, thy Power, thy Wisdom, thy Truth: all wondrously speaking and wondrously creating. Who shall comprehend such things and who shall tell of it? What is it that shineth through me and striketh my heart without injury, so that I both shudder and burn? I shudder because I am unlike it; I burn because I am like it. It is Wisdom itself that shineth through me, clearing away my fog, which so readily overwhelms me so that I faint in it, in the darkness and burden of my punishment. For my strength is brought down in neediness, so that I cannot endure even my blessings until thou, O Lord, who hast been gracious to all my iniquities, also healest all my infirmities—for it is thou who "shalt redeem my life from corruption, and crown me with loving-kindness and tender mercy, and shalt satisfy my desire with good things so that my youth shall be renewed like the eagle's." [22] For by this hope we are saved, and through patience we await thy promises. Let him that is able hear thee speaking to his inner mind. I will cry out with confidence because of thy own oracle, "How wonderful are thy works, O Lord; in wisdom thou hast made them all." [23] And this Wisdom is the Beginning, and in that Beginning thou hast made heaven and earth.

CHAPTER X

12. Now, are not those still full of their old carnal nature [24] who ask us: "What was God doing *before* he made heaven and earth? For if he was idle," they say, "and doing nothing, then

---

[21] Cf. John 3:29.   [22] Cf. Ps. 103:4, 5 (mixed text).   [23] Ps. 104:24.

[24] *Pleni vetustatis suae.* In *Sermon* CCLXVII, 2 (*PL* 38, c. 1230), Augustine has a similar usage. Speaking of those who pour new wine into old containers, he says: *Carnalitas vetustas est, gratia novitas est,* "Carnality is the old nature; grace is the new"; cf. Matt. 9:17.

why did he not continue in that state forever—doing nothing, as he had always done? If any new motion has arisen in God, and a new will to form a creature, which he had never before formed, how can that be a true eternity in which an act of will occurs that was not there before? For the will of God is not a created thing, but comes before the creation—and this is true because nothing could be created unless the will of the Creator came before it. The will of God, therefore, pertains to his very Essence. Yet if anything has arisen in the Essence of God that was not there before, then that Essence cannot truly be called eternal. But if it was the eternal will of God that the creation should come to be, why, then, is not the creation itself also from eternity?" [25]

CHAPTER XI

13. Those who say these things do not yet understand thee, O Wisdom of God, O Light of souls. They do not yet understand how the things are made that are made by and in thee. They endeavor to comprehend eternal things, but their heart still flies about in the past and future motions of created things, and is still unstable. Who shall hold it and fix it so that it may come to rest for a little; and then, by degrees, glimpse the glory of that eternity which abides forever; and then, comparing eternity with the temporal process in which nothing abides, they may see that they are incommensurable? They would see that a long time does not become long, except from the many separate events that occur in its passage, which cannot be simultaneous. In the Eternal, on the other hand, nothing passes away, but the whole is simultaneously present. But no temporal process is wholly simultaneous. Therefore, let it [26] see that all time past is forced to move on by the incoming future; that all the future follows from the past; and that all, past and future, is created and issues out of that which is forever present. Who will hold the heart of man that it may stand still and see how the eternity which always stands still is itself neither future nor past but expresses itself in the times that are future and past? Can my hand do this, or can the hand of my mouth bring about so difficult a thing even by persuasion?

[25] The notion of the eternity of this world was widely held in Greek philosophy, in different versions, and was incorporated into the Manichean rejection of the Christian doctrine of *creatio ex nihilo* which Augustine is citing here. He returns to the question, and his answer to it, again in *De civitate Dei*, XI, 4–8.

[26] The unstable "heart" of those who confuse time and eternity.

CHAPTER XII

14. How, then, shall I respond to him who asks, "What was God doing *before* he made heaven and earth?" I do not answer, as a certain one is reported to have done facetiously (shrugging off the force of the question). "He was preparing hell," he said, "for those who pry too deep." It is one thing to see the answer; it is another to laugh at the questioner—and for myself I do not answer these things thus. More willingly would I have answered, "I do not know what I do not know," than cause one who asked a deep question to be ridiculed—and by such tactics gain praise for a worthless answer.

Rather, I say that thou, our God, art the Creator of every creature. And if in the term "heaven and earth" every creature is included, I make bold to say further: "Before God made heaven and earth, he did not make anything at all. For if he did, what did he make unless it were a creature?" I do indeed wish that I knew all that I desire to know to my profit as surely as I know that no creature was made before any creature was made.

CHAPTER XIII

15. But if the roving thought of someone should wander over the images of past time, and wonder that thou, the Almighty God, the All-creating and All-sustaining, the Architect of heaven and earth, didst for ages unnumbered abstain from so great a work before thou didst actually do it, let him awake and consider that he wonders at illusions. For in what temporal medium could the unnumbered ages that thou didst not make pass by, since thou art the Author and Creator of all the ages? Or what periods of time would those be that were not made by thee? Or how could they have already passed away if they had not already been? Since, therefore, thou art the Creator of all times, if there was any time *before* thou madest heaven and earth, why is it said that thou wast abstaining from working? For thou madest that very time itself, and periods could not pass by *before* thou madest the whole temporal procession. But if there was no time *before* heaven and earth, how, then, can it be asked, "What wast thou doing then?" For there was no "then" when there was no time.

16. Nor dost thou precede any given period of time by another period of time. Else thou wouldst not precede all periods

of time. In the eminence of thy ever-present eternity, thou precedest all times past, and extendest beyond all future times, for they are still to come—and when they have come, they will be past. But "Thou art always the Selfsame and thy years shall have no end." [27] Thy years neither go nor come; but ours both go and come in order that all separate moments may come to pass. All thy years stand together as one, since they are abiding. Nor do thy years past exclude the years to come because thy years do not pass away. All these years of ours shall be with thee, when all of them shall have ceased to be. Thy years are but a day, and thy day is not recurrent, but always today. Thy "today" yields not to tomorrow and does not follow yesterday. Thy "today" is eternity. Therefore, thou didst generate the Coeternal, to whom thou didst say, "This day I have begotten thee." [28] Thou madest all time and before all times thou art, and there was never a time when there was no time.

CHAPTER XIV

17. There was no time, therefore, when thou hadst not made anything, because thou hadst made time itself. And there are no times that are coeternal with thee, because thou dost abide forever; but if times should abide, they would not be times.

For what is time? Who can easily and briefly explain it? Who can even comprehend it in thought or put the answer into words? Yet is it not true that in conversation we refer to nothing more familiarly or knowingly than time? And surely we understand it when we speak of it; we understand it also when we hear another speak of it.

What, then, is time? If no one asks me, I know what it is. If I wish to explain it to him who asks me, I do not know. Yet I say with confidence that I know that if nothing passed away, there would be no past time; and if nothing were still coming, there would be no future time; and if there were nothing at all, there would be no present time.

But, then, how is it that there are the two times, past and future, when even the past is now no longer and the future is now not yet? But if the present were always present, and did not pass into past time, it obviously would not be time but eternity. If, then, time present—if it be time—comes into existence only because it passes into time past, how can we say that

[27] Cf. Ps. 102:27.   [28] Ps. 2:7.

even this *is*, since the cause of its being is that it will cease to be? Thus, can we not truly say that time *is* only as it tends toward nonbeing?

CHAPTER XV

18. And yet we speak of a long time and a short time; but never speak this way except of time past and future. We call a hundred years ago, for example, a long time past. In like manner, we should call a hundred years hence a long time to come. But we call ten days ago a short time past; and ten days hence a short time to come. But in what sense is something long or short that is nonexistent? For the past is not now, and the future is not yet. Therefore, let us not say, "It *is* long"; instead, let us say of the past, "It *was* long," and of the future, "It *will be* long." And yet, O Lord, my Light, shall not thy truth make mockery of man even here? For that long time past: was it long when it was already past, or when it was still present? For it might have been long when there was a period that could be long, but when it was past, it no longer was. In that case, that which was not at all could not be long. Let us not, therefore, say, "Time past was long," for we shall not discover what it was that was long because, since it is past, it no longer exists. Rather, let us say that "time *present* was long, because when it was present it *was* long." For then it had not yet passed on so as not to be, and therefore it still was in a state that could be called long. But after it passed, it ceased to be long simply because it ceased to be.

19. Let us, therefore, O human soul, see whether present time can be long, for it has been given you to feel and measure the periods of time. How, then, will you answer me?

Is a hundred years when present a long time? But, first, see whether a hundred years can be present at once. For if the first year in the century is current, then it is present time, and the other ninety and nine are still future. Therefore, they are not yet. But, then, if the second year is current, one year is already past, the second present, and all the rest are future. And thus, if we fix on any middle year of this century as present, those before it are past, those after it are future. Therefore, a hundred years cannot be present all at once.

Let us see, then, whether the year that is now current can be present. For if its first month is current, then the rest are future; if the second, the first is already past, and the remainder are not yet. Therefore, the current year is not present all at once. And if it is not present as a whole, then the year is not present. For it

takes twelve months to make the year, from which each individual month which is current is itself present one at a time,
but the rest are either past or future.

20. Thus it comes out that time present, which we found was
the only time that could be called "long," has been cut down
to the space of scarcely a single day. But let us examine even
that, for one day is never present as a whole. For it is made up
of twenty-four hours, divided between night and day. The first
of these hours has the rest of them as future, and the last of them
has the rest as past; but any of those between has those that
preceded it as past and those that succeed it as future. And that
one hour itself passes away in fleeting fractions. The part of it
that has fled is past; what remains is still future. If any fraction of
time be conceived that cannot now be divided even into the most
minute momentary point, this alone is what we may call time
present. But this flies so rapidly from future to past that it cannot
be extended by any delay. For if it is extended, it is then divided
into past and future. But the present has no extension[29] whatever.

Where, therefore, is that time which we may call "long"? Is
it future? Actually we do not say of the future, "It is long," for
it has not yet come to be, so as to be long. Instead, we say, "It
will be long." *When* will it be? For since it is future, it will not
be long, for what may be long is not yet. It will be long only
when it passes from the future which is not as yet, and will have
begun to be present, so that there can be something that may
be long. But in that case, time present cries aloud, in the words
we have already heard, that it cannot be "long."

CHAPTER XVI

21. And yet, O Lord, we do perceive intervals of time, and
we compare them with each other, and we say that some are
longer and others are shorter. We even measure how much
longer or shorter this time may be than that time. And we say
that this time is twice as long, or three times as long, while this
other time is only just as long as that other. But we measure the
passage of time when we measure the intervals of perception.
But who can measure times past which are no longer, or
times future which are not yet—unless perhaps someone will
dare to say that what does not exist can be measured? Therefore, while time is passing, it can be perceived and measured;
but when it is past, it cannot, since it is not.

[29] *Spatium*, which means extension either in space or time.

CHAPTER XVII

22. I am seeking the truth, O Father; I am not affirming it.
O my God, direct and rule me.

Who is there who will tell me that there are not three times—
as we learned when boys and as we have also taught boys—
time past, time present, and time future? Who can say that
there is only time present because the other two do not exist?
Or do they also exist; but when, from the future, time becomes
present, it proceeds from some secret place; and when, from
times present, it becomes past, it recedes into some secret place?
For where have those men who have foretold the future seen the
things foretold, if then they were not yet existing? For what
does not exist cannot be seen. And those who tell of things past
could not speak of them as if they were true, if they did not see
them in their minds. These things could in no way be discerned
if they did not exist. There are therefore times present and times
past.

CHAPTER XVIII

23. Give me leave, O Lord, to seek still further. O my Hope,
let not my purpose be confounded. For if there are times past
and future, I wish to know where they are. But if I have not yet
succeeded in this, I still know that wherever they are, they are
not there as future or past, but as present. For if they are there
as future, they are there as "not yet"; if they are there as past,
they are there as "no longer." Wherever they are and whatever
they are they exist therefore only as present. Although we tell
of past things as true, they are drawn out of the memory—not
the things themselves, which have already passed, but words
constructed from the images of the perceptions which were
formed in the mind, like footprints in their passage through the
senses. My childhood, for instance, which is no longer, still
exists in time past, which does not now exist. But when I call to
mind its image and speak of it, I see it in the present because it
is still in my memory. Whether there is a similar explanation for
the foretelling of future events—that is, of the images of things
which are not yet seen as if they were already existing—I confess, O my God, I do not know. But this I certainly do know:
that we generally think ahead about our future actions, and
this premeditation is in time present; but that the action which
we premeditate is not yet, because it is still future. When we

shall have started the action and have begun to do what we were premeditating, then that action will be in time present, because then it is no longer in time future.

24. Whatever may be the manner of this secret foreseeing of future things, nothing can be seen except what exists. But what exists now is not future, but present. When, therefore, they say that future events are seen, it is not the events themselves, for they do not exist as yet (that is, they are still in time future), but perhaps, instead, their causes and their signs are seen, which already do exist. Therefore, to those already beholding these causes and signs, they are not future, but present, and from them future things are predicted because they are conceived in the mind. These conceptions, however, exist *now*, and those who predict those things see these conceptions before them in time present.

Let me take an example from the vast multitude and variety of such things. I see the dawn; I predict that the sun is about to rise. What I see is in time present, what I predict is in time future—not that the sun is future, for it already exists; but its rising is future, because it is not yet. Yet I could not predict even its rising, unless I had an image of it in my mind; as, indeed, I do even now as I speak. But that dawn which I see in the sky is not the rising of the sun (though it does precede it), nor is it a conception in my mind. These two[30] are seen in time present, in order that the event which is in time future may be predicted.

Future events, therefore, are not yet. And if they are not yet, they do not exist. And if they do not exist, they cannot be seen at all, but they can be predicted from things present, which now are and are seen.

CHAPTER XIX

25. Now, therefore, O Ruler of thy creatures, what is the mode by which thou teachest souls those things which are still future? For thou hast taught thy prophets. How dost thou, to whom nothing is future, teach future things—or rather teach things present from the signs of things future? For what does not exist certainly cannot be taught. This way of thine is too far from my sight; it is too great for me, I cannot attain to it.[31] But I shall be enabled by thee, when thou wilt grant it, O sweet Light of my secret eyes.

[30] The breaking light and the image of the rising sun.
[31] Cf. Ps. 139:6.

CHAPTER XX

26. But even now it is manifest and clear that there are
neither times future nor times past. Thus it is not properly said
that there are three times, past, present, and future. Perhaps it
might be said rightly that there are three times: a time present
of things past; a time present of things present; and a time
present of things future. For these three do coexist somehow in
the soul, for otherwise I could not see them. The time present of
things past is memory; the time present of things present is direct
experience; the time present of things future is expectation.[32]
If we are allowed to speak of these things so, I see three times,
and I grant that there are three. Let it still be said, then, as our
misapplied custom has it: "There are three times, past, present,
and future." I shall not be troubled by it, nor argue, nor object
—always provided that what is said is understood, so that
neither the future nor the past is said to exist now. There are
but few things about which we speak properly—and many
more about which we speak improperly—though we understand
one another's meaning.

CHAPTER XXI

27. I have said, then, that we measure periods of time as they
pass so that we can say that this time is twice as long as that one
or that this is just as long as that, and so on for the other fractions of time which we can count by measuring.

So, then, as I was saying, we measure periods of time as they
pass. And if anyone asks me, "How do you know this?", I can
answer: "I know because we measure. We could not measure
things that do not exist, and things past and future do not exist."
But how do we measure present time since it has no extension?
It is measured while it passes, but when it has passed it is not
measured; for then there is nothing that could be measured.
But whence, and how, and whither does it pass while it is being
measured? Whence, but from the future? Which way, save
through the present? Whither, but into the past? Therefore,
from what is not yet, through what has no length, it passes into
what is now no longer. But what do we measure, unless it is a

32 *Memoria, contuitus,* and *expectatio:* a pattern that corresponds vaguely to the
movement of Augustine's thought in the *Confessions:* from direct experience
back to the supporting memories and forward to the outreach of hope
and confidence in God's provident grace.

time of some length? For we cannot speak of single, and double, and triple, and equal, and all the other ways in which we speak of time, except in terms of the length of the periods of time. But in what "length," then, do we measure passing time? Is it in the future, from which it passes over? But what does not yet exist cannot be measured. Or, is it in the present, through which it passes? But what has no length we cannot measure. Or is it in the past into which it passes? But what is no longer we cannot measure.

CHAPTER XXII

28. My soul burns ardently to understand this most intricate enigma. O Lord my God, O good Father, I beseech thee through Christ, do not close off these things, both the familiar and the obscure, from my desire. Do not bar it from entering into them; but let their light dawn by thy enlightening mercy, O Lord. Of whom shall I inquire about these things? And to whom shall I confess my ignorance of them with greater profit than to thee, to whom these studies of mine (ardently longing to understand thy Scriptures) are not a bore? Give me what I love, for I do love it; and this thou hast given me. O Father, who truly knowest how to give good gifts to thy children, give this to me. Grant it, since I have undertaken to understand it, and hard labor is my lot until thou openest it. I beseech thee, through Christ and in his name, the Holy of Holies, let no man interrupt me. "For I have believed, and therefore do I speak."[33] This is my hope; for this I live: that I may contemplate the joys of my Lord.[34] Behold, thou hast made my days grow old, and they pass away—and how I do not know.

We speak of this time and that time, and these times and those times: "How long ago since he said this?" "How long ago since he did this?" "How long ago since I saw that?" "This syllable is twice as long as that single short syllable." These words we say and hear, and we are understood and we understand. They are quite commonplace and ordinary, and still the meaning of these very same things lies deeply hid and its discovery is still to come.

CHAPTER XXIII

29. I once heard a learned man say that the motions of the sun, moon, and stars constituted time; and I did not agree. For

33 Cf. Ps. 116:10.   34 Cf. Matt. 25:21, 23.

why should not the motions of all bodies constitute time? What
if the lights of heaven should cease, and a potter's wheel still
turn round: would there be no time by which we might measure
those rotations and say either that it turned at equal intervals,
or, if it moved now more slowly and now more quickly, that
some rotations were longer and others shorter? And while we
were saying this, would we not also be speaking in time? Or
would there not be in our words some syllables that were long
and others short, because the first took a longer time to sound,
and the others a shorter time? O God, grant men to see in a
small thing the notions that are common [35] to all things, both
great and small. Both the stars and the lights of heaven are "for
signs and seasons, and for days and years." [36] This is doubtless
the case, but just as I should not say that the circuit of that
wooden wheel was a day, neither would that learned man say
that there was, therefore, no time.

30. I thirst to know the power and the nature of time, by
which we measure the motions of bodies, and say, for example,
that this motion is twice as long as that. For I ask, since the
word "day" refers not only to the length of time that the sun is
above the earth (which separates day from night), but also
refers to the sun's entire circuit from east all the way around to
east—on account of which we can say, "So many days have
passed" (the nights being included when we say, "So many
days," and their lengths not counted separately)—since, then,
the day is ended by the motion of the sun and by his passage
from east to east, I ask whether the motion itself is the day, or
whether the day is the period in which that motion is completed;
or both? For if the sun's passage is the day, then there would be
a day even if the sun should finish his course in as short a period
as an hour. If the motion itself is the day, then it would not be
a day if from one sunrise to another there were a period no
longer than an hour. But the sun would have to go round
twenty-four times to make just one day. If it is both, then that
could not be called a day if the sun ran his entire course in the
period of an hour; nor would it be a day if, while the sun stood
still, as much time passed as the sun usually covered during his
whole course, from morning to morning. I shall, therefore, not
ask any more what it is that is called a day, but rather what time
is, for it is by time that we measure the circuit of the sun, and

35 *Communes notitias*, the universal principles of "common sense." This idea
became a basic category in scholastic epistemology.
36 Gen. 1:14.

would be able to say that it was finished in half the period of time that it customarily takes if it were completed in a period of only twelve hours. If, then, we compare these periods, we could call one of them a single and the other a double period, as if the sun might run his course from east to east sometimes in a single period and sometimes in a double period.

Let no man tell me, therefore, that the motions of the heavenly bodies constitute time. For when the sun stood still at the prayer of a certain man in order that he might gain his victory in battle, the sun stood still but time went on. For in as long a span of time as was sufficient the battle was fought and ended.[37]

I see, then, that time is a certain kind of extension. But do I see it, or do I only seem to? Thou, O Light and Truth, wilt show me.

CHAPTER XXIV

31. Dost thou command that I should agree if anyone says that time is "the motion of a body"? Thou dost not so command. For I hear that no body is moved but in time; this thou tellest me. But that the motion of a body itself is time I do not hear; thou dost not say so. For when a body is moved, I measure by time how long it was moving from the time when it began to be moved until it stopped. And if I did not see when it began to be moved, and if it continued to move so that I could not see when it stopped, I could not measure the movement, except from the time when I began to see it until I stopped. But if I look at it for a long time, I can affirm only that the time is long but not how long it may be. This is because when we say, "How long?", we are speaking comparatively as: "This is as long as that," or, "This is twice as long as that"; or other such similar ratios. But if we were able to observe the point in space where and from which the body, which is moved, comes and the point to which it is moved; or if we can observe its parts moving as in a wheel, we can say how long the movement of the body took or the movement of its parts from this place to that. Since, therefore, the motion of a body is one thing, and the norm by which we measure how long it takes is another thing, we cannot see which of these two is to be called time. For, although a body is sometimes moved and sometimes stands still, we measure not only its motion but also its rest as well; and both by time! Thus we say, "It stood still as long as it moved,"

[37] Cf. Josh. 10:12–14.

or, "It stood still twice or three times as long as it moved"— or any other ratio which our measuring has either determined or imagined, either roughly or precisely, according to our custom. Therefore, time is not the motion of a body.

CHAPTER XXV

32. And I confess to thee, O Lord, that I am still ignorant as to what time is. And again I confess to thee, O Lord, that I know that I am speaking all these things in time, and that I have already spoken of time a long time, and that "very long" is not long except when measured by the duration of time. How, then, do I know this, when I do not know what time is? Or, is it possible that I do not know how I can express what I do know? Alas for me! I do not even know the extent of my own ignorance. Behold, O my God, in thy presence I do not lie. As my heart is, so I speak. Thou shalt light my candle; thou, O Lord my God, wilt enlighten my darkness.[38]

CHAPTER XXVI

33. Does not my soul most truly confess to thee that I do measure intervals of time? But what is it that I thus measure, O my God, and how is it that I do not know what I measure? I measure the motion of a body by time, but the time itself I do not measure. But, truly, could I measure the motion of a body— how long it takes, how long it is in motion from this place to that—unless I could measure the time in which it is moving?

How, then, do I measure this time itself? Do we measure a longer time by a shorter time, as we measure the length of a crossbeam in terms of cubits?[39] Thus, we can say that the length of a long syllable is measured by the length of a short syllable and thus say that the long syllable is double. So also we measure the length of poems by the length of the lines, and the length of the line by the length of the feet, and the length of the feet by the length of the syllable, and the length of the long syllables by the length of the short ones. We do not measure by pages— for in that way we would measure space rather than time—but when we speak the words as they pass by we say: "It is a long stanza, because it is made up of so many verses; they are long

38 Cf. Ps. 18:28.
39 *Cubitum*, literally the distance between the elbow and the tip of the middle finger; in the imperial system of weights and measures it was 17.5 inches.

verses because they consist of so many feet; they are long feet because they extend over so many syllables; this is a long syllable because it is twice the length of a short one."

But no certain measure of time is obtained this way; since it is possible that if a shorter verse is pronounced slowly, it may take up more time than a longer one if it is pronounced hurriedly. The same would hold for a stanza, or a foot, or a syllable. From this it appears to me that time is nothing other than extendedness; [40] but extendedness of what I do not know. This is a marvel to me. The extendedness may be of the mind itself. For what is it I measure, I ask thee, O my God, when I say either, roughly, "This time is longer than that," or, more precisely, "This is *twice* as long as that." I know that I am measuring time. But I am not measuring the future, for it is not yet; and I am not measuring the present because it is extended by no length; and I am not measuring the past because it no longer is. What is it, therefore, that I am measuring? Is it time in its passage, but not time past [*praetereuntia tempora, non praeterita*]? This is what I have been saying.

CHAPTER XXVII

34. Press on, O my mind, and attend with all your power. God is our Helper: "it is he that hath made us and not we ourselves." [41] Give heed where the truth begins to dawn. [42] Suppose now that a bodily voice begins to sound, and continues to sound —on and on—and then ceases. Now there is silence. The voice is past, and there is no longer a sound. It was future before it sounded, and could not be measured because it was not yet; and now it cannot be measured because it is no longer. Therefore, while it was sounding, it might have been measured because then there was something that could be measured. But even then it did not stand still, for it was in motion and was passing away. Could it, on that account, be any more readily measured? For while it was passing away, it was being extended into some interval of time in which it might be measured, since the present has no length. Supposing, though, that it might have been measured—then also suppose that another voice had begun to sound and is still sounding without any interruption

40 *Distentionem*, "spread-out-ness"; cf. Descartes' notion of *res extensae*, and its relation to time. 41 Ps. 100:3.

42 Here Augustine begins to summarize his own answers to the questions he has raised in his analysis of time.

to break its continued flow. We can measure it only while it is sounding, for when it has ceased to sound it will be already past and there will not be anything there that can be measured. Let us measure it exactly; and let us say how much it is. But while it is sounding, it cannot be measured except from the instant when it began to sound, down to the final moment when it left off. For we measure the time interval itself from some beginning point to some end. This is why a voice that has not yet ended cannot be measured, so that one could say how long or how briefly it will continue. Nor can it be said to be equal to another voice or single or double in comparison to it or anything like this. But when it is ended, it is no longer. How, therefore, may it be measured? And yet we measure times; not those which are not yet, nor those which no longer are, nor those which are stretched out by some delay, nor those which have no limit. Therefore, we measure neither times future nor times past, nor times present, nor times passing by; and yet we do measure times.

35. *Deus Creator omnium* [43]: this verse of eight syllables alternates between short and long syllables. The four short ones—that is, the first, third, fifth, and seventh—are single in relation to the four long ones—that is, the second, fourth, sixth, and eighth. Each of the long ones is double the length of each of the short ones. I affirm this and report it, and common sense perceives that this indeed is the case. By common sense, then, I measure a long syllable by a short one, and I find that it is twice as long. But when one sounds after another, if the first be short and the latter long, how can I hold the short one and how can I apply it to the long one as a measure, so that I can discover that the long one is twice as long, when, in fact, the long one does not begin to sound until the short one leaves off sounding? That same long syllable I do not measure as present, since I cannot measure it until it is ended; but its ending is its passing away.

What is it, then, that I can measure? Where is the short syllable by which I measure? Where is the long one that I am measuring? Both have sounded, have flown away, have passed on, and are no longer. And still I measure, and I confidently answer—as far as a trained ear can be trusted—that this syllable is single and that syllable double. And I could not do this unless they both had passed and were ended. Therefore I do not

[43] The same hymn of Ambrose quoted above, Bk. IX, Ch. XII, 32, and analyzed again in *De musica*, VI, 2:2.

measure them, for they do not exist any more. But I measure something in my memory which remains fixed.

36. It is in you, O mind of mine, that I measure the periods of time. Do not shout me down that it exists [objectively]; do not overwhelm yourself with the turbulent flood of your impressions. In you, as I have said, I measure the periods of time. I measure as time present the impression that things make on you as they pass by and what remains after they have passed by —I do not measure the things themselves which have passed by and left their impression on you. This is what I measure when I measure periods of time. Either, then, these are the periods of time or else I do not measure time at all.

What are we doing when we measure silence, and say that this silence has lasted as long as that voice lasts? Do we not project our thought to the measure of a sound, as if it were then sounding, so that we can say something concerning the intervals of silence in a given span of time? For, even when both the voice and the tongue are still, we review—in thought— poems and verses, and discourse of various kinds or various measures of motions, and we specify their time spans—how long this is in relation to that—just as if we were speaking them aloud. If anyone wishes to utter a prolonged sound, and if, in forethought, he has decided how long it should be, that man has already in silence gone through a span of time, and committed his sound to memory. Thus he begins to speak and his voice sounds until it reaches the predetermined end. It has truly sounded and will go on sounding. But what is already finished has already sounded and what remains will still sound. Thus it passes on, until the present intention carries the future over into the past. The past increases by the diminution of the future until by the consumption of all the future all is past.[44]

CHAPTER XXVIII

37. But how is the future diminished or consumed when it does not yet exist? Or how does the past, which exists no longer, increase, unless it is that in the mind in which all this happens there are three functions? For the mind expects, it attends, and it remembers; so that what it expects passes into what it remembers by way of what it attends to. Who denies that future

[44] This theory of time is worth comparing with its most notable restatement in modern poetry, in T. S. Eliot's *Four Quartets* and especially "Burnt Norton."

things do not exist as yet? But still there is already in the mind the expectation of things still future. And who denies that past things now exist no longer? Still there is in the mind the memory of things past. Who denies that time present has no length, since it passes away in a moment? Yet, our attention has a continuity and it is through this that what is present may proceed to become absent. Therefore, future time, which is nonexistent, is not long; but "a long future" is "a long expectation of the future." Nor is time past, which is now no longer, long; a "long past" is "a long memory of the past."

38. I am about to repeat a psalm that I know. Before I begin, my attention encompasses the whole, but once I have begun, as much of it as becomes past while I speak is still stretched out in my memory. The span of my action is divided between my memory, which contains what I have repeated, and my expectation, which contains what I am about to repeat. Yet my attention is continually present with me, and through it what was future is carried over so that it becomes past. The more this is done and repeated, the more the memory is enlarged— and expectation is shortened—until the whole expectation is exhausted. Then the whole action is ended and passed into memory. And what takes place in the entire psalm takes place also in each individual part of it and in each individual syllable. This also holds in the even longer action of which that psalm is only a portion. The same holds in the whole life of man, of which all the actions of men are parts. The same holds in the whole age of the sons of men, of which all the lives of men are parts.

CHAPTER XXIX

39. But "since thy loving-kindness is better than life itself,"[45] observe how my life is but a stretching out, and how thy right hand has upheld me in my Lord, the Son of Man, the Mediator between thee, the One, and us, the many—in so many ways and by so many means. Thus through him I may lay hold upon him in whom I am also laid hold upon; and I may be gathered up from my old way of life to follow that One and to forget that which is behind, no longer stretched out but now pulled together again—stretching forth not to what shall be and shall pass away but to those things that *are* before me. Not distractedly now, but intently, I follow on for the prize of my heavenly calling,[46] where I may hear the sound of thy praise

[45] Ps. 63:3.   [46] Cf. Phil. 3:12-14.

and contemplate thy delights, which neither come to be nor pass away.

But now my years are spent in mourning.[47] And thou, O Lord, art my comfort, my eternal Father. But I have been torn between the times, the order of which I do not know, and my thoughts, even the inmost and deepest places of my soul, are mangled by various commotions until I shall flow together into thee, purged and molten in the fire of thy love.

CHAPTER XXX

40. And I will be immovable and fixed in thee, and thy truth will be my mold. And I shall not have to endure the questions of those men who, as if in a morbid disease, thirst for more than they can hold and say, "What did God make before he made heaven and earth?" or, "How did it come into his mind to make something when he had never before made anything?" Grant them, O Lord, to consider well what they are saying; and grant them to see that where there is no time they cannot say "never." When, therefore, he is said "never to have made" something—what is this but to say that it was made in no time at all? Let them therefore see that there could be no time without a created world, and let them cease to speak vanity of this kind. Let them also be stretched out to those things which are before them, and understand that thou, the eternal Creator of all times, art before all times and that no times are coeternal with thee; nor is any creature, even if there is a creature "above time."

CHAPTER XXXI

41. O Lord my God, what a chasm there is in thy deep secret! How far short of it have the consequences of my sins cast me? Heal my eyes, that I may enjoy thy light. Surely, if there is a mind that so greatly abounds in knowledge and foreknowledge, to which all things past and future are as well known as one psalm is well known to me, that mind would be an exceeding marvel and altogether astonishing. For whatever is past and whatever is yet to come would be no more concealed from him than the past and future of that psalm were hidden from me when I was chanting it: how much of it had been sung from the beginning and what and how much still remained till the end.

[47] Cf. Ps. 31:10.

But far be it from thee, O Creator of the universe, and Creator of our souls and bodies—far be it from thee that thou shouldst merely know all things past and future. Far, far more wonderfully, and far more mysteriously thou knowest them. For it is not as the feelings of one singing familiar songs, or hearing a familiar song in which, because of his expectation of words still to come and his remembrance of those that are past, his feelings are varied and his senses are divided. This is not the way that anything happens to thee, who art unchangeably eternal, that is, the truly eternal Creator of minds. As in the beginning thou knewest both the heaven and the earth without any change in thy knowledge, so thou didst make heaven and earth in their beginnings without any division in thy action.[48] Let him who understands this confess to thee; and let him who does not understand also confess to thee! Oh, exalted as thou art, still the humble in heart are thy dwelling place! For thou liftest them who are cast down and they fall not for whom thou art the Most High.[49]

[48] Note here the preparation for the transition from this analysis of time in Bk. XI to the exploration of the mystery of creation in Bks. XII and XIII.
[49] *Celsitudo*, an honorific title, somewhat like "Your Highness."

BOOK TWELVE

The mode of creation and the truth of Scripture. Augustine explores the relation of the visible and formed matter of heaven and earth to the prior matrix from which it was formed. This leads to an intricate analysis of "unformed matter" and the primal "possibility" from which God created, itself created de nihilo. *He finds a reference to this in the misconstrued Scriptural phrase "the heaven of heavens." Realizing that his interpretation of Gen.* 1:1, 2, *is not self-evidently the only possibility, Augustine turns to an elaborate discussion of the multiplicity of perspectives in hermeneutics and, in the course of this, reviews the various possibilities of true interpretation of his Scripture text. He emphasizes the importance of tolerance where there are plural options, and confidence where basic Christian faith is concerned.*

CHAPTER I

1. My heart is deeply stirred, O Lord, when in this poor life of mine the words of thy Holy Scripture strike upon it. This is why the poverty of the human intellect expresses itself in an abundance of language. Inquiry is more loquacious than discovery. Demanding takes longer than obtaining; and the hand that knocks is more active than the hand that receives. But we have the promise, and who shall break it? "If God be for us, who can be against us?" [1] "Ask, and you shall receive; seek, and you shall find; knock, and it shall be opened unto you; for everyone that asks receives, and he who seeks finds, and to him that knocks, it shall be opened." [2] These are thy own promises, and who need fear to be deceived when truth promises?

[1] Rom. 8:31. [2] Matt. 7:7, 8.

CHAPTER II

2. In lowliness my tongue confesses to thy exaltation, for thou madest heaven and earth. This heaven which I see, and this earth on which I walk—from which came this "earth" that I carry about me—thou didst make.

But where is that heaven of heavens, O Lord, of which we hear in the words of the psalm, "The heaven of heavens is the Lord's, but the earth he hath given to the children of men"? [3] Where is the heaven that we cannot see, in relation to which all that we can see is earth? For this whole corporeal creation has been beautifully formed—though not everywhere in its entirety—and our earth is the lowest of these levels. Still, compared with that heaven of heavens, even the heaven of our own earth is only earth. Indeed, it is not absurd to call each of those two great bodies [4] "earth" in comparison with that ineffable heaven which is the Lord's, and not for the sons of men.

CHAPTER III

3. And truly this earth was invisible and unformed, [5] and there was an inexpressibly profound abyss [6] above which there was no light since it had no form. Thou didst command it

[3] Vulgate, Ps. 113:16 (cf. Ps. 115:16, K. J.; see also Ps. 148:4, both Vulgate and K.J.): *Caelum caeli domino*, etc. Augustine finds a distinction here for which the Hebrew text gives no warrant. שָׁמַיִם לַיהוָה הַשָּׁמַיִם is a typical Hebrew nominal sentence and means simply "The heavens are the heavens of Yahweh"; cf. the Soncino edition of The Psalms, edited by A. Cohen; cf. also R.S.V., Ps. 115:16. The LXX reading (ὁ οὐρανὸς τοῦ οὐρανοῦ) seems to rest on a variant Hebrew text which read שְׁמֵי הַשָּׁמַיִם. This idiomatic construction does not mean "the heavens of the heavens" (as it is too literally translated in the LXX), but rather "highest heaven." This is a familiar way, in Hebrew, of emphasizing a superlative (e.g., "King of kings," "Song of songs"). The singular thing can be described superlatively only in terms of itself!   [4] Earth and sky.

[5] It is interesting that Augustine should have preferred the *invisibilis et incomposita* of the Old Latin version of Gen. 1:2 over the *inanis et vacua* of the Vulgate, which was surely accessible to him. Since this is to be a key phrase in the succeeding exegesis this reading can hardly have been the casual citation of the old and familiar version. Is it possible that Augustine may have had the sensibilities and associations of his readers in mind—for many of them may have not known Jerome's version or, at least, not very well?

[6] *Abyssus*, literally, the unplumbed depths of the sea, and as a constant meaning here, "the depths beyond measure."

written that "darkness was on the face of the deep."[7] What else is darkness except the absence of light? For if there had been light, where would it have been except by being over all, showing itself rising aloft and giving light? Therefore, where there was no light as yet, why was it that darkness was present, unless it was that light was absent? Darkness, then, was heavy upon it, because the light from above was absent; just as there is silence where there is no sound. And what is it to have silence anywhere but simply not to have sound? Hast thou not, O Lord, taught this soul which confesses to thee? Hast thou not thus taught me, O Lord, that before thou didst form and separate this formless matter there was *nothing*: neither color, nor figure, nor body, nor spirit? Yet it was not absolutely nothing; it was a certain formlessness without any shape.

CHAPTER IV

4. What, then, should that formlessness be called so that somehow it might be indicated to those of sluggish mind, unless we use some word in common speech? But what can be found anywhere in the world nearer to a total formlessness than the earth and the abyss? Because of their being on the lowest level, they are less beautiful than are the other and higher parts, all translucent and shining. Therefore, why may I not consider the formlessness of matter—which thou didst create without shapely form, from which to make this shapely world—as fittingly indicated to men by the phrase, "The earth invisible and unformed"?

CHAPTER V

5. When our thought seeks something for our sense to fasten to [in this concept of unformed matter], and when it says to itself, "It is not an intelligible form, such as life or justice, since it is the material for bodies; and it is not a former perception, for there is nothing in the invisible and unformed which can be seen and felt"—while human thought says such things to itself, it may be attempting either to know by being ignorant or by knowing how not to know.

CHAPTER VI

6. But if, O Lord, I am to confess to thee, by my mouth and my pen, the whole of what thou hast taught me concerning this

[7] Gen. 1:2.

unformed matter, I must say first of all that when I first heard of such matter and did not understand it—and those who told me of it could not understand it either—I conceived of it as having countless and varied forms. Thus, I did not think about it rightly. My mind in its agitation used to turn up all sorts of foul and horrible "forms"; but still they were "forms." And still I called it formless, not because it was unformed, but because it had what seemed to me a kind of form that my mind turned away from, as bizarre and incongruous, before which my human weakness was confused. And even what I did conceive of as unformed was so, not because it was deprived of all form, but only as it compared with more beautiful forms. Right reason, then, persuaded me that I ought to remove altogether all vestiges of form whatever if I wished to conceive matter that was wholly unformed; and this I could not do. For I could more readily imagine that what was deprived of all form simply did not exist than I could conceive of anything between form and nothing—something which was neither formed nor nothing, something that was unformed and nearly nothing.

Thus my mind ceased to question my spirit—filled as it was with the images of formed bodies, changing and varying them according to its will. And so I applied myself to the bodies themselves and looked more deeply into their mutability, by which they cease to be what they had been and begin to be what they were not. This transition from form to form I had regarded as involving something like a formless condition, though not actual nothingness.[8]

But I desired to know, not to guess. And, if my voice and my pen were to confess to thee all the various knots thou hast untied for me about this question, who among my readers could endure to grasp the whole of the account? Still, despite this, my heart will not cease to give honor to thee or to sing thy praises concerning those things which it is not able to express.[9]

For the mutability of mutable things carries with it the possibility of all those forms into which mutable things can be changed. But this mutability—what is it? Is it soul? Is it body?

---

[8] Augustine may not have known the Platonic doctrine of nonbeing (cf. *Sophist*, 236C–237B), but he clearly is deeply influenced here by Plotinus; cf. *Enneads*, II, 4:8f., where matter is analyzed as a substratum without quantity or quality; and 4:15: "Matter, then, must be described as τὸ ἄπειρον (the indefinite). . . . Matter is indeterminateness and nothing else." In short, *materia informis* is sheer possibility; not anything and not nothing!

[9] *Dictare:* was Augustine dictating his *Confessions?* It is very probable.

Is it the external appearance of soul or body? Could it be said, "Nothing was something," and "That which is, is not"? If this were possible, I would say that this was it, and in some such manner it must have been in order to receive these visible and composite forms.[10]

CHAPTER VII

7. Whence and how was this, unless it came from thee, from whom all things are, in so far as they are? But the farther something is from thee, the more unlike thee it is—and this is not a matter of distance or place.

Thus it was that thou, O Lord, who art not one thing in one place and another thing in another place but the Selfsame, and the Selfsame, and the Selfsame—"Holy, Holy, Holy, Lord God Almighty"[11]—thus it was that in the beginning, and through thy Wisdom which is from thee and born of thy substance, thou didst create something and that out of nothing.[12] For thou didst create the heaven and the earth—not out of thyself, for then they would be equal to thy only Son and thereby to thee. And there is no sense in which it would be right that anything should be equal to thee that was not of thee. But what else besides thee was there out of which thou mightest create these things, O God, one Trinity, and trine Unity?[13] And, therefore, it was out of nothing at all that thou didst create the heaven and earth—something great and something small—for thou art Almighty and Good, and able to make all things good: even the great heaven and the small earth. Thou wast, and there was nothing else from which thou didst create heaven and earth: these two things, one near thee, the other near to nothing; the one to which only thou art superior, the other to which nothing else is inferior.

CHAPTER VIII

8. That heaven of heavens was thine, O Lord, but the earth which thou didst give to the sons of men to be seen and touched was not then in the same form as that in which we now see it and touch it. For then it was invisible and unformed and there was an abyss over which there was no light. The darkness was truly *over* the abyss, that is, more than just *in* the abyss. For this abyss of waters which now is visible has even in its depths a certain light appropriate to its nature, perceptible in some

[10] *Visibiles et compositas*, the opposite of "invisible and unformed."
[11] Isa. 6:3; Rev. 4:8.   [12] *De nihilo.*   [13] *Trina unitas.*

fashion to fishes and the things that creep about on the bottom of it. But then the entire abyss was almost nothing, since it was still altogether unformed. Yet even there, there was something that had the possibility of being formed. For thou, O Lord, hadst made the world out of unformed matter, and this thou didst make out of nothing and didst make it into almost nothing. From it thou hast then made these great things which we, the sons of men, marvel at. For this corporeal heaven is truly marvelous, this firmament between the water and the waters which thou didst make on the second day after the creation of light, saying, "Let it be done," and it was done.[14] This firmament thou didst call heaven, that is, the heaven of this earth and sea which thou madest on the third day, giving a visible shape to the unformed matter which thou hadst made before all the days. For even before any day thou hadst already made a heaven, but that was the heaven of this heaven: for in the beginning thou hadst made heaven and earth.

But this earth itself which thou hadst made was unformed matter; it was invisible and unformed, and darkness was over the abyss. Out of this invisible and unformed earth, out of this formlessness which is almost nothing, thou didst then make all these things of which the changeable world consists—and yet does not fully consist in itself[15]—for its very changeableness appears in this, that its times and seasons can be observed and numbered. The periods of time are measured by the changes of things, while the forms, whose matter is the invisible earth of which we have spoken, are varied and altered.

CHAPTER IX

9. And therefore the Spirit, the Teacher of thy servant,[16] when he mentions that "in the beginning thou madest heaven and earth," says nothing about times and is silent as to the days. For, clearly, that heaven of heavens which thou didst create in the beginning is in some way an intellectual creature, although in no way coeternal with thee, O Trinity. Yet it is nonetheless a partaker in thy eternity. Because of the sweetness of its most happy contemplation of thee, it is greatly restrained in its own mutability and cleaves to thee without any lapse from the time in which it was created, surpassing all the rolling change of

---

[14] Cf. Gen. 1:6.
[15] *Constat et non constat*, the created earth really exists but never is self-sufficient.   [16] Moses.

time. But this shapelessness—this earth invisible and unformed —was not numbered among the days itself. For where there is no shape or order there is nothing that either comes or goes, and where this does not occur there certainly are no days, nor any vicissitude of duration.

CHAPTER X

10. O Truth, O Light of my heart, let not my own darkness speak to me! I had fallen into that darkness and was darkened thereby. But in it, even in its depths, I came to love thee. I went astray and still I remembered thee. I heard thy voice behind me, bidding me return, though I could scarcely hear it for the tumults of my boisterous passions. And now, behold, I am returning, burning and thirsting after thy fountain. Let no one hinder me; here will I drink and so have life. Let me not be my own life; for of myself I have lived badly. I was death to myself; in thee I have revived. Speak to me; converse with me. I have believed thy books, and their words are very deep.

CHAPTER XI

11. Thou hast told me already, O Lord, with a strong voice in my inner ear, that thou art eternal and alone hast immortality. Thou art not changed by any shape or motion, and thy will is not altered by temporal process, because no will that changes is immortal. This is clear to me, in thy sight; let it become clearer and clearer, I beseech thee. In that light let me abide soberly under thy wings.

Thou hast also told me, O Lord, with a strong voice in my inner ear, that thou hast created all natures and all substances, which are not what thou art thyself; and yet they do exist. Only that which is nothing at all is not from thee, and that motion of the will away from thee, who art, toward something that exists only in a lesser degree—such a motion is an offense and a sin. No one's sin either hurts thee or disturbs the order of thy rule, either first or last. All this, in thy sight, is clear to me. Let it become clearer and clearer, I beseech thee, and in that light let me abide soberly under thy wings.

12. Likewise, thou hast told me, with a strong voice in my inner ear, that this creation—whose delight thou alone art—is not coeternal with thee. With a most persevering purity it draws its support from thee and nowhere and never betrays its own mutability, for thou art ever present with it; and it cleaves to

thee with its entire affection, having no future to expect and no past that it remembers; it is varied by no change and is extended by no time.

O blessed one—if such there be—clinging to thy blessedness! It is blest in thee, its everlasting Inhabitant and its Light. I cannot find a term that I would judge more fitting for "the heaven of the heavens of the Lord" than "Thy house"—which contemplates thy delights without any declination toward anything else and which, with a pure mind in most harmonious stability, joins all together in the peace of those saintly spirits who are citizens of thy city in those heavens that are above this visible heaven.

13. From this let the soul that has wandered far away from thee understand—if now it thirsts for thee; if now its tears have become its bread, while daily they say to it, "Where is your God?"[17]; if now it requests of thee just one thing and seeks after this: that it may dwell in thy house all the days of its life (and what is its life but thee? And what are thy days but thy eternity, like thy years which do not fail, since thou art the Selfsame?)—from this, I say, let the soul understand (as far as it can) how far above all times thou art in thy eternity; and how thy house has never wandered away from thee; and, although it is not coeternal with thee, it continually and unfailingly clings to thee and suffers no vicissitudes of time. This, in thy sight, is clear to me; may it become clearer and clearer to me, I beseech thee, and in this light may I abide soberly under thy wings.

14. Now I do not know what kind of formlessness there is in these mutations of these last and lowest creatures. Yet who will tell me, unless it is someone who, in the emptiness of his own heart, wanders about and begins to be dizzy in his own fancies? Who except such a one would tell me whether, if all form were diminished and consumed, formlessness alone would remain, through which a thing was changed and turned from one species into another, so that sheer formlessness would then be characterized by temporal change? And surely this could not be, because without motion there is no time, and where there is no form there is no change.

CHAPTER XII

15. These things I have considered as thou hast given me ability, O my God, as thou hast excited me to knock, and as

[17] Ps. 42:3, 10.

thou hast opened to me when I knock. Two things I find which thou hast made, not within intervals of time, although neither is coeternal with thee. One of them is so formed that, without any wavering in its contemplation, without any interval of change—mutable but not changed—it may fully enjoy thy eternity and immutability. The other is so formless that it could not change from one form to another (either of motion or of rest), and so time has no hold upon it. But thou didst not leave this formless, for, before any "day" in the beginning, thou didst create heaven and earth—these are the two things of which I spoke.

But "the earth was invisible and unformed, and darkness was over the abyss." By these words its formlessness is indicated to us—so that by degrees they may be led forward who cannot wholly conceive of the privation of all form without arriving at nothing. From this formlessness a second heaven might be created and a second earth—visible and well formed, with the ordered beauty of the waters, and whatever else is recorded as created (though not without days) in the formation of this world. And all this because such things are so ordered that in them the changes of time may take place through the ordered processes of motion and form.

CHAPTER XIII

16. Meanwhile this is what I understand, O my God, when I hear thy Scripture saying, "In the beginning God made the heaven and the earth, but the earth was invisible and unformed, and darkness was over the abyss." It does not say on what day thou didst create these things. Thus, for the time being I understand that "heaven of heavens" to mean the intelligible heaven, where to understand is to know all at once—not "in part," not "darkly," not "through a glass"—but as a simultaneous whole, in full sight, "face to face."[18] It is not this thing now and then another thing, but (as we said) knowledge all at once without any temporal change. And by the invisible and unformed earth, I understand that which suffers no temporal vicissitude. Temporal change customarily means having one thing now and another later; but where there is no form there can be no distinction between this or that. It is, then, by means of these two—one thing well formed in the beginning and

[18] I Cor. 13:12.

another thing wholly unformed, the one heaven (that is, the heaven of heavens) and the other one earth (but the earth invisible and unformed)—it is by means of these two notions that I am able to understand why thy Scripture said, without mention of days, "In the beginning God created the heaven and the earth." For it immediately indicated which earth it was speaking about. When, on the second day, the firmament is recorded as having been created and called heaven, this suggests to us which heaven it was that he was speaking about earlier, without specifying a day.

CHAPTER XIV

17. Marvelous is the depth of thy oracles. Their surface is before us, inviting the little ones; and yet wonderful is their depth, O my God, marvelous is their depth! It is a fearful thing to look into them: an awe of honor and a tremor of love. Their enemies I hate vehemently. Oh, if thou wouldst slay them with thy twoedged sword, so that they should not be enemies! For I would prefer that they should be slain to themselves, that they might live to thee. But see, there are others who are not critics but praisers of the book of Genesis; they say: "The Spirit of God who wrote these things by his servant Moses did not wish these words to be understood like this. He did not wish to have it understood as you say, but as we say." To them, O God of us all, thyself being the judge, I give answer.

CHAPTER XV

18. "Will you say that these things are false which Truth tells me, with a loud voice in my inner ear, about the very eternity of the Creator: that his essence is changed in no respect by time and that his will is not distinct from his essence? Thus, he doth not will one thing now and another thing later, but he willeth once and for all everything that he willeth—not again and again; and not now this and now that. Nor does he will afterward what he did not will before, nor does he cease to will what he had willed before. Such a will would be mutable and no mutable thing is eternal. But our God is eternal.

"Again, he tells me in my inner ear that the expectation of future things is turned to sight when they have come to pass. And this same sight is turned into memory when they have passed. Moreover, all thought that varies thus is mutable, and nothing mutable is eternal. But our God is eternal." These things I sum up and put together, and I conclude that my God, the eternal God, hath not made any creature by any new will, and his knowledge does not admit anything transitory.

19. "What, then, will you say to this, you objectors? Are these things false?" "No," they say. "What then? Is it false that every entity already formed and all matter capable of receiving form is from him alone who is supremely good, because he is supreme?" "We do not deny this, either," they say. "What then? Do you deny this: that there is a certain sublime created order which cleaves with such a chaste love to the true and truly eternal God that, although it is not coeternal with him, yet it does not separate itself from him, and does not flow away into any mutation of change or process but abides in true contemplation of him alone?" If thou, O God, dost show thyself to him who loves thee as thou hast commanded—and art sufficient for him—then, such a one will neither turn himself away from thee nor turn away toward himself. This is "the house of God." It is not an earthly house and it is not made from any celestial matter; but it is a spiritual house, and it partakes in thy eternity because it is without blemish forever. For thou hast made it steadfast forever and ever; thou hast given it a law which will not be removed. Still, it is not coeternal with thee, O God, since it is not without beginning—it was created.

20. For, although we can find no time before it (for wisdom was created before all things),[19] this is certainly not that Wisdom which is absolutely coeternal and equal with thee, our God, its Father, the Wisdom through whom all things were created and in whom, in the beginning, thou didst create the heaven and earth. This is truly the created Wisdom, namely, the intelligible nature which, in its contemplation of light, is light. For this is also called wisdom, even if it is a created wisdom. But the difference between the Light that lightens and that which is enlightened is as great as is the difference between the Wisdom that creates and that which is created. So also is the difference between the Righteousness that justifies and the righteousness that is made by justification. For we also are called thy righteousness, for a certain servant of thine says, "That we might be made the righteousness of God in him."[20] Therefore, there is a certain created wisdom that was created before all things: the rational and intelligible mind of that

[19] Cf. Ecclus. 1:4.   [20] II Cor. 5:21.

chaste city of thine. It is our mother which is above and is free [21] and "eternal in the heavens" [22]—but in what heavens except those which praise thee, the "heaven of heavens"? This also is the "heaven of heavens" which is the Lord's—although we find no time before it, since what has been created before all things also precedes the creation of time. Still, the eternity of the Creator himself is before it, from whom it took its beginning as created, though not in time (since time as yet was not), even though time belongs to its created nature.

21. Thus it is that the intelligible heaven came to be from thee, our God, but in such a way that it is quite another being than thou art; it is not the Selfsame. Yet we find that time is not only not *before* it, but not even *in* it, thus making it able to behold thy face forever and not ever be turned aside. Thus, it is varied by no change at all. But there is still in it that mutability in virtue of which it could become dark and cold, if it did not, by cleaving to thee with a supernal love, shine and glow from thee like a perpetual noon. O house full of light and splendor! "I have loved your beauty and the place of the habitation of the glory of my Lord," [23] your builder and possessor. In my wandering let me sigh for you; this I ask of him who made you, that he should also possess me in you, seeing that he hath also made me. "I have gone astray like a lost sheep [24]; yet upon the shoulders of my Shepherd, who is your builder, I have hoped that I may be brought back to you." [25]

22. "What will you say to me now, you objectors to whom I spoke, who still believe that Moses was the holy servant of God, and that his books were the oracles of the Holy Spirit? Is it not in this 'house of God'—not coeternal with God, yet in its own mode 'eternal in the heavens'—that you vainly seek for temporal change? You will not find it there. It rises above all extension and every revolving temporal period, and it rises to what is forever good and cleaves fast to God."

"It is so," they reply. "What, then, about those things which my heart cried out to my God, when it heard, within, the voice of his praise? What, then, do you contend is false in them? Is it because matter was unformed, and since there was no form there was no order? But where there was no order there could have been no temporal change. Yet even this 'almost

21 Cf. Gal. 4:26.   22 II Cor. 5:1.
23 Cf. Ps. 26:8.   24 Ps. 119:176.
25 To "the house of God."

nothing,' since it was not altogether nothing, was truly from him from whom everything that exists is in whatever state it is." "This also," they say, "we do not deny."

CHAPTER XVI

23. Now, I would like to discuss a little further, in thy presence, O my God, with those who admit that all these things are true that thy Truth has indicated to my mind. Let those who deny these things bark and drown their own voices with as much clamor as they please. I will endeavor to persuade them to be quiet and to permit thy word to reach them. But if they are unwilling, and if they repel me, I ask of thee, O my God, that thou shouldst not be silent to me.[26] Speak truly in my heart; if only thou wouldst speak thus, I would send them away, blowing up the dust and raising it in their own eyes. As for myself I will enter into my closet[27] and there sing to thee the songs of love, groaning with groanings that are unutterable now in my pilgrimage,[28] and remembering Jerusalem with my heart uplifted to Jerusalem my country, Jerusalem my mother[29]; and to thee thyself, the Ruler of the source of Light, its Father, Guardian, Husband; its chaste and strong delight, its solid joy and all its goods ineffable—and all of this at the same time, since thou art the one supreme and true Good! And I will not be turned away until thou hast brought back together all that I am from this dispersion and deformity to the peace of that dearest mother, where the first fruits of my spirit are to be found and from which all these things are promised me which thou dost conform and confirm forever, O my God, my Mercy. But as for those who do not say that all these things which are true are false, who still honor thy Scripture set before us by the holy Moses, who join us in placing it on the summit of authority for us to follow, and yet who oppose us in some particulars, I say this: "Be thou, O God, the judge between my confessions and their gainsaying."

---

[26] Cf. Ps. 28:1.

[27] *Cubile*, i.e., the heart.

[28] Cf. Rom. 8:26.

[29] The heavenly Jerusalem of Gal. 4:26, which had become a favorite Christian symbol of the peace and blessedness of heaven; cf. the various versions of the hymn "Jerusalem, My Happy Home" in Julian's *Dictionary of Hymnology*, pp. 580–583. The original text is found in the *Liber meditationum*, erroneously ascribed to Augustine himself.

CHAPTER XVII

24. For they say: "Even if these things are true, still Moses did not refer to these two things when he said, by divine revelation, 'In the beginning God created the heaven and the earth.' By the term 'heaven' he did not mean that spiritual or intelligible created order which always beholds the face of God. And by the term 'earth' he was not referring to unformed matter."

"What then do these terms mean?"

They reply, "That man [Moses] meant what we mean; this is what he was saying in those terms."

"What is that?"

"By the terms of heaven and earth," they say, "he wished first to indicate universally and briefly this whole visible world; then after this, by an enumeration of the days, he could point out, one by one, all the things that it has pleased the Holy Spirit to reveal in this way. For the people to whom he spoke were rude and carnal, so that he judged it prudent that only those works of God which were visible should be mentioned to them."

But they do agree that the phrases, "The earth was invisible and unformed," and "The darkened abyss," may not inappropriately be understood to refer to this unformed matter— and that out of this, as it is subsequently related, all the visible things which are known to all were made and set in order during those specified "days."

25. But now, what if another one should say, "This same formlessness and chaos of matter was first mentioned by the name of heaven and earth because, out of it, this visible world —with all its entities which clearly appear in it and which we are accustomed to be called by the name of heaven and earth— was created and perfected"? And what if still another should say: "The invisible and visible nature is quite fittingly called heaven and earth. Thus, the whole creation which God has made in his wisdom—that is, in the beginning—was included under these two terms. Yet, since all things have been made, not from the essence of God, but from nothing; and because they are not the same reality that God is; and because there is in them all a certain mutability, whether they abide as the eternal house of God abides or whether they are changed as the soul and body of man are changed—then the common matter of all things invisible and visible (still formless but capable of

receiving form) from which heaven and earth were to be created (that is, the creature already fashioned, invisible as well as visible)—all this was spoken of in the same terms by which the invisible and unformed earth and the darkness over the abyss would be called. There was this difference, however: that the invisible and unformed earth is to be understood as having corporeal matter before it had any manner of form; but the darkness over the abyss was *spiritual* matter, before its unlimited fluidity was harnessed, and before it was enlightened by Wisdom."

26. And if anyone wished, he might also say, "The entities already perfected and formed, invisible and visible, are not signified by the terms 'heaven and earth,' when it reads, 'In the beginning God created the heaven and the earth'; instead, the unformed beginning of things, the matter capable of receiving form and being made was called by these terms—because the chaos was contained in it and was not yet distinguished by qualities and forms, which have now been arranged in their own orders and are called heaven and earth: the former a spiritual creation, the latter a physical creation."

CHAPTER XVIII

27. When all these things have been said and considered, I am unwilling to contend about words, for such contention is profitable for nothing but the subverting of the hearer.[30] But the law is profitable for edification if a man use it lawfully: for the end of the law "is love out of a pure heart, and a good conscience, and faith unfeigned." [31] And our Master knew it well, for it was on these two commandments that he hung all the Law and the Prophets. And how would it harm me, O my God, thou Light of my eyes in secret, if while I am ardently confessing these things—since many different things may be understood from these words, all of which may be true—what harm would be done if I should interpret the meaning of the sacred writer differently from the way some other man interprets? Indeed, all of us who read are trying to trace out and understand what our author wished to convey; and since we believe that he speaks truly we dare not suppose that he has spoken anything that we either know or suppose to be false. Therefore, since every person tries to understand in the Holy Scripture what the writer understood, what harm is done if a man understands what thou,

30 Cf. II Tim. 2:14. 31 I Tim. 1:5.

the Light of all truth-speaking minds, showest him to be true, although the author he reads did not understand this aspect of the truth even though he did understand the truth in a different meaning? [32]

CHAPTER XIX [33]

28. For it is certainly true, O Lord, that thou didst create the heaven and the earth. It is also true that "the beginning" is thy wisdom in which thou didst create all things. It is likewise true that this visible world has its own great division (the heaven and the earth) and these two terms include all entities that have been made and created. It is further true that everything mutable confronts our minds with a certain lack of form, whereby it receives form, or whereby it is capable of taking form. It is true, yet again, that what cleaves to the changeless form so closely that even though it is mutable it is not changed is not subject to temporal process. It is true that the formlessness which is almost nothing cannot have temporal change in it. It is true that that from which something is made can, in a manner of speaking, be called by the same name as the thing that is made from it. Thus that formlessness of which heaven and earth were made might be called "heaven and earth." It is true that of all things having form nothing is nearer to the unformed than the earth and the abyss. It is true that not only every created and formed thing but also everything capable of creation and of form were created by Thee, from whom all things are.[34] It is true, finally, that everything that is formed from what is formless was formless before it was formed.

CHAPTER XX

29. From all these truths, which are not doubted by those to whom thou hast granted insight in such things in their inner eye and who believe unshakably that thy servant Moses spoke

---

[32] This is the basis of Augustine's defense of allegory as both legitimate and profitable in the interpretation of Scripture. He did not mean that there is a plurality of literal truths in Scripture but a multiplicity of perspectives on truth which amounted to different levels and interpretations of truth. This gave Augustine the basis for a positive tolerance of varying interpretations which did hold fast to the essential common premises about God's primacy as Creator; cf. M. Pontet, *L'Exégèse de Saint Augustin prédicateur* (Lyons, 1944), chs. II and III.

[33] In this chapter, Augustine summarizes what he takes to be the Christian consensus on the questions he has explored about the relation of the intellectual and corporeal creations.   [34] Cf. I Cor. 8:6.

in the spirit of truth—from all these truths, then, one man takes the sense of "In the beginning God created the heaven and the earth" to mean, "In his Word, coeternal with himself, God made both the intelligible and the tangible, the spiritual and the corporeal creation." Another takes it in a different sense, that "In the beginning God created the heaven and the earth" means, "In his Word, coeternal with himself, God made the universal mass of this corporeal world, with all the observable and known entities that it contains." Still another finds a different meaning, that "In the beginning God created the heaven and the earth" means, "In his Word, coeternal with himself, God made the unformed matter of the spiritual and corporeal creation." Another can take the sense that "In the beginning God created the heaven and the earth" means, "In his Word, coeternal with himself, God made the unformed matter of the physical creation, in which heaven and earth were as yet indistinguished; but now that they have come to be separated and formed, we can now perceive them both in the mighty mass of this world."[35] Another takes still a further meaning, that "In the beginning God created heaven and earth" means, "In the very beginning of creating and working, God made that unformed matter which contained, undifferentiated, heaven and earth, from which both of them were formed, and both now stand out and are observable with all the things that are in them."

CHAPTER XXI

30. Again, regarding the interpretation of the following words, one man selects for himself, from all the various truths, the interpretation that "the earth was invisible and unformed and darkness was over the abyss" means, "That corporeal entity which God made was as yet the formless matter of physical things without order and without light." Another takes it in a different sense, that "But the earth was invisible and unformed, and darkness was over the abyss" means, "This totality called heaven and earth was as yet unformed and lightless matter, out of which the corporeal heaven and the corporeal earth were to be made, with all the things in them that are known to our physical senses." Another takes it still differently and says that "But the earth was invisible and unformed, and darkness was over the abyss" means, "This totality called heaven and earth was as yet an unformed and lightless matter,

[35] *Mole mundi.*

from which were to be made that intelligible heaven (which is also called 'the heaven of heavens') and the earth (which refers to the whole physical entity, under which term may be included this corporeal heaven)—that is, He made the intelligible heaven from which every invisible and visible creature would be created." He takes it in yet another sense who says that "But the earth was invisible and unformed, and darkness was over the abyss" means, "The Scripture does not refer to that formlessness by the term 'heaven and earth'; that formlessness itself already existed. This it called the invisible 'earth' and the unformed and lightless 'abyss,' from which—as it had said before—God made the heaven and the earth (namely, the spiritual and the corporeal creation)." Still another says that "But the earth was invisible and formless, and darkness was over the abyss" means, "There was already an unformed matter from which, as the Scripture had already said, God made heaven and earth, namely, the entire corporeal mass of the world, divided into two very great parts, one superior, the other inferior, with all those familiar and known creatures that are in them."

CHAPTER XXII

31. Now suppose that someone tried to argue against these last two opinions as follows: "If you will not admit that this formlessness of matter appears to be called by the term 'heaven and earth,' then there was something that God had not made out of which he did make heaven and earth. And Scripture has not told us that God made *this* matter, unless we understand that it is implied in the term 'heaven and earth' (or the term 'earth' alone) when it is said, 'In the beginning God created the heaven and earth.' Thus, in what follows—'the earth was invisible and unformed'—even though it pleased Moses thus to refer to unformed matter, yet we can only understand by it that which God himself hath made, as it stands written in the previous verse, 'God made heaven and earth.'" Those who maintain either one or the other of these two opinions which we have set out above will answer to such objections: "We do not deny at all that this unformed matter was created by God, from whom all things are, and are very good—because we hold that what is created and endowed with form is a higher good; and we also hold that what is made capable of being created and endowed with form, though it is a lesser good, is still a good. But the Scripture has not said specifically that God made this formlessness

—any more than it has said it specifically of many other things, such as the orders of 'cherubim' and 'seraphim' and those others of which the apostle distinctly speaks: 'thrones,' 'dominions,' 'principalities,' 'powers' [36]—yet it is clear that God made all of these. If in the phrase 'He made heaven and earth' all things are included, what are we to say about the waters upon which the Spirit of God moved? For if they are understood as included in the term 'earth,' then how can unformed matter be meant by the term 'earth' when we see the waters so beautifully formed? Or, if it be taken thus, why, then, is it written that out of the same formlessness the firmament was made and called heaven, and yet is it not specifically written that the waters were made? For these waters, which we perceive flowing in so beautiful a fashion, are not formless and invisible. But if they received that beauty at the time God said of them, 'Let the waters which are under the firmament be gathered together,'[37] thus indicating that their gathering together was the same thing as their reception of form, what, then, is to be said about the waters that are *above* the firmament? Because if they are unformed, they do not deserve to have a seat so honorable, and yet it is not written by what specific word they were formed. If, then, Genesis is silent about anything that God hath made, which neither sound faith nor unerring understanding doubts that God hath made, let not any sober teaching dare to say that these waters were coeternal with God because we find them mentioned in the book of Genesis and do not find it mentioned *when* they were created. If Truth instructs us, why may we not interpret that unformed matter which the Scripture calls the earth—invisible and unformed—and the lightless abyss as having been made by God from nothing; and thus understand that they are not coeternal with him, although the narrative fails to tell us precisely when they were made?"

CHAPTER XXIII

32. I have heard and considered these theories as well as my weak apprehension allows, and I confess my weakness to Thee, O Lord, though already thou knowest it. Thus I see that two sorts of disagreements may arise when anything is related by signs, even by trustworthy reporters. There is one disagreement about the truth of the things involved; the other concerns the meaning of the one who reports them. It is one thing to inquire

[36] Cf. Col. 1:16.   [37] Gen. 1:9.

as to what is true about the formation of the Creation. It is another thing, however, to ask what that excellent servant of thy faith, Moses, would have wished for the reader and hearer to understand from these words. As for the first question, let all those depart from me who imagine that Moses spoke things that are false. But let me be united with them in thee, O Lord, and delight myself in thee with those who feed on thy truth in the bond of love. Let us approach together the words of thy book and make diligent inquiry in them for thy meaning through the meaning of thy servant by whose pen thou hast given them to us.

CHAPTER XXIV

33. But in the midst of so many truths which occur to the interpreters of these words (understood as they can be in different ways), which one of us can discover that single interpretation which warrants our saying confidently that Moses thought *thus* and that in this narrative he wishes *this* to be understood, as confidently as he would say that *this* is true, whether Moses thought the one or the other. For see, O my God, I am thy servant, and I have vowed in this book an offering of confession to thee,[38] and I beseech thee that by thy mercy I may pay my vow to thee. Now, see, could I assert that Moses meant nothing else than *this* [i.e., my interpretation] when he wrote, "In the beginning God created the heaven and the earth," as confidently as I can assert that thou in thy immutable Word hast created all things, invisible and visible? No, I cannot do this because it is not as clear to me that *this* was in his mind when he wrote these things, as I see it to be certain in thy truth. For his thoughts might be set upon the very beginning of the creation when he said, "In the beginning"; and he might have wished it understood that, in this passage, "heaven and earth" refers to no formed and perfect entity, whether spiritual or corporeal, but each of them only newly begun and still formless. Whichever of these possibilities has been mentioned I can see that it might have been said truly. But which of them he did actually intend to express in these words I do not clearly see. However, whether it was one of these or some other meaning which I have not mentioned that this great man saw in his mind when he used these words I have no doubt whatever that he saw it truly and expressed it suitably.

[38] Note how this reiterates a constant theme in the *Confessions* as a whole; a further indication that Bk. XII is an integral part of the single whole.

CHAPTER XXV

34. Let no man fret me now by saying, "Moses did not mean what *you* say, but what *I* say." Now if he asks me, "How do you know that Moses meant what you deduce from his words?", I ought to respond calmly and reply as I have already done, or even more fully if he happens to be untrained. But when he says, "Moses did not mean what *you* say, but what *I* say," and then does not deny what either of us says but allows that *both* are true—then, O my God, life of the poor, in whose breast there is no contradiction, pour thy soothing balm into my heart that I may patiently bear with people who talk like this! It is not because they are godly men and have seen in the heart of thy servant what they say, but rather they are proud men and have not considered Moses' meaning, but only love their own— not because it is true but because it is their own. Otherwise they could equally love another true opinion, as I love what they say when what they speak is true—not because it is theirs but because it is true, and therefore not theirs but true. And if they love an opinion because it is true, it becomes both theirs and mine, since it is the common property of all lovers of the truth.[39] But I neither accept nor approve of it when they contend that Moses did not mean what I say but what they say—and this because, even if it were so, such rashness is born not of knowledge, but of impudence. It comes not from vision but from vanity.

And therefore, O Lord, thy judgments should be held in awe, because thy truth is neither mine nor his nor anyone else's; but it belongs to all of us whom thou hast openly called to have it in common; and thou hast warned us not to hold on to it as our own special property, for if we do we lose it. For if anyone arrogates to himself what thou hast bestowed on all to enjoy, and if he desires something for his own that belongs to all, he is forced away from what is common to all to what is, indeed, his very own—that is, from truth to falsehood. For he who tells a lie speaks of his own thought.[40]

35. Hear, O God, best judge of all! O Truth itself, hear what I say to this disputant. Hear it, because I say it in thy presence and before my brethren who use the law rightly to the end of love. Hear and give heed to what I shall say to him, if it pleases thee.

---

[39] Cf. *De libero arbitrio*, II, 8:20, 10:28.   [40] Cf. John 8:44.

For I would return this brotherly and peaceful word to him: "If we both see that what you say is true, and if we both say that what I say is true, where is it, I ask you, that we see this? Certainly, I do not see it in you, and you do not see it in me, but both of us see it in the unchangeable truth itself, which is above our minds." [41] If, then, we do not disagree about the true light of the Lord our God, why do we disagree about the thoughts of our neighbor, which we cannot see as clearly as the immutable Truth is seen? If Moses himself had appeared to us and said, "This is what I meant," it would not be in order that we should see it but that we should believe him. Let us not, then, "go beyond what is written and be puffed up for the one against the other." [42] Let us, instead, "love the Lord our God with all our heart, with all our soul, and with all our mind, and our neighbor as ourself." [43] Unless we believe that whatever Moses meant in these books he meant to be ordered by these two precepts of love, we shall make God a liar, if we judge of the soul of his servant in any other way than as he has taught us. See now, how foolish it is, in the face of so great an abundance of true opinions which can be elicited from these words, rashly to affirm that Moses especially intended only *one* of these interpretations; and then, with destructive contention, to violate love itself, on behalf of which he had said all the things we are endeavoring to explain!

CHAPTER XXVI

36. And yet, O my God, thou exaltation of my humility and rest of my toil, who hearest my confessions and forgivest my sins, since thou commandest me to love my neighbor as myself, I cannot believe that thou gavest thy most faithful servant Moses a lesser gift than I should wish and desire for myself from thee, if I had been born in his time, and if thou hadst placed me in the position where, by the use of my heart and my tongue, those books might be produced which so long after were to profit all nations throughout the whole world—from such a great pinnacle of authority—and were to surmount the words of all false and proud teachings. If I had been Moses—and we

---

41 The essential thesis of the *De Magistro*; it has important implications both for Augustine's epistemology and for his theory of Christian nurture; cf. the *De catechizandis rudibus*.

42 I Cor. 4:6.

43 Cf. Deut. 6:5; Lev. 19:18; see also Matt. 22:37, 39.

all come from the same mass,[44] and what is man that thou art mindful of him? [45]—if I had been Moses at the time that he was, and if I had been ordered by thee to write the book of Genesis, I would surely have wished for such a power of expression and such an art of arrangement to be given me, that those who cannot as yet understand *how* God createth would still not reject my words as surpassing their powers of understanding. And I would have wished that those who are already able to do this would find fully contained in the laconic speech of thy servant whatever truths they had arrived at in their own thought; and if, in the light of the Truth, some other man saw some further meaning, that too would be found congruent to my words.

CHAPTER XXVII

37. For just as a spring dammed up is more plentiful and affords a larger supply of water for more streams over wider fields than any single stream led off from the same spring over a long course—so also is the narration of thy minister: it is intended to benefit many who are likely to discourse about it and, with an economy of language, it overflows into various streams of clear truth, from which each one may draw out for himself that particular truth which he can about these topics—this one that truth, that one another truth, by the broader survey of various interpretations. For some people, when they read or hear these words,[46] think that God, like some sort of man or like some sort of huge body, by some new and sudden decision, produced outside himself and at a certain distance two great bodies: one above, the other below, within which all created things were to be contained. And when they hear, "God said, 'Let such and such be done,' and it was done," they think of words begun and ended, sounding in time and then passing away, followed by the coming into being of what was commanded. They think of other things of the same sort which their familiarity with the world suggests to them.

In these people, who are still little children and whose weakness is borne up by this humble language as if on a mother's breast, their faith is built up healthfully and they come to possess and to hold as certain the conviction that God made all entities that their senses perceive all around them in such marvelous variety. And if one despises these words as if they were

---

[44] Cf. Rom. 9:21.   [45] Cf. Ps. 8:4.
[46] "In the beginning God created," etc.

trivial, and with proud weakness stretches himself beyond his fostering cradle, he will, alas, fall away wretchedly. Have pity, O Lord God, lest those who pass by trample on the unfledged bird,[47] and send thy angel who may restore it to its nest, that it may live until it can fly.

CHAPTER XXVIII

38. But others, to whom these words are no longer a nest but, rather, a shady thicket, spy the fruits concealed in them and fly around rejoicing and search among them and pluck them with cheerful chirpings. For when they read or hear these words, O God, they see that all times past and times future are transcended by thy eternal and stable permanence, and they see also that there is no temporal creature that is not of thy making. By thy will, since it is the same as thy being, thou hast created all things, not by any mutation of will and not by any will that previously was nonexistent—and not out of thyself, but in thy own likeness, thou didst make from nothing the form of all things. This was an unlikeness which was capable of being formed by thy likeness through its relation to thee, the One, as each thing has been given form appropriate to its kind according to its preordained capacity. Thus, all things were made very good, whether they remain around thee or whether, removed in time and place by various degrees, they cause or undergo the beautiful changes of natural process.

They see these things and they rejoice in the light of thy truth to whatever degree they can.

39. Again, one of these men[48] directs his attention to the verse, "In the beginning God made the heaven and the earth," and he beholds Wisdom as the true "beginning," because it also speaks to us. Another man directs his attention to the same words, and by "beginning" he understands simply the commencement of creation, and interprets it thus: "In the beginning he made," as if it were the same thing as to say, "At the first moment, God made. . . ." And among those who interpret "In the beginning" to mean that in thy wisdom thou hast created the heaven and earth, one believes that the matter out of which heaven and earth were to be created is what is referred to by the phrase "heaven and earth." But another believes that these entities were already formed and distinct. Still another

47 An echo of Job 39:13-16.
48 The thicket denizens mentioned above.

will understand it to refer to one formed entity—a spiritual one, designated by the term "heaven"—and to another unformed entity of corporeal matter, designated by the term "earth." But those who understand the phrase "heaven and earth" to mean the yet unformed matter from which the heaven and the earth were to be formed do not take it in a simple sense: one man regards it as that from which the intelligible and tangible creations are both produced; and another only as that from which the tangible, corporeal world is produced, containing in its vast bosom these visible and observable entities. Nor are they in simple accord who believe that "heaven and earth" refers to the created things already set in order and arranged. One believes that it refers to the invisible and visible world; another, only to the visible world, in which we admire the luminous heavens and the darkened earth and all the things that they contain.

CHAPTER XXIX

40. But he who understands "In the beginning he made" as if it meant, "At first he made," can truly interpret the phrase "heaven and earth" as referring only to the "matter" of heaven and earth, namely, of the prior universal, which is the intelligible and corporeal creation. For if he would try to interpret the phrase as applying to the universe already formed, it then might rightly be asked of him, "If God first made this, what then did he do afterward?" And, after the universe, he will find nothing. But then he must, however unwillingly, face the question, How is this the first if there is nothing afterward? But when he said that God made matter first formless and then formed, he is not being absurd if he is able to discern what precedes by eternity, and what proceeds in time; what comes from choice, and what comes from origin. In eternity, God is before all things; in the temporal process, the flower is before the fruit; in the act of choice, the fruit is before the flower; in the case of origin, sound is before the tune. Of these four relations, the first and last that I have referred to are understood with much difficulty. The second and third are very easily understood. For it is an uncommon and lofty vision, O Lord, to behold thy eternity immutably making mutable things, and thereby standing always before them. Whose mind is acute enough to be able, without great labor, to discover how the sound comes before the tune? For a tune is a formed sound; and an unformed thing

may exist, but a thing that does not exist cannot be formed. In the same way, matter is prior to what is made from it. It is not prior because it makes its product, for it is itself made; and its priority is not that of a time interval. For in time we do not first utter formless sounds without singing and then adapt or fashion them into the form of a song, as wood or silver from which a chest or vessel is made. Such materials precede in time the forms of the things which are made from them. But in singing this is not so. For when a song is sung, its sound is heard at the same time. There is not first a formless sound, which afterward is formed into a song; but just as soon as it has sounded it passes away, and you cannot find anything of it which you could gather up and shape. Therefore, the song is absorbed in its own sound and the "sound" of the song *is* its "matter." But the sound is formed in order that it may be a tune. This is why, as I was saying, the matter of the sound is prior to the form of the tune. It is not "before" in the sense that it has any power of making a sound or tune. Nor is the sound itself the composer of the tune; rather, the sound is sent forth from the body and is ordered by the soul of the singer, so that from it he may form a tune. Nor is the sound first in time, for it is given forth together with the tune. Nor is it first in choice, because a sound is no better than a tune, since a tune is not merely a sound but a beautiful sound. But it is first in origin, because the tune is not formed in order that it may become a sound, but the sound is formed in order that it may become a tune.

From this example, let him who is able to understand see that the matter of things was first made and was called "heaven and earth" because out of it the heaven and earth were made. This primal formlessness was not made first in time, because the form of things gives rise to time; but now, in time, it is intuited together with its form. And yet nothing can be related of this unformed matter unless it is regarded as if it were the first in the time series though the last in value—because things formed are certainly superior to things unformed—and it is preceded by the eternity of the Creator, so that from nothing there might be made that from which something might be made.

CHAPTER XXX

41. In this discord of true opinions let Truth itself bring concord, and may our God have mercy on us all, that we may use the law rightly to the end of the commandment which is pure

love. Thus, if anyone asks me which of these opinions was the meaning of thy servant Moses, these would not be my confessions did I not confess to thee that I do not know. Yet I do know that those opinions are true—with the exception of the carnal ones—about which I have said what I thought was proper. Yet those little ones of good hope are not frightened by these words of thy Book, for they speak of high things in a lowly way and of a few basic things in many varied ways. But let all of us, whom I acknowledge to see and speak the truth in these words, love one another and also love thee, our God, O Fountain of Truth—as we will if we thirst not after vanity but for the Fountain of Truth. Indeed, let us so honor this servant of thine, the dispenser of this Scripture, full of thy Spirit, so that we will believe that when thou didst reveal thyself to him, and he wrote these things down, he intended through them what will chiefly minister both for the light of truth and to the increase of our fruitfulness.

CHAPTER XXXI

42. Thus, when one man says, "Moses meant what *I* mean," and another says, "No, he meant what *I* do," I think that I speak more faithfully when I say, "Why could he not have meant both if both opinions are true?" And if there should be still a third truth or a fourth one, and if anyone should seek a truth quite different in those words, why would it not be right to believe that Moses saw all these different truths, since through him the one God has tempered the Holy Scriptures to the understanding of many different people, who should see truths in it even if they are different? Certainly—and I say this fearlessly and from my heart—if I were to write anything on such a supreme authority, I would prefer to write it so that, whatever of truth anyone might apprehend from the matter under discussion, my words should re-echo in the several minds rather than that they should set down one true opinion so clearly on one point that I should exclude the rest, even though they contained no falsehood that offended me. Therefore, I am unwilling, O my God, to be so headstrong as not to believe that this man [Moses] has received at least this much from thee. Surely when he was writing these words, he saw fully and understood all the truth we have been able to find in them, and also much besides that we have not been able to discern, or are not yet able to find out, though it is there in them still to be found.

CHAPTER XXXII

43. Finally, O Lord—who art God and not flesh and blood —if any man sees anything less, can anything lie hid from "thy good Spirit" who shall "lead me into the land of uprightness,"[49] which thou thyself, through those words, wast revealing to future readers, even though he through whom they were spoken fixed on only one among the many interpretations that might have been found? And if this is so, let it be agreed that the meaning he saw is more exalted than the others. But to us, O Lord, either point out the same meaning or any other true one, as it pleases thee. Thus, whether thou makest known to us what thou madest known to that man of thine, or some other meaning by the agency of the same words, still do thou feed us and let error not deceive us. Behold, O Lord, my God, how much we have written concerning these few words—how much, indeed! What strength of mind, what length of time, would suffice for all thy books to be interpreted in this fashion?[50] Allow me, therefore, in these concluding words to confess more briefly to thee and select some one, true, certain, and good sense that thou shalt inspire, although many meanings offer themselves and many indeed are possible.[51] This is the faith of my confession, that if I could say what thy servant meant, that is truest and best, and for that I must strive. Yet if I do not succeed, may it be that I shall say at least what thy Truth wished to say to me through its words, just as it said what it wished to Moses.

[49] Cf. Ps. 143:10.
[50] Something of an understatement! It is interesting to note that Augustine devotes more time and space to these opening verses of Genesis than to any other passage in the entire Bible—and he never commented on the *full* text of Genesis. Cf. Karl Barth's 274 pages devoted to Gen., chs. 1;2, in the *Kirchliche Dogmatik*, III, 1, pp. 103–377.
[51] Transition, in preparation for the concluding book (XIII), which undertakes a constructive resolution to the problem of the analysis of the mode of creation made here in Bk. XII.

BOOK THIRTEEN

The mysteries and allegories of the days of creation. Augustine undertakes to interpret Gen. 1:2–31 in a mystical and allegorical fashion so as to exhibit the profundities of God's power and wisdom and love. He is also interested in developing his theories of hermeneutics on his favorite topic: creation. He finds the Trinity in the account of creation and he ponders the work of the Spirit moving over the waters. In the firmament he finds the allegory of Holy Scripture and in the dry land and bitter sea he finds the division between the people of God and the conspiracy of the unfaithful. He develops the theme of man's being made in the image and likeness of God. He brings his survey to a climax and his confessions to an end with a meditation on the goodness of all creation and the promised rest and blessedness of the eternal Sabbath, on which God, who is eternal rest, "rested."

CHAPTER I

1. I call on thee, my God, my Mercy, who madest me and didst not forget me, though I was forgetful of thee. I call thee into my soul, which thou didst prepare for thy reception by the desire which thou inspirest in it. Do not forsake me when I call on thee, who didst anticipate me before I called and who didst repeatedly urge with manifold calling that I should hear thee afar off and be turned and call upon thee, who callest me. For thou, O Lord, hast blotted out all my evil deserts, not punishing me for what my hands have done; and thou hast anticipated all my good deserts so as to recompense me for what thy hands have done—the hands which made me. Before I was, thou wast, and I was not anything at all that thou shouldst grant me being. Yet, see how I exist by reason of thy goodness, which made provision for all that thou madest me to be and all that thou

madest me from. For thou didst not stand in need of me, nor am I the kind of good entity which could be a help to thee, my Lord and my God. It is not that I may serve thee as if thou wert fatigued in working, or as if thy power would be the less if it lacked my assistance. Nor is the service I pay thee like the cultivation of a field, so that thou wouldst go untended if I did not tend thee.[1] Instead, it is that I may serve and worship thee to the end that I may have my well-being from thee, from whom comes my capacity for well-being.

CHAPTER II

2. Indeed, it is from the fullness of thy goodness that thy creation exists at all: to the end that the created good might not fail to be, even though it can profit thee nothing, and is nothing of thee nor equal to thee—since its created existence comes from thee.

For what did the heaven and earth, which thou didst make in the beginning, ever deserve from thee? Let them declare— these spiritual and corporeal entities, which thou madest in thy wisdom—let them declare what they merited at thy hands, so that the inchoate and the formless, whether spiritual or corporeal, would deserve to be held in being in spite of the fact that they tend toward disorder and extreme unlikeness to thee? An unformed spiritual entity is more excellent than a formed corporeal entity; and the corporeal, even when unformed, is more excellent than if it were simply nothing at all. Still, these formless entities are held in their state of being by thee, until they are recalled to thy unity and receive form and being from thee, the one sovereign Good. What have they deserved of thee, since they would not even be unformed entities except from thee?

3. What has corporeal matter deserved of thee—even in its invisible and unformed state—since it would not exist even in this state if thou hadst not made it? And, if it did not exist, it could not merit its existence from thee.

Or, what has that formless spiritual creation deserved of thee —that it should flow lightlessly like the abyss—since it is so unlike thee and would not exist at all if it had not been turned by the Word which made it that same Word, and, illumined by that

---

1 This is a compound—and untranslatable—Latin pun: *neque ut sic te colam quasi terram, ut sis uncultus si non te colam.*

Word, had been "made light" [2]—although not as thy equal but only as an image of that Form [of Light] which is equal to thee? For, in the case of a body, its being is not the same thing as its being beautiful; else it could not then be a deformed body. Likewise, in the case of a created spirit, living is not the same state as living wisely; else it could then be immutably wise. But the true good of every created thing is always to cleave fast to thee, lest, in turning away from thee, it lose the light it had received in being turned by thee, and so relapse into a life like that of the dark abyss.

As for ourselves, who are a spiritual creation by virtue of our souls, when we turned away from thee, O Light, we were in that former life of darkness; and we toil amid the shadows of our darkness until—through thy only Son—we become thy righteousness,[3] like the mountains of God. For we, like the great abyss,[4] have been the objects of thy judgments.

CHAPTER III

4. Now what thou saidst in the beginning of the creation— "Let there be light: and there was light"—I interpret, not unfitly, as referring to the spiritual creation, because it already had a kind of life which thou couldst illuminate. But, since it had not merited from thee that it should be a life capable of enlightenment, so neither, when it already began to exist, did it merit from thee that it should be enlightened. For neither could its formlessness please thee until it became light—and it became light, not from the bare fact of existing, but by the act of turning its face to the light which enlightened it, and by cleaving to it. Thus it owed the fact that it lived, and lived happily, to nothing whatsoever but thy grace, since it had been turned, by a change for the better, toward that which cannot be changed for either better or worse. Thou alone art, because

---

[2] Cf. *Enneads*, I, 2:4: "What the soul now sees, it certainly always possessed, but as lying in the darkness. . . . To dispel the darkness and thus come to knowledge of its inner content, it must thrust toward the light." Compare the notions of the *initiative* of such movements in the soul in Plotinus and Augustine.

[3] Cf. II Cor. 5:21.

[4] Cf. Ps. 36:6 and see also Augustine's *Exposition on the Psalms*, XXXVI, 8, where he says that "the great preachers [receivers of God's illumination] are the mountains of God," for they first catch the light on their summits. The abyss he called "the depth of sin" into which the evil and unfaithful fall.

thou alone art without complication. For thee it is not one thing to live and another thing to live in blessedness; for thou art thyself thy own blessedness.

CHAPTER IV

5. What, therefore, would there have been lacking in thy good, which thou thyself art, even if these things had never been made or had remained unformed? Thou didst not create them out of any lack but out of the plenitude of thy goodness, ordering them and turning them toward form,[5] but not because thy joy had to be perfected by them. For thou art perfect, and their imperfection is displeasing. Therefore were they perfected by thee and became pleasing to thee—but not as if thou wert before that imperfect and had to be perfected in their perfection. For thy good Spirit which moved over the face of the waters[6] was not borne up by them as if he rested on them. For those in whom thy good Spirit is said to rest he actually causes to rest in himself. But thy incorruptible and immutable will—in itself all-sufficient for itself—moved over that life which thou hadst made: in which living is not at all the same thing as living happily, since that life still lives even as it flows in its own darkness. But it remains to be turned to him by whom it was made and to live more and more like "the fountain of life," and in his light "to see light,"[7] and to be perfected, and enlightened, and made blessed.

CHAPTER V

6. See now,[8] how the Trinity appears to me in an enigma. And thou art the Trinity, O my God, since thou, O Father—in the beginning of our wisdom, that is, in thy wisdom born of thee, equal and coeternal with thee, that is, thy Son—created the heaven and the earth. Many things we have said about the heaven of heavens, and about the earth invisible and unformed,

---

5 Cf. *Timaeus*, 29D–30A, "He [the Demiurge-Creator] was good: and in the good no jealousy . . . can ever arise. So, being without jealousy, he desired that all things should come as near as possible to being like himself. . . . He took over all that is visible . . . and brought it from order to order, since he judged that order was in every way better" (F. M. Cornford, *Plato's Cosmology*, New York, 1937, p. 33). Cf. *Enneads*, V, 4:1, and Athanasius, *On the Incarnation*, III, 3.

6 Cf. Gen. 1:2.   7 Cf. Ps. 36:9.

8 In this passage in Genesis on the creation.

and about the shadowy abyss—speaking of the aimless flux of its being spiritually deformed unless it is turned to him from whom it has its life (such as it is) and by his Light comes to be a life suffused with beauty. Thus it would be a [lower] heaven of that [higher] heaven, which afterward was made between water and water.[9]

And now I came to recognize, in the name of God, the Father who made all these things, and in the term "the Beginning" to recognize the Son, through whom he made all these things; and since I did believe that my God was the Trinity, I sought still further in his holy Word, and, behold, "Thy Spirit moved over the waters." Thus, see the Trinity, O my God: Father, Son, and Holy Spirit, the Creator of all creation!

CHAPTER VI

7. But why, O truth-speaking Light? To thee I lift up my heart—let it not teach me vain notions. Disperse its shadows and tell me, I beseech thee, by that Love which is our mother; tell me, I beseech thee, the reason why—after the reference to heaven and to the invisible and unformed earth, and darkness over the abyss—thy Scripture should then at long last refer to thy Spirit? Was it because it was appropriate that he should first be shown to us as "moving over"; and this could not have been said unless something had already been mentioned over which thy Spirit could be understood as "moving"? For he did not "move over" the Father and the Son, and he could not properly be said to be "moving over" if he were "moving over" nothing. Thus, what it was he was "moving over" had to be mentioned first and he whom it was not proper to mention otherwise than as "moving over" could then be mentioned. But why was it not fitting that he should have been introduced in some other way than in this context of "moving over"?

CHAPTER VII

8. Now let him who is able follow thy apostle with his understanding when he says, "Thy love is shed abroad in our hearts by the Holy Spirit, who is given to us"[10] and who teacheth us about spiritual gifts[11] and showeth us a more

---

[9] Cf. Gen. 1:6.   [10] Rom. 5:5.   [11] I Cor. 12:1.

excellent way of love; and who bows his knee unto thee for us, that we may come to the surpassing knowledge of the love of Christ.[12] Thus, from the beginning, he who is above all was "moving over" the waters.

To whom shall I tell this? How can I speak of the weight of concupiscence which drags us downward into the deep abyss, and of the love which lifts us up by thy Spirit who moved over the waters? To whom shall I tell this? How shall I tell it? For concupiscence and love are not certain "places" into which we are plunged and out of which we are lifted again. What could be more like, and yet what more unlike? They are both feelings; they are both loves. The uncleanness of our own spirit flows downward with the love of worldly care; and the sanctity of thy Spirit raises us upward by the love of release from anxiety— that we may lift our hearts to thee where thy Spirit is "moving over the waters." Thus, we shall have come to that supreme rest where our souls shall have passed through the waters which give no standing ground.[13]

CHAPTER VIII

9. The angels fell, and the soul of man fell; thus they indicate to us the deep darkness of the abyss, which would have still contained the whole spiritual creation if thou hadst not said, in the beginning, "Let there be light: and there was light"—and if every obedient mind in thy heavenly city had not adhered to thee and had not reposed in thy Spirit, which moved immutable over all things mutable. Otherwise, even the heaven of heavens itself would have been a dark shadow, instead of being, as it is now, light in the Lord.[14] For even in the restless misery of the fallen spirits, who exhibit their own darkness when they are stripped of the garments of thy light, thou showest clearly how noble thou didst make the rational creation, for whose rest and beatitude nothing suffices save thee thyself. And certainly it is not itself sufficient for its beatitude. For it is thou, O our God, who wilt enlighten our darkness; from thee shall come our garments of light; and then our darkness shall be as the noonday. Give thyself to me, O my God, restore thyself to me! See, I love thee; and if it be too little, let me love thee still more strongly. I cannot measure my love so that I may come to know how

12 Cf. Eph. 3:14, 19.   13 Cf. the Old Latin version of Ps. 123:5.
14 Cf. Eph. 5:8.

much there is still lacking in me before my life can run to thy embrace and not be turned away until it is hidden in "the covert of thy presence."[15] Only this I know, that my existence is my woe except in thee—not only in my outward life, but also within my inmost self—and all abundance I have which is not my God is poverty.

CHAPTER IX

10. But was neither the Father nor the Son "moving over the waters"? If we understand this as a motion in space, as a body moves, then not even the Holy Spirit "moved." But if we understand the changeless supereminence of the divine Being above every changeable thing, then Father, Son, and Holy Spirit "moved over the waters."

Why, then, is this said of thy Spirit alone? Why is it said of him only—as if he had been in a "place" that is not a place—about whom alone it is written, "He is thy gift"? It is in thy gift that we rest. It is there that we enjoy thee. Our rest *is* our "place." Love lifts us up toward that place, and thy good Spirit lifts our lowliness from the gates of death.[16] Our peace rests in the goodness of will. The body tends toward its own place by its own gravity. A weight does not tend downward only, but moves to its own place. Fire tends upward; a stone tends downward. They are propelled by their own mass; they seek their own places. Oil poured under the water rises above the water; water poured on oil sinks under the oil. They are moved by their own mass; they seek their own places. If they are out of order, they are restless; when their order is restored, they are at rest. My weight is my love. By it I am carried wherever I am carried. By thy gift,[17] we are enkindled and are carried upward. We burn inwardly and move forward. We ascend thy ladder which is in our heart, and we sing a canticle of degrees[18]; we glow inwardly with thy fire—with thy good fire[19]—and we go forward because we go up to the peace of Jerusalem[20]; for I was glad when they said to me, "Let us go into the house of the Lord."[21] There thy good pleasure will settle us so that we will desire nothing more than to dwell there forever.[22]

[15] Cf. Ps. 31:20.   [16] Cf. Ps. 9:13.   [17] The Holy Spirit.
[18] *Canticum graduum.* Psalms 119 to 133 as numbered in the Vulgate were regarded as a single series of ascending steps by which the soul moves up toward heaven; cf. *The Exposition on the Psalms, loc. cit.*
[19] Tongues of fire, symbol of the descent of the Holy Spirit; cf. Acts 2:3, 4.
[20] Cf. Ps. 122:6.   [21] Ps. 122:1.   [22] Cf. Ps. 23:6.

CHAPTER X

11. Happy would be that creature who, though it was in itself other than thou, still had known no other state than this from the time it was made, so that it was never without thy gift which moves over everything mutable—who had been borne up by the call in which thou saidst, "Let there be light: and there was light." [23] For in us there is a distinction between the time when we were darkness and the time when we were made light. But we are not told what would have been the case with that creature if the light had not been made. It is spoken of as though there had been something of flux and darkness in it beforehand so that the cause by which it was made to be otherwise might be evident. This is to say, by being turned to the unfailing Light it might become light. Let him who is able understand this; and let him who is not ask of thee. Why trouble me, as if *I* could "enlighten every man that comes into the world" [24]?

CHAPTER XI

12. Who can understand the omnipotent Trinity? And yet who does not speak about it, if indeed it is of it that he speaks? Rare is the soul who, when he speaks of it, also knows of what he speaks. And men contend and strive, but no man sees the vision of it without peace.

I could wish that men would consider three things which are within themselves. These three things are quite different from the Trinity, but I mention them in order that men may exercise their minds and test themselves and come to realize how different from it they are. [25]

The three things I speak of are: to be, to know, and to will. For I am, and I know, and I will. I am a knowing and a willing being; I know that I am and that I will; and I will to be and to know. In these three functions, therefore, let him who can see how integral a life is; for there is one life, one mind, one essence. Finally, the distinction does not separate the things, and yet it is a distinction. Surely a man has this distinction before his mind; let him look into himself and see, and tell me. But when he discovers and can say anything about any one of these, let him not think that he has thereby discovered what is

[23] Gen. 1:3.   [24] John 1:9.
[25] Cf. the detailed analogy from self to Trinity in *De Trinitate*, IX–XII.

Immutable above them all, which *is* immutably and *knows* immutably and *wills* immutably. But whether there is a Trinity there because these three functions exist in the one God, or whether all three are in each Person so that they are each threefold, or whether both these notions are true and, in some mysterious manner, the Infinite is in itself its own Selfsame object—at once one and many, so that by itself it is and knows itself and suffices to itself without change, so that the Selfsame is the abundant magnitude of its Unity—who can readily conceive? Who can in any fashion express it plainly? Who can in any way rashly make a pronouncement about it?

CHAPTER XII

13. Go forward in your confession, O my faith; say to the Lord your God, "Holy, holy, holy, O Lord my God, in thy name we have been baptized, in the name of the Father, Son, and Holy Spirit." In thy name we baptize, in the name of the Father, the Son, and the Holy Spirit. For among us also God in his Christ made "heaven and earth," namely, the spiritual and carnal members of his Church. And true it is that before it received "the form of doctrine," our "earth" [26] was "invisible and unformed," and we were covered with the darkness of our ignorance; for thou dost correct man for his iniquity,[27] and "thy judgments are a great abyss." [28] But because thy Spirit was moving over these waters, thy mercy did not forsake our wretchedness, and thou saidst, "Let there be light; repent, for the kingdom of heaven is at hand." [29] Repent, and let there be light. Because our soul was troubled within us, we remembered thee, O Lord, from the land of Jordan, and from the mountain [30] —and as we became displeased with our darkness we turned to thee, "and there was light." And behold, we were heretofore in darkness, but now we are light in the Lord.[31]

CHAPTER XIII

14. But even so, we still live by faith and not by sight, for we are saved by hope; but hope that is seen is not hope. Thus far deep calls unto deep, but now in "the noise of thy waterfalls." [32]

---

26 I.e., the Church. 27 Cf. Ps. 39:11. 28 Ps. 36:6.
29 Gen. 1:3 and Matt. 4:17; 3:2.
30 Cf. Ps. 42:5, 6. 31 Cf. Eph. 5:8. 32 Ps. 42:7.

And thus far he who said, "I could not speak to you as if you were spiritual ones, but only as if you were carnal"[33]—thus far even he does not count himself to have apprehended, but forgetting the things that are behind and reaching forth to the things that are before, he presses on to those things that are ahead,[34] and he groans under his burden and his soul thirsts after the living God as the stag pants for the water brooks,[35] and says, "When shall I come?"[36]—"desiring to be further clothed by his house which is from heaven."[37] And he called to this lower deep, saying, "Be not conformed to this world, but be transformed by the renewing of your mind."[38] And "be not children in understanding, although in malice be children," in order that "in understanding you may become perfect."[39] "O foolish Galatians, who has bewitched you?"[40] But this is not now only in his own voice but in thy voice, who sent thy Spirit from above through Him who both "ascended up on high"[41] and opened up the floodgates of his gifts, that the force of his streams might make glad the city of God.[42]

For that city and for him sighs the Bridegroom's friend,[43] who has now the first fruits of the Spirit laid up with him, but who is still groaning within himself and waiting for adoption, that is, the redemption of his body.[44] To Him he sighs, for he is a member of the Bride[45]; for him he is jealous, not for himself, but because not in his own voice but in the voice of thy waterfalls he calls on that other deep, of which he is jealous and in fear; for he fears lest, as the serpent seduced Eve by his subtlety, his mind should be corrupted from the purity which is in our Bridegroom, thy only Son. What a light of beauty that will be when "we shall see him as he is"[46]!—and when these tears shall pass away which "have been my meat day and night, while they continually say unto me, 'Where is your God?'"[47]

CHAPTER XIV

15. And I myself say: "O my God, where art thou? See now, where art thou?" In thee I take my breath for a little while, when I pour out my soul beyond myself in the voice of joy and

---

[33] Cf. I Cor. 3:1. [34] Cf. Phil. 3:13. [35] Cf. Ps. 42:1.
[36] Ps. 42:2. [37] Cf. II Cor. 5:1–4. [38] Rom. 12:2.
[39] I Cor. 14:20. [40] Gal. 3:1. [41] Eph. 4:8, 9.
[42] Cf. Ps. 46:4. [43] Cf. John 3:29. [44] Cf. Rom. 8:23.
[45] I.e., the Body of Christ. [46] I John 3:2. [47] Ps. 42:3.

praise, in the voice of him that keeps holyday.[48] And still it is cast down because it relapses and becomes an abyss, or rather it feels that it still is an abyss. My faith speaks to my soul—the faith that thou dost kindle to light my path in the night: "Why are you cast down, O my soul, and why are you disquieted in me? Hope in God."[49] For his word is a lamp to your feet.[50] Hope and persevere until the night passes—that mother of the wicked; until the Lord's wrath subsides—that wrath whose children once we were, of whom we were beforehand in darkness, whose residue we still bear about us in our bodies, dead because of sin.[51] Hope and endure until the day breaks and the shadows flee away.[52] Hope in the Lord: in the morning I shall stand in his presence and keep watch[53]; I shall forever give praise to him. In the morning I shall stand and shall see my God, who is the health of my countenance,[54] who also will quicken our mortal bodies by the Spirit that dwells in us,[55] because in mercy he was moving over our lightless and restless inner deep. From this we have received an earnest, even now in this pilgrimage, that we are now in the light, since already we are saved by hope and are children of the light and children of the day—not children of the night, nor of the darkness,[56] which we have been hitherto. Between those children of the night and ourselves, in this still uncertain state of human knowledge, only thou canst rightly distinguish—thou who dost test the heart and who dost call the light day, and the darkness night.[57] For who can see us clearly but thee? What do we have that we have not received from thee, who madest from the same lump some vessels to noble, and others to ignoble, use[58]?

CHAPTER XV

16. Now who but thee, our God, didst make for us that firmament of the authority of thy divine Scripture to be over us? For "the heaven shall be folded up like a scroll"[59]; but now it is stretched over us like a skin. Thy divine Scripture is of more sublime authority now that those mortal men through whom thou didst dispense it to us have departed this life. And thou knowest, O Lord, thou knowest how thou didst clothe men with skins when they became mortal because of sin.[60] In some-

[48] Cf. Ps. 42:4.
[49] Ps. 43:5.
[50] Cf. Ps. 119:105.
[51] Cf. Rom. 8:10.
[52] Cf. S. of Sol. 2:17.
[53] Cf. Ps. 5:3.
[54] Ps. 43:5.
[55] Cf. Rom. 8:11.
[56] I Thess. 5:5.
[57] Cf. Gen. 1:5.
[58] Cf. Rom. 9:21.
[59] Isa. 34:4.
[60] Cf. Gen. 3:21.

thing of the same way, thou hast stretched out the firmament of thy Book as a skin—that is to say, thou hast spread thy harmonious words over us through the ministry of mortal men. For by their very death that solid firmament of authority in thy sayings, spoken forth by them, stretches high over all that now drift under it; whereas while they lived on earth their authority was not so widely extended. Then thou hadst not yet spread out the heaven like a skin; thou hadst not yet spread abroad everywhere the fame of their death.

17. Let us see, O Lord, "the heavens, the work of thy fingers," [61] and clear away from our eyes the fog with which thou hast covered them. In them[62] is that testimony of thine which gives wisdom even to the little ones. O my God, out of the mouth of babes and sucklings, perfect thy praise.[63] For we know no other books that so destroy man's pride, that so break down the adversary and the self-defender who resists thy reconciliation by an effort to justify his own sins. I do not know, O Lord, I do not know any other such pure words that so persuade me to confession and make my neck submissive to thy yoke, and invite me to serve thee for nothing else than thy own sake. Let me understand these things, O good Father. Grant this to me, since I am placed under them; for thou hast established these things for those placed under them.

18. There are other waters that are above this firmament, and I believe that they are immortal and removed from earthly corruption. Let them praise thy name—this supercelestial society, thy angels, who have no need to look up at this firmament or to gain a knowledge of thy Word by reading it— let them praise thee. For they always behold thy face and read therein, without any syllables in time, what thy eternal Will intends. They read, they choose, they love.[64] They are always reading, and what they read never passes away. For by choosing and by loving they read the very immutability of thy counsel. Their book is never closed, nor is the scroll folded up, because thou thyself art this to them, and art this to them eternally; because thou didst range them above this firmament which thou madest firm over the infirmities of the people below the heavens, where they might look up and learn thy mercy, which proclaims in time thee who madest all times. "For thy mercy, O Lord, is in the heavens, and thy faithfulness reaches to the clouds."[65] The clouds pass away, but the heavens

[61] Ps. 8:3. [62] "The heavens," i.e., the Scriptures.
[63] Cf. Ps. 8:2. [64] *Legunt, eligunt, diligunt.* [65] Ps. 36:5.

remain. The preachers of thy Word pass away from this life into another; but thy Scripture is spread abroad over the people, even to the end of the world. Indeed, both heaven and earth shall pass away, but thy words shall never pass away.[66] The scroll shall be rolled together, and the "grass" over which it was spread shall, with all its goodliness, pass away; but thy Word remains forever[67]—thy Word which now appears to us in the dark image of the clouds and through the glass of heaven, and not as it really is. And even if we are the well-beloved of thy Son, it has not yet appeared what we shall be.[68] He hath seen us through the entanglement[69] of our flesh, and he is fair-speaking, and he hath enkindled us, and we run after his fragrance.[70] But "when he shall appear, then we shall be like him, for we shall see him as he is."[71] As he *is*, O Lord, we shall see him—although that time is not yet.

CHAPTER XVI

19. For just as thou art the utterly Real, thou alone dost fully know, since thou art immutably, and thou knowest immutably, and thou willest immutably. And thy Essence knows and wills immutably. Thy Knowledge is and wills immutably. Thy Will is and knows immutably. And it does not seem right to thee that the immutable Light should be known by the enlightened but mutable creature in the same way as it knows itself. Therefore, to thee my soul is as a land where no water is [72]; for, just as it cannot enlighten itself by itself, so it cannot satisfy itself by itself. Thus the fountain of life is with thee, and "in thy light shall we see light."[73]

CHAPTER XVII

20. Who has gathered the "embittered ones" [74] into a single society? For they all have the same end, which is temporal and

---

[66] Cf. Matt. 24:35.   [67] Cf. Isa. 40:6–8.   [68] Cf. I John 3:2.
[69] *Retia*, literally "a net"; such as those used by *retiarii*, the gladiators who used nets to entangle their opponents.   [70] Cf. S. of Sol. 1:3, 4.
[71] I John 3:2.   [72] Cf. Ps. 63:1.   [73] Ps. 36:9.
[74] *Amaricantes*, a figure which Augustine develops both in the *Exposition of the Psalms* and *The City of God*. Commenting on Ps. 65, Augustine says: "For the sea, by a figure, is used to indicate this world, with its bitter saltiness and troubled storms, where men with perverse and depraved appetites have become like fishes devouring one another." In *The City of God*, he speaks of the bitterness of life in the *civitas terrena*; cf. XIX, 5.

earthly happiness. This is their motive for doing everything, although they may fluctuate within an innumerable diversity of concerns. Who but thee, O Lord, gathered them together, thou who saidst, "Let the waters be gathered together into one place and let the dry land appear"—athirst for thee? For the sea also is thine, and thou madest it, and thy hands formed the dry land.[75] For it is not the bitterness of men's wills but the gathering together of the waters which is called "the sea"; yet thou dost curb the wicked lusts of men's souls and fix their bounds: how far they are allowed to advance, and where their waves will be broken against each other—and thus thou makest it "a sea," by the providence of thy governance of all things.

21. But as for the souls that thirst after thee and who appear before thee—separated from "the society of the [bitter] sea" by reason of their different ends—thou waterest them by a secret and sweet spring, so that "the earth" may bring forth her fruit and—thou, O Lord, commanding it—our souls may bud forth in works of mercy after their kind.[76] Thus we shall love our neighbor in ministering to his bodily needs, for in this way the soul has seed in itself after its kind when in our own infirmity our compassion reaches out to the relief of the needy, helping them even as we would desire to be helped ourselves if we were in similar need. Thus we help, not only in easy problems (as is signified by "the herb yielding its seed") but also in the offering of our best strength in affording them the aid of protection (such as "the tree bearing its fruit"). This is to say, we seek to rescue him who is suffering injury from the hands of the powerful—furnishing him with the sheltering protection which comes from the strong arm of a righteous judgment.[77]

CHAPTER XVIII

22. Thus, O Lord, thus I beseech thee: let it happen as thou hast prepared it, as thou givest joy and the capacity for joy. Let truth spring up out of the earth, and let righteousness look down from heaven,[78] and let there be lights in the firmament.[79]

Let us break our bread with the hungry, let us bring the

[75] Cf. Ps. 95:5.　　　　[76] Cf. Gen. 1:10f.
[77] In this way, Augustine sees an analogy between the good earth bearing its fruits and the ethical "fruit-bearing" of the Christian love of neighbor.
[78] Cf. Ps. 85:11.　　　　[79] Cf. Gen. 1:14.

shelterless poor to our house; let us clothe the naked, and never despise those of our own flesh.[80] See from the fruits which spring forth from the earth how good it is. Thus let our temporal light break forth, and let us from even this lower level of fruitful action come to the joy of contemplation and hold on high the Word of Life. And let us at length appear like "lights in the world," [81] cleaving to the firmament of thy Scripture.

For in it thou makest it plain to us how we may distinguish between things intelligible and things tangible, as if between the day and the night—and to distinguish between souls who give themselves to things of the mind and others absorbed in things of sense. Thus it is that now thou art not alone in the secret of thy judgment as thou wast before the firmament was made, and before thou didst divide between the light and the darkness. But now also thy spiritual children, placed and ranked in this same firmament—thy grace being thus manifest throughout the world—may shed light upon the earth, and may divide between the day and night, and may be for the signs of the times[82]; because old things have passed away, and, lo, all things are become new[83]; and because our salvation is nearer than when we believed; and because "the night is far spent and the day is at hand" [84]; and because "thou crownest the year with blessing," [85] sending the laborers into thy harvest, in which others have labored in the sowing and sending laborers also to make new sowings whose harvest shall not be until the end of time. Thus thou dost grant the prayers of him who seeks, and thou dost bless the years of the righteous man. But thou art always the Selfsame, and in thy years which fail not thou preparest a granary for our transient years. For by an eternal design thou spreadest the heavenly blessings on the earth in their proper seasons.

23. For "to one there is given by thy Spirit the word of wisdom" [86] (which resembles the greater light—which is for those whose delight is in the clear light of truth—as the light which is given for the ruling of the day[87]). But to another the word of knowledge is given by the same Spirit (as it were, the "lesser light"); to another, faith; to another, the gift of healing;

---

[80] Cf. Isa. 58:7. [81] Cf. Phil. 2:15. [82] Cf. Gen. 1:19.
[83] Cf. II Cor. 5:17. [84] Cf. Rom. 13:11, 12. [85] Ps. 65:11.
[86] For this whole passage, cf. the parallel developed here with I Cor. 12:7–11.
[87] *In principio diei*, an obvious echo to the Vulgate *ut praesset diei* of Gen. 1:16. Cf. Gibb and Montgomery, p. 424 (see Bibl.), for a comment on *in principio diei* and *in principio noctis*, below.

to another, the power of working miracles; to another, the gift of prophecy; to another, the discerning of spirits; to another, other kinds of tongues—and all these gifts may be compared to "the stars." For in them all the one and selfsame Spirit is at work, dividing to every man his own portion, as He wills, and making stars to appear in their bright splendor for the profit of souls. But the word of knowledge, *scientia*, in which is contained all the mysteries[88] which change in their seasons like the moon; and all the other promises of gifts, which when counted are like the stars—all of these fall short of that splendor of Wisdom in which the day rejoices and are only for the ruling of the night. Yet they are necessary for those to whom thy most prudent servant could not speak as to the spiritually mature, but only as if to carnal men—even though he could speak wisdom among the perfect.[89] Still the natural man—as a babe in Christ, and a drinker of milk, until he is strong enough for solid meat, and his eye is able to look into the sun—do not leave him in a lightless night. Instead, let him be satisfied with the light of the moon and the stars. In thy book thou dost discuss these things with us wisely, our God—in thy book, which is thy "firmament"—in order that we may be able to view all things in admiring contemplation, although thus far we must do so through signs and seasons and in days and years.

CHAPTER XIX

24. But, first, "wash yourselves and make you clean; put away iniquity from your souls and from before my eyes"[90]—so that "the dry land" may appear. "Learn to do well, judge the fatherless, plead for the widow,"[91] that the earth may bring forth the green herb for food and fruit-bearing trees. "And come, let us reason together, saith the Lord"[92]—that there may be lights in the firmament of heaven and that they may shine upon the earth.

There was that rich man who asked of the good Teacher what he should do to attain eternal life. Let the good Teacher (whom the rich man thought a man and nothing more) give him an answer—he is good for he is God. Let him answer him

---

[88] *Sacramenta;* but cf. Augustine's discussion of *sacramenta* in the Old Testament in the *Exposition of the Psalms*, LXXIV, 2: "The sacraments of the Old Testament promised a Saviour; the sacraments of the New Testament give salvation." [89] Cf. I Cor. 3:1; 2:6.
[90] Isa. 1:16. [91] Isa. 1:17. [92] Isa. 1:18.

that, if he would enter into life, he must keep the commandments: let him put away from himself the bitterness of malice and wickedness; let him not kill, nor commit adultery, nor steal, nor bear false witness[93]—that "the dry land" may appear and bring forth the honoring of fathers and mothers and the love of neighbor. "All these," he replied, "I have kept." Where do so many thorns come from, if the earth is really fruitful? Go, uproot the brier patch of avarice; "sell what you have, and be filled with fruit by giving to the poor, and you shall have treasure in heaven; and follow" the Lord if you would be perfect and joined with those in whose midst he speaketh wisdom— who know how to give rightly to the day and to the night—and you will also understand, so that for you also there may be lights in the firmament of heaven—which will not be there, however, unless your heart is there also. And your heart will not be there unless your treasure is there,[94] as you have heard from the good Teacher. But "the barren earth"[95] was grieved, and the briers choked the word.[96]

25. But you, O elect people, set in the firmament of the world,[97] who have forsaken all that you may follow the Lord: follow him now, and confound the mighty! Follow him, O beautiful feet,[98] and shine in the firmament, that the heavens may declare his glory, dividing the light of the perfect ones[99] —though not yet so perfect as the angels—from the darkness of the little ones—who are nevertheless not utterly despised. Shine over all the earth, and let the day be lighted by the sun, utter the Word of wisdom to the day ("day unto day utters speech"[1]); and let the night, lighted by the moon, display the Word of knowledge to the night. The moon and the stars give light for the night; the night does not put them out, and they illumine it in its proper mode. For lo, it is as if God were saying, "Let there be lights in the firmament of the heaven": and suddenly there came a sound from heaven, as if it were a rushing mighty wind, and there appeared cloven tongues of fire, and they sat on each of them.[2] And then they were made to be lights in the firmament of heaven, having the Word of life. Run to and fro

---

[93] Cf. for this syntaxis, Matt. 19:16–22 and Ex. 20:13–16.
[94] Cf. Matt. 6:21.　　[95] I.e., the rich young ruler.　　[96] Cf. Matt. 13:7.
[97] Reading here, with Knöll and the *Sessorianus, in firmamento mundi*.
[98] Cf. Isa. 52:7.
[99] *Perfectorum*. Is this a conscious use, in a Christian context, of the distinction he had known so well among the Manicheans—between the *perfecti* and the *auditores*?
[1] Ps. 19:2.　　　　　　　　　[2] Cf. Acts 2:2, 3.

everywhere, you holy fires, you lovely fires, for you are the light of the world and you are not to be hid under a peck measure.[3] He to whom you cleave is raised on high, and he hath raised you on high. Run to and fro; make yourselves known among all the nations!

CHAPTER XX

26. Also let the sea conceive and bring forth your works, and let the waters bear the moving creatures that have life.[4] For by separating the precious from the vile you are made the mouth of God[5] by whom he said, "Let the waters bring forth." This does not refer to the living creatures which the earth brings forth, but to the creeping creatures that have life and the fowls that fly over the earth. For, by the ministry of thy holy ones, thy mysteries have made their way amid the buffeting billows of the world, to instruct the nations in thy name, in thy Baptism. And among these things many great and marvelous works have been wrought, which are analogous to the huge whales. The words of thy messengers have gone flying over the earth, high in the firmament of thy Book which is spread over them as the authority beneath which they are to fly wheresoever they go. For "there is no speech nor language where their voice is not heard," because "their sound has gone out through all the earth, and their words to the end of the world"[6]—and this because thou, O Lord, hast multiplied these things by thy blessing.

27. Am I speaking falsely? Am I mingling and confounding and not rightly distinguishing between the knowledge of these things in the firmament of heaven and those corporeal works in the swelling sea and beneath the firmament of heaven? For there are those things, the knowledge of which is solid and defined. It does not increase from generation to generation and thus they stand, as it were, as lights of wisdom and knowledge. But there are many and varied physical processes that manifest these selfsame principles. And thus one thing growing from another is multiplied by thy blessing, O God, who dost so refresh our easily wearied mortal senses that in our mental cognition a single thing may be figured and signified in many different ways by different bodily motions.

"The waters" have brought forth these mysteries, but only at thy word. The needs of the people who were alien to the eternity of thy truth have called them forth, but only in thy

3 Cf. Matt. 5:14, 15.   4 Cf. Gen. 1:20.
5 Cf. Jer. 15:19.   6 Ps. 19:4.

gospel, since it was these "waters" which cast them up—the waters whose stagnant bitterness was the reason why they came forth through thy Word.

28. Now all the things that thou hast made are fair, and yet, lo, thou who didst make all things art inexpressibly fairer. And if Adam had not fallen away from thee, that brackish sea—the human race—so deeply prying, so boisterously swelling, so restlessly moving, would never have flowed forth from his belly. Thus, there would have been no need for thy ministers to use corporeal and tangible signs in the midst of many "waters" in order to show forth their mystical deeds and words. For this is the way I interpret the phrases "creeping creatures" and "flying fowl." Still, men who have been instructed and initiated and made dependent on thy corporeal mysteries would not be able to profit from them if it were not that their soul has a higher life and unless, after the word of its admission, it did not look beyond toward its perfection.

CHAPTER XXI

29. And thus, in thy Word, it was not the depth of the sea but "the earth," [7] separated from the brackishness of the water, that brought forth, not "the creeping and the flying creature that has life," but "the living soul" itself! [8]

And now this soul no longer has need of baptism, as the heathen had, or as it did when it was covered with the waters—and there can be no other entrance into the Kingdom of Heaven, since thou hast appointed that baptism should be the entrance. Nor does it seek great, miraculous works by which to buttress faith. For such a soul does not refuse to believe unless it sees signs and marvels, now that "the faithful earth" is separated from "the waters" of the sea, which have been made bitter by infidelity. Thus, for them, "tongues are for a sign, not to those who believe but to those who do not believe." [9]

And the earth which thou hast founded above the waters does not stand in need of those flying creatures which the waters brought forth at thy word. Send forth thy word into it by the agency of thy messengers. For we only tell of their works, but it is thou who dost the works in them, so that they may bring forth "a living soul" in the earth.

[7] That is, the Church.
[8] An allegorical ideal type of the *perfecti* in the Church.
[9] I Cor. 14:22.

The earth brings forth "the living soul" because "the earth" is the cause of such things being done by thy messengers, just as the sea was the cause of the production of the creeping creatures having life and the flying fowl under the firmament of heaven. "The earth" no longer needs them, although it feeds on the Fish which was taken out of the deep,[10] set out on that table which thou preparest in the presence of those who believe. To this end he was raised from the deep: that he might feed "the dry land." And "the fowl," even though they were bred in the sea, will yet be multiplied on the earth. The preaching of the first evangelists was called forth by reason of man's infidelity, but the faithful also are exhorted and blessed by them in manifold ways, day by day. "The living soul" has its origin from "the earth," because only to the faithful is there any profit in restraining themselves from the love of this world, so that their soul may live to thee. This soul was dead while it was living in pleasures—in pleasures that bear death in them—whereas thou, O Lord, art the living delight of the pure heart.

30. Now, therefore, let thy ministers do their work on "the earth"—not as they did formerly in "the waters" of infidelity, when they had to preach and speak by miracles and mysteries and mystical expressions, in which ignorance—the mother of wonder—gives them an attentive ear because of its fear of occult and strange things. For this is the entry into faith for the sons of Adam who are forgetful of thee, who hide themselves from thy face, and who have become a darkened abyss. Instead, let thy ministers work even as on "the dry land," safe from the whirlpools of the abyss. Let them be an example unto the faithful by living before them and stirring them up to imitation.

For in such a setting, men will heed, not with the mere intent to hear, but also to act. Seek the Lord and your soul shall live[11] and "the earth" may bring forth "the living soul." Be not conformed to this world;[12] separate yourselves from it. The soul lives by avoiding those things which bring death if they are loved. Restrain yourselves from the unbridled wildness of pride, from the indolent passions of luxury, and from what is falsely called knowledge.[13] Thus may the wild beast be tamed, the cattle

---

[10] The fish was an early Christian rebus for "Jesus Christ." The Greek word for fish, ἰχθύς, was arranged acrostically to make the phrase Ἰησοῦς Χριστός, Θεοῦ Υἱός, Σωτήρ; cf. Smith and Cheetham, *Dictionary of Christian Antiquities*, pp. 673 f.; see also Cabrol, *Dictionnaire d'archéologie chrétienne*, Vol. 14, cols. 1246–1252, for a full account of the symbolism and pictures of early examples.

[11] Cf. Ps. 69:32.   [12] Cf. Rom. 12:2.   [13] Cf. I Tim. 6:20.

subdued, and the serpent made harmless. For, in allegory, these figures are the motions of our mind: that is to say, the haughtiness of pride, the delight of lust, and the poison of curiosity are motions of the dead soul—not so dead that it has lost all motion, but dead because it has deserted the fountain of life, and so has been taken up by this transitory world and conformed to it.

31. But thy Word, O God, is a fountain of life eternal, and it does not pass away. Therefore, this desertion is restrained by thy Word when it says to us, "Be not conformed to this world," to the end that "the earth" may bring forth a "living soul" in the fountain of life—a soul disciplined by thy Word, by thy evangelists, by the following of the followers of thy Christ. For this is the meaning of "after his kind." A man tends to follow the example of his friend. Thus, he [Paul] says, "Become as I am, because I have become as you are."[14]

Thus, in this "living soul" there shall be good beasts, acting meekly. For thou hast commanded this, saying: "Do your work in meekness and you shall be loved by all men."[15] And the cattle will be good, for if they eat much they shall not suffer from satiety; and if they do not eat at all they will suffer no lack. And the serpents will be good, not poisonous to do harm, but only cunning in their watchfulness—exploring only as much of this temporal nature as is necessary in order that the eternal nature may "be clearly seen, understood through the things that have been made."[16] For all these animals will obey reason when, having been restrained from their death-dealing ways, they live and become good.

CHAPTER XXII

32. Thus, O Lord, our God, our Creator, when our affections have been turned from the love of the world, in which we died by living ill; and when we began to be "a living soul" by living well; and when the word, "Be not conformed to this world," which thou didst speak through thy apostle, has been fulfilled in us, then will follow what thou didst immediately add when thou saidst, "But be transformed by the renewing of your mind."[17] This will not now be "after their kind," as if we were following the neighbor who went before us, or as if we were living after the example of a better man—for thou didst not say, "Let man be made after his kind," but rather, "Let us

14 Gal. 4:12.　　　　　　　　15 Cf. Ecclus. 3:19.
16 Rom. 1:20.　　　　　　　　17 Rom. 12:2.

make man in our own image and our own likeness,"[18] so that then we may be able to prove what thy will is.

This is why thy minister—begetting children by the gospel so that he might not always have them babes whom he would have to feed with milk and nurse as children—this is why he said, "Be transformed by the renewing of your minds, that you may prove what is the good and acceptable and perfect will of God."[19] Therefore thou didst not say, "Let man be made," but rather, "Let us make man." And thou didst not say, "After his kind," but after "our image" and "likeness." Indeed, it is only when man has been renewed in his mind, and comes to behold and apprehend thy truth, that he does not need another man as his director, to show him how to imitate human examples. Instead, by thy guidance, he proves what is thy good and acceptable and perfect will. And thou dost teach him, now that he is able to understand, to see the trinity of the Unity and the unity of the Trinity.

This is why the statement in the plural, "Let us make man," is also connected with the statement in the singular, "And God made man." Thus it is said in the plural, "After our likeness," and then in the singular, "After the image of God." Man is thus transformed in the knowledge of God, according to the image of Him who created him. And now, having been made spiritual, he judges all things—that is, all things that are appropriate to be judged—and he himself is judged of no man.[20]

CHAPTER XXIII

33. Now this phrase, "he judges all things," means that man has dominion over the fish of the sea, and over the fowl of the air, and over all cattle and wild beasts, and over all the earth, and over every creeping thing that creeps on the earth. And he does this by the power of reason in his mind by which he perceives "the things of the Spirit of God."[21] But, when man was put in this high office, he did not understand what was involved and thus was reduced to the level of the brute beasts, and made like them.[22]

Therefore in thy Church, O our God, by the grace thou hast given us—since we are thy workmanship, created in good works (not only those who are in spiritual authority but also those who are spiritually subject to them)—thou madest man male and

---

[18] Gen. 1:26. [19] Rom. 12:2 (mixed text).
[20] Cf. I Cor. 2:15. [21] I Cor. 2:14. [22] Cf. Ps. 49:20.

female. Here all are equal in thy spiritual grace where, as far as sex is concerned, there is neither male nor female, just as there is neither Jew nor Greek, nor bond nor free. Spiritual men, therefore, whether those who are in authority or those who are subject to authority, judge spiritually. They do not judge by the light of that spiritual knowledge which shines in the firmament, for it is inappropriate for them to judge by so sublime an authority. Nor does it behoove them to judge concerning thy Book itself, although there are some things in it which are not clear. Instead, we submit our understanding to it and believe with certainty that what is hidden from our sight is still rightly and truly spoken. In this way, even though a man is now spiritual and renewed by the knowledge of God according to the image of him who created him, he must be a doer of the law rather than its judge.[23] Neither does the spiritual man judge concerning that division between spiritual and carnal men which is known to thy eyes, O God, and which may not, as yet, be made manifest to us by their external works, so that we may know them by their fruits; yet thou, O God, knowest them already and thou hast divided and called them secretly, before the firmament was made. Nor does a man, even though he is spiritual, judge the disordered state of society in this world. For what business of his is it to judge those who are without, since he cannot know which of them may later on come into the sweetness of thy grace, and which of them may continue in the perpetual bitterness of their impiety?

34. Man, then, even if he was made after thy own image, did not receive the power of dominion over the lights of heaven, nor over the secret heaven, nor over the day and the night which thou calledst forth before the creation of the heaven, nor over the gathering together of the waters which is the sea. Instead, he received dominion over the fish of the sea, and the fowls of the air; and over all cattle, and all the earth; and over all creeping things which creep on the earth.

Indeed, he judges and approves what he finds right and disapproves what he finds amiss, whether in the celebration of those mysteries by which are initiated those whom thy mercy hast sought out in the midst of many waters; or in that sacrament in which is exhibited the Fish itself[24] which, being raised from the depths, the pious "earth"[25] feeds upon; or, in the signs and symbols of words, which are subject to the authority of thy Book—such signs as burst forth and sound from the

[23] Cf. James 4:11.   [24] See above, p. 317.   [25] I.e., the Church.

mouth, as if it were "flying" under the firmament, interpreting, expounding, discoursing, disputing, blessing, invoking thee, so that the people may answer, "Amen." [26] The reason that all these words have to be pronounced vocally is because of the abyss of this world and the blindness of our flesh in which thoughts cannot be seen directly,[27] but have to be spoken aloud in our ears. Thus, although the flying fowl are multiplied on the earth, they still take their origins from the waters.

The spiritual man also judges by approving what is right and reproving what he finds amiss in the works and morals of the faithful, such as in their almsgiving, which is signified by the phrase, "The earth bringing forth its fruit." And he judges of the "living soul," which is then made to live by the disciplining of her affections in chastity, in fasting, and in holy meditation. And he also judges concerning all those things which are perceived by the bodily senses. For it can be said that he should judge in all matters about which he also has the power of correction.

CHAPTER XXIV

35. But what is this; what kind of mystery is this? Behold, O Lord, thou dost bless men in order that they may be "fruitful and multiply, and replenish the earth." In this art thou not making a sign to us that we may understand something [allegorically]? Why didst thou not also bless the light, which thou calledst "the day," nor the firmament of heaven, nor the lights, nor the stars, nor the earth, nor the sea? I might reply, O our God, that thou in creating us after thy own image—I might reply that thou didst will to bestow this gift of blessing upon man alone, if thou hadst not similarly blessed the fishes and the whales, so that they too should be fruitful and multiply and replenish the waters of the sea; and also the fowls, so that they should be multiplied on the earth. In like fashion, I might say that this blessing properly belonged only to such creatures as are propagated from their own kind, if I could find it given also as a blessing to trees, and plants, and the beasts of the earth. But this "increase and multiply" was not said to plants or trees or beasts or serpents—although all of these, along with fishes and birds and men, do actually increase by propagation and so preserve their species.

36. What, then, shall I say, O Truth, O my Life: that it was

26 Cf. I Cor. 14:16.
27 Another reminder that, ideally, knowledge is immediate and direct.

idly and vainly said? Surely not this, O Father of piety; far be it from a servant of thy Word to say anything like this! But if I do not understand what thou meanest by that phrase, let those who are better than I—that is, those more intelligent than I—interpret it better, in the degree that thou hast given each of us the ability to understand.

But let also my confession be pleasing in thy eyes, for I confess to thee that I believe, O Lord, that thou hast not spoken thus in vain. Nor will I be silent as to what my reading has suggested to me. For it is valid, and I do not see anything to prevent me from thus interpreting the figurative sayings in thy books. For I know that a thing that is understood in only one way in the mind may be expressed in many different ways by the body; and I know that a thing that has only one manner of expression through the body may be understood in the mind in many different ways. For consider this single example—the love of God and of our neighbor—by how many different mysteries and countless languages, and, in each language, by how many different ways of speaking, this is signified corporeally! In similar fashion, the "young fish" in "the waters" increase and multiply. On the other hand, whoever you are who reads this, observe and behold what Scripture declares, and how the voice pronounces it *in only one way*, "In the beginning God created heaven and earth." [28] Is this not understood in many different ways by different kinds of true interpretations which do not involve the deceit of error? Thus the offspring of men are fruitful and do multiply. [29]

37. If, then, we consider the nature of things, in their strictly literal sense, and not allegorically, the phrase, "Be fruitful and multiply," applies to all things that are begotten by seed. But if we treat these words figuratively, as I judge that the Scripture intended them to be—since it cannot be for nothing that this blessing is attributed only to the offspring of marine life and man—then we discover that the characteristic of fecundity belongs also to the spiritual and physical creations (which are signified by "heaven and earth"), and also in righteous and unrighteous souls (which are signified by "light and darkness")

[28] Here, again, as in a coda, Augustine restates his central theme and motif in the whole of his "confessions": the primacy of God, His constant creativity, his mysterious, unwearied, unfrustrated redemptive love. All are summed up in this mystery of creation in which the purposes of God are announced and from which all Christian hope takes its premise.

[29] That is, from basic and essentially simple ideas, they proliferate the multiple—and valid—implications and corollaries.

and in the sacred writers through whom the law is uttered (who are signified by "the firmament established between the waters and the waters"); and in the earthly commonwealth still steeped in their bitterness (which is signified by "the sea"); and in the zeal of holy souls (signified by "the dry land"); and the works of mercy done in this present life (signified by "the seed-bearing herbs and fruit-bearing trees"); and in spiritual gifts which shine out for our edification (signified by "the lights of heaven"); and to human affections ruled by temperance (signified by "the living soul"). In all these instances we meet with multiplicity and fertility and increase; but the particular way in which "Be fruitful and multiply" can be exemplified differs widely. Thus a single category may include many things, and we cannot discover them except through their signs displayed corporeally and by the things being excogitated by the mind.

We thus interpret the phrase, "The generation of the waters," as referring to the corporeally expressed signs [of fecundity], since they are made necessary by the degree of our involvement in the flesh. But the power of human generation refers to the process of mental conception; this we see in the fruitfulness of reason. Therefore, we believe that to both of these two kinds it has been said by thee, O Lord, "Be fruitful and multiply." In this blessing, I recognize that thou hast granted us the faculty and power not only to express what we understand by a single idea in many different ways but also to understand in many ways what we find expressed obscurely in a single statement. Thus the waters of the sea are replenished, and their waves are symbols of diverse meanings. And thus also the earth is also replenished with human offspring. Its dryness is the symbol of its thirst for truth, and of the fact that reason rules over it.

CHAPTER XXV

38. I also desire to say, O my Lord God, what the following Scripture suggests to me. Indeed, I will speak without fear, for I will speak the truth, as thou inspirest me to know what thou dost will that I should say concerning these words. For I do not believe I can speak the truth by any other inspiration than thine, since thou art the Truth, and every man a liar.[30] Hence, he that speaks a lie, speaks out of himself. Therefore, if I am to speak the truth, I must speak of thy truth.

[30] Cf. Rom. 3:4.

Behold, thou hast given us for our food every seed-bearing herb on the face of the earth, and all trees that bear in themselves seed of their own kind; and not to us only, but to all the fowls of the air and the beasts of the field and all creeping things.[31] Still, thou hast not given these things to the fishes and great whales. We have said that by these fruits of the earth the works of mercy were signified and figured forth in an allegory: thus, from the fruitful earth, things are provided for the necessities of life. Such an "earth" was the godly Onesiphorus, to whose house thou gavest mercy because he often refreshed Paul and was not ashamed of his bonds.[32] This was also the way of the brethren from Macedonia, who bore such fruit and supplied to him what he lacked. But notice how he grieves for certain "trees," which did not give him the fruit that was due, when he said, "At my first answer no man stood with me, but all men forsook me: I pray God, that it be not laid up to their charge."[33] For we owe "fruits" to those who minister spiritual doctrine to us through their understanding of the divine mysteries. We owe these to them as men. We owe these fruits, also, to "the living souls" since they offer themselves as examples for us in their own continence. And, finally, we owe them likewise to "the flying creatures" because of their blessings which are multiplied on the earth, for "their sound has gone forth into all the earth."[34]

CHAPTER XXVI

39. Those who find their joy in it are fed by these "fruits"; but those whose god is their belly find no joy in them. For in those who offer these fruits, it is not the fruit itself that matters, but the spirit in which they give them. Therefore, he who serves God and not his own belly may rejoice in them, and I plainly see why. I see it, and I rejoice with him greatly. For he [Paul] had received from the Philippians the things they had sent by Epaphroditus; yet I see why he rejoiced. He was fed by what he found his joy in; for, speaking truly, he says, "I rejoice in the Lord greatly, that now at the last your care of me has flourished again, in which you were once so careful, but it had become a weariness to you.[35] These Philippians, in their extended period of weariness in well-doing, had become weak and were, so to say, dried up; they were no longer bringing forth the fruits of good works. And now Paul rejoices in them—and

[31] Cf. Gen. 1:29, 30.   [32] Cf. II Tim. 1:16.
[33] II Tim. 4:16.   [34] Cf. Ps. 19:4.   [35] Phil. 4:10 (mixed text).

not just for himself alone—because they were flourishing again in ministering to his needs. Therefore he adds: "I do not speak in respect of my want, for I have learned in whatsoever state I am therewith to be content. I know both how to be abased and how to abound; everywhere and in all things I am instructed both to be full and to be hungry, both to abound and to suffer need. I can do all things through Christ who strengtheneth me." [36]

40. Where do you find joy in all things, O great Paul? What is the cause of your joy? On what do you feed, O man, renewed now in the knowledge of God after the image of him who created you, O living soul of such great continence—O tongue like a winged bird, speaking mysteries? What food is owed such creatures; what is it that feeds you? It is joy! For hear what follows: "Nevertheless, you have done well in that you have shared with me in my affliction." [37] This is what he finds his joy in; this is what he feeds on. They have done well, not merely because his need had been relieved—for he says to them, "You have opened my heart when I was in distress"—but because he knew both how to abound and how to suffer need, in thee who didst strengthen him. And so he said, "You [Philippians] know also that in the beginning of the gospel, when I departed from Macedonia, no church shared with me in regard to giving and receiving, except you only. For even in Thessalonica you sent time and time again, according to my need." [38] He now finds his joy in the fact that they have returned once again to these good works, and he is made glad that they are flourishing again, as a fruitful field when it recovers its fertility.

41. Was it on account of his own needs alone that he said, "You have sent me gifts according to my needs?" Does he find joy in that? Certainly not for that alone. But how do we know this? We know it because he himself adds, "Not because I desire a gift, but because I desire fruit." [39]

Now I have learned from thee, O my God, how to distinguish between the terms "gift" and "fruit." A "gift" is the thing itself, given by one who bestows life's necessities on another—such as money, food, drink, clothing, shelter, and aid. But "the fruit" is the good and right will of the giver. For the good Teacher not only said, "He that receives a prophet," but he added, "In the name of a prophet." And he did not say only, "He who receives a righteous man," but added, "In the name of a righteous

---

[36] Phil. 4: 11–13.
[37] Phil. 4:14.
[38] Phil. 4:15–17.
[39] Phil. 4:17.

man." [40] Thus, surely, the former shall receive the reward of a prophet; the latter, that of a righteous man. Nor did he say only, "Whoever shall give a cup of cold water to one of these little ones to drink," but added, "In the name of a disciple"; and concluded, "Truly I tell you he shall not lose his reward." The "gift" involves receiving a prophet, receiving a righteous man, handing a cup of cold water to a disciple: but the "fruit" is to do all this in the name of a prophet, in the name of a righteous man, in the name of a disciple. Elijah was fed by the widow with "fruit," for she knew that she was feeding a man of God and this is why she fed him. But he was fed by the raven with a "gift." The inner man of Elijah was not fed by this "gift," but only the outer man, which otherwise might have perished from the lack of such food.

CHAPTER XXVII

42. Therefore I will speak before thee, O Lord, what is true, in order that the uninstructed [41] and the infidels, who require the mysteries of initiation and great works of miracles—which we believe are signified by the phrase, "Fishes and great whales"—may be helped in being gained [for the Church] when they endeavor to provide that thy servants are refreshed in body, or otherwise aided in this present life. For they do not really know why this should be done, and to what end. Thus the former do not feed the latter, and the latter do not feed the former; for neither do the former offer their "gifts" through a holy and right intent, nor do the others rejoice in the gifts of those who do not as yet see the "fruit." For it is on the "fruit" that the mind is fed, and by which it is gladdened. And, therefore, fishes and whales are not fed on such food as the earth alone brings forth when they have been separated and divided from the bitterness of "the waters" of the sea.

CHAPTER XXVIII

43. And thou, O God, didst see everything that thou hadst made and, behold, it was very good. [42] We also see the whole

[40] Cf. Matt. 10:41, 42.
[41] *Idiotae*: there is some evidence that this term was used to designate pagans who had a nominal connection with the Christian community but had not formally enrolled as catechumens. See Th. Zahn in *Neue kirkliche Zeitschrift* (1899), pp. 42–43.
[42] Gen. 1:31.

creation and, behold, it is all very good. In each separate kind
of thy work, when thou didst say, "Let them be made," and
they were made, thou didst see that it was good. I have counted
seven times where it is written that thou didst see what thou
hadst made was "good." And there is the eighth time when thou
didst see *all* things that thou hadst made and, behold, they were
not only good but also *very* good; for they were now seen as
a totality. Individually they were only good; but taken as a
totality they were both good and very good. Beautiful bodies
express this truth; for a body which consists of several parts,
each of which is beautiful, is itself far more beautiful than any
of its individual parts separately, by whose well-ordered union
the whole is completed even though these parts are separately
beautiful.

CHAPTER XXIX

44. And I looked attentively to find whether it was seven or
eight times that thou didst see thy works were good, when they
were pleasing to thee, but I found that there was no "time" in
thy seeing which would help me to understand in what sense
thou hadst looked so many "times" at what thou hadst made.
And I said: "O Lord, is not this thy Scripture true, since thou
art true, and thy truth doth set it forth? Why, then, dost thou
say to me that in thy seeing there are no times, while this
Scripture tells me that what thou madest each day thou didst see
to be good; and when I counted them I found how many
'times'?" To these things, thou didst reply to me, for thou art
my God, and thou dost speak to thy servant with a strong voice
in his inner ear, my deafness, and crying: "O man, what my
Scripture says, I say. But it speaks in terms of time, whereas
time does not affect my Word—my Word which exists co-
eternally with myself. Thus the things you see through my
Spirit, I see; just as what you say through my Spirit, I say. But
while you see those things in time, I do not see them in time;
and when you speak those things in time, I do not speak them in
time."

CHAPTER XXX

45. And I heard this, O Lord my God, and drank up a drop
of sweetness from thy truth, and understood that there are some
men to whom thy works are displeasing, who say that many of
them thou didst make under the compulsion of necessity—such
as the pattern of the heavens and the courses of the stars—and

that thou didst not make them out of what was thine, but that they were already created elsewhere and from other sources. It was thus [they say] that thou didst collect and fashion and weave them together, as if from thy conquered enemies thou didst raise up the walls of the universe; so that, built into the ramparts of the building, they might not be able a second time to rebel against thee. And, even of other things, they say that thou didst neither make them nor arrange them—for example, all flesh and all the very small living creatures, and all things fastened to the earth by their roots. But [they say] a hostile mind and an alien nature—not created by thee and in every way contrary to thee—begot and framed all these things in the nether parts of the world.[43] They who speak thus are mad [*insani*], since they do not see thy works through thy Spirit, nor recognize thee in them.

CHAPTER XXXI

46. But for those who see these things through thy Spirit, it is thou who seest them in them. When, therefore, they see that these things are good, it is thou who seest that they are good; and whatsoever things are pleasing because of thee, it is thou who dost give us pleasure in those things. Those things which please us through thy Spirit are pleasing to thee in us. "For what man knows the things of a man except the spirit of a man which is in him? Even so, no man knows the things of God, but the Spirit of God. Now we have not received the spirit of the world, but the Spirit of God, that we might know the things that are freely given to us from God."[44] And I am admonished to say: "Yes, truly. No man knows the things of God, but the Spirit of God: but how, then, do we also know what things are given us by God?" The answer is given me: "Because we know these things by his Spirit; for no one knows but the Spirit of God." But just as it is truly said to those who were to speak through the Spirit of God, "It is not you who speak," so it is also truly said to them who know through the Spirit of God, "It is not you yourselves who know," and just as rightly it may be said to those who perceive through the Spirit of God that a thing is good; it is not they who see, but God who seeth that it is good.

It is, therefore, one thing to think like the men who judge

---

[43] A reference to the Manichean cosmogony and similar dualistic doctrines of "creation."　　　　[44] I Cor. 2:11, 12.

something to be bad when it is good, as do those whom we have already mentioned. It is quite another thing that a man should see as good what is good—as is the case with many whom thy creation pleases because it is good, yet what pleases them in it is not thee, and so they would prefer to find their joy in thy creatures rather than to find their joy in thee. It is still another thing that when a man sees a thing to be good, God should see in him that it is good—that truly he may be loved in what he hath made, he who cannot be loved except through the Holy Spirit which he hath given us: "Because the love of God is shed abroad in our hearts by the Holy Spirit who is given to us." [45] It is by him that we see whatever we see to be good in any degree, since it is from him, who doth not exist in any particular degree but who simply is what he is. [46]

CHAPTER XXXII

47. Thanks be to thee, O Lord! We see the heaven and the earth, either the corporeal part—higher and lower—or the spiritual and physical creation. And we see the light made and divided from the darkness for the adornment of these parts, from which the universal mass of the world or the universal creation is constituted. We see the firmament of heaven, either the original "body" of the world between the spiritual (higher) waters and the corporeal (lower) waters [47] or the expanse of air —which is also called "heaven"—through which the fowls of heaven wander, between the waters which move in clouds above them and which drop down in dew on clear nights, and those waters which are heavy and flow along the earth. We see the waters gathered together in the vast plains of the sea; and the dry land, first bare and then formed, so as to be visible and well-ordered; and the soil of herbs and trees. We see the light shining from above—the sun to serve the day, the moon and the stars to give cheer in the night; and we see by all these that the intervals of time are marked and noted. We see on every side the watery elements, fruitful with fishes, beasts, and birds—and we notice that the density of the atmosphere which supports the

[45] Rom. 5:5.

[46] *Sed quod est, est.* Note the variant text in Skutella, *op. cit.: sed est, est.* This is obviously an echo of the Vulgate Ex. 3:14: *ego sum qui sum.*

[47] Augustine himself had misgivings about this passage. In the *Retractations*, he says that this statement was made "without due consideration." But he then adds, with great justice: "However, the point in question is very obscure" (*res autem in abdito est valde*); cf. *Retract.*, 2:6.

flights of birds is increased by the evaporation of the waters. We see the face of the earth, replete with earthly creatures; and man, created in thy image and likeness, in the very image and likeness of thee—that is, having the power of reason and understanding—by virtue of which he has been set over all irrational creatures. And just as there is in his soul one element which controls by its power of reflection and another which has been made subject so that it should obey, so also, physically, the woman was made for the man; for, although she had a like nature of rational intelligence in the mind, still in the sex of her body she should be similarly subject to the sex of her husband, as the appetite of action is subjected to the deliberation of the mind in order to conceive the rules of right action. These things we see, and each of them is good; and the whole is very good!

CHAPTER XXXIII

48. Let thy works praise thee, that we may love thee; and let us love thee that thy works may praise thee—those works which have a beginning and an end in time—a rising and a setting, a growth and a decay, a form and a privation. Thus, they have their successions of morning and evening, partly hidden, partly plain. For they were made from nothing by thee, and not from thyself, and not from any matter that is not thine, or that was created beforehand. They were created from concreated matter—that is, matter that was created by thee at the same time that thou didst form its formlessness, without any interval of time. Yet, since the matter of heaven and earth is one thing and the form of heaven and earth is another thing, thou didst create matter out of absolutely nothing (*de omnino nihilo*), but the form of the world thou didst form from formless matter (*de informi materia*). But both were done at the same time, so that form followed matter with no delaying interval.

CHAPTER XXXIV

49. We have also explored the question of what thou didst desire to figure forth, both in the creation and in the description of things in this particular order. And we have seen that things taken separately are good, and all things taken together are very good, both in heaven and earth. And we have seen that this was wrought through thy Word, thy only Son, the head and the body of the Church, and it signifies thy predestination before

all times, without morning and evening. But when, in time, thou didst begin to unfold the things destined before time, so that thou mightest make hidden things manifest and mightest reorder our disorders—since our sins were over us and we had sunk into profound darkness away from thee, and thy good Spirit was moving over us to help us in due season—thou didst justify the ungodly and also didst divide them from the wicked; and thou madest the authority of thy Book a firmament between those above who would be amenable to thee and those beneath who would be subject to them. And thou didst gather the society of unbelievers [48] into a conspiracy, in order that the zeal of the faithful might become manifest and that they might bring forth works of mercy unto thee, giving their earthly riches to the poor to obtain heavenly riches. Then thou didst kindle the lights in the firmament, which are thy holy ones, who have the Word of Life and who shine with an exalted authority, warranted to them by their spiritual gifts. And then, for the instruction of the unbelieving nations, thou didst out of physical matter produce the mysteries and the visible miracles and the sounds of words in harmony with the firmament of thy Book, through which the faithful should be blessed. After this thou didst form "the living soul" of the faithful, through the ordering of their passions by the strength of continence. And then thou didst renew, after thy image and likeness, the mind which is faithful to thee alone, which needs to imitate no human authority. Thus, thou didst subordinate rational action to the higher excellence of intelligence, as the woman is subordinate to the man. Finally, in all thy ministries which were needed to perfect the faithful in this life, thou didst will that these same faithful ones should themselves bring forth good things, profitable for their temporal use and fruitful for the life to come. We see all these things, and they are very good, because thou seest them thus in us—thou who hast given us thy Spirit, by which we may see them so and love thee in them.

CHAPTER XXXV

50. O Lord God, grant us thy peace—for thou hast given us all things. Grant us the peace of quietness, the peace of the Sabbath, the peace without an evening. All this most beautiful array of things, all so very good, will pass away when all their courses are finished—for in them there is both morning and evening.

[48] See above, *amaricantes*, Ch. XVII, 20.

CHAPTER XXXVI

51. But the seventh day is without an evening, and it has no setting, for thou hast sanctified it with an everlasting duration. After all thy works of creation, which were very good, thou didst rest on the seventh day, although thou hadst created them all in unbroken rest—and this so that the voice of thy Book might speak to us with the prior assurance that after our works —and they also are very good because thou hast given them to us—we may find our rest in thee in the Sabbath of life eternal. [49]

CHAPTER XXXVII

52. For then also thou shalt so rest in us as now thou workest in us; and, thus, that will be thy rest through us, as these are thy works through us. But thou, O Lord, workest evermore and art always at rest. Thou seest not in time, thou movest not in time, thou restest not in time. And yet thou makest all those things which are seen in time—indeed, the very times themselves— and everything that proceeds in and from time.

CHAPTER XXXVIII

53. We can see all those things which thou hast made because they are—but they are because thou seest them. [50] And we see with our eyes that they are, and we see with our minds that they are good. But thou sawest them as made when thou sawest that they would be made.

And now, in this present time, we have been moved to do well, now that our heart has been quickened by thy Spirit; but in the former time, having forsaken thee, we were moved to do evil. [51] But thou, O the one good God, hast never ceased to do good! And we have accomplished certain good works by thy good gifts, and even though they are not eternal, still we hope, after these things here, to find our rest in thy great sanctification. But thou art the Good, and needest no rest, and art always at rest, because thou thyself art thy own rest.

[49] Cf. this *requiescamus in te* with the *requiescat in te* in Bk. I, Ch. I.
[50] Cf. *The City of God*, XI, 10, on Augustine's notion that the world exists as a thought in the mind of God.
[51] Another conscious connection between Bk. XIII and Bks. I–X.

What man will teach men to understand this? And what angel will teach the angels? Or what angels will teach men? We must ask it of thee; we must seek it in thee; we must knock for it at thy door. Only thus shall we receive; only thus shall we find; only thus shall thy door be opened.[52]

[52] This final ending is an antiphon to Bk. XII, Ch. I, 1 above.

ENCHIRIDION

Enchiridion

On Faith, Hope, and Love

CHAPTER I

THE OCCASION AND PURPOSE OF THIS "MANUAL"

1. I cannot say, my dearest son Laurence, how much your learning pleases me, and how much I desire that you should be wise—though not one of those of whom it is said: "Where is the wise? Where is the scribe? Where is the disputant of this world? Hath not God made foolish the wisdom of this world?" [1] Rather, you should be one of those of whom it is written, "The multitude of the wise is the health of the world" [2]; and also you should be the kind of man the apostle wishes those men to be to whom he said,[3] "I would have you be wise in goodness and simple in evil." [4]

2. Human wisdom consists in piety. This you have in the book of the saintly Job, for there he writes that Wisdom herself said to man, "Behold, piety is wisdom." [5] If, then, you ask what kind of piety she was speaking of, you will find it more distinctly designated by the Greek term θεοσέβεια, literally, "the service of God." The Greek has still another word for "piety," εὐσέβεια, which also signifies "proper service." This too refers chiefly to the service of God. But no term is better than θεοσέβεια, which clearly expresses the idea of the man's service of God as the source of human wisdom.

When you ask me to be brief, you do not expect me to speak of great issues in a few sentences, do you? Is not this rather what you desire: a brief summary or a short treatise on the proper mode of worshiping [serving] God?

---

[1] I Cor. 1:20.   [2] Wis. 6:26 (Vulgate).   [3] Rom. 16:19.
[4] A later interpolation, not found in the best MSS., adds, "As no one can exist from himself, so also no one can be wise in himself save only as he is enlightened by Him of whom it is written, 'All wisdom is from God' [Ecclus. 1:1]."   [5] Job 28:28.

3. If I should answer, "God should be worshiped in faith, hope, love," you would doubtless reply that this was shorter than you wished, and might then beg for a brief explication of what each of these three means: What should be believed, what should be hoped for, and what should be loved? If I should answer these questions, you would then have everything you asked for in your letter. If you have kept a copy of it, you can easily refer to it. If not, recall your questions as I discuss them.

4. It is your desire, as you wrote, to have from me a book, a sort of *enchiridion*,[6] as it might be called—something to have "at hand"—that deals with your questions. What is to be sought after above all else? What, in view of the divers heresies, is to be avoided above all else? How far does reason support religion; or what happens to reason when the issues involved concern faith alone; what is the beginning and end of our endeavor? What is the most comprehensive of all explanations? What is the certain and distinctive foundation of the catholic faith? You would have the answers to all these questions if you really understood what a man should believe, what he should hope for, and what he ought to love. For these are the chief things—indeed, the only things—to seek for in religion. He who turns away from them is either a complete stranger to the name of Christ or else he is a heretic. Things that arise in sensory experience, or that are analyzed by the intellect, may be demonstrated by the reason. But in matters that pass beyond the scope of the physical senses, which we have not settled by our own understanding, and cannot—here we must believe, without hesitation, the witness of those men by whom the Scriptures (rightly called divine) were composed, men who were divinely aided in their senses and their minds to see and even to foresee the things about which they testify.

5. But, as this faith, which works by love,[7] begins to penetrate the soul, it tends, through the vital power of goodness, to change into sight, so that the holy and perfect in heart catch glimpses of that ineffable beauty whose full vision is our highest happiness. Here, then, surely, is the answer to your question about the beginning and the end of our endeavor. We begin in faith, we are perfected in sight.[8] This likewise is the most comprehensive of all explanations. As for the certain and distinctive foundation of the catholic faith, it is Christ. "For other foundation," said the apostle, "can no man lay save that which has been laid,

---

[6] A transliteration of the Greek ἐγχειρίδιον, literally, a handbook or manual.   [7] Cf. Gal. 5:6.   [8] Cf. I Cor. 13:10, 11.

which is Christ Jesus." [9] Nor should it be denied that this is the distinctive basis of the catholic faith, just because it appears that it is common to us and to certain heretics as well. For if we think carefully about the meaning of Christ, we shall see that among some of the heretics who wish to be called Christians, the *name* of Christ is held in honor, but the reality itself is not among them. To make all this plain would take too long—because we would then have to review all the heresies that have been, the ones that now exist, and those which could exist under the label "Christian," and we would have to show that what we have said of all is true of each of them. Such a discussion would take so many volumes as to make it seem endless. [10]

6. You have asked for an *enchiridion*, something you could carry around, not just baggage for your bookshelf. Therefore we may return to these three ways in which, as we said, God should be served: faith, hope, love. It is easy to *say* what one ought to believe, what to hope for, and what to love. But to defend our doctrines against the calumnies of those who think differently is a more difficult and detailed task. If one is to have this wisdom, it is not enough just to put an *enchiridion* in the hand. It is also necessary that a great zeal be kindled in the heart.

CHAPTER II

The Creed and the Lord's Prayer as Guides to the Interpretation of the Theological Virtues of Faith, Hope, and Love

7. Let us begin, for example, with the Symbol [11] and the Lord's Prayer. What is shorter to hear or to read? What is more easily memorized? Since through sin the human race stood grievously burdened by great misery and in deep need of mercy, a prophet, preaching of the time of God's grace, said, "And it shall be that all who invoke the Lord's name will be saved." [12] Thus, we have the Lord's Prayer. Later, the apostle, when he wished to commend this same grace, remembered this prophetic testimony and promptly added, "But how shall they invoke him in whom they have not believed?" [13] Thus, we have the

[9] I Cor. 3:11.
[10] Already, very early in his ministry (397), Augustine had written *De agone Christiano*, in which he had reviewed and refuted a full score of heresies threatening the orthodox faith.
[11] The Apostles' Creed. Cf. Augustine's early essay *On Faith and the Creed*.
[12] Joel 2:32.   [13] Rom. 10:14.

Symbol. In these two we have the three theological virtues working together: faith believes; hope and love pray. Yet without faith nothing else is possible; thus faith prays too. This, then, is the meaning of the saying, "How shall they invoke him in whom they have not believed?"

8. Now, is it possible to hope for what we do not believe in? We can, of course, believe in something that we do not hope for. Who among the faithful does not believe in the punishment of the impious? Yet he does not hope for it, and whoever believes that such a punishment is threatening him and draws back in horror from it is more rightly said to fear than to hope. A poet, distinguishing between these two feelings, said,

"Let those who dread be allowed to hope," [14]

but another poet, and a better one, did not put it rightly:

"Here, if I could have hoped for [i.e., foreseen]
    such a grievous blow . . ." [15]

Indeed, some grammarians use this as an example of inaccurate language and comment, "He said 'to hope' when he should have said 'to fear.' "

Therefore faith may refer to evil things as well as to good, since we believe in both the good and evil. Yet faith is good, not evil. Moreover, faith refers to things past and present and future. For we believe that Christ died; this is a past event. We believe that he sitteth at the Father's right hand; this is present. We believe that he will come as our judge; this is future. Again, faith has to do with our own affairs and with those of others. For everyone believes, both about himself and other persons— and about things as well—that at some time he began to exist and that he has not existed forever. Thus, not only about men, but even about angels, we believe many things that have a bearing on religion.

But hope deals only with good things, and only with those which lie in the future, and which pertain to the man who cherishes the hope. Since this is so, faith must be distinguished from hope: they are different terms and likewise different concepts. Yet faith and hope have this in common: they refer to

[14] Lucan, *Pharsalia*, II, 15.
[15] Virgil, *Aeneid*, IV, 419. The context of this quotation is Dido's lament over Aeneas' prospective abandonment of her. She is saying that if she could have foreseen such a disaster, she would have been able to bear it. Augustine's criticism here is a literalistic quibble.

what is not seen, whether this unseen is believed in or hoped for. Thus in the Epistle to the Hebrews, which is used by the enlightened defenders of the catholic rule of faith, faith is said to be "the conviction of things not seen."[16] However, when a man maintains that neither words nor witnesses nor even arguments, but only the evidence of present experience, determine his faith, he still ought not be be called absurd or told, "You have seen; therefore you have not believed." For it does not follow that unless a thing is not seen it cannot be believed. Still it is better for us to use the term "faith," as we are taught in "the sacred eloquence,"[17] to refer to things not seen. And as for hope, the apostle says: "Hope that is seen is not hope. For if a man sees a thing, why does he hope for it? If, however, we hope for what we do not see, we then wait for it in patience."[18] When, therefore, our good is believed to be future, this is the same thing as hoping for it.

What, then, shall I say of love, without which faith can do nothing? There can be no true hope without love. Indeed, as the apostle James says, "Even the demons believe and tremble."[19] Yet they neither hope nor love. Instead, believing as we do that what we hope for and love is coming to pass, they tremble. Therefore, the apostle Paul approves and commends the faith that works by love and that cannot exist without hope. Thus it is that love is not without hope, hope is not without love, and neither hope nor love are without faith.

CHAPTER III

God the Creator of All; and the Goodness of All Creation

9. Wherefore, when it is asked what we ought to believe in matters of religion, the answer is not to be sought in the exploration of the nature of things [rerum natura], after the manner of those whom the Greeks called "physicists."[20] Nor should we be dismayed if Christians are ignorant about the

---

16 Heb. 11:1.
17 Sacra eloquia—a favorite phrase of Augustine's for the Bible.
18 Rom. 8:24, 25 (Old Latin).   19 James 2:19.
20 One of the standard titles of early Greek philosophical treatises was περὶ φύσεως, which would translate into Latin as De rerum natura. This is, in fact, the title of Lucretius' famous poem, the greatest philosophical work written in classical Latin.

properties and the number of the basic elements of nature, or about the motion, order, and deviations of the stars, the map of the heavens, the kinds and nature of animals, plants, stones, springs, rivers, and mountains; about the divisions of space and time, about the signs of impending storms, and the myriad other things which these "physicists" have come to understand, or think they have. For even these men, gifted with such superior insight, with their ardor in study and their abundant leisure, exploring some of these matters by human conjecture and others through historical inquiry, have not yet learned everything there is to know. For that matter, many of the things they are so proud to have discovered are more often matters of opinion than of verified knowledge.

For the Christian, it is enough to believe that the cause of all created things, whether in heaven or on earth, whether visible or invisible, is nothing other than the goodness of the Creator, who is the one and the true God.[21] Further, the Christian believes that nothing exists save God himself and what comes from him; and he believes that God is triune, i.e., the Father, and the Son begotten of the Father, and the Holy Spirit proceeding from the same Father, but one and the same Spirit of the Father and the Son.

10. By this Trinity, supremely and equally and immutably good, were all things created. But they were not created supremely, equally, nor immutably good. Still, each single created thing is good, and taken as a whole they are very good, because together they constitute a universe of admirable beauty.

11. In this universe, even what is called evil, when it is rightly ordered and kept in its place, commends the good more eminently, since good things yield greater pleasure and praise when compared to the bad things. For the Omnipotent God, whom even the heathen acknowledge as the Supreme Power over all, would not allow any evil in his works, unless in his omnipotence and goodness, as the Supreme Good, he is able to bring forth good out of evil. What, after all, is anything we call evil except the privation of good? In animal bodies, for instance, sickness and wounds are nothing but the privation of health. When a cure is effected, the evils which were present (i.e., the sickness and the wounds) do not retreat and go elsewhere. Rather, they simply do not exist any more. For such

[21] This basic motif appears everywhere in Augustine's thought as the very foundation of his whole system.

evil is not a substance; the wound or the disease is a defect of the bodily substance which, as a substance, is good. Evil, then, is an accident, i.e., a privation of that good which is called health. Thus, whatever defects there are in a soul are privations of a natural good. When a cure takes place, they are not transferred elsewhere but, since they are no longer present in the state of health, they no longer exist at all.[22]

CHAPTER IV

THE PROBLEM OF EVIL

12. All of nature, therefore, is good, since the Creator of all nature is supremely good. But nature is not supremely and immutably good as is the Creator of it. Thus the good in created things can be diminished and augmented. For good to be diminished is evil; still, however much it is diminished, something must remain of its original nature as long as it exists at all. For no matter what kind or however insignificant a thing may be, the good which is its "nature" cannot be destroyed without the thing itself being destroyed. There is good reason, therefore, to praise an uncorrupted thing, and if it were indeed an incorruptible thing which could not be destroyed, it would doubtless be all the more worthy of praise. When, however, a thing is corrupted, its corruption is an evil because it is, by just so much, a privation of the good. Where there is no privation of the good, there is no evil. Where there is evil, there is a corresponding diminution of the good. As long, then, as a thing is being corrupted, there is good in it of which it is being deprived; and in this process, if something of its being remains that cannot be further corrupted, this will then be an incorruptible entity [*natura incorruptibilis*], and to this great good it will have come through the process of corruption. But even if the corruption is not arrested, it still does not cease having some good of which it cannot be further deprived. If, however, the corruption comes

[22] This section (Chs. III and IV) is the most explicit statement of a major motif which pervades the whole of Augustinian metaphysics. We see it in his earliest writings, *Soliloquies*, I, 2, and *De ordine*, II, 7. It is obviously a part of the Neoplatonic heritage which Augustine appropriated for his Christian philosophy. The good is positive, constructive, essential; evil is privative, destructive, parasitic on the good. It has its origin, not in nature, but in the will. Cf. *Confessions*, Bk. VII, Chs. III, V, XII–XVI; *On Continence*, 14–16; *On the Gospel of John*, Tractate XCVIII, 7; *City of God*, XI, 17; XII, 7–9.

to be total and entire, there is no good left either, because it is no longer an entity at all. Wherefore corruption cannot consume the good without also consuming the thing itself. Every actual entity [*natura*] is therefore good; a greater good if it cannot be corrupted, a lesser good if it can be. Yet only the foolish and unknowing can deny that it is still good even when corrupted. Whenever a thing is consumed by corruption, not even the corruption remains, for it is nothing in itself, having no subsistent being in which to exist.

13. From this it follows that there is nothing to be called evil if there is nothing good. A good that wholly lacks an evil aspect is entirely good. Where there is some evil in a thing, its good is defective or defectible. Thus there can be no evil where there is no good. This leads us to a surprising conclusion: that, since every being, in so far as it is a being, is good, if we then say that a defective thing is bad, it would seem to mean that we are saying that what is evil is good, that only what is good is ever evil and that there is no evil apart from something good. This is because every actual entity is good [*omnis natura bonum est.*] Nothing evil exists *in itself*, but only as an evil aspect of some actual entity. Therefore, there can be nothing evil except something good. Absurd as this sounds, nevertheless the logical connections of the argument compel us to it as inevitable. At the same time, we must take warning lest we incur the prophetic judgment which reads: "Woe to those who call evil good and good evil: who call darkness light and light darkness; who call the bitter sweet and the sweet bitter." [23] Moreover the Lord himself saith: "An evil man brings forth evil out of the evil treasure of his heart." [24] What, then, is an evil man but an evil entity [*natura mala*], since man is an entity? Now, if a man is something good because he is an entity, what, then, is a bad man except an evil good? When, however, we distinguish between these two concepts, we find that the bad man is not bad because he is a man, nor is he good because he is wicked. Rather, he is a good entity in so far as he is a man, evil in so far as he is wicked. Therefore, if anyone says that simply to be a man is evil, or that to be a wicked man is good, he rightly falls under the prophetic judgment: "Woe to him who calls evil good and good evil." For this amounts to finding fault with God's work, because man is an entity of God's creation. It also means that we are praising the defects in this particular man *because* he is a wicked person. Thus, every entity, even if it is a defective

[23] Isa. 5:20.   [24] Matt. 12:35.

one, in so far as it is an entity, is good. In so far as it is defective, it is evil.

14. Actually, then, in these two contraries we call evil and good, the rule of the logicians fails to apply.[25] No weather is both dark and bright at the same time; no food or drink is both sweet and sour at the same time; no body is, at the same time and place, both white and black, nor deformed and well-formed at the same time. This principle is found to apply in almost all disjunctions: two contraries cannot coexist in a single thing. Nevertheless, while no one maintains that good and evil are not contraries, they can not only coexist, but the evil cannot exist at all without the good, or in a thing that is not a good. On the other hand, the good can exist without evil. For a man or an angel could exist and yet not be wicked, whereas there cannot be wickedness except in a man or an angel. It is good to be a man, good to be an angel; but evil to be wicked. These two contraries are thus coexistent, so that if there were no good in what is evil, then the evil simply could not be, since it can have no mode in which to exist, nor any source from which corruption springs, unless it be something corruptible. Unless this something is good, it cannot be corrupted, because corruption is nothing more than the deprivation of the good. Evils, therefore, have their source in the good, and unless they are parasitic on something good, they are not anything at all. There is no other source whence an evil thing can come to be. If this is the case, then, in so far as a thing is an entity, it is unquestionably good. If it is an incorruptible entity, it is a great good. But even if it is a corruptible entity, it still has no mode of existence except as an aspect of something that is good. Only by corrupting something good can corruption inflict injury.

15. But when we say that evil has its source in the good, do not suppose that this denies our Lord's judgment: "A good tree cannot bear evil fruit."[26] This cannot be, even as the Truth himself declareth: "Men do not gather grapes from thorns," since thorns cannot bear grapes. Nevertheless, from good soil we can see both vines and thorns spring up. Likewise, just as a bad tree does not grow good fruit, so also an evil will does not produce good deeds. From a human nature, which is good in itself, there can spring forth either a good or an evil will. There was no other place from whence evil could have arisen in the first place except from the nature—good in itself—of an angel or

25 This refers to Aristotle's well-known principle of "the excluded middle."
26 Matt. 7:18.

a man. This is what our Lord himself most clearly shows in the passage about the trees and the fruits, for he said: "Make the tree good and the fruits will be good, or make the tree bad and its fruits will be bad."[27] This is warning enough that bad fruit cannot grow on a good tree nor good fruit on a bad one. Yet from that same earth to which he was referring, both sorts of trees can grow.

CHAPTER V

THE KINDS AND DEGREES OF ERROR

16. This being the case, when that verse of Maro's gives us pleasure,

"Happy is he who can understand the causes of things,"[28]

it still does not follow that our felicity depends upon our knowing the causes of the great physical processes in the world, which are hidden in the secret maze of nature,

"Whence earthquakes, whose force swells the sea to flood,
    so that they burst their bounds and then subside again," [29]

and other such things as this.

But we ought to know the causes of good and evil in things, at least as far as men may do so in this life, filled as it is with errors and distress, in order to avoid these errors and distresses. We must always aim at that true felicity wherein misery does not distract, nor error mislead. If it is a good thing to understand the causes of physical motion, there is nothing of greater concern in these matters which we ought to understand than our own health. But when we are in ignorance of such things, we seek out a physician, who has seen how the secrets of heaven and earth still remain hidden from us, and what patience there must be in unknowing.

17. Although we should beware of error wherever possible, not only in great matters but in small ones as well, it is impossible not to be ignorant of many things. Yet it does not follow that one falls into error out of ignorance alone. If someone thinks he knows what he does not know, if he approves as true what is actually false, this then is error, in the proper sense of the term. Obviously, much depends on the question involved in the error,

[27] Cf. Matt. 12:33.   [28] Virgil, *Georgics*, II, 490.   [29] *Ibid.*, 479.

for in one and the same question one naturally prefers the instructed to the ignorant, the expert to the blunderer, and this with good reason. In a complex issue, however, as when one man knows one thing and another man knows something else, if the former knowledge is more useful and the latter is less useful or even harmful, who in this latter case would not prefer ignorance? There are some things, after all, that it is better not to know than to know. Likewise, there is sometimes profit in error—but on a journey, not in morals.[30] This sort of thing happened to us once, when we mistook the way at a crossroads and did not go by the place where an armed gang of Donatists lay in wait to ambush us. We finally arrived at the place where we were going, but only by a roundabout way, and upon learning of the ambush, we were glad to have erred and gave thanks to God for our error. Who would doubt, in such a situation, that the erring traveler is better off than the unerring brigand? This perhaps explains the meaning of our finest poet, when he speaks for an unhappy lover:

> "When I saw [her] I was undone,
>   and fatal error swept me away," [31]

for there is such a thing as a fortunate mistake which not only does no harm but actually does some good.

But now for a more careful consideration of the truth in this business. To err means nothing more than to judge as true what is in fact false, and as false what is true. It means to be certain about the uncertain, uncertain about the certain, whether it be certainly true or certainly false. This sort of error in the mind is deforming and improper, since the fitting and proper thing would be to be able to say, in speech or judgment: "Yes, yes. No, no."[32] Actually, the wretched lives we lead come partly from this: that sometimes if they are not to be entirely lost, error is unavoidable. It is different in that higher life where Truth itself is the life of our souls, where none deceives and none is deceived. In this life men deceive and are deceived, and are actually worse off when they deceive by lying than when they are deceived by believing lies. Yet our rational mind shrinks from falsehood, and naturally avoids error as much as it can, so

30 *Sed in via pedum, non in via morum.*
31 Virgil, *Eclogue*, VIII, 42. The context of the passage is Damon's complaint over his faithless Nyssa; he is here remembering the first time he ever saw her—when he was twelve! Cf. *Theocritus*, II, 82.
32 Cf. Matt. 5:37.

that even a deceiver is unwilling to be deceived by somebody else.[33] For the liar thinks he does not deceive himself and that he deceives only those who believe him. Indeed, he does not err in his lying, if he himself knows what the truth is. But he is deceived in this, that he supposes that his lie does no harm to himself, when actually every sin harms the one who commits it more that it does the one who suffers it.

CHAPTER VI

THE PROBLEM OF LYING

18. Here a most difficult and complex issue arises which I once dealt with in a large book, in response to the urgent question whether it is ever the duty of a righteous man to lie.[34] Some go so far as to contend that in cases concerning the worship of God or even the nature of God, it is sometimes a good and pious deed to speak falsely. It seems to me, however, that every lie is a sin, albeit there is a great difference depending on the intention and the topic of the lie. He does not sin as much who lies in the attempt to be helpful as the man who lies as a part of a deliberate wickedness. Nor does one who, by lying, sets a traveler on the wrong road do as much harm as one who, by a deceitful lie, perverts the way of a life. Obviously, no one should be adjudged a liar who speaks falsely what he sincerely supposes is the truth, since in his case he does not deceive but rather is deceived. Likewise, a man is not a liar, though he could be charged with rashness, when he incautiously accepts as true what is false. On the other hand, however, that man is a liar in his own conscience who speaks the truth supposing that it is a falsehood. For as far as his soul is concerned, since he did not say what he believed, he did not tell the truth, even though the truth did come out in what he said. Nor is a man to be cleared of the charge of lying whose mouth unknowingly speaks the truth while his conscious intention is to lie. If we do not con-

[33] Cf. *Confessions*, Bk. X, Ch. XXIII.

[34] *Ad consentium contra mendacium*, CSEL (J. Zycha, ed.), Vol. 41, pp. 469–528; also Migne, *PL*, 40, c. 517–548; English translation by H. B. Jaffee in Deferrari, *St. Augustine: Treatises on Various Subjects* (The Fathers of the Church, New York, 1952), pp. 113–179. This had been written about a year earlier than the *Enchiridion*. Augustine had also written another treatise *On Lying* much earlier, c. 395; see *De mendacio* in CSEL (J. Zycha, ed.), Vol. 41, pp. 413–466; Migne, *PL*, 40, c. 487–518; English translation by M. S. Muldowney in Deferrari, *op. cit.*, pp. 47–109. This summary of his position here represents no change of view whatever on this question.

sider the things spoken of, but only the intentions of the one speaking, he is the better man who unknowingly speaks falsely —because he judges his statement to be true—than the one who unknowingly speaks the truth while in his heart he is attempting to deceive. For the first man does not have one intention in his heart and another in his word, whereas the other, whatever be the facts in his statement, still "has one thought locked in his heart, another ready on his tongue," [35] which is the very essence of lying. But when we do consider the things spoken of, it makes a great difference in what respect one is deceived or lies. To be deceived is a lesser evil than to lie, as far as a man's intentions are concerned. But it is far more tolerable that a man should lie about things not connected with religion than for one to be deceived in matters where faith and knowledge are prerequisite to the proper service of God. To illustrate what I mean by examples: If one man lies by saying that a dead man is alive, and another man, being deceived, believes that Christ will die again after some extended future period—would it not be incomparably better to lie in the first case than to be deceived in the second? And would it not be a lesser evil to lead someone into the former error than to be led by someone into the latter?

19. In some things, then, we are deceived in great matters; in others, small. In some of them no harm is done; in others, even good results. It is a great evil for a man to be deceived so as not to believe what would lead him to life eternal, or what would lead to eternal death. But it is a small evil to be deceived by crediting a falsehood as the truth in a matter where one brings on himself some temporal setback which can then be turned to good use by being borne in faithful patience—as for example, when someone judges a man to be good who is actually bad, and consequently has to suffer evil on his account. Or, take the man who believes a bad man to be good, yet suffers no harm at his hand. He is not badly deceived nor would the prophetic condemnation fall on him: "Woe to those who call evil good." For we should understand that this saying refers to the things in which men are evil and not to the men themselves. Hence, he who calls adultery a good thing may be rightly accused by the prophetic word. But if he calls a man good supposing him to be chaste and not knowing that he is an adulterer, such a man is not deceived in his doctrine of good and evil, but only as to the secrets of human conduct. He calls the

[35] Sallust, *The War with Catiline*, X, 6-7.

man good on the basis of what he supposed him to be, and this is undoubtedly a good thing. Moreover, he calls adultery bad and chastity good. But he calls this particular man good in ignorance of the fact that he is an adulterer and not chaste. In similar fashion, if one escapes an injury through an error, as I mentioned before happened to me on that journey, there is even something good that accrues to a man through his mistakes. But when I say that in such a case a man may be deceived without suffering harm therefrom, or even may gain some benefit thereby, I am not saying that error is not a bad thing, nor that it is a positively good thing. I speak only of the evil which did not happen or the good which did happen, through the error, which was not caused by the error itself but which came out of it. Error, in itself and by itself, whether a great error in great matters or a small error in small affairs, is always a bad thing. For who, except in error, denies that it is bad to approve the false as though it were the truth, or to disapprove the truth as though it were falsehood, or to hold what is certain as if it were uncertain, or what is uncertain as if it were certain? It is one thing to judge a man good who is actually bad—this is an error. It is quite another thing not to suffer harm from something evil if the wicked man whom we supposed to be good actually does nothing harmful to us. It is one thing to suppose that this particular road is the right one when it is not. It is quite another thing that, from this error—which is a bad thing— something good actually turns out, such as being saved from the onslaught of wicked men.

CHAPTER VII

Disputed Questions About the Limits of Knowledge and Certainty in Various Matters

20. I do not rightly know whether errors of this sort should be called sins—when one thinks well of a wicked man, not knowing what his character really is, or when, instead of our physical perception, similar perceptions occur which we experience in the spirit (such as the illusion of the apostle Peter when he thought he was seeing a vision but was actually being liberated from fetters and chains by the angel [36]) or in perceptual illusions when we think something is smooth which is actually rough, or something sweet which is bitter, something fragrant which is

[36] Cf. Acts 12:9.

putrid, that a noise is thunder when it is actually a wagon passing by, when one takes this man for that, or when two men look alike, as happens in the case of twins—whence our poet speaks of "a pleasant error for parents" 37—I say I do not know whether these and other such errors should be called sins.

Nor am I at the moment trying to deal with that knottiest of questions which baffled the most acute men of the Academy, whether a wise man ought ever to affirm anything positively lest he be involved in the error of affirming as true what may be false, since all questions, as they assert, are either mysterious [occulta] or uncertain. On these points I wrote three books in the early stages of my conversion because my further progress was being blocked by objections like this which stood at the very threshold of my understanding. 38 It was necessary to overcome the despair of being unable to attain to truth, which is what their arguments seemed to lead one to. Among them every error is deemed a sin, and this can be warded off only by a systematic suspension of positive assent. Indeed they say it is an error if someone believes in what is uncertain. For them, however, nothing is certain in human experience, because of the deceitful likeness of falsehood to the truth, so that even if what appears to be true turns out to be true indeed, they will still dispute it with the most acute and even shameless arguments.

Among us, on the other hand, "the righteous man lives by faith." 39 Now, if you take away positive affirmation, 40 you take away faith, for without positive affirmation nothing is believed. And there are truths about things unseen, and unless they are believed, we cannot attain to the happy life, which is nothing less than life eternal. It is a question whether we ought to argue with those who profess themselves ignorant not only about the eternity yet to come but also about their present existence, for they [the Academics] even argue that they do not know what they cannot help knowing. For no one can "not know" that he himself is alive. If he is not alive, he cannot "not know" about it or anything else at all, because either to know or to "not

37 Virgil, *Aeneid*, X, 392.
38 This refers to one of the first of the Cassiciacum dialogues, *Contra Academicos*. The gist of Augustine's refutation of skepticism is in III, 23 ff. Throughout his whole career he continued to maintain this position: that certain knowledge begins with self-knowledge. Cf. *Confessions*, Bk. V, Ch. X, 19; see also *City of God*, XI, xxvii.
39 Hab. 2:4; Rom. 1:17.
40 A direct contrast between *suspensus assensio*—the watchword of the Academics—and *assensio*, the badge of Christian certitude.

know" implies a living subject. But, in such a case, by not positively affirming that they are alive, the skeptics ward off the appearance of error in themselves, yet they do make errors simply by showing themselves alive; one cannot err who is not alive. That we live is therefore not only true, but it is altogether certain as well. And there are many things that are thus true and certain concerning which, if we withhold positive assent, this ought not to be regarded as a higher wisdom but actually a sort of dementia.

21. In those things which do not concern our attainment of the Kingdom of God, it does not matter whether they are believed in or not, or whether they are true or are supposed to be true or false. To err in such questions, to mistake one thing for another, is not to be judged as a sin or, if it is, as a small and light one. In sum, whatever kind or how much of an error these miscues may be, it does not involve the way that leads to God, which is the faith of Christ which works through love. This way of life was not abandoned in that error so dear to parents concerning the twins.[41] Nor did the apostle Peter deviate from this way when he thought he saw a vision and so mistook one thing for something else. In his case, he did not discover the actual situation until after the angel, by whom he was freed, had departed from him. Nor did the patriarch Jacob deviate from this way when he believed that his son, who was in fact alive, had been devoured by a wild beast. We may err through false impressions of this kind, with our faith in God still safe, nor do we thus leave the way that leads us to him. Nevertheless, such mistakes, even if they are not sins, must still be listed among the evils of this life, which is so readily subject to vanity that we judge the false for true, reject the true for the false, and hold as uncertain what is actually certain. For even if these mistakes do not affect that faith by which we move forward to affirm truth and eternal beatitude, yet they are not unrelated to the misery in which we still exist. Actually, of course, we would be deceived in nothing at all, either in our souls or our physical senses, if we were already enjoying that true and perfected happiness.

22. Every lie, then, must be called a sin, because every man ought to speak what is in his heart—not only when he himself knows the truth, but even when he errs and is deceived, as a man may be. This is so whether it be true or is only supposed to be true when it is not. But a man who lies says the opposite of what is in his heart, with the deliberate intent to deceive. Now

[41] See above, VII, 20.

clearly, language, in its proper function, was developed not as a means whereby men could deceive one another, but as a medium through which a man could communicate his thought to others. Wherefore to use language in order to deceive, and not as it was designed to be used, is a sin.

Nor should we suppose that there is any such thing as a lie that is not a sin, just because we suppose that we can sometimes help somebody by lying. For we could also do this by stealing, as when a secret theft from a rich man who does not feel the loss is openly given to a pauper who greatly appreciates the gain. Yet no one would say that such a theft was not a sin. Or again, we could also "help" by committing adultery, if someone appeared to be dying for love if we would not consent to her desire and who, if she lived, might be purified by repentance. But it cannot be denied that such an adultery would be a sin. If, then, we hold chastity in such high regard, wherein has truth offended us so that although chastity must not be violated by adultery, even for the sake of some other good, yet truth may be violated by lying? That men have made progress toward the good, when they will not lie save for the sake of human values, is not to be denied. But what is rightly praised in such a forward step, and perhaps even rewarded, is their good will and not their deceit. The deceit may be pardoned, but certainly ought not to be praised, especially among the heirs of the New Covenant to whom it has been said, "Let your speech be yes, yes; no, no: for what is more than this comes from evil." [42] Yet because of what this evil does, never ceasing to subvert this mortality of ours, even the joint heirs of Christ themselves pray, "Forgive us our debts." [43]

CHAPTER VIII

The Plight of Man After the Fall

23. With this much said, within the necessary brevity of this kind of treatise, as to what we need to know about the causes of good and evil—enough to lead us in the way toward the Kingdom, where there will be life without death, truth without error, happiness without anxiety—we ought not to doubt in any way that the cause of everything pertaining to our good is nothing other than the bountiful goodness of God himself. The cause of evil is the defection of the will of a being who is mutably good

[42] Matt. 5:37.   [43] Matt. 6:12.

from the Good which is immutable. This happened first in the case of the angels and, afterward, that of man.

24. This was the primal lapse of the rational creature, that is, his first privation of the good. In train of this there crept in, even without his willing it, ignorance of the right things to do and also an appetite for noxious things. And these brought along with them, as their companions, error and misery. When these two evils are felt to be imminent, the soul's motion in flight from them is called fear. Moreover, as the soul's appetites are satisfied by things harmful or at least inane—and as it fails to recognize the error of its ways—it falls victim to unwholesome pleasures or may even be exhilarated by vain joys. From these tainted springs of action—moved by the lash of appetite rather than a feeling of plenty—there flows out every kind of misery which is now the lot of rational natures.

25. Yet such a nature, even in its evil state, could not lose its appetite for blessedness. There are the evils that both men and angels have in common, for whose wickedness God hath condemned them in simple justice. But man has a unique penalty as well: he is also punished by the death of the body. God had indeed threatened man with death as penalty if he should sin. He endowed him with freedom of the will in order that he might rule him by rational command and deter him by the threat of death. He even placed him in the happiness of paradise in a sheltered nook of life [in umbra vitae] where, by being a good steward of righteousness, he would rise to better things.

26. From this state, after he had sinned, man was banished, and through his sin he subjected his descendants to the punishment of sin and damnation, for he had radically corrupted them, in himself, by his sinning. As a consequence of this, all those descended from him and his wife (who had prompted him to sin and who was condemned along with him at the same time)—all those born through carnal lust, on whom the same penalty is visited as for disobedience—all these entered into the inheritance of original sin. Through this involvement they were led, through divers errors and sufferings (along with the rebel angels, their corruptors and possessors and companions), to that final stage of punishment without end. "Thus by one man, sin entered into the world and death through sin; and thus death came upon all men, since all men have sinned." [44] By "the world" in this passage the apostle is, of course, referring to the whole human race.

[44] Rom. 5:12.

27. This, then, was the situation: the whole mass of the human race stood condemned, lying ruined and wallowing in evil, being plunged from evil into evil and, having joined causes with the angels who had sinned, it was paying the fully deserved penalty for impious desertion. Certainly the anger of God rests, in full justice, on the deeds that the wicked do freely in blind and unbridled lust; and it is manifest in whatever penalties they are called on to suffer, both openly and secretly. Yet the Creator's goodness does not cease to sustain life and vitality even in the evil angels, for were *this* sustenance withdrawn, they would simply cease to exist. As for mankind, although born of a corrupted and condemned stock, he still retains the power to form and animate his seed, to direct his members in their temporal order, to enliven his senses in their spatial relations, and to provide bodily nourishment. For God judged it better to bring good out of evil than not to permit any evil to exist. And if he had willed that there should be no reformation in the case of men, as there is none for the wicked angels, would it not have been just if the nature that deserted God and, through the evil use of his powers, trampled and transgressed the precepts of his Creator, which could have been easily kept—the same creature who stubbornly turned away from His Light and violated the image of the Creator in himself, who had in the evil use of his free will broken away from the wholesome discipline of God's law—would it not have been just if such a being had been abandoned by God wholly and forever and laid under the everlasting punishment which he deserved? Clearly God would have done this if he were only just and not also merciful and if he had not willed to show far more striking evidence of his mercy by pardoning some who were unworthy of it.

CHAPTER IX

The Replacement of the Fallen Angels by Elect Men (28–30); The Necessity of Grace (30–32)

28. While some of the angels deserted God in impious pride and were cast into the lowest darkness from the brightness of their heavenly home, the remaining number of the angels persevered in eternal bliss and holiness with God. For these faithful angels were not descended from a single angel, lapsed and damned. Hence, the original evil did not bind them in the fetters of inherited guilt, nor did it hand the whole company

over to a deserved punishment, as is the human lot. Instead, when he who became the devil first rose in rebellion with his impious company and was then with them prostrated, the rest of the angels stood fast in pious obedience to the Lord and so received what the others had not had—a sure knowledge of their everlasting security in his unfailing steadfastness.

29. Thus it pleased God, Creator and Governor of the universe, that since the whole multitude of the angels had not perished in this desertion of him, those who had perished would remain forever in perdition, but those who had remained loyal through the revolt should go on rejoicing in the certain knowledge of the bliss forever theirs. From the other part of the rational creation —that is, mankind—although it had perished as a whole through sins and punishments, both original and personal, God had determined that a portion of it would be restored and would fill up the loss which that diabolical disaster had caused in the angelic society. For this is the promise to the saints at the resurrection, that they shall be equal to the angels of God.[45]

Thus the heavenly Jerusalem, our mother and the commonwealth of God, shall not be defrauded of her full quota of citizens, but perhaps will rule over an even larger number. We know neither the number of holy men nor of the filthy demons, whose places are to be filled by the sons of the holy mother, who seemed barren in the earth, but whose sons will abide time without end in the peace the demons lost. But the number of those citizens, whether those who now belong or those who will in the future, is known to the mind of the Maker, "who calleth into existence things which are not, as though they were,"[46] and "ordereth all things in measure and number and weight."[47]

30. But now, can that part of the human race to whom God hath promised deliverance and a place in the eternal Kingdom be restored through the merits of their own works? Of course not! For what good works could a lost soul do except as he had been rescued from his lostness? Could he do this by the determination of his free will? Of course not! For it was in the evil use of his free will that man destroyed himself and his will at the same time. For as a man who kills himself is still alive when he kills himself, but having killed himself is then no longer alive and cannot resuscitate himself after he has destroyed his own life—so also sin which arises from the action of the free will turns out to be victor over the will and the free will is destroyed. "By whom a man is overcome, to this one he then is bound as

45 Cf. Luke 20:36.   46 Rom. 4:17.   47 Wis. 11:20.

slave." [48] This is clearly the judgment of the apostle Peter. And since it is true, I ask you what kind of liberty can one have who is bound as a slave except the liberty that loves to sin?

He serves freely who freely does the will of his master. Accordingly he who is slave to sin is free to sin. But thereafter he will not be free to do right unless he is delivered from the bondage of sin and begins to be the servant of righteousness. This, then, is true liberty: the joy that comes in doing what is right. At the same time, it is also devoted service in obedience to righteous precept.

But how would a man, bound and sold, get back his liberty to do good, unless he could regain it from Him whose voice saith, "If the Son shall make you free, then you will be free indeed" [49]? But before this process begins in man, could anyone glory in his good works as if they were acts of his free will, when he is not yet free to act rightly? He could do this only if, puffed up in proud vanity, he were merely boasting. This attitude is what the apostle was reproving when he said, "By grace you have been saved by faith." [50]

31. And lest men should arrogate to themselves saving faith as their own work and not understand it as a divine gift, the same apostle who says somewhere else that he had "obtained mercy of the Lord to be trustworthy" [51] makes here an additional comment: "And this is not of yourselves; rather it is a gift of God—not because of works either, lest any man should boast." [52] But then, lest it be supposed that the faithful are lacking in good works, he added further, "For we are his workmanship, created in Christ Jesus to good works, which God hath prepared beforehand for us to walk in them." [53]

We are then truly free when God ordereth our lives, that is, formeth and createth us not as men—this he hath already done —but also as good men, which he is now doing by his grace, that we may indeed be new creatures in Christ Jesus. [54] Accordingly, the prayer: "Create in me a clean heart, O God." [55] This does not mean, as far as the natural human heart is concerned, that God hath not already created this.

32. Once again, lest anyone glory, if not in his own works, at least in the determination of his free will, as if some merit had originated from him and as if the freedom to do good works had been bestowed on him as a kind of reward, let him

[48] II Peter 2:19.   [49] John 8:36.   [50] Eph. 2:8.
[51] I Cor. 7:25.   [52] Eph. 2:8, 9.   [53] Eph. 2:10.
[54] Cf. Gal. 6:15; II Cor. 5:17.   [55] Ps. 51:10.

hear the same herald of grace, announcing: "For it is God who is at work in you both to will and to do according to his good will." [56] And, in another place: "It is not therefore a matter of man's willing, or of his running, but of God's showing mercy." [57] Still, it is obvious that a man who is old enough to exercise his reason cannot believe, hope, or love unless he wills it, nor could he run for the prize of his high calling in God without a decision of his will. In what sense, therefore, is it "not a matter of human willing or running but of God's showing mercy," unless it be that "the will itself is prepared by the Lord," even as it is written? [58] This saying, therefore, that "it is not a matter of human willing or running but of God's showing mercy," means that the action is from both, that is to say, from the will of man and from the mercy of God. Thus we accept the dictum, "It is not a matter of human willing or running but of God's showing mercy," as if it meant, "The will of man is not sufficient by itself unless there is also the mercy of God." By the same token, the mercy of God is not sufficient by itself unless there is also the will of man. But if we say rightly that "it is not a matter of human willing or running but of God's showing mercy," because the will of man alone is not enough, why, then, is not the contrary rightly said, "It is not a matter of God's showing mercy but of a man's willing," since the mercy of God by itself alone is not enough? Now, actually, no Christian would dare to say, "It is not a matter of God's showing mercy but of man's willing," lest he explicitly contradict the apostle. The conclusion remains, therefore, that this saying: "Not man's willing or running but God's showing mercy," is to be understood to mean that the whole process is credited to God, who both prepareth the will to receive divine aid and aideth the will which has been thus prepared. [59]

[56] Phil. 2:13.   [57] Rom. 9:16.   [58] Prov. 8:35 (LXX).

[59] From the days at Cassiciacum till the very end, Augustine toiled with the mystery of the primacy of God's grace and the reality of human freedom. Of two things he was unwaveringly sure, even though they involved him in a paradox and the appearance of confusion. The first is that God's grace is not only primary but also sufficient as the ground and source of human willing. And against the Pelagians and other detractors from grace, he did not hesitate to insist that grace is irresistible and inviolable. Cf. *On Grace and Free Will*, 29, 41–43; *On the Predestination of the Saints*, 19:10; *On the Gift of Perseverance*, 41; *On the Soul and Its Origin*, 16; and even the *Enchiridion*, XXIV, 97.

But he never drew from this deterministic emphasis the conclusion that man is unfree and everywhere roundly rejects the not illogical corollary of his theonomism, that man's will counts for little or nothing except as

For a man's good will comes before many other gifts from God, but not all of them. One of the gifts it does not antedate is—just itself! Thus in the Sacred Eloquence we read both, "His mercy goes before me," [60] and also, "His mercy shall follow me." [61] It predisposes a man before he wills, to prompt his willing. It follows the act of willing, lest one's will be frustrated. Otherwise, why are we admonished to pray for our enemies, [62] who are plainly not now willing to live piously, unless it be that God is even now at work in them and in their wills? [63] Or again, why are we admonished to ask in order to receive, unless it be that He who grants us what we will is he through whom it comes to pass that we will? We pray for enemies, therefore, that the mercy of God should go before them, as it goes before us; we pray for ourselves that his mercy shall follow us.

CHAPTER X

JESUS CHRIST THE MEDIATOR

33. Thus it was that the human race was bound in a just doom and all men were children of wrath. Of this wrath it is written: "For all our days are wasted; we are ruined in thy wrath; our years seem like a spider's web." [64] Likewise Job spoke of this wrath: "Man born of woman is of few days and full of trouble." [65] And even the Lord Jesus said of it: "He that believes in the Son has life everlasting, but he that believes not does not have life. Instead, the wrath of God abides in him." [66] He does not say, "It will come," but, "It now abides." Indeed every man is born into this state. Wherefore the apostle says, "For we too were by nature children of wrath even as the others." [67] Since men are in this state of wrath through original sin—a condition made still graver and more pernicious as they compounded more and worse sins with it—a Mediator was required; that is to say, a Reconciler who by offering a unique sacrifice,

passive agent of God's will. He insists on responsibility on man's part in responding to the initiatives of grace. For this emphasis, which is characteristically directed to the faithful themselves, see *On the Psalms*, LXVIII, 7–8; *On the Gospel of John*, Tractate, 53:6–8; and even his severest anti-Pelagian tracts: *On Grace and Free Will*, 6–8, 10, 31 and *On Admonition and Grace*, 2–8.

[60] Ps. 58:11 (Vulgate). [61] Ps. 23:6. [62] Cf. Matt. 5:44.
[63] The theme that he had explored in *Confessions*, Bks. I–IX. See especially Bk. V, Chs. X, XIII; Bk. VII, Ch. VIII; Bk. IX, Ch. I.
[64] Cf. Ps. 90:9. [65] Job 14:1. [66] John 3:36. [67] Eph. 2:3.

of which all the sacrifices of the Law and the Prophets were shadows, should allay that wrath. Thus the apostle says, "For if, when we were enemies, we were reconciled to God by the death of his Son, even more now being reconciled by his blood we shall be saved from wrath through him." [68] However, when God is said to be wrathful, this does not signify any such perturbation in him as there is in the soul of a wrathful man. His verdict, which is always just, takes the name "wrath" as a term borrowed from the language of human feelings. This, then, is the grace of God through Jesus Christ our Lord—that we are reconciled to God through the Mediator and receive the Holy Spirit so that we may be changed from enemies into sons, "for as many as are led by the Spirit of God, they are the sons of God." [69]

34. It would take too long to say all that would be truly worthy of this Mediator. Indeed, men cannot speak properly of such matters. For who can unfold in cogent enough fashion this statement, that "the Word became flesh and dwelt among us," [70] so that we should then believe in "the only Son of God the Father Almighty, born of the Holy Spirit and Mary the Virgin." Yet it is indeed true that the Word was made flesh, the flesh being assumed by the Divinity, not the Divinity being changed into flesh. Of course, by the term "flesh" we ought here to understand "man," an expression in which the part signifies the whole, just as it is said, "Since by the works of the law no flesh shall be justified," [71] which is to say, no *man* shall be justified. Yet certainly we must say that in that assumption nothing was lacking that belongs to human nature.

But it was a nature entirely free from the bonds of all sin. It was not a nature born of both sexes with fleshly desires, with the burden of sin, the guilt of which is washed away in regeneration. Instead, it was the kind of nature that would be fittingly born of a virgin, conceived by His mother's faith and not her fleshly desires. Now if in his being born, her virginity had been destroyed, he would not then have been born of a virgin. It would then be false (which is unthinkable) for the whole Church to confess him "born of the Virgin Mary." This is the Church which, imitating his mother, daily gives birth to his members yet remains virgin. Read, if you please, my letter on the virginity of Saint Mary written to that illustrious man, Volusianus, whom I name with honor and affection. [72]

---

[68] Rom. 5:9, 10.   [69] Rom. 8:14.   [70] John 1:14.   [71] Rom. 3:20.
[72] *Epistle* CXXXVII, written in 412 in reply to a list of queries sent to Augustine by the proconsul of Africa.

35. Christ Jesus, Son of God, is thus both God and man. He was God before all ages; he is man in this age of ours. He is God because he is the Word of God, for "the Word was God." [73] Yet he is man also, since in the unity of his Person a rational soul and body is joined to the Word.

Accordingly, in so far as he is God, he and the Father are one. Yet in so far as he is man, the Father is greater than he. Since he was God's only Son—not by grace but by nature—to the end that he might indeed be the fullness of all grace, he was also made Son of Man—and yet he was in the one nature as well as in the other, one Christ. "For being in the form of God, he judged it not a violation to be what he was by nature, the equal of God. Yet he emptied himself, taking on the form of a servant," [74] yet neither losing nor diminishing the form of God. [75] Thus he was made less and remained equal, and both these in a unity as we said before. But he is one of these because he is the Word; the other, because he was a man. As the Word, he is the equal of the Father; as a man, he is less. He is the one Son of God, and at the same time Son of Man; the one Son of Man, and at the same time God's Son. These are not two sons of God, one God and the other man, but *one* Son of God—God without origin, man with a definite origin—our Lord Jesus Christ.

CHAPTER XI

THE INCARNATION AS PRIME EXAMPLE OF THE ACTION OF GOD'S GRACE

36. In this the grace of God is supremely manifest, commended in grand and visible fashion; for what had the human nature in the man Christ merited, that it, and no other, should be assumed into the unity of the Person of the only Son of God? What good will, what zealous strivings, what good works preceded this assumption by which that particular man deserved to become one Person with God? Was he a man before the union, and was this singular grace given him as to one particularly deserving before God? Of course not! For, from the moment he began to be a man, that man began to be nothing

---

[73] John 1:1.   [74] Phil. 2:6, 7.
[75] These metaphors for contrasting the "two natures" of Jesus Christ were favorite figures of speech in Augustine's Christological thought. Cf. *On the Gospel of John*, Tractate 78; *On the Trinity*, I, 7; II, 2; IV, 19–20; VII, 3; *New Testament Sermons*, 76, 14.

other than God's Son, the only Son, and this because the Word of God assuming him became flesh, yet still assuredly remained God. Just as every man is a personal unity—that is, a unity of rational soul and flesh—so also is Christ a personal unity: Word and man.

Why should there be such great glory to a human nature— and this undoubtedly an act of grace, no merit preceding it— unless it be that those who consider such a question faithfully and soberly might have here a clear manifestation of God's great and sole grace, and this in order that they might understand how they themselves are justified from their sins by the selfsame grace which made it so that the man Christ had no power to sin? Thus indeed the angel hailed his mother when announcing to her the future birth: "Hail," he said, "full of grace." And shortly thereafter, "You have found favor with God." [76] And this was said of her, that she was full of grace, since she was to be mother of her Lord, indeed the Lord of all. Yet, concerning Christ himself, when the Evangelist John said, "And the Word became flesh and dwelt among us," he added, "and we beheld his glory, a glory as of the only Son of the Father, full of grace and truth." [77] When he said, "The Word was made flesh," this means, "Full of grace." When he also said, "The glory of the only begotten of the Father," this means, "Full of truth." Indeed it was Truth himself, God's only-begotten Son—and, again, this not by grace but by nature— who, by grace, assumed human nature into such a personal unity that he himself became the Son of Man as well.

37. This same Jesus Christ, God's one and only Son our Lord, was born of the Holy Spirit and the Virgin Mary. Now obviously the Holy Spirit is God's gift, a gift that is itself equal to the Giver; wherefore the Holy Spirit is God also, not inferior to the Father and the Son. Now what does this mean, that Christ's birth in respect to his human nature was of the Holy Spirit, save that this was itself also a work of grace?

For when the Virgin asked of the angel the manner by which what he announced would come to pass (since she had known no man), the angel answered: "The Holy Spirit shall come upon you and the power of the Most High shall overshadow you; therefore the Holy One which shall be born of you shall be called the Son of God." [78] And when Joseph wished to put her away, suspecting adultery (since he knew she was not pregnant by him), he received a similar answer from the angel: "Do not

[76] Luke 1:28–30.·   [77] John 1:14.   [78] Luke 1:35.

fear to take Mary as your wife; for that which is conceived in her is of the Holy Spirit" [79]—that is, "What you suspect is from another man is of the Holy Spirit."

CHAPTER XII

THE ROLE OF THE HOLY SPIRIT

38. Are we, then, to say that the Holy Spirit is the Father of Christ's human nature, so that as God the Father generated the Word, so the Holy Spirit generated the human nature, and that from both natures Christ came to be one, Son of God the Father as the Word, Son of the Holy Spirit as man? Do we suppose that the Holy Spirit is his Father through begetting him of the Virgin Mary? Who would dare to say such a thing? There is no need to show by argument how many absurd consequences such a notion has, when it is so absurd in itself that no believer's ear can bear to hear it. Actually, then, as we confess our Lord Jesus Christ, who is God from God yet born as man of the Holy Spirit and the Virgin Mary, there is in each nature (in both the divine and the human) the only Son of God the Father Almighty, from whom proceeds the Holy Spirit.

How, then, do we say that Christ is born of the Holy Spirit, if the Holy Spirit did not beget him? Is it because he made him? This might be, since through our Lord Jesus Christ—in the form of God—all things were made. Yet in so far as he is man, he himself was made, even as the apostle says: "He was made of the seed of David according to the flesh." [80] But since that creature which the Virgin conceived and bore, though it was related to the Person of the Son alone, was made by the whole Trinity—for the works of the Trinity are not separable—why is the Holy Spirit named as the One who made it? Is it, perhaps, that when any One of the Three is named in connection with some divine action, the whole Trinity is to be understood as involved in that action? This is true and can be shown by examples, but we should not dwell too long on this kind of solution.

For what still concerns us is how it can be said, "Born of the Holy Spirit," when he is in no wise the Son of the Holy Spirit? Now, just because God made [*fecit*] this world, one could not say that the world is the son of God, or that it is "born" of

God. Rather, one says it was "made" or "created" or "founded" or "established" by him, or however else one might like to speak of it. So, then, when we confess, "Born of the Holy Spirit and the Virgin Mary," the sense in which he is not the Son of the Holy Spirit and yet is the son of the Virgin Mary, when he was born both of him and of her, is difficult to explain. But there is no doubt as to the fact that he was not born from him as Father as he was born of her as mother.

39. Consequently we should not grant that whatever is born of something should therefore be called the son of that thing. Let us pass over the fact that a son is "born" of a man in a different sense than a hair is, or a louse, or a maw worm—none of these is a son. Let us pass over these things, since they are an unfitting analogy in so great a matter. Yet it is certain that those who are born of water and of the Holy Spirit would not properly be called sons of the water by anyone. But it does make sense to call them sons of God the Father and of Mother Church. Thus, therefore, the one born of the Holy Spirit is the son of God the Father, not of the Holy Spirit.

What we said about the hair and the other things has this much relevance, that it reminds us that not everything which is "born" of something is said to be "son" to him from which it is "born." Likewise, it does not follow that those who are called sons of someone are always said to have been born of him, since there are some who are adopted. Even those who are called "sons of Gehenna" are not born *of* it, but have been destined *for* it, just as the sons of the Kingdom are destined for that.

40. Wherefore, since a thing may be "born" of something else, yet not in the fashion of a "son," and conversely, since not everyone who is called son is born of him whose son he is called —this is the very mode in which Christ was "born" of the Holy Spirit (yet not as a son), and of the Virgin Mary as a son—this suggests to us the grace of God by which a certain human person, no merit whatever preceding, at the very outset of his existence, was joined to the Word of God in such a unity of person that the selfsame one who is Son of Man should be Son of God, and the one who is Son of God should be Son of Man. Thus, in his assumption of human nature, grace came to be natural to that nature, allowing no power to sin. This is why grace is signified by the Holy Spirit, because he himself is so perfectly God that he is also called God's Gift. Still, to speak adequately of this—even if one could—would call for a very long discussion.

CHAPTER XIII

BAPTISM AND ORIGINAL SIN

41. Since he was begotten and conceived in no pleasure of carnal appetite—and therefore bore no trace of original sin—he was, by the grace of God (operating in a marvelous and an ineffable manner), joined and united in a personal unity with the only-begotten Word of the Father, a Son not by grace but by nature. And although he himself committed no sin, yet because of "the likeness of sinful flesh" [81] in which he came, he was himself called sin and was made a sacrifice for the washing away of sins.

Indeed, under the old law, sacrifices for sins were often called sins.[82] Yet he of whom those sacrifices were mere shadows was himself actually made sin. Thus, when the apostle said, "For Christ's sake, we beseech you to be reconciled to God," he straightway added, "Him, who knew no sin, he made to be sin for us that we might be made to be the righteousness of God in him." [83] He does not say, as we read in some defective copies, "He who knew no sin did sin for us," as if Christ himself committed sin for our sake. Rather, he says, "He [Christ] who knew no sin, he [God] made to be sin for us." The God to whom we are to be reconciled hath thus made him the sacrifice for sin by which we may be reconciled.

He himself is therefore sin as we ourselves are righteousness—not our own but God's, not in ourselves but in him. Just as he was sin—not his own but ours, rooted not in himself but in us—so he showed forth through the likeness of sinful flesh, in which he was crucified, that since sin was not in him he could then, so to say, die to sin by dying in the flesh, which was "the likeness of sin." And since he had never lived in the old manner of sinning, he might, in his resurrection, signify the new life which is ours, which is springing to life anew from the old death in which we had been dead to sin.

42. This is the meaning of the great sacrament of baptism, which is celebrated among us. All who attain to this grace die thereby to sin—as he himself is said to have died to sin because he died in the flesh, that is, "in the likeness of sin"—and they are thereby alive by being reborn in the baptismal font, just as

---

[81] Rom. 8:3.   [82] Cf. Hos. 4:8.   [83] II Cor. 5:20, 21.

he rose again from the sepulcher. This is the case no matter what the age of the body.

43. For whether it be a newborn infant or a decrepit old man —since no one should be barred from baptism—just so, there is no one who does not die to sin in baptism. Infants die to original sin only; adults, to all those sins which they have added, through their evil living, to the burden they brought with them at birth.

44. But even these are frequently said to die to sin, when without doubt they die not to one but to many sins, and to all the sins which they have themselves already committed by thought, word, and deed. Actually, by the use of the singular number the plural number is often signified, as the poet said,

"And they fill the belly with the armed warrior," [84]

although they did this with many warriors. And in our own Scriptures we read: "Pray therefore to the Lord that he may take from us the serpent." [85] It does not say "serpents," as it might, for they were suffering from many serpents. There are, moreover, innumerable other such examples.

Yet, when the original sin is signified by the use of the plural number, as we say when infants are baptized "unto the remission of sins," instead of saying "unto the remission of sin," then we have the converse expression in which the singular is expressed by the plural number. Thus in the Gospel, it is said of Herod's death, "For they are dead who sought the child's life" [86]; it does not say, "He is dead." And in Exodus: "They made," [Moses] says, "to themselves gods of gold," when they had made one calf. And of this calf, they said: "These are thy gods, O Israel, which brought you out of the land of Egypt," [87] here also putting the plural for the singular.

45. Still, even in that one sin—which "entered into the world by one man and so spread to all men," [88] and on account of which infants are baptized—one can recognize a plurality of sins, if that single sin is divided, so to say, into its separate elements. For there is pride in it, since man preferred to be under his own rule rather than the rule of God; and sacrilege too, for man did not acknowledge God; and murder, since he cast himself down to death; and spiritual fornication, for the integrity of the human mind was corrupted by the seduction of the serpent; and theft, since the forbidden fruit was snatched; and avarice,

---

[84] Virgil, *Aeneid*, II, 1, 20.   [85] Num. 21:7 (LXX).
[86] Matt. 2:20.   [87] Ex. 32:4.   [88] Rom. 5:12.

since he hungered for more than should have sufficed for him—and whatever other sins that could be discovered in the diligent analysis of that one sin.

46. It is also said—and not without support—that infants are involved in the sins of their parents, not only of the first pair, but even of their own, of whom they were born. Indeed, that divine judgment, "I shall visit the sins of the fathers on their children," [89] definitely applies to them before they come into the New Covenant by regeneration. This Covenant was foretold by Ezekiel when he said that the sons should not bear their fathers' sins, nor the proverb any longer apply in Israel, "Our fathers have eaten sour grapes and the children's teeth are set on edge." [90]

This is why each one of them must be born again, so that he may thereby be absolved of whatever sin was in him at the time of birth. For the sins committed by evil-doing after birth can be healed by repentance—as, indeed, we see it happen even after baptism. For the new birth [regeneratio] would not have been instituted except for the fact that the first birth [generatio] was tainted—and to such a degree that one born of even a lawful wedlock said, "I was conceived in iniquities; and in sins did my mother nourish me in her womb." [91] Nor did he say "in iniquity" or "in sin," as he might have quite correctly; rather, he preferred to say "iniquities" and "sins," because, as I explained above, there are so many sins in that one sin—which has passed into all men, and which was so great that human nature was changed and by it brought under the necessity of death—and also because there are other sins, such as those of parents, which, even if they cannot change our nature in the same way, still involve the children in guilt, unless the gracious grace and mercy of God interpose.

47. But, in the matter of the sins of one's other parents, those who stand as one's forebears from Adam down to one's own parents, a question might well be raised: whether a man at birth is involved in the evil deeds of all his forebears, and their multiplied original sins, so that the later in time he is born, the worse estate he is born in; or whether, on this very account, God threatens to visit the sins of the parents as far as—but no farther than—the third and fourth generations, because in his mercy he will not continue his wrath beyond that. It is not his purpose that those not given the grace of regeneration be crushed under too heavy a burden in their eternal damnation,

[89] Deut. 5:9.   [90] Ezek. 18:2.   [91] Ps. 51:5.

as they would be if they were bound to bear, as original guilt, all the sins of their ancestors from the beginning of the human race, and to pay the due penalty for them. Whether yet another solution to so difficult a problem might or might not be found by a more diligent search and interpretation of Holy Scripture, I dare not rashly affirm.

CHAPTER XIV

The Mysteries of Christ's Mediatorial Work (48–49) and Justification (50–55)

48. That one sin, however, committed in a setting of such great happiness, was itself so great that by it, in one man, the whole human race was originally and, so to say, radically condemned. It cannot be pardoned and washed away except through "the one mediator between God and men, the man Christ Jesus," [92] who alone could be born in such a way as not to need to be reborn.

49. They were not reborn, those who were baptized by John's baptism, by which Christ himself was baptized.[93] Rather, they were *prepared* by the ministry of this forerunner, who said, "Prepare a way for the Lord," [94] for Him in whom alone they could be reborn.

For his baptism is not with water alone, as John's was, but with the Holy Spirit as well. Thus, whoever believes in Christ is reborn by that same Spirit, of whom Christ also was born, needing not to be reborn. This is the reason for the Voice of the Father spoken over him at his baptism, "Today have I begotten thee," [95] which pointed not to that particular day on which he was baptized, but to that "day" of changeless eternity, in order to show us that this Man belonged to the personal Unity of the Only Begotten. For a day that neither begins with the close of yesterday nor ends with the beginning of tomorrow is indeed an eternal "today."

Therefore, he chose to be baptized in water by John, not thereby to wash away any sin of his own, but to manifest his great humility. Indeed, baptism found nothing in him to wash away, just as death found nothing to punish. Hence, it was in authentic justice, and not by violent power, that the devil was overcome and conquered: for, as he had most unjustly slain Him

[92] I Tim. 2:5.
[93] Matt. 3:13.
[94] Luke 3:4; Isa. 40:3.
[95] Ps. 2:7; Heb. 5:5; cf. Mark 1:9-11.

who was in no way deserving of death, he also did most 'justly lose those whom he had justly held in bondage as punishment for their sins. Wherefore, He took upon himself both baptism and death, not out of a piteous necessity but through his own free act of showing mercy—as part of a definite plan whereby One might take away the sin of the world, just as one man had brought sin into the world, that is, the whole human race.

50. There is a difference, however. The first man brought sin into the world, whereas this One took away not only that one sin but also all the others which he found added to it. Hence, the apostle says, "And the gift [of grace] is not like the effect of the one that sinned: for the judgment on that one trespass was condemnation; but the gift of grace is for many offenses, and brings justification." [96] Now it is clear that the one sin originally inherited, even if it were the only one involved, makes men liable to condemnation. Yet grace justifies a man for many offenses, both the sin which he originally inherited in common with all the others and also the multitude of sins which he has committed on his own.

51. However, when he [the apostle] says, shortly after, "Therefore, as the offense of one man led all men to condemnation, so also the righteousness of one man leads all men to the life of justification," [97] he indicates sufficiently that everyone born of Adam is subject to damnation, and no one, unless reborn of Christ, is free from such a damnation.

52. And after this discussion of punishment through one man and grace through the Other, as he deemed sufficient for that part of the epistle, the apostle passes on to speak of the great mystery of holy baptism in the cross of Christ, and to do this so that we may understand nothing other in the baptism of Christ than the likeness of the death of Christ. The death of Christ crucified is nothing other than the likeness of the forgiveness of sins—so that in the very same sense in which the death is real, so also is the forgiveness of our sins real, and in the same sense in which his resurrection is real, so also in us is there authentic justification.

He asks: "What, then, shall we say? Shall we continue in sin, that grace may abound?" [98]—for he had previously said, "But where sin abounded, grace did much more abound." [99] And therefore he himself raised the question whether, because of the abundance of grace that follows sin, one should then continue in sin. But he answers, "God forbid!" and adds, "How shall

[96] Rom. 5:16.   [97] Rom. 5:18.   [98] Rom. 6:1.   [99] Rom. 5:20.

we, who are dead to sin, live any longer therein?"[1] Then, to show that we are dead to sin, "Do you not know that all we who were baptized in Christ Jesus were baptized into his death?"[2]

If, therefore, the fact that we are baptized into the death of Christ shows that we are dead to sin, then certainly infants who are baptized in Christ die to sin, since they are baptized into his own death. For there is no exception in the saying, "All we who are baptized into Christ Jesus are baptized into his death." And the effect of this is to show that we are dead to sin.

Yet what sin do infants die to in being reborn except that which they inherit in being born? What follows in the epistle also pertains to this: "Therefore we were buried with him by baptism into death; that, as Christ was raised up from the dead by the glory of the Father, even so we also should walk in the newness of life. For if we have been united with him in the likeness of his death, we shall be also united with him in the likeness of his resurrection, knowing this, that our old man is crucified with him, that the body of sin might be destroyed, that henceforth we should not serve sin. For he that is dead is freed from sin. Now if we are dead with Christ, we believe that we shall also live with him: knowing that Christ, being raised from the dead, dies no more; death has no more dominion over him. For the death he died, he died to sin, once for all; but the life he lives, he lives unto God. So also, reckon yourselves also to be dead to sin, but alive unto God through Christ Jesus."[3]

Now, he had set out to prove that we should not go on sinning, in order that thereby grace might abound, and had said, "If we have died to sin, how, then, shall we go on living in it?" And then to show that we were dead to sin, he had added, "Know you not, that as many of us as were baptized into Jesus Christ were baptized into his death?" Thus he concludes the passage as he began it. Indeed, he introduced the death of Christ in order to say that even he died to sin. To what sin, save that of the flesh in which he existed, not as sinner, but in "the likeness of sin" and which was, therefore, called by the name of sin? Thus, to those baptized into the death of Christ—into which not only adults but infants as well are baptized—he says, "So also you should reckon yourselves to be dead to sin, but alive to God in Christ Jesus."

53. Whatever was done, therefore, in the crucifixion of Christ, his burial, his resurrection on the third day, his ascension into heaven, his being seated at the Father's right hand—

[1] Rom. 6:2.   [2] Rom. 6:3.   [3] Rom. 6:4–11.

all these things were done thus, that they might not only signify their mystical meanings but also serve as a model for the Christian life which we lead here on the earth. Thus, of his crucifixion it was said, "And they that are Jesus Christ's have crucified their own flesh, with the passions and lusts thereof" [4]; and of his burial, "For we are buried with Christ by baptism into death"; of his resurrection, "Since Christ is raised from the dead through the glory of the Father, so we also should walk with him in newness of life"; of his ascension and session at the Father's right hand: "But if you have risen again with Christ, seek the things which are above, where Christ is sitting at the right hand of God. Set your affection on things above, not on things on the earth. For you are dead, and your life is hid with Christ in God." [5]

54. Now what we believe concerning Christ's future actions, since we confess that he will come again from heaven to judge the living and the dead, does not pertain to this life of ours as we live it here on earth, because it belongs not to his deeds already done, but to what he will do at the close of the age. To this the apostle refers and goes on to add, "When Christ, who is your life, shall appear, you shall then also appear with him in glory." [6]

55. There are two ways to interpret the affirmation that he "shall judge the living and the dead." On the one hand, we may understand by "the living" those who are not yet dead but who will be found living in the flesh when he comes; and we may understand by "the dead" those who have left the body, or who shall have left it before his coming. Or, on the other hand, "the living" may signify "the righteous," and "the dead" may signify "the unrighteous"—since the righteous are to be judged as well as the unrighteous. For sometimes the judgment of God is passed upon the evil, as in the word, "But they who have done evil [shall come forth] to the resurrection of judgment." [7] And sometimes it is passed upon the good, as in the word, "Save me, O God, by thy name, and judge me in thy strength." [8] Indeed, it is by the judgment of God that the distinction between good and evil is made, to the end that, being freed from evil and not destroyed with the evildoers, the good may be set apart at his right hand. [9] This is why the psalmist cried, "Judge me, O God," and, as if to explain what he had said, "and defend my cause against an unholy nation." [10]

[4] Gal. 5:24.   [5] Col. 3:1–3.   [6] Col. 3:4.   [7] John 5:29.
[8] Ps. 54:1.   [9] Cf. Matt. 25:32, 33.   [10] Ps. 43:1.

CHAPTER XV

THE HOLY SPIRIT (56) AND THE CHURCH (57–60)

56. Now, when we have spoken of Jesus Christ, the only Son of God our Lord, in the brevity befitting our confession of faith, we go on to affirm that we believe also in the Holy Spirit, as completing the Trinity which is God; and after that we call to mind our faith "in holy Church." By this we are given to understand that the rational creation belonging to the free Jerusalem ought to be mentioned in a subordinate order to the Creator, that is, the supreme Trinity. For, of course, all that has been said about the man Christ Jesus refers to the unity of the Person of the Only Begotten.

Thus, the right order of the Creed demanded[11] that the Church be made subordinate to the Trinity, as a house is subordinate to him who dwells in it, the temple to God, and the city to its founder. By the Church here we are to understand the whole Church, not just the part that journeys here on earth from rising of the sun to its setting, praising the name of the Lord [12] and singing a new song of deliverance from its old captivity, but also that part which, in heaven, has always, from creation, held fast to God, and which never experienced the evils of a fall. This part, composed of the holy angels, remains in blessedness, and it gives help, even as it ought, to the other part still on pilgrimage. For both parts together will make one eternal consort, as even now they are one in the bond of love— the whole instituted for the proper worship of the one God.[13] Wherefore, neither the whole Church nor any part of it wishes to be worshiped as God nor to be God to anyone belonging to the temple of God—the temple that is being built up of "the gods" whom the uncreated God created.[14] Consequently, if the Holy Spirit were creature and not Creator, he would obviously be a rational creature, for this is the highest of the levels of creation. But in this case he would not be set in the rule of faith *before* the Church, since he would then belong *to* the Church, in

---

[11] Reading the classical Latin form *poscebat* (as in Scheel and *PL*) for the late form *poxebat* (as in Rivière and many old MSS.).

[12] Cf. Ps. 113:3.

[13] Here reading *unum deum* (with Rivière and *PL*) against *deum* (in Scheel).

[14] A hyperbolic expression referring to "the saints." Augustine's Scriptural backing for such an unusual phrase is Ps. 82:6 and John 10:34f. But note the firm distinction between *ex diis quos facit* and *non factus Deus*.

that part of it which is in heaven. He would not have a temple, for he himself would be a temple. Yet, in fact, he hath a temple of which the apostle speaks, "Know you not that your body is the temple of the Holy Spirit, who is in you, whom you have from God?" [15] In another place, he says of this body, "Know you not that your bodies are members of Christ?" [16] How, then, is he not God who has a temple? Or how can he be less than Christ whose members are his temple? It is not that he has one temple and God another temple, since the same apostle says: "Know you not that you are the temple of God," and then, as if to prove his point, added, "and that the Spirit of God dwelleth in you?"

God therefore dwelleth in his temple, not the Holy Spirit only, but also Father and Son, who saith of his body—in which he standeth as Head of the Church on earth "that in all things he may be pre-eminent" [17]—"Destroy this temple and in three days I will raise it up again." [18] Therefore, the temple of God— that is, of the supreme Trinity as a whole—is holy Church, the Universal Church in heaven and on the earth.

57. But what can we affirm about that part of the Church in heaven, save that in it no evil is to be found, nor any apostates, nor will there be again, since that time when "God did not spare the sinning angels"—as the apostle Peter writes— "but casting them out, he delivered them into the prisons of darkness in hell, to be reserved for the sentence in the Day of Judgment" [19]?

58. Still, how is life ordered in that most blessed and supernal society? What differences are there in rank among the angels, so that while all are called by the general title "angels" —as we read in the Epistle to the Hebrews, "But to which of the angels said he at any time, 'Sit at my right hand'?" [20]; this expression clearly signifies that all are angels without exception —yet there are archangels there as well? Again, should these archangels be called "powers" [virtutes], so that the verse, "Praise him, all his angels; praise him, all his powers," [21] would mean the same thing as, "Praise him, all his angels; praise him, all his archangels"? Or, what distinctions are implied by the four designations by which the apostle seems to encompass the entire heavenly society, "Be they thrones or dominions, principalities, or powers" [22]? Let them answer these questions who

---

15 I Cor. 6:19.   16 I Cor. 6:15.   17 Col. 1:18.   18 John 2:19.
19 II Peter 2:4 (Old Latin).   20 Heb. 1:13.
21 Ps. 148:2 (LXX).   22 Col. 1:16.

can, if they can indeed prove their answers. For myself, I confess to ignorance of such matters. I am not even certain about another question: whether the sun and moon and all the stars belong to that same heavenly society—although they seem to be nothing more than luminous bodies, with neither perception nor understanding.

59. Furthermore, who can explain the kind of bodies in which the angels appeared to men, so that they were not only visible, but tangible as well? And, again, how do they, not by impact of physical stimulus but by spiritual force, bring certain visions, not to the physical eyes but to the spiritual eyes of the mind, or speak something, not to the ears, as from outside us, but actually from within the human soul, since they are present within it too? For, as it is written in the book of the Prophets: "And the angel that spoke in me, said to me . . ." [23] He does not say, "Spoke *to* me" but "Spoke *in* me." How do they appear to men in sleep, and communicate through dreams, as we read in the Gospel: "Behold, the angel of the Lord appeared to him in his sleep, saying . . ." [24]? By these various modes of presentation, the angels seem to indicate that they do not have tangible bodies. Yet this raises a very difficult question: How, then, did the patriarchs wash the angels' feet? [25] How, also, did Jacob wrestle with the angel in such a tangible fashion? [26]

To ask such questions as these, and to guess at the answers as one can, is not a useless exercise in speculation, so long as the discussion is moderate and one avoids the mistake of those who think they know what they do not know.

CHAPTER XVI

PROBLEMS ABOUT HEAVENLY AND EARTHLY DIVISIONS OF THE CHURCH

60. It is more important to be able to discern and tell when Satan transforms himself as an angel of light, lest by this deception he should seduce us into harmful acts. For, when he deceives the corporeal senses, and does not thereby turn the mind from that true and right judgment by which one leads the life of faith, there is no danger to religion. Or if, feigning himself to be good, he does or says things that would fit the character of the good angels, even if then we believe him good, the error is

[23] Zech. 1:9.   [24] Matt. 1:20.   [25] Gen. 18:4; 19:2.   [26] Gen. 32:24.

neither dangerous nor fatal to the Christian faith. But when, by these alien wiles, he begins to lead us into his own ways, then great vigilance is required to recognize him and not follow after. But how few men are there who are able to avoid his deadly stratagems, unless God guides and preserves them! Yet the very difficulty of this business is useful in this respect: it shows that no man should rest his hopes in himself, nor one man in another, but all who are God's should cast their hopes on him. And that this latter is obviously the best course for us no pious man would deny.

61. This part of the Church, therefore, which is composed of the holy angels and powers of God will become known to us as it really is only when, at the end of the age, we are joined to it, to possess, together with it, eternal bliss. But the other part which, separated from this heavenly company, wanders through the earth is better known to us because we are in it, and because it is composed of men like ourselves. This is the part that has been redeemed from all sin by the blood of the sinless Mediator, and its cry is: "If God be for us, who is against us? He that spared not his own Son, but delivered him up for us all. . . ." [27] Now Christ did not die for the angels. But still, what was done for man by his death for man's redemption and his deliverance from evil was done for the angels also, because by it the enmity caused by sin between men and the angels is removed and friendship restored. Moreover, this redemption of mankind serves to repair the ruins left by the angelic apostasy.

62. Of course, the holy angels, taught by God—in the eternal contemplation of whose truth they are blessed— know how many of the human race are required to fill up the full census of that commonwealth. This is why the apostle says "that all things are restored to unity in Christ, both those in heaven and those on the earth in him." [28] The part in heaven is indeed restored when the number lost from the angelic apostasy are replaced from the ranks of mankind. The part on earth is restored when those men predestined to eternal life are redeemed from the old state of corruption.

Thus by the single sacrifice, of which the many victims of the law were only shadows, the heavenly part is set at peace with the earthly part and the earthly reconciled to the heavenly. Wherefore, as the same apostle says: "For it pleased God that all plenitude of being should dwell in him and by him to reconcile all things to himself, making peace with them by the

27 Rom. 8:31, 32.   28 Cf. Eph. 1:10.

blood of his cross, whether those things on earth or those in heaven." [29]

63. This peace, as it is written, "passes all understanding." It cannot be known by us until we have entered into it. For how is the heavenly realm set at peace, save together with us; that is, by concord with us? For in that realm there is always peace, both among the whole company of rational creatures and between them and their Creator. This is the peace that, as it is said, "passes all understanding." But obviously this means *our* understanding, not that of those who always see the Father's face. For no matter how great our understanding may be, "we know in part, and we see in a glass darkly." [30] But when we shall have become "equal to God's angels," [31] then, even as they do, "we shall see face to face." [32] And we shall then have as great amity toward them as they have toward us; for we shall come to love them as much as we are loved by them.

In this way their peace will become known to us, since ours will be like theirs in kind and measure—nor will it then surpass our understanding. But the peace of God, which is there, will still doubtless surpass our understanding and theirs as well. For, of course, in so far as a rational creature is blessed, this blessedness comes, not from himself, but from God. Hence, it follows that it is better to interpret the passage, "The peace of God which passes all understanding," so that from the word "all" not even the understanding of the holy angels should be excepted. Only God's understanding is excepted; for, of course, his peace does not surpass his own understanding.

CHAPTER XVII

FORGIVENESS OF SINS IN THE CHURCH

64. The angels are in concord with us even now, when our sins are forgiven. Therefore, in the order of the Creed, after the reference to "holy Church" is placed the reference to "forgiveness of sins." For it is by this that the part of the Church on earth stands; it is by this that "what was lost and is found again" [33] is not lost again. Of course, the gift of baptism is an exception. It is an antidote given us against original sin, so that what is contracted by birth is removed by the new birth—

[29] Col. 1:19, 20.
[31] Cf. Luke 20:36.
[33] Cf. Luke 15:24.

[30] Cf. I Cor. 13:9, 12.
[32] I Cor. 13:12.

though it also takes away actual sins as well, whether of heart, word, or deed. But except for this great remission—the beginning point of a man's renewal, in which all guilt, inherited and acquired, is washed away—the rest of life, from the age of accountability (and no matter how vigorously we progress in righteousness), is not without the need for the forgiveness of sins. This is the case because the sons of God, as long as they live this mortal life, are in a conflict with death. And although it is truly said of them, "As many as are led by the Spirit of God, they are the sons of God," [34] yet even as they are being led by the Spirit of God and, as sons of God, advance toward God, they are also being led by their own spirits so that, weighed down by the corruptible body and influenced by certain human feelings, they thus fall away from themselves and commit sin. But it matters *how much*. Although every crime is a sin, not every sin is a crime. Thus we can say of the life of holy men even while they live in this mortality, that they are found without crime. "But if we say that we have no sin," as the great apostle says, "we deceive even ourselves, and the truth is not in us." [35]

65. Nevertheless, no matter how great our crimes, their forgiveness should never be despaired of in holy Church for those who truly repent, each according to the measure of his sin. And, in the act of repentance,[36] where a crime has been committed of such gravity as also to cut off the sinner from the body of Christ, we should not consider the measure of time as much as the measure of sorrow. For, "a contrite and humbled heart God will not despise." [37]

Still, since the sorrow of one heart is mostly hid from another, and does not come to notice through words and other such signs—even when it is plain to Him of whom it is said, "My groaning is not hid from thee"[38]—times of repentance have been rightly established by those set over the churches, that satisfaction may also be made in the Church, in which the sins are forgiven. For, of course, outside her they are not forgiven. For she alone has received the pledge of the Holy Spirit,[39] without whom there is no forgiveness of sins. Those forgiven thus obtain life everlasting.

66. Now the remission of sins has chiefly to do with the future judgment. In this life the Scripture saying holds true:

---

[34] Rom. 8:14.   [35] I John 1:8.

[36] In *actione poenitentiae*; cf. Luther's similar conception of *poenitentiam agite* in the *95 Theses* and in *De poenitentia*.

[37] Ps. 51:17.   [38] Ps. 38:9.   [39] II Cor. 1:22.

"A heavy yoke is on the sons of Adam, from the day they come forth from their mother's womb till the day of their burial in the mother of us all." [40] Thus we see even infants, after the washing of regeneration, tortured by divers evil afflictions. This helps us to understand that the whole import of the sacraments of salvation has to do more with the hope of future goods than with the retaining or attaining of present goods.

Indeed, many sins seem to be ignored and go unpunished; but their punishment is reserved for the future. It is not in vain that the day when the Judge of the living and the dead shall come is rightly called the Day of Judgment. Just so, on the other hand, some sins are punished here, and, if they are forgiven, will certainly bring no harm upon us in the future age. Hence, referring to certain temporal punishments, which are visited upon sinners in this life, the apostle, speaking to those whose sins are blotted out and not reserved to the end, says: "For if we judge ourselves truly we should not be judged by the Lord. But when we are judged, we are chastised by the Lord, that we may not be condemned along with this world." [41]

CHAPTER XVIII [42]

FAITH AND WORKS

67. There are some, indeed, who believe that those who do not abandon the name of Christ, and who are baptized in his laver in the Church, who are not cut off from it by schism or heresy, who may then live in sins however great, not washing them away by repentance, nor redeeming them by alms—and who obstinately persevere in them to life's last day—even these will still be saved, "though as by fire." They believe that such people will be punished by fire, prolonged in proportion to their sins, but still not eternal.

---

[40] Ecclus. 40:1 (Vulgate). [41] I Cor. 11:31, 32.

[42] This chapter supplies an important clue to the date of the *Enchiridion* and an interesting side light on Augustine's inclination to re-use "good material." In his treatise on *The Eight Questions of Dulcitius* (*De octo Dulcitii quaestionibus*), I: 10–13, Augustine quotes this entire chapter as a part of his answer to the question whether those who sin after baptism are ever delivered from hell. The date of the *De octo* is 422 or, possibly, 423; thus we have a *terminus ad quem* for the date of the *Enchiridion*. Still the best text of *De octo* is Migne, *PL*, 40, c. 147–170, and the best English translation is in Deferrari, *St. Augustine: Treatises on Various Subjects* (The Fathers of the Church, New York, 1952), pp. 427–466.

But those who believe thus, and still are Catholics, are deceived, as it seems to me, by a kind of merely human benevolence. For the divine Scripture, when consulted, answers differently. Moreover, I have written a book about this question, entitled *Faith and Works*,[43] in which, with God's help, I have shown as best I could that, according to Holy Scripture, the faith that saves is the faith that the apostle Paul adequately describes when he says, "For in Christ Jesus neither circumcision avails anything, nor uncircumcision, but the faith which works through love."[44] But if faith works evil and not good, then without doubt, according to the apostle James "it is dead in itself."[45] He then goes on to say, "If a man says he has faith, yet has not works, can his faith be enough to save him?"[46]

Now, if the wicked man were to be saved by fire on account of his faith only, and if this is the way the statement of the blessed Paul should be understood—"But he himself shall be saved, yet so as by fire"[47]—then faith without works would be sufficient to salvation. But then what the apostle James said would be false. And also false would be another statement of the same Paul himself: "Do not err," he says; "neither fornicators, nor idolaters, nor adulterers, nor the unmanly, nor homosexuals, nor thieves, nor the covetous, nor drunkards, nor revilers, nor extortioners, shall inherit the Kingdom of God."[48] Now, if those who persist in such crimes as these are nevertheless saved by their faith in Christ, would they not then be in the Kingdom of God?

68. But, since these fully plain and most pertinent apostolic testimonies cannot be false, that one obscure saying about those who build on "the foundation, which is Christ, not gold, silver, and precious stones, but wood, hay, and stubble"[49]—for it is about these it is said that they will be saved as by fire, not perishing on account of the saving worth of their foundation— such a statement must be interpreted so that it does not contradict these fully plain testimonies.

In fact, wood and hay and stubble may be understood, without absurdity, to signify such an attachment to those worldly

---

[43] A short treatise, written in 413, in which Augustine seeks to combine the Pauline and Jacobite emphases by analyzing what kind of faith and what kind of works are *both* essential to salvation. The best text is that of Joseph Zycha in *CSEL*, Vol. 41, pp. 35–97; but see also Migne, *PL*, 40, c. 197–230. There is an English translation by C. L. Cornish in *A Library of Fathers of the Holy Catholic Church; Seventeen Short Treatises*, pp. 37–84.
[44] Gal. 5:6.   [45] James 2:17.   [46] James 2:14.
[47] I Cor. 3:15.   [48] I Cor. 6:9, 10.   [49] I Cor. 3:11, 12.

things—albeit legitimate in themselves—that one cannot suffer their loss without anguish in the soul. Now, when such anguish "burns," and Christ still holds his place as foundation in the heart—that is, if nothing is preferred to him and if the man whose anguish "burns" would still prefer to suffer loss of the things he greatly loves than to lose Christ—then one is saved, "by fire." But if, in time of testing, he should prefer to hold onto these temporal and worldly goods rather than to Christ, he does not have him as foundation—because he has put "things" in the first place—whereas in a building nothing comes before the foundations.

Now, this fire, of which the apostle speaks, should be understood as one through which both kinds of men must pass: that is, the man who builds with gold, silver, and precious stones on this foundation and also the man who builds with wood, hay, and stubble. For, when he had spoken of this, he added: "The fire shall try every man's work, of what sort it is. If any man's work abides which he has built thereupon, he shall receive a reward. If any man's work burns up, he shall suffer loss; but he himself shall be saved, yet so as by fire." [50] Therefore the fire will test the work, not only of the one, but of both.

The fire is a sort of trial of affliction, concerning which it is clearly written elsewhere: "The furnace tries the potter's vessels and the trial of affliction tests righteous men." [51] This kind of fire works in the span of this life, just as the apostle said, as it affects the two different kinds of faithful men. There is, for example, the man who "thinks of the things of God, how he may please God." Such a man builds on Christ the foundation, with gold, silver, and precious stones. The other man "thinks about the things of the world, how he may please his wife" [52]; that is, he builds upon the same foundation with wood, hay, and stubble. The work of the former is not burned up, since he has not loved those things whose loss brings anguish. But the work of the latter is burned up, since things are not lost without anguish when they have been loved with a possessive love. But because, in this second situation, he prefers to suffer the loss of these things rather than losing Christ, and does not desert Christ from fear of losing such things—even though he may grieve over his loss—"he is saved," indeed, "yet so as by fire." He "burns" with grief, for the things he has loved and lost, but this does not subvert nor consume him, secured as he is by the stability and the indestructibility of his foundation.

[50] I Cor. 3:11-15.   [51] Ecclus. 27:5.   [52] Cf. I Cor. 7:32, 33.

69. It is not incredible that something like this should occur after this life, whether or not it is a matter for fruitful inquiry. It may be discovered or remain hidden whether some of the faithful are sooner or later to be saved by a sort of purgatorial fire, in proportion as they have loved the goods that perish, and in proportion to their attachment to them. However, this does not apply to those of whom it was said, "They shall not possess the Kingdom of God,"[53] unless their crimes are remitted through due repentance. I say "due repentance" to signify that they must not be barren of almsgiving, on which divine Scripture lays so much stress that our Lord tells us in advance that, on the bare basis of fruitfulness in alms, he will impute merit to those on his right hand; and, on the same basis of unfruitfulness, demerit to those on his left—when he shall say to the former, "Come, blessed of my Father, receive the Kingdom," but to the latter, "Depart into everlasting fire."[54]

CHAPTER XIX

ALMSGIVING AND FORGIVENESS

70. We must beware, however, lest anyone suppose that unspeakable crimes such as they commit who "will not possess the Kingdom of God" can be perpetrated daily and then daily redeemed by almsgiving. Of course, life must be changed for the better, and alms should be offered as propitiation to God for our past sins. But he is not somehow to be bought off, as if we always had a license to commit crimes with impunity. For, "he has given no man a license to sin"[55]—although, in his mercy, he does blot out sins already committed, if due satisfaction for them is not neglected.

71. For the passing and trivial sins of every day, from which no life is free, the everyday prayer of the faithful makes satisfaction. For they can say, "Our Father who art in heaven," who have already been reborn to such a Father "by water and the Spirit."[56] This prayer completely blots out our minor and everyday sins. It also blots out those sins which once made the life of the faithful wicked, but from which, now that they have changed for the better by repentance, they have departed. The condition of this is that just as they truly say, "Forgive us our

[53] See above, XVIII, 67.   [54] Matt. 25:34, 41.
[55] Ecclus. 15:20.   [56] John 3:5.

debts" (since there is no lack of debts to be forgiven), so also they truly say, "As we forgive our debtors" [57]; that is, if what is said is also done. For to forgive a man who seeks forgiveness is indeed to give alms.

72. Accordingly, what our Lord says—"Give alms and, behold, all things are clean to you" [58]—applies to all useful acts of mercy. Therefore, not only the man who gives food to the hungry, drink to the thirsty, clothing to the naked, hospitality to the wayfarer, refuge to the fugitive; who visits the sick and the prisoner, redeems the captive, bears the burdens of the weak, leads the blind, comforts the sorrowful, heals the sick, shows the errant the right way, gives advice to the perplexed, and does whatever is needful for the needy [59]—not only does this man give alms, but the man who forgives the trespasser also gives alms as well. He is also a giver of alms who, by blows or other discipline, corrects and restrains those under his command, if at the same time he forgives from the heart the sin by which he has been wronged or offended, or prays that it be forgiven the offender. Such a man gives alms, not only in that he forgives and prays, but also in that he rebukes and administers corrective punishment, since in this he shows mercy.

Now, many benefits are bestowed on the unwilling, when their interests and not their preferences are consulted. And men frequently are found to be their own enemies, while those they suppose to be their enemies are their true friends. And then, by mistake, they return evil for good, when a Christian ought not to return evil even for evil. Thus, there are many kinds of alms, by which, when we do them, we are helped in obtaining forgiveness of our own sins.

73. But none of these alms is greater than the forgiveness from the heart of a sin committed against us by someone else. It is a smaller thing to wish well or even to do well to one who has done you no evil. It is far greater—a sort of magnificent goodness—to love your enemy, and always to wish him well and, as you can, *do* well to him who wishes you ill and who does you harm when he can. Thus one heeds God's command: "Love your enemies, do good to them that hate you, and pray for them that persecute you." [60]

Such counsels are for the perfect sons of God. And although

---

[57] Matt. 6:9–12.   [58] Cf. Luke 11:41.

[59] This is a close approximation of the medieval lists of "The Seven Works of Mercy." Cf. J. T. McNeill, *A History of the Cure of Souls*, pp. 155, 161. (Harper & Brothers, 1951, New York.)   [60] Matt. 5:44.

all the faithful should strive toward them and through prayer to God and earnest endeavor bring their souls up to this level, still so high a degree of goodness is not possible for so great a multitude as we believe are heard when, in prayer, they say, "Forgive us our debts, as we forgive our debtors." Accordingly, it cannot be doubted that the terms of this pledge are fulfilled if a man, not yet so perfect that he already loves his enemies, still forgives from the heart one who has sinned against him and who now asks his forgiveness. For he surely seeks forgiveness when he asks for it when he prays, saying, "As we forgive our debtors." For this means, "Forgive us our debts when we ask for forgiveness, as we also forgive our debtors when they ask for forgiveness."

74. Again, if one seeks forgiveness from a man against whom he sinned—moved by his sin to seek it—he should no longer be regarded as an enemy, and it should not now be as difficult to love him as it was when he was actively hostile.

Now, a man who does not forgive from the heart one who asks forgiveness and is repentant of his sins can in no way suppose that his own sins are forgiven by the Lord, since the Truth cannot lie, and what hearer and reader of the gospel has not noted who it was who said, "I am the Truth"[61]? It is, of course, the One who, when he was teaching the prayer, strongly emphasized this sentence which he put in it, saying: "For if you forgive men their trespasses, your Heavenly Father will also forgive you your trespasses. But if you will not forgive men, neither will your Father forgive you your offenses."[62] He who is not awakened by such great thundering is not asleep, but dead. And yet such a word has power to awaken even the dead.

CHAPTER XX

SPIRITUAL ALMSGIVING

75. Now, surely, those who live in gross wickedness and take no care to correct their lives and habits, who yet, amid their crimes and misdeeds, continue to multiply their alms, flatter themselves in vain with the Lord's words, "Give alms; and, behold, all things are clean to you." They do not understand how far this saying reaches. In order for them to understand, let them notice to whom it was that he said it. For this is the context of

---

[61] John 14:6.   [62] Matt. 6:14, 15.

it in the Gospel: "As he was speaking, a certain Pharisee asked him to dine with him. And he went in and reclined at the table. And the Pharisee began to wonder and ask himself why He had not washed himself before dinner. But the Lord said to him: 'Now you Pharisees clean the outside of the cup and the dish, but within you are still full of extortion and wickedness. Foolish ones! Did not He who made the outside make the inside too? Nevertheless, give for alms what remains within; and, behold, all things are clean to you.' " [63] Should we interpret this to mean that to the Pharisees, who had not the faith of Christ, all things are clean if only they give alms, as they deem it right to give them, even if they have not believed in him, nor been reborn of water and the Spirit? But all are unclean who are not made clean by the faith of Christ, of whom it is written, "Cleansing their hearts by faith."[64] And as the apostle said, "But to them that are unclean and unbelieving nothing is clean; both their minds and consciences are unclean." [65] How, then, should all things be clean to the Pharisees, even if they gave alms, but were not believers? Or, how could they be believers, if they were unwilling to believe in Christ and to be born again in his grace? And yet, what they heard is true: "Give alms; and behold, all things are clean to you."

76. He who would give alms as a set plan of his life should begin with himself and give them to himself. For almsgiving is a work of mercy, and the saying is most true: "Have mercy upon your own soul, pleasing God." [66] The purpose of the new birth is that we should become pleasing to God, who is justly displeased with the sin we contracted in birth. This is the first almsgiving, which we give to ourselves—when through the mercy of a merciful God we come to inquire about our wretchedness and come to acknowledge the just verdict by which we were put in need of that mercy, of which the apostle says, "Judgment came by that one trespass to condemnation." [67] And the same herald of grace then adds (in a word of thanksgiving for God's great love), "But God commendeth his love toward us in that, while we were yet sinners, Christ died for us." [68] Thus, when we come to a valid estimate of our wretchedness and begin to love God with the love he himself giveth us, we then begin to live piously and righteously.

But the Pharisees, while they gave as alms a tithing of even the least of their fruits, disregarded this "judgment and love

---

[63] Luke 11:37–41.   [64] Acts 15:9.   [65] Titus 1:15.
[66] Ecclus. 30:24 (Vulgate).   [67] Rom. 5:16.   [68] Rom. 5:8.

of God." Therefore, they did not begin their almsgiving with themselves, nor did they, first of all, show mercy toward themselves. In reference to this right order of self-love, it was said, "You shall love your neighbor as yourself." [69]

Therefore, when the Lord had reproved the Pharisees for washing themselves on the outside while inwardly they were still full of extortion and wickedness, he then admonished them also to give those alms which a man owes first to himself—to make clean the inner man: "However," he said, "give what remains as alms, and, behold, all things are clean to you." Then, to make plain the import of his admonition, which they had ignored, and to show them that he was not ignorant of their kind of almsgiving, he adds, "But woe to you, Pharisees" [70]—as if to say, "I am advising you to give the kind of alms which shall make all things clean to you." "But woe to you, for you tithe mint and rue and every herb"—"I know these alms of yours and you need not think I am admonishing you to give them up" —"and then neglect justice and the love of God." "*This* kind of almsgiving would make you clean from all inward defilement, just as the bodies which you wash are made clean by you." For the word "all" here means both "inward" and "outward"—as elsewhere we read, "Make clean the inside, and the outside will become clean." [71]

But, lest it appear that he was rejecting the kind of alms we give of the earth's bounty, he adds, "These things you should do"—that is, pay heed to the judgment and love of God—and "not omit the others"—that is, alms done with the earth's bounty.

77. Therefore, let them not deceive themselves who suppose that by giving alms—however profusely, and whether of their fruits or money or anything else—they purchase impunity to continue in the enormity of their crimes and the grossness of their wickedness. For not only do they do such things, but they also love them so much that they would always choose to continue in them—if they could do so with impunity. "But he who loves iniquity hates his own soul." [72] And he who hates his own soul is not merciful but cruel to it. For by loving it after the world's way he hates it according to God's way of judging. Therefore, if one really wished to give alms to himself, that all things might become clean to him, he would hate his soul after the world's way and love it according to God's way. No one,

[69] Luke 10:27.   [70] Luke 11:42.
[71] Matt. 23:26.   [72] Ps. 10:6 (Vulgate).

however, gives any alms at all unless he gives from the store of Him who needs not anything. "Accordingly," it is said, "His mercy shall go before me." [73]

CHAPTER XXI

PROBLEMS OF CASUISTRY

78. What sins are trivial and what are grave, however, is not for human but for divine judgment to determine. For we see that, in respect of some sins, even the apostle, by pardoning them, has conceded this point. Such a case is seen in what the venerable Paul says to married folks: "Do not deprive one another, except by consent for a time to give yourselves to prayer, and then return together lest Satan tempt you at the point of self-control." [74] One could consider that it is not a sin for a married couple to have intercourse, not only for the sake of procreating children—which is the good of marriage—but also for the sake of the carnal pleasure involved. Thus, those whose self-control is weak could avoid fornication, or adultery, and other kinds of impurity too shameful to name, into which their lust might drag them through Satan's tempting. Therefore one could, as I said, consider this not a sin, had the apostle not added, "But I say this as a concession, not as a rule." Who, then, denies that it is a sin when he agrees that apostolic authority for doing it is given only by "concession"?

Another such case is seen where he says, "Dare any of you, having a case against another, bring it to be judged before the unrighteous and not the saints?" [75] And a bit later: "If, therefore, you have cases concerning worldly things," he says, "you appoint those who are contemptible in the Church's eyes. I say this to shame you. Can it be that there is not a wise man among you, who could judge between his brethren? But brother goes to law with brother, and that in the presence of unbelievers." [76] And here it might be thought that it was not a sin to bring suit against a brother, and that the only sin consisted in wishing it judged outside the Church, if the apostle had not added immediately, "Now therefore the whole fault among you is that you have lawsuits with one another." [77] Then, lest someone excuse himself on this point by saying that he had a just cause

---

[73] Ps. 58:11 (Vulgate); cf. Ps. 59:10 (R.S.V.).
[74] I Cor. 7:5 (mixed text).   [75] I Cor. 6:1.
[76] I Cor. 6:4-6.   [77] I Cor. 6:7a.

and was suffering injustice which he wished removed by judicial sentence, the apostle directly resists such thoughts and excuses by saying: "Why not rather suffer iniquity? Why not rather be defrauded?" [78] Thus we are brought back to that saying of the Lord: "If anyone would take your tunic and contend in court with you, let go your cloak also." [79] And in another place: "If a man takes away your goods, seek them not back." [80] Thus, he forbids his own to go to court with other men in secular suits. And it is because of this teaching that the apostle says that this kind of action is "a fault." Still, when he allows such suits to be decided in the Church, brothers judging brothers, yet sternly forbids such a thing outside the Church, it is clear that some concession is being made here for the infirmities of the weak.

Because of these and similar sins—and of others even less than these, such as offenses in words and thoughts—and because, as the apostle James confesses, "we all offend in many things," [81] it behooves us to pray to the Lord daily and often, and say, "Forgive us our debts," and not lie about what follows this petition, "As we also forgive our debtors."

79. There are, however, some sins that could be deemed quite trifling if the Scriptures did not show that they are more serious than we think. For who would suppose that one saying to his brother, "You fool," is "in danger of hell-fire," if the Truth had not said it? Still, for the hurt he immediately supplied a medicine, adding the precept of brotherly reconciliation: "If, therefore, you are offering a gift at the altar, and remember there that your brother has something against you," [82] etc.

Or who would think how great a sin it is to observe days and months and years and seasons—as those people do who will or will not begin projects on certain days or in certain months or years, because they follow vain human doctrines and suppose that various seasons are lucky or unlucky—if we did not infer the magnitude of this evil from the apostle's fear, in saying to such men, "I fear for you, lest perhaps I have labored among you in vain" [83]?

80. To this one might add those sins, however grave and terrible, which, when they come to be habitual, are then believed to be trivial or no sins at all. And so far does this go that

[78] I Cor. 6:7b.
[80] Luke 6:30.
[82] Matt. 5:22, 23.
[79] Matt. 5:40.
[81] James 3:2 (Vulgate).
[83] Gal. 4:11 (Vulgate).

such sins are not only not kept secret, but are even proclaimed and published abroad—cases of which it is written, "The sinner is praised in the desires of his soul; and he that works iniquity is blessed." [84]

In the divine books such iniquity is called a "cry" (clamor). You have such a usage in the prophet Isaiah's reference to the evil vineyard: "I looked that he should perform justice, yet he did iniquity; not justice but a cry." [85] So also is that passage in Genesis: "The cry of Sodom and Gomorrah is multiplied," [86] for among these people such crimes were not only unpunished, but were openly committed, as if sanctioned by law.

So also in our times so many evils, even if not like those [of old], have come to be public customs that we not only do not dare excommunicate a layman; we do not dare degrade a clergyman for them. Thus, several years ago, when I was expounding the Epistle to the Galatians, where the apostle says, "I fear for you, lest perchance I have labored in vain among you," I was moved to exclaim: "Woe to the sins of men! We shrink from them only when we are not accustomed to them. As for those sins to which we are accustomed—although the blood of the Son of God was shed to wash them away—although they are so great that the Kingdom of God is wholly closed to them, yet, living with them often we come to tolerate them, and, tolerating them, we even practice some of them! But grant, O Lord, that we do not practice any of them which we could prohibit!" I shall someday know whether immoderate indignation moved me here to speak rashly.

CHAPTER XXII

THE TWO CAUSES OF SIN

81. I shall now mention what I have often discussed before in other places in my short treatises. [87] We sin from two causes: either from not seeing what we ought to do, or else from not doing what we have already seen we ought to do. Of these two, the first is ignorance of the evil; the second, weakness.

---

[84] Ps. 10:3 (Vulgate).　　　　[85] Isa. 5:7 (LXX).
[86] Gen. 18:20 (Vulgate with one change).
[87] For example, Contra Faust., XXII, 78; De pecc. meritis et remissione, I, xxxix, 70; ibid., II, xxii, 26; Quaest. in Heptateuch, 4:24; De libero arbitrio, 3:18, 55; De div. quaest., 83: 26; De natura et gratia, 67: 81; Contra duas ep. Pelag., I:3, 7; I: 13: 27.

We must surely fight against both; but we shall as surely be defeated unless we are divinely helped, not only to see what we ought to do, but also, as sound judgment increases, to make our love of righteousness victor over our love of those things because of which—either by desiring to possess them or by fearing to lose them—we fall, open-eyed, into known sin. In this latter case, we are not only sinners—which we are even when we sin through ignorance—but also lawbreakers: for we do not do what we should, and we do what we know already we should not.

Accordingly, we should pray for pardon if we have sinned, as we do when we say, "Forgive us our debts as we also forgive our debtors." But we should also pray that God should guide us away from sin, and this we do when we say, "Lead us not into temptation"—and we should make our petitions to Him of whom it is said in the psalm, "The Lord is my light and my salvation" [88]; that, as Light, he may take away our ignorance, as Salvation, our weakness.

82. Now, penance itself is often omitted because of weakness, even when in Church custom there is an adequate reason why it should be performed. For shame is the fear of displeasing men, when a man loves their good opinion more than he regards judgment, which would make him humble himself in penitence. Wherefore, not only for one to repent, but also in order that he may be enabled to do so, the mercy of God is prerequisite. Otherwise, the apostle would not say of some men, "In case God giveth them repentance." [89] And, similarly, that Peter might be enabled to weep bitterly, the Evangelist tells, "The Lord looked at him." [90]

83. But the man who does not believe that sins are forgiven in the Church, who despises so great a bounty of the divine gifts and ends, and persists to his last day in such an obstinacy of mind—that man is guilty of the unpardonable sin against the Holy Spirit, in whom Christ forgiveth sins. [91] I have discussed this difficult question, as clearly as I could, in a little book devoted exclusively to this very point. [92]

[88] Ps. 27:1. [89] II Tim. 2:25 (mixed text).
[90] Cf. Luke 22:61. [91] Cf. John 20:22, 23.
[92] This *libellus* is included in Augustine's *Sermons* (LXXI, *PL*, 38, col. 445–467), to which Possidius gave the title *De blasphemia in Spiritum Sanctum*. English translation in *N–PNF*, 1st Series, Vol. VI, Sermon XXI, pp. 318–332.

CHAPTER XXIII

THE REALITY OF THE RESURRECTION

84. Now, with respect to the resurrection of the body—and by this I do not mean the cases of resuscitation after which people died again, but a resurrection to eternal life after the fashion of Christ's own body—I have not found a way to discuss it briefly and still give satisfactory answers to all the questions usually raised about it. Yet no Christian should have the slightest doubt as to the fact that the bodies of all men, whether already or yet to be born, whether dead or still to die, will be resurrected.

85. Once this fact is established, then, first of all, comes the question about abortive fetuses, which are indeed "born" in the mother's womb, but are never so that they could be "reborn." For, if we say that there is a resurrection for them, then we can agree that at least as much is true of fetuses that are fully formed. But, with regard to undeveloped fetuses, who would not more readily think that they perish, like seeds that did not germinate? [93]

But who, then, would dare to deny—though he would not dare to affirm it either—that in the resurrection day what is lacking in the forms of things will be filled out? Thus, the perfection which time would have accomplished will not be lacking, any more than the blemishes wrought by time will still be present. Nature, then, will be cheated of nothing apt and fitting which time's passage would have brought, nor will anything remain disfigured by anything adverse and contrary which time has wrought. But what is not yet a whole will become whole, just as what has been disfigured will be restored to its full figure.

86. On this score, a corollary question may be most carefully discussed by the most learned men, and still I do not know that any man can answer it, namely: When does a human being begin to live in the womb? Is there some form of hidden life, not yet apparent in the motions of a living thing? To deny, for example, that those fetuses ever lived at all which are cut away limb by limb and cast out of the wombs of pregnant women, lest the mothers die also if the fetuses were left there dead, would seem much too rash. But, in any case, once a man begins to live, it is thereafter possible for him to die. And, once dead, whereso-

[93] *Sicut semina quae concepta non fuerint.*

ever death overtook him, I cannot find the basis on which he would not have a share in the resurrection of the dead.

87. By the same token, the resurrection is not to be denied in the cases of monsters which are born and live, even if they quickly die, nor should we believe that they will be raised as they were, but rather in an amended nature and free from faults. Far be it from us to say of that double-limbed man recently born in the Orient—about whom most reliable brethren have given eyewitness reports and the presbyter Jerome, of holy memory, has left a written account [94]—far be it from us, I say, to suppose that at the resurrection there will be one double man, and not rather two men, as there would have been if they had actually been born twins. So also in other cases, which, because of some excess or defect or gross deformity, are called monsters: at the resurrection they will be restored to the normal human physiognomy, so that every soul will have its own body and not two bodies joined toether, even though they were born this way. Every soul will have, as its own, all that is required to complete a whole human body.

88. Moreover, with God, the earthly substance from which the flesh of mortal man is produced does not perish. Instead, whether it be dissolved into dust or ashes, or dispersed into vapors and the winds, or converted into the substance of other bodies (or even back into the basic elements themselves), or has served as food for beasts or even men and been turned into their flesh—in an instant of time this matter returns to the soul that first animated it, and that caused it to become a man, to live and to grow.

89. This earthly matter which becomes a corpse upon the soul's departure will not, at the resurrection, be so restored that the parts into which it was separated and which have become parts of other things must necessarily return to the same parts of the body in which they were situated—though they do return to the body from which they were separated. Otherwise, to suppose that the hair recovers what frequent clippings have taken off, or the nails get back what trimming has pared off, makes for a wild and wholly unbecoming image in the minds of those who speculate this way and leads them thus to disbelieve in the resurrection. But take the example of a statue made of fusible metal: if it were melted by heat or pounded into dust, or reduced to a shapeless mass, and an artist wished to restore it

[94] Jerome, *Epistle to Vitalis, Ep. LXXII*, 2; *PL*, 22, 674. Augustine also refers to similar phenomena in *The City of God*, XVI, viii, 2.

again from the mass of the same material, it would make no difference to the wholeness of the restored statue which part of it was remade of what part of the metal, so long as the statue, as restored, had been given all the material of which it was originally composed. Just so, God—an artist who works in marvelous and mysterious ways—will restore our bodies, with marvelous and mysterious celerity, out of the whole of the matter of which it was originally composed. And it will make no difference, in the restoration, whether hair returns to hair and nails to nails, or whether the part of this original matter that had perished is turned back into flesh and restored to other parts of the body. The main thing is that the providence of the [divine] Artist takes care that nothing unbecoming will result.

90. Nor does it follow that the stature of each person will be different when brought to life anew because there were differences in stature when first alive, nor that the lean will be raised lean or the fat come back to life in their former obesity. But if this is in the Creator's plan, that each shall retain his special features and the proper and recognizable likeness of his former self—while an equality of physical endowment will be preserved—then the matter of which each resurrection body is composed will be so disposed that none shall be lost, and any defect will be supplied by Him who can create out of nothing as he wills.

But if in the bodies of those rising again there is to be an intelligible inequality, such as between voices that fill out a chorus, this will be managed by disposing the matter of each body so to bring men into their place in the angelic band and impose nothing on their senses that is inharmonious. For surely nothing unseemly will be there, and whatever is there will be fitting, and this because the unfitting will simply not be.

91. The bodies of the saints, then, shall rise again free from blemish and deformity, just as they will be also free from corruption, encumbrance, or handicap. Their facility [*facilitas*] will be as complete as their felicity [*felicitas*]. This is why their bodies are called "spiritual," though undoubtedly they will be bodies and not spirits. For just as now the body is called "animate" [*animale*], though it is a body and not a "spirit" [*anima*], so then it will be a "spiritual body," but still a body and not a spirit.

Accordingly, then, as far as the corruption which weighs down the soul and the vices through which "the flesh lusts against the spirit"[95] are concerned, there will be no "flesh," but only

95 Gal. 5:17.

body, since there are bodies that are called "heavenly bodies." [96] This is why it is said, "Flesh and blood shall not inherit the Kingdom of God," and then, as if to expound what was said, it adds, "Neither shall corruption inherit incorruption." [97] What the writer first called "flesh and blood" he later called "corruption," and what he first called "the Kingdom of God" he then later called "incorruption."

But, as far as the substance of the resurrection body is concerned, it will even then still be "flesh." This is why the body of Christ is called "flesh" even after the resurrection. Wherefore the apostle also says, "What is sown a natural body [*corpus animale*] rises as a spiritual body [*corpus spirituale*]." [98] For there will then be such a concord between flesh and spirit—the spirit quickening the servant flesh without any need of sustenance therefrom—that there will be no further conflict within ourselves. And just as there will be no more external enemies to bear with, so neither shall we have to bear with ourselves as enemies within.

92. But whoever are not liberated from that mass of perdition (brought to pass through the first man) by the one Mediator between God and man, they will also rise again, each in his own flesh, but only that they may be punished together with the devil and his angels. Whether these men will rise again with all their faults and deformities, with their diseased and deformed members—is there any reason for us to labor such a question? For obviously the uncertainty about their bodily form and beauty need not weary us, since their damnation is certain and eternal. And let us not be moved to inquire how their body can be incorruptible if it can suffer—or corruptible if it cannot die. For there is no true life unless it be lived in happiness; no true incorruptibility save where health is unscathed by pain. But where an unhappy being is not allowed to die, then death itself, so to say, dies not; and where pain perpetually afflicts but never destroys, corruption goes on endlessly. This state is called, in the Scripture, "the second death." [99]

93. Yet neither the first death, in which the soul is compelled to leave its body, nor the second death, in which it is not allowed to leave the body undergoing punishment, would have befallen man if no one had sinned. Surely, the lightest of all punishments will be laid on those who have added no further sin to that originally contracted. Among the rest, who have added further

[96] I Cor. 15:40. [97] I Cor. 15:50.
[98] I Cor. 15:44. [99] Rev. 2:11; 20:6, 14.

sins to that one, they will suffer a damnation somewhat more tolerable in proportion to the lesser degree of their iniquity.

CHAPTER XXIV

THE SOLUTION TO PRESENT SPIRITUAL ENIGMAS TO BE AWAITED IN THE LIFE OF THE WORLD TO COME

94. And thus it will be that while the reprobated angels and men go on in their eternal punishment, the saints will go on learning more fully the blessings which grace has bestowed upon them. Then, through the actual realities of their experience, they will see more clearly the meaning of what is written in The Psalms: "I will sing to thee of mercy and judgment, O Lord" [1]—since no one is set free save by unmerited mercy and no one is damned save by a merited condemnation.

95. Then what is now hidden will not be hidden: when one of two infants is taken up by God's mercy and the other abandoned through God's judgment—and when the chosen one knows what would have been his just deserts in judgment—why was the one chosen rather than the other, when the condition of the two was the same? Or again, why were miracles not wrought in the presence of certain people who would have repented in the face of miraculous works, while miracles were wrought in the presence of those who were not about to believe. For our Lord saith most plainly: "Woe to you, Chorazin; woe to you, Bethsaida. For if in Tyre and Sidon had been wrought the miracles done in your midst, they would have repented long ago in sackcloth and ashes." [2] Now, obviously, God did not act unjustly in not willing their salvation, even though they could have been saved, if he willed it so. [3]

---

[1] Ps. 100:1 (Vulgate); cf. Ps. 101:1 (R.S.V.).   [2] Matt. 11:21.

[3] This is one of the rare instances in which a textual variant in Augustine's text affects a basic issue in the interpretation of his doctrine. All but one of the major old editions, up to and including Migne, here read: *Nec utique deus injuste noluit salvos fiere eum possent salvi esse SI VELLENT* (if *they* willed it). This would mean the attribution of a decisive role in human salvation to the human will and would thus stand out in bold relief from his general stress in the rest of the *Enchiridion* and elsewhere on the primacy and even irresistibility of grace. The Jansenist edition of Augustine, by Arnauld in 1648, read *SI VELLET* (if *He* willed it) and the reading became the subject of acrimonious controversy between the Jansenists and the Molinists. The Maurist edition reads *si vellet*, on the strength of much additional MS. evidence that had not been available up to that time. In

Then, in the clearest light of wisdom, will be seen what now the pious hold by faith, not yet grasping it in clear understanding—how certain, immutable, and effectual is the will of God, how there are things he can do but doth not will to do, yet willeth nothing he cannot do, and how true is what is sung in the psalm: "But our God is above in heaven; in heaven and on earth he hath done all things whatsoever that he would." [4] This obviously is not true, if there is anything that he willed to do and did not do, or, what were worse, if he did not do something because man's will prevented him, the Omnipotent, from doing what he willed. Nothing, therefore, happens unless the Omnipotent wills it to happen. He either allows it to happen or he actually causes it to happen.

96. Nor should we doubt that God doth well, even when he alloweth whatever happens ill to happen. For he alloweth it only through a just judgment—and surely all that is just is good. Therefore, although evil, in so far as it is evil, is not good, still it is a good thing that not only good things exist but evil as well. For if it were not good that evil things exist, they would certainly not be allowed to exist by the Omnipotent Good, for whom it is undoubtedly as easy not to allow to exist what he does not will, as it is for him to do what he does will.

Unless we believe this, the very beginning of our Confession of Faith is imperiled—the sentence in which we profess to believe in God the Father Almighty. For he is called Almighty for no other reason than that he can do whatsoever he willeth and because the efficacy of his omnipotent will is not impeded by the will of any creature.

97. Accordingly, we must now inquire about the meaning of what was said most truly by the apostle concerning God, "Who willeth that all men should be saved." [5] For since not all—not even a majority—are saved, it would indeed appear that the fact that what God willeth to happen does not happen is due to an embargo on God's will by the human will.

modern times, the *si vellet* reading has come to have the overwhelming support of the critical editors, although Rivière still reads *si vellent*. Cf. Scheel, 76–77 (See Bibl.); Rivière, 402–403; J.=G. Krabinger, *S. Aurelii Augustini Enchiridion* (Tübingen, 1861), p. 116; Faure-Passaglia, *S. Aurelii Augustini Enchiridion* (Naples, 1847), p. 178; and H. Hurter, *Sanctorum Patrum opuscula selecta* (Innsbruck, 1895), p. 123.

[4] Cf. Ps. 113:11 (a mixed text; composed inexactly from Ps. 115:3 and Ps. 135:6; an interesting instance of Augustine's sense of liberty with the texts of Scripture. Here he is doubtless quoting from memory).

[5] I Tim. 2:4.

Now, when we ask for the reason why not all are saved, the customary answer is: "Because they themselves have not willed it." But this cannot be said of infants, who have not yet come to the power of willing or not willing. For, if we could attribute to their wills the infant squirmings they make at baptism, when they resist as hard as they can, we would then have to say that they were saved against their will. But the Lord's language is clearer when, in the Gospel, he reproveth the unrighteous city: "How often," he saith, "would I have gathered your children together, as a hen gathers her chicks, and you would not."[6] This sounds as if God's will had been overcome by human wills and as if the weakest, by not willing, impeded the Most Powerful so that he could not do what he willed. And where is that omnipotence by which "whatsoever he willed in heaven and on earth, he has done," if he willed to gather the children of Jerusalem together, and did not do so? Or, is it not rather the case that, although Jerusalem did not will that her children be gathered together by him, yet, despite her unwillingness, God did indeed gather together those children of hers whom he would? It is not that "in heaven and on earth" he hath willed and done some things, and willed other things and not done them. Instead, "all things whatsoever he willed, he hath done."

CHAPTER XXV

PREDESTINATION AND THE JUSTICE OF GOD

98. Furthermore, who would be so impiously foolish as to say that God cannot turn the evil wills of men—as he willeth, when he willeth, and where he willeth—toward the good? But, when he acteth, he acteth through mercy; when he doth not act, it is through justice. For, "he hath mercy on whom he willeth; and whom he willeth, he hardeneth."[7]

Now when the apostle said this, he was commending grace, of which he had just spoken in connection with the twin children in Rebecca's womb: "Before they had yet been born, or had done anything good or bad, in order that the electing purpose of God might continue—not through works but through the divine calling—it was said of them, 'The elder shall serve the younger.' "[8] Accordingly, he refers to another prophetic witness, where it is written, "Jacob I loved, but Esau have I

---

[6] Matt. 23:37.   [7] Rom. 9:18.   [8] Rom. 9:11, 12.

hated." 9 Then, realizing how what he said could disturb those whose understanding could not penetrate to this depth of grace, he adds: "What therefore shall we say to this? Is there unrighteousness in God? God forbid!" 10 Yet it does seem unfair that, without any merit derived from good works or bad, God should love the one and hate the other. Now, if the apostle had wished us to understand that there were future good deeds of the one, and evil deeds of the other—which God, of course, foreknew—he would never have said "not of good works" but rather "of *future* works." Thus he would have solved the difficulty; or, rather, he would have left no difficulty to be solved. As it is, however, when he went on to exclaim, "God forbid!"—that is, "God forbid that there should be unfairness in God"—he proceeds immediately to add (to prove that no unfairness in God is involved here), "For he says to Moses, 'I will have mercy on whom I will have mercy, and I will show pity to whom I will show pity.' " 11 Now, who but a fool would think God unfair either when he imposes penal judgment on the deserving or when he shows mercy to the undeserving? Finally, the apostle concludes and says, "Therefore, it is not a question of him who wills nor of him who runs but of God's showing mercy."12

Thus, both the twins were "by nature children of wrath," 13 not because of any works of their own, but because they were both bound in the fetters of damnation originally forged by Adam. But He who said, "I will have mercy on whom I will have mercy," loved Jacob in unmerited mercy, yet hated Esau with merited justice. Since this judgment [of wrath] was due them both, the former learned from what happened to the other that the fact that he had not, with equal merit, incurred the same penalty gave him no ground to boast of his own distinctive merits—but, instead, that he should glory in the abundance of divine grace, because "it is not a question of him who wills nor of him who runs, but of God's showing mercy." 14 And, indeed, the whole visage of Scripture and, if I may speak so, the lineaments of its countenance, are found to exhibit a mystery, most profound and salutary, to admonish all who carefully look thereupon "that he who glories, should glory in the Lord." 15

9 Cf. Mal. 1:2, 3 and Rom. 9:13.   10 Rom. 9:14.   11 Rom. 9:15.
12 Rom. 9:15; see above, IX, 32.   13 Eph. 2:3.   14 Rom. 9:16.
15 I Cor. 1:31; cf. Jer. 9:24. The *religious* intention of Augustine's emphasis upon divine sovereignty and predestination is never so much to account for the doom of the wicked as to underscore the sheer and wonderful gratuity of salvation.

99. Now, after the apostle had commended God's mercy in saying, "So then, there is no question of him who wills nor of him who runs, but of God's showing mercy," next in order he intends to speak also of his judgment—for where his mercy is not shown, it is not unfairness but justice. For with God there is no injustice. Thus, he immediately added, "For the Scripture says to Pharaoh, 'For this very purpose I raised you up, that I may show through you my power, and that my name may be proclaimed in all the earth.'"[16] Then, having said this, he draws a conclusion that looks both ways, that is, toward mercy and toward judgment: "Therefore," he says, "he hath mercy on whom he willeth, and whom he willeth he hardeneth." He showeth mercy out of his great goodness; he hardeneth out of no unfairness at all. In this way, neither does he who is saved have a basis for glorying in any merit of his own; nor does the man who is damned have a basis for complaining of anything except what he has fully merited. For grace alone separates the redeemed from the lost, all having been mingled together in the one mass of perdition, arising from a common cause which leads back to their common origin. But if any man hears this in such a way as to say: "Why then does he find fault? For who resists his will?"[17]—as if to make it seem that man should not therefore be blamed for being evil *because* God "hath mercy on whom he willeth and whom he willeth he hardeneth"—God forbid that we should be ashamed to give the same reply as we see the apostle giving: "O man, who are you to reply to God? Does the molded object say to the molder, 'Why have you made me like this?' Or is not the potter master of his clay, to make from the same mass one vessel for honorable, another for ignoble, use?"[18]

There are some stupid men who think that in this part of the argument the apostle had no answer to give; and, for lack of a reasonable rejoinder, simply rebuked the audacity of his gainsayer. But what he said—"O man, who are you?"— has actually great weight and in an argument like this recalls man, in a single word, to consider the limits of his capacity and, at the same time, supplies an important explanation.

For if one does not understand these matters, who is he to talk back to God? And if one does understand, he finds no better ground even then for talking back. For if he understands, he sees that the whole human race was condemned in its apos-

16 Rom. 9:17; cf. Ex. 9:16.   17 Rom. 9:19.
18 Rom. 9:20, 21.

tate head by a divine judgment so just that not even if a single member of the race were ever saved from it, no one could rail against God's justice. And he also sees that those who are saved had to be saved on such terms that it would show—by contrast with the greater number of those not saved but simply abandoned to their wholly just damnation—what the whole mass deserved and to what end God's merited judgment would have brought them, had not his undeserved mercy interposed. Thus every mouth of those disposed to glory in their own merits should be stopped, so that "he that glories may glory in the Lord."[19]

CHAPTER XXVI

The Triumph of God's Sovereign Good Will

100. These are "the great works of the Lord, well-considered in all his acts of will"[20]—and so wisely well-considered that when his angelic and human creation sinned (that is, did not do what he willed, but what it willed) he could still accomplish what he himself had willed and this through the same creaturely will by which the first act contrary to the Creator's will had been done. As the Supreme Good, he made good use of evil deeds, for the damnation of those whom he had justly predestined to punishment and for the salvation of those whom he had mercifully predestined to grace.

For, as far as they were concerned, they did what God did not will that they do, but as far as God's omnipotence is concerned, they were quite unable to achieve their purpose. In their very act of going against his will, his will was thereby accomplished. This is the meaning of the statement, "The works of the Lord are great, well-considered in all his acts of will"—that in a strange and ineffable fashion even that which is done against his will is not done without his will. For it would not be done without his allowing it—and surely his permission is not unwilling but willing—nor would he who is good allow the evil to be done, unless in his omnipotence he could bring good even out of evil.

101. Sometimes, however, a man of good will wills something that God doth not will, even though God's will is much more, and much more certainly, good—for under no circumstances can it ever be evil. For example, it is a good son's will that his father

---

[19] I Cor. 1:31.   [20] Ps. 110:2 (Vulgate).

live, whereas it is God's good will that he should die. Or, again, it can happen that a man of evil will can will something that God also willeth with a good will—as, for example, a bad son wills that his father die and this is also God's will. Of course, the former wills what God doth not will, whereas the latter does will what God willeth. Yet the piety of the one, though he wills not what God willeth, is more consonant with God's will than is the impiety of the other, who wills the same thing that God willeth. There is a very great difference between what is fitting for man to will and what is fitting for God—and also between the ends to which a man directs his will—and this difference determines whether an act of will is to be approved or disapproved. Actually, God achieveth some of his purposes—which are, of course, all good—through the evil wills of bad men. For example, it was through the ill will of the Jews that, by the good will of the Father, Christ was slain for us—a deed so good that when the apostle Peter would have nullified it he was called "Satan" by him who had come in order to be slain.[21] How good seemed the purposes of the pious faithful who were unwilling that the apostle Paul should go to Jerusalem, lest there he should suffer the things that the prophet Agabus had predicted![22] And yet God had willed that he should suffer these things for the sake of the preaching of Christ, and for the training of a martyr for Christ. And this good purpose of his he achieved, not through the good will of the Christians, but through the ill will of the Jews. Yet they were more fully his who did not will what he willed than were those who were willing instruments of his purpose—for while he and the latter did the very same thing, he worked through them with a good will, whereas they did his good will with their ill will.

102. But, however strong the wills either of angels or of men, whether good or evil, whether they will what God willeth or will something else, the will of the Omnipotent is always undefeated. And this will can never be evil, because even when it inflicts evils, it is still just; and obviously what is just is not evil. Therefore, whether through pity "he hath mercy on whom he willeth," or in justice "whom he willeth, he hardeneth," the omnipotent God never doth anything except what he doth will, and doth everything that he willeth.

[21] Matt. 16:23.   [22] Acts 21:10–12.

CHAPTER XXVII

Limits of God's Plan for Human Salvation

103. Accordingly, when we hear and read in sacred Scripture that God "willeth that all men should be saved," [23] although we know well enough that not all men are saved, we are not on that account to underrate the fully omnipotent will of God. Rather, we must understand the Scripture, "Who will have all men to be saved," as meaning that no man is saved unless God willeth his salvation: not that there is no man whose salvation he doth not will, but that no one is saved unless He willeth it. Moreover, his will should be sought in prayer, because if he willeth, then what he willeth must necessarily be. And, indeed, it was of prayer to God that the apostle was speaking when he made that statement. Thus, we are also to understand what is written in the Gospel about Him "who enlighteneth every man." [24] This means that there is no man who is enlightened except by God.

In any case, the word concerning God, "who will have all men to be saved," does not mean that there is no one whose salvation he doth not will—he who was unwilling to work miracles among those who, he said, would have repented if he had wrought them—but by "all men" we are to understand the whole of mankind, in every single group into which it can be divided: kings and subjects; nobility and plebeians; the high and the low; the learned and unlearned; the healthy and the sick; the bright, the dull, and the stupid; the rich, the poor, and the middle class; males, females, infants, children, the adolescent, young adults and middle-aged and very old; of every tongue and fashion, of all the arts, of all professions, with the countless variety of wills and minds and all the other things that differentiate people. For from which of these groups doth not God will that some men from every nation should be saved through his only-begotten Son our Lord? Therefore, he doth save them since the Omnipotent cannot will in vain, whatsoever he willeth.

Now, the apostle had enjoined that prayers should be offered "for all men" [25] and especially "for kings and all those of exalted station," [26] whose worldly pomp and pride could be supposed to be a sufficient cause for them to despise the humility of the Christian faith. Then, continuing his argument, "for this

[23] I Tim. 2:4.   [24] John 1:9.   [25] I Tim. 2:1.   [26] I Tim. 2:2.

A.C.E.—26

is good and acceptable in the sight of God our Saviour" [27]—
that is, to pray even for such as these [kings]—the apostle, to
remove any warrant for despair, added, "Who willeth that all
men be saved and come to the knowledge of the truth." [28] Truly,
then, God hath judged it good that through the prayers of the
lowly he would deign to grant salvation to the exalted—a paradox we have already seen exemplified. Our Lord also useth the
same manner of speech in the Gospel, where he saith to the
Pharisees, "You tithe mint and rue and every herb." [29] Obviously, the Pharisees did not tithe what belonged to others, nor
all the herbs of all the people of other lands. Therefore, just as
we should interpret "every herb" to mean "every kind of
herb," so also we can interpret "all men" to mean "all kinds of
men." We could interpret it in any other fashion, as long as
we are not compelled to believe that the Omnipotent hath
willed anything to be done which was not done. "He hath
done all things in heaven and earth, whatsoever he willed," [30] as
Truth sings of him, and surely he hath not willed to do anything
that he hath not done. There must be no equivocation on this
point.

CHAPTER XXVIII

The Destiny of Man

104. Consequently, God would have willed to preserve even
the first man in that state of salvation in which he was created
and would have brought him in due season, after the begetting
of children, to a better state without the intervention of death—
where he not only would have been unable to sin, but would
not have had even the will to sin—if he had foreknown that
man would have had a steadfast will to continue without sin,
as he had been created to do. But since he did foreknow that
man would make bad use of his free will—that is, that he would
sin—God prearranged his own purpose so that he could do good
to man, even in man's doing evil, and so that the good will of
the Omnipotent should be nullified by the bad will of men, but
should nonetheless be fulfilled.

105. Thus it was fitting that man should be created, in the
first place, so that he could will both good and evil—not without
reward, if he willed the good; not without punishment, if he
willed the evil. But in the future life he will not have the power
to will evil; and yet this will not thereby restrict his free will.

[27] I Tim. 2:3. [28] I Tim. 2:4. [29] Luke 11:42. [30] Ps. 135:6.

Indeed, his will will be much freer, because he will then have no power whatever to serve sin. For we surely ought not to find fault with such a will, nor say it is no will, or that it is not rightly called free, when we so desire happiness that we not only are unwilling to be miserable, but have no power whatsoever to will it.

And, just as in our present state, our soul is unable to will unhappiness for ourselves, so then it will be forever unable to will iniquity. But the ordered course of God's plan was not to be passed by, wherein he willed to show how good the rational creature is that is able not to sin, although one unable to sin is better.[31] So, too, it was an inferior order of immortality—but yet it was immortality—in which man was capable of not dying, even if the higher order which is to be is one in which man will be incapable of dying.[32]

106. Human nature lost the former kind of immortality through the misuse of free will. It is to receive the latter through grace—though it was to have obtained it through merit, if it had not sinned. Not even then, however, could there have been any merit without grace. For although sin had its origin in free will alone, still free will would not have been sufficient to maintain justice, save as divine aid had been afforded man, in the gift of participation in the immutable good. Thus, for example, the power to die when he wills it is in a man's own hands—since there is no one who could not kill himself by not eating (not to mention other means). But the bare will is not sufficient for maintaining life, if the aids of food and other means of preservation are lacking.

Similarly, man in paradise was capable of self-destruction by abandoning justice by an act of will; yet if the life of justice was to be maintained, his will alone would not have sufficed, unless He who made him had given him aid. But, after the Fall, God's mercy was even more abundant, for then the will itself had to be freed from the bondage in which sin and death are the masters. There is no way at all by which it can be freed by itself, but only through God's grace, which is made effectual in

---

[31] Another example of Augustine's wordplay. Man's original capacities included both the power not to sin and the power to sin (*posse non peccare et posse peccare*). In Adam's original sin, man lost the *posse non peccare* (the power not to sin) and retained the *posse peccare* (the power to sin)—which he continues to exercise. In the fulfillment of grace, man will have the *posse peccare* taken away and receive the highest of all, the power not to be able to sin, *non posse peccare*. Cf. *On Correction and Grace* XXXIII.

[32] Again, a wordplay between *posset non mori* and *non possit mori*.

the faith of Christ. Thus, as it is written, even the will by which "the will itself is prepared by the Lord"[33] so that we may receive the other gifts of God through which we come to the Gift eternal—this too comes from God.

107. Accordingly, even the life eternal, which is surely the wages of good works, is called a *gift* of God by the apostle. "For the wages of sin," he says, "is death; but the gift of God is eternal life in Christ Jesus our Lord."[34] Now, wages for military service are paid as a just debit, not as a gift. Hence, he said "the wages of sin is death," to show that death was not an unmerited punishment for sin but a just debit. But a gift, unless it be gratuitous, is not grace. We are, therefore, to understand that even man's merited goods are gifts from God, and when life eternal is given through them, what else do we have but "grace upon grace returned"[35]?

Man was, therefore, made upright, and in such a fashion that he could either continue in that uprightness—though not without divine aid—or become perverted by his own choice. Whichever of these two man had chosen, God's will would be done, either by man or at least *concerning* him. Wherefore, since man chose to do his own will instead of God's, God's will *concerning* him was done; for, from the same mass of perdition that flowed out of that common source, God maketh "one vessel for honorable, another for ignoble use"[36]; the ones for honorable use through his mercy, the ones for ignoble use through his judgment; lest anyone glory in man, or—what is the same thing—in himself.

108. Now, we could not be redeemed, even through "the one Mediator between God and man, Man himself, Christ Jesus,"[37] if he were not also God. For when Adam was made—being made an upright man—there was no need for a mediator. Once sin, however, had widely separated the human race from God, it was necessary for a mediator, who alone was born, lived, and was put to death without sin, to reconcile us to God, and provide even for our bodies a resurrection to life eternal—and all this in order that man's pride might be exposed and healed through God's humility. Thus it might be shown man how far he had departed from God, when by the incarnate God he is recalled to God; that man in his contumacy might be furnished an example of obedience by the God-Man; that the fount of grace might be opened up; that even the resurrection of the

---

[33] Prov. 8:35 (LXX).   [34] Rom. 6:23.   [35] Cf. John 1:16.
[36] Rom. 9:21.   [37] I Tim. 2:5 (mixed text).

body—itself promised to the redeemed—might be previewed in the resurrection of the Redeemer himself; that the devil might be vanquished by that very nature he was rejoicing over having deceived—all this, however, without giving man ground for glory in himself, lest pride spring up anew. And if there are other advantages accruing from so great a mystery of the Mediator, which those who profit from them can see or testify— even if they cannot be described—let them be added to this list.

CHAPTER XXIX

"The Last Things"

109. Now, for the time that intervenes between man's death and the final resurrection, there is a secret shelter for his soul, as each is worthy of rest or affliction according to what it has merited while it lived in the body.

110. There is no denying that the souls of the dead are benefited by the piety of their living friends, when the sacrifice of the Mediator is offered for the dead, or alms are given in the church. But these means benefit only those who, when they were living, have merited that such services could be of help to them. For there is a mode of life that is neither so good as not to need such helps after death nor so bad as not to gain benefit from them after death. There is, however, a good mode of life that does not need such helps, and, again, one so thoroughly bad that, when such a man departs this life, such helps avail him nothing. It is here, then, in this life, that all merit or demerit is acquired whereby a man's condition in the life hereafter is improved or worsened. Therefore, let no one hope to obtain any merit with God after he is dead that he has neglected to obtain here in this life.

So, then, those means which the Church constantly uses in interceding for the dead are not opposed to that statement of the apostle when he said, "For all of us shall stand before the tribunal of Christ, so that each may receive according to what he has done in the body, whether good or evil." [38] For each man has for himself while living in the body earned the merit whereby these means can benefit him [after death]. For they do not benefit all. And yet why should they not benefit all, unless it be because of the different kinds of lives men lead in the body? Accordingly, when sacrifices, whether of the altar or of

[38] Rom. 14:10; II Cor. 5:10.

alms, are offered for the baptized dead, they are thank offerings for the very good, propitiations for the not-so-very-bad [*non valde malis*], and, as for the very bad—even if they are of no help to the dead—they are at least a sort of consolation to the living. Where they are of value, their benefit consists either in obtaining a full forgiveness or, at least, in making damnation more tolerable.

111. After the resurrection, however, when the general judgment has been held and finished, the boundary lines will be set for the two cities: the one of Christ, the other of the devil; one for the good, the other for the bad—both including angels and men. In the one group, there will be no will to sin, in the other, no power to sin, nor any further possibility of dying. The citizens of the first commonwealth will go on living truly and happily in life eternal. The second will go on, miserable in death eternal, with no power to die to it. The condition of both societies will then be fixed and endless. But in the first city, some will outrank others in bliss, and in the second, some will have a more tolerable burden of misery than others.

112. It is quite in vain, then, that some—indeed very many— yield to merely human feelings and deplore the notion of the eternal punishment of the damned and their interminable and perpetual misery. They do not believe that such things will be. Not that they would go counter to divine Scripture— but, yielding to their own human feelings, they soften what seems harsh and give a milder emphasis to statements they believe are meant more to terrify than to express the literal truth. "God will not forget," they say, "to show mercy, nor in his anger will he shut up his mercy." This is, in fact, the text of a holy psalm.[39] But there is no doubt that it is to be interpreted to refer to those who are called "vessels of mercy,"[40] those who are freed from misery not by their own merits but through God's mercy. Even so, if they suppose that the text applies to all men, there is no ground for them further to suppose that there can be an end for those of whom it is said, "Thus these shall go into everlasting punishment."[41] Otherwise, it can as well be thought that there will also be an end to the happiness of those of whom the antithesis was said: "But the righteous into life eternal."

But let them suppose, if it pleases them, that, for certain intervals of time, the punishments of the damned are somewhat mitigated. Even so, the wrath of God must be understood as

39 Cf. Ps. 77:9.   40 Rom. 9:23.   41 Matt. 25:46.

still resting on them. And this is damnation—for this anger, which is not a violent passion in the divine mind, is called "wrath" in God. Yet even in his wrath—his wrath resting on them—he does not "shut up his mercy." This is not to put an end to their eternal afflictions, but rather to apply or interpose some little respite in their torments. For the psalm does not say, "To put an end to his wrath," or, "*After* his wrath," but, "*In* his wrath." Now, if this wrath were all there is [in man's damnation], and even if it were present only in the slightest degree conceivable—still, to be lost out of the Kingdom of God, to be an exile from the City of God, to be estranged from the life of God, to suffer loss of the great abundance of God's blessings which he has hidden for those who fear him and prepared for those who hope in him [42]—this would be a punishment so great that, if it be eternal, no torments that we know could be compared to it, no matter how many ages they continued.

113. The eternal death of the damned—that is, their estrangement from the life of God—will therefore abide without end, and it will be common to them all, no matter what some people, moved by their human feelings, may wish to think about gradations of punishment, or the relief or intermission of their misery. In the same way, the eternal life of the saints will abide forever, and also be common to all of them no matter how different the grades of rank and honor in which they shine forth in their effulgent harmony.

CHAPTER XXX

The Principles of Christian Living: Faith and Hope

114. Thus, from our confession of *faith*, briefly summarized in the Creed (which is milk for babes when pondered at the carnal level but food for strong men when it is considered and studied spiritually), there is born the good *hope* of the faithful, accompanied by a holy *love*.[43] But of these affirmations, all of which ought *faithfully* to be believed, only those which have to do with *hope* are contained in the Lord's Prayer. For "cursed is everyone," as the divine eloquence testified, "who rests his hope in man."[44] Thus, he who rests his hope in himself is bound by the bond of this curse. Therefore, we should seek

---

42 Cf. Ps. 31:19.
43 Note the artificial return to the triadic scheme of the treatise: faith, hope, and love.   44 Jer. 17:5.

from none other than the Lord God whatever it is that we hope to do well, or hope to obtain as reward for our good works.

115. Accordingly, in the Evangelist Matthew, the Lord's Prayer may be seen to contain seven petitions: three of them ask for eternal goods, the other four for temporal goods, which are, however, necessary for obtaining the eternal goods.

For when we say: "Hallowed be thy name. Thy Kingdom come. Thy will be done on earth, as it is in heaven" [45]—this last being wrongly interpreted by some as meaning "in body and spirit"—these blessings will be retained forever. They begin in this life, of course; they are increased in us as we make progress, but in their perfection—which is to be hoped for in the other life—they will be possessed forever! But when we say: "Give us this day our daily bread. And forgive us our debts, as we forgive our debtors. And lead us not into temptation, but deliver us from evil," [46] who does not see that all these pertain to our needs in the present life? In that life eternal—where we all hope to be—the hallowing of God's name, his Kingdom, and his will, in our spirit and body will abide perfectly and immortally. But in this life we ask for "daily bread" because it is necessary, in the measure required by soul and body, whether we take the term in a spiritual or bodily sense, or both. And here too it is that we petition for forgiveness, where the sins are committed; here too are the temptations that allure and drive us to sinning; here, finally, the evil from which we wish to be freed. But in that other world none of these things will be found.

116. However, the Evangelist Luke, in his version of the Lord's Prayer, has brought together, not seven, but five petitions. Yet, obviously, there is no discrepancy here, but rather, in his brief way, the Evangelist has shown us how the seven petitions should be understood. Actually, God's name is even now hallowed in the spirit, but the Kingdom of God is yet to come in the resurrection of the body. Therefore, Luke was seeking to show that the third petition ["Thy will be done"] is a repetition of the first two, and makes this better understood by omitting it. He then adds three other petitions, concerning daily bread, forgiveness of sins, and avoidance of temptation. [47] However, what Matthew puts in the last place, "But deliver us from evil," Luke leaves out, in order that we might understand that it was included in what was previously said about temptation. This is, indeed, why Matthew said, *"But* deliver us," instead of, *"And* deliver us," as if to indicate that there is only one

[45] Matt. 6:9, 10.   [46] Matt. 6:11–13.   [47] Luke 11:2–4.

petition—"Will not this, but that"—so that anyone would realize that he is being delivered from evil in that he is not being led into temptation.

CHAPTER XXXI

LOVE

117. And now regarding *love*, which the apostle says is greater than the other two—that is, faith and hope—for the more richly it dwells in a man, the better the man in whom it dwells. For when we ask whether someone is a good man, we are not asking what he believes, or hopes, but what he loves. Now, beyond all doubt, he who loves aright believes and hopes rightly. Likewise, he who does not love believes in vain, even if what he believes is true; he hopes in vain, even if what he hopes for is generally agreed to pertain to true happiness, unless he believes and hopes for this: that he may through prayer obtain the gift of love. For, although it is true that he cannot hope without love, it may be that there is something without which, if he does not love it, he cannot realize the object of his hopes. An example of this would be if a man hopes for life eternal—and who is there who does not love that?—and yet does not love *righteousness*, without which no one comes to it.

Now this is the true faith of Christ which the apostle commends: faith that works through love. And what it yet lacks in love it asks that it may receive, it seeks that it may find, and knocks that it may be opened unto it.[48] For faith achieves what the law commands [*fides namque impetrat quod lex imperat*]. And, without the gift of God—that is, without the Holy Spirit, through whom love is shed abroad in our hearts—the law may bid but it cannot aid [*jubere lex poterit, non juvare*]. Moreover, it can make of man a transgressor, who cannot then excuse himself by pleading ignorance. For appetite reigns where the love of God does not.[49]

118. When, in the deepest shadows of ignorance, he lives according to the flesh with no restraint of reason—this is the primal state of man.[50] Afterward, when "through the law the knowledge of sin"[51] has come to man, and the Holy Spirit has not yet come to his aid—so that even if he wishes to live according to the law, he is vanquished—man sins knowingly and

---

48 Matt. 7:7.   49 Another wordplay on *cupiditas* and *caritas*.
50 An interesting resemblance here to Freud's description of the Id, the primal core of our unconscious life.   51 Rom. 3:20.

is brought under the spell and made the slave of sin, "for by whatever a man is vanquished, of this master he is the slave" [52]. The effect of the knowledge of the law is that sin works in man the whole round of concupiscence, which adds to the guilt of the first transgression. And thus it is that what was written is fulfilled: "The law entered in, that the offense might abound." [53] This is the *second* state of man. [54]

But if God regards a man with solicitude so that he then believes in God's help in fulfilling His commands, and if a man begins to be led by the Spirit of God, then the mightier power of love struggles against the power of the flesh. [55] And although there is still in man a power that fights against him—his infirmity being not yet fully healed—yet he [the righteous man] lives by faith and lives righteously in so far as he does not yield to evil desires, conquering them by his love of righteousness. This is the *third* stage of the man of good hope.

A final peace is in store for him who continues to go forward in this course toward perfection through steadfast piety. This will be perfected beyond this life in the repose of the spirit, and, at the last, in the resurrection of the body.

Of these four different stages of man, the first is before the law, the second is under the law, the third is under grace, and the fourth is in full and perfect peace. Thus, also, the history of God's people has been ordered by successive temporal epochs, as it pleased God, who "ordered all things in measure and number and weight." [56] The first period was before the law; the second under the law, which was given through Moses; the next, under grace which was revealed through the first Advent of the Mediator. [57] This grace was not previously absent from those to whom it was to be imparted, although, in conformity to the temporal dispensations, it was veiled and hidden. For none of the righteous men of antiquity could find salvation apart from the faith of Christ. And, unless Christ had also been known to them, he could not have been prophesied to us—sometimes openly and sometimes obscurely—through their ministry.

119. Now, in whichever of these four "ages"—if one can call them that—the grace of regeneration finds a man, then and there all his past sins are forgiven him and the guilt he con-

---

[52] II Peter 2:19.   [53] Rom. 5:20.
[54] Compare the psychological notion of the effect of external moral pressures and their power to arouse guilt feelings, as in Freud's notion of "superego."   [55] Gal. 5:17.
[56] Wis. 11:21 (Vulgate).   [57] Cf. John 1:17.

tracted in being born is removed by his being reborn. And so true is it that "the Spirit breatheth where he willeth"[58] that some men have never known the second "age" of slavery under the law, but begin to have divine aid directly under the new commandment.

120. Yet, before a man can receive the commandment, he must, of course, live according to the flesh. But, once he has been imbued with the sacrament of rebirth, no harm will come to him even if he then immediately depart this life—"Wherefore on this account Christ died and rose again, that he might be the Lord of both the living and the dead."[59] Nor will the kingdom of death have dominion over him for whom He, who was "free among the dead,"[60] died.

CHAPTER XXXII

The End of All the Law

121. All the divine precepts are, therefore, referred back to *love*, of which the apostle says, "Now the end of the commandment is love, out of a pure heart, and a good conscience and a faith unfeigned."[61] Thus every commandment harks back to love. For whatever one does either in fear of punishment or from some carnal impulse, so that it does not measure up to the standard of love which the Holy Spirit sheds abroad in our hearts—whatever it is, it is not yet done as it should be, although it may seem to be. Love, in this context, of course includes both the love of God and the love of our neighbor and, indeed, "on these two commandments hang all the Law and the Prophets"[62]—and, we may add, the gospel and the apostles, for from nowhere else comes the voice, "The end of the commandment is love,"[63] and, "God is love."[64]

Therefore, whatsoever things God commands (and one of these is, "Thou shalt not commit adultery"[65]) and whatsoever things are not positively ordered but are strongly advised as good spiritual counsel (and one of these is, "It is a good thing for a man not to touch a woman"[66])—all of these imperatives are rightly obeyed only when they are measured by the standard of our love of God and our love of our neighbor in God [*propter Deum*]. This applies both in the present age and in the world

[58] John 3:8.   [59] Rom. 14:9.   [60] Cf. Ps. 88:5.
[61] I Tim. 1:5.   [62] Matt. 22:40.   [63] I Tim. 1:5.
[64] I John 4:16.   [65] Ex. 20:14; Matt. 5:27; etc.   [66] I Cor. 7:1.

to come. Now we love God in faith; then, at sight. For, though mortal men ourselves, we do not know the hearts of mortal men. But then "the Lord will illuminate the hidden things in the darkness and will make manifest the cogitations of the heart; and then shall each one have his praise from God" [67]—for what will be praised and loved in a neighbor by his neighbor is just that which, lest it remain hidden, God himself will bring to light. Moreover, passion decreases as love increases [68] until love comes at last to that fullness which cannot be surpassed, "for greater love than this no one has, that a man lay down his life for his friends." [69] Who, then, can explain how great the power of love will be, when there will be no passion [*cupiditas*] for it to restrain or overcome? For, then, the supreme state of true health [*summa sanitas*] will have been reached, when the struggle with death shall be no more.

CHAPTER XXXIII

CONCLUSION

122. But somewhere this book must have an end. You can see for yourself whether you should call it an *Enchiridion*, or use it as one. But since I have judged that your zeal in Christ ought not to be spurned and since I believe and hope for good things for you through the help of our Redeemer, and since I love you greatly as one of the members of his body, I have written this book for you—may its usefulness match its prolixity!—on Faith, Hope, and Love.

[67] I Cor. 4:5.   [68] *Minuitur autem cupiditas caritate crescente.*   [69] John 15:13.

SELECTED BIBLIOGRAPHY

The literature on Augustine is enormous; in a short list, one cannot include all of even the best books and articles. The following titles will, however, serve as a useful and reliable introduction. Thereafter, the interested student should be qualified to guide himself.

The Confessions
TEXTS

Saint Augustin: Confessions; texte établi et traduit par Pierre de Labriolle. Cinquième édition revue et corrigée (Paris, "Les Belles Lettres," 1950). Tome I, Livres I-VIII; Tome II, Livres IX-XIII.

S. Aureli Augustini Confessionum Libri Tredecim, post Pium Knöll iteratis curis edidit Martinus Skutella (Lipsiae in aedibus B. G. Teubneri, 1934).

Confessions, opera et studio monachorum S. Benedicti a congregatione S. Mauri (*Opera Omnia*, I, Paris, 1679); reprinted in J. P. Migne, *Patrologia Latina*, Tomus XXXII, col. 659-866 (Paris, 1845).

Sancti Aureli Augustini Confessionum Libri Tredecim, recensuit et commentario critico instruxit Pius Knöll (Vienna, 1896).

The Confessions of Augustine, Latin text edited by John Gibb and William Montgomery, 2d ed. (Cambridge, 1927).

The Enchiridion

Augustins Enchiridion, herausgegeben von Otto Scheel (dritte Auflage, Tübingen, J. C. B. Mohr [Paul Siebeck], 1937).

Enchiridion sive De Fide, Spe et Charitate, texte, traduction, notes par J. Rivière; Tome IX: *Exposés généraux de la foi; première série: Opuscules*, Œuvres de Saint Augustin, Bibliothèque Augustinienne, Paris, 1947, pp. 77-447 (Paris, Desclée, De Brouwer et Cie, 1947).

S. Aurelii Augustini Enchiridion ad Laurentium sive De Fide, Spe et Charitate; Migne, *Patrologia Latina*, Tomus XL, col. 231-290.

The Confessions   TRANSLATIONS

Matthew, Sir Tobie, *Confessions* (London, 1620). The first translation into English—by a Roman priest.

Watts, William, *Confessions* (London, 1631). First Anglican translation.

Pusey, E. B., *The Confessions of St. Augustine* (Library of the Fathers, I–II, London, 1838; frequently reprinted thereafter).

Biggs, Charles, *The Confessions of Saint Augustine*; Books I–IX (London, 1900).

Pilkington, J. G., *The Confessions of St. Augustine* (A Select Library of the Nicene and Post-Nicene Fathers of the Christian Church, Vol. I, New York, 1907).

Rouse, W. H. D., *St. Augustine's Confessions.* Loeb Classical Library, 2 vols. (London, William Heinemann, Ltd., 1912); a revision of Watts.

Sheed, F. J., *The Confessions of St. Augustine* (New York, Sheed & Ward, 1943).

Bourke, V. J., *Saint Augustine: Confessions.* The Fathers of the Church, Vol. 21 (New York, Fathers of the Church, Inc., 1953).

The Enchiridion

Cornish, J. C., *St. Augustine, The Enchiridion to Laurentius.* The Library of the Fathers (Oxford, 1847); an extremely literal translation.

Shaw, J. F., *The Enchiridion of Augustine Addressed to Laurentius Being a Treatise on Faith, Hope and Love* (Edinburgh, 1883); reprinted in the Nicene and Post-Nicene Fathers, First Series, Vol. IV.

Arand, Louis A., *St. Augustine: Faith, Hope and Charity* (Westminster, Md., The Newman Press, 1947); in Ancient Christian Writers, Vol. III.

Peebles, Bernard M., *St. Augustine: Faith, Hope and Charity* (New York, Fathers of the Church, Inc., 1947); in The Fathers of the Church, Vol. IV.

Evans, Ernest, *Saint Augustine's Enchiridion or Manual to Laurentius Concerning Faith, Hope and Charity* (London, S.P.C.K., 1953).

Oates, Whitney J., ed., *Basic Writings of Saint Augustine*; 2 vols. (New York, Random House, Inc., 1948); Vol. I contains *The Confessions* and *The Enchiridion*.

BOOKS AND ARTICLES

Abercrombie, Nigel, *Saint Augustine and French Classical Thought* (Oxford, Clarendon Press, 1938); the most useful study of the influence of Cicero and the Stoics on Augustine—and of Augustine's influence in the Renaissance and after.

Adam, Karl, *St. Augustine, the Odyssey of His Soul* (New York, The Macmillan Company, 1932).

Alfaric, Prosper, *L'Évolution intellectuelle de Saint Augustine*, Vol I. (Paris, 1918); maintains the thesis that Augustine's "conversion" in 386 was to "Platonism."

Battenhouse, Roy (ed.), *A Companion to the Study of St. Augustine* (New York, Oxford University Press, 1954); a survey and contemporary interpretation.

Bourke, Vernon J., *Augustine's Quest of Wisdom* (Milwaukee, Bruce Publishing Company, 1945); a general survey of Augustine's life and writings.

Boyer, Charles, *Christianisme et néo-platonisme dans la formation de Saint Augustin* (Paris, Beauchesne, 1920); the "case" against Alfaric.

Burkitt, F. C., *The Religion of the Manichees* (Cambridge University Press, 1925).

Cayré, F., *Initiation à la philosophie de Saint Augustin* (Paris, Desclée, De Brouwer et Cie, 1947); the first volume in a series of studies by the group sponsoring the Bibliothèque Augustinienne.

Cochrane, Charles N., *Christianity and Classical Culture: A Study of Thought and Action from Augustus to Augustine* (London, Oxford University Press, 1939); indispensable review of Augustine's "mission" in the Graeco-Roman world.

Courcelle, Pierre, *Recherches sur les Confessions de Saint Augustine* (Paris, E. De Boccard, 1950); most detailed study of *The Confessions*.

Cushman, Robert E., "Faith and Reason in the Thought of St. Augustine," in *Church History*, XIX, 4, 1950, pp. 271–294; basic study of the primacy of faith in Augustine's epistemology.

D'Arcy, M. C., et al., *A Monument to St. Augustine* (London, Sheed & Ward, 1930).

Dinkler, Erich, *Die Anthropologie Augustins* (Stuttgart, Kolhammer, 1934). Brilliant essay which stresses the existentialist character of Augustinian thought.

Gilson, Étienne, *Introduction à l'étude de Saint Augustin;* 3d ed. (Paris, J. Vrin, 1949); the most substantial analysis and summary of Augustine's "system"; useful bibliography.

Guitton, Jean, *Le Temps et l'éternité dans la philosophie de Plotin et de Saint Augustin* (Paris, J. Vrin, 1938); a classic study of Augustine's philosophical background and his inner life of devotion.

Henry, Paul, "Augustine and Plotinus," in *The Journal of Theological Studies*, XXXVIII, 1937, pp. 1–23. Excellent and just estimate of the influence of Plotinus on Augustine.

Hrdlicka, C. L., *A Study of the Late Latin Vocabulary and of the Prepositions and Demonstrative Pronouns in the Confessions of St. Augustine* (Washington, The Catholic University Press, 1931); the Catholic University of American Patristic Studies, XXXI.

Marrou, Henri-Irénée, *Saint Augustin et la fin de la culture antique* (Paris, E. De Boccard, 1938); excellent study of Augustine as literary artist, philosopher, and "man of his age."

Mausbach, J., *Die Ethik des hlg. Augustinus*; 2 vols. (Freiburg, Herder & Co., 1929). The most complete summary of Augustine's ethical concepts and teachings.

Milne, C. H., *A Reconstruction of the Old Latin Text or Texts of the Gospels Used by St. Augustine with a Study of Their Character* (Cambridge University Press, 1926).

Montgomery, W., *St. Augustine: Aspects of His Life and Thought* (London, Hodder and Stoughton, 1914).

Pontet, Maurice, *L'Exégèse de Saint Augustin prédicateur* (Lyons, Aubier, 1946); definitive study of Augustine's doctrine and use of Scripture.

Pope, Hugh, *Saint Augustine of Hippo* (Westminster, Md., The Newman Press, 1949); disparate essays which are, nevertheless, very readable and informative.

Portalié, E., "Augustin" in *Dictionnaire vacant de théologie catholique*. A long and very judicious monograph; a short book in itself; stresses the essential agreement of Augustine and Thomas Aquinas.

Verheijen, Melchior, *Eloquentia Pedisequa; observations sur le style des Confessions de Saint Augustin* (Nijmegen, Dekker and van de Vegt, N. V., 1949); excellent linguistic study, illuminating many theological problems.

Wagner, M. M., "Plan in the Confessions of St. Augustine," in *The Philological Quarterly*, XXIII, 1944, pp. 1–23.

INDEXES

GENERAL INDEX

BIBLICAL REFERENCES